PAULINE THEOLOGY
Volume 3

Society of Biblical Literature

Symposium Series

Christopher R. Matthews, Editor

Number 23

Pauline Theology
Volume 3

PAULINE THEOLOGY

Volume 3
Romans

Edited by
David M. Hay and
E. Elizabeth Johnson

Society of Biblical Literature
Atlanta

PAULINE THEOLOGY

Volume 3

Romans

Edited by
David M. Hay and
E. Elizabeth Johnson

First edition published by Fortress Press, 1995.

Interior design and typesetting: The HK Scriptorium, Inc.

Library of Congress Cataloging-in-Publication Data
Pauline theology.
   p. cm. — (Society of Biblical Literature symposium series ; no. 21–23)
   Originally published: Minneapolis : Fortress Press, c1991–c1997.
   Contents: v. 1. Thessalonians, Philippians, Galatians, Philemon/ Jouette M. Bassler, editor—v. 2. 1 and 2 Corinthians / David M. Hay, editor—v. 3. Romans / David M. Hay and E. Elizabeth Johnson, editors.
   ISBN 1-58983-052-0 (v. 1 : pbk. : alk. paper)—ISBN 1-58983-053-9 (v. 2 : pbk. : alk. paper)—ISBN 1-58983-054-7 (v. 3 : pbk. : alk. paper)
   1. Bible. N.T. Epistles of Paul—Theology. I. Bassler, Jouette M. II. Hay, David M., 1935– III. Johnson, E. Elizabeth. IV. Symposium series (Society of Biblical Literature); no. 21–23

BS2651.P284 2002
227'.06—dc21   2002029413

Printed in the United States of America
on acid-free paper

Contents

Preface

FOR CENTURIES many expert readers of the New Testament have tended to assert that Romans is not only Paul's most important letter but that it is also a comprehensive statement of his mature theology.[1] General studies of the apostle's theology have often followed the outline of Romans, referring to passages in the other letters to clarify or expand on the ideas in Romans. This anthology of essays on the letter was produced by a team of scholars seeking to explore the thought of Romans by itself, as though the other letters were unknown, and without making initial assumptions that Romans is a first-century equivalent of one of the *Summas* of Aquinas or the *Christian Institutes* of Calvin.

This is the third in a series of volumes that has grown out of the work of the Pauline Theology Group of the Society of Biblical Literature. Most of the essays published here were presented in their initial form at the 1992 and 1993 annual meetings of the society. The authors, however, were given a chance to reconsider theses and reshape sentences on the basis of conversations at those meetings. The ambience of lively debate is retained by the format of this volume, involving as it does an alternation of essays and responses written to them. The respondents, however, were asked not only to react to the essays of others but also to define alternative interpretations of their own. The result is that for each major section of Romans the readers will find two contrasting exegetical essays, and they will easily detect that the writers were listening to each other as well as to other voices.

Whereas the first volume in this series dealt with five letters (1–2 Thessalonians, Galatians, Philippians, Philemon) and the second with two (1–2 Corinthians), this volume deals with only one. The essays in the earlier volumes dealt with specific letters and treated them as wholes. In this volume, by

[1]See, e.g., Rudolf Bultmann, *Theology of the New Testament* (New York: Scribners, 1951) 1.190.

contrast, most of the essays treat sections of Romans rather than the whole letter.

The writers of the essays in this volume take different approaches and arrive at differing interpretations of Paul's thought. Yet some general tendencies in this work may be usefully noted at the outset, tendencies reflecting broad developments in New Testament studies since the 1970s. Great emphasis is placed on Romans as a letter written in a very particular historical situation, reflecting the concerns of Paul at a special time in his apostolic career as well as the situation of Christians in Rome. Romans 16 is now widely recognized as authentic, with the implication that Paul is well acquainted with a considerable number of influential Christians in Rome. The references to his travel plans in chap. 15 are taken as hints of the practical missionary orientation of Paul's thought. Chapters 9–11 are now widely read as integrally linked with the argument of 1:18–8:39, not as a mere "appendix." The methods of rhetorical criticism and social-history investigation are freely employed. Classic theological issues like law versus gospel and justification by faith are not neglected, but they are linked with fresh thinking about the apostle's ideas about Jewish–Christian relations, his emphasis on theocentric language, and the cross-cultural conflicts that existed already in the churches of his time.

Leander Keck argues that the current—very proper—respect for Romans as a contingent letter rather than a systematic treatise may result in unwise and unfounded dependence on one historical reconstruction of its occasion or another. He urges instead that interpreters of Romans focus on the text and the apparent function of its argumentation, since it is "the inner logic" of Paul's gospel rather than the immediate situation which governs the letter's content. N. T. Wright, on the other hand, sees a dual occasion of the letter in Paul's plans for a Spanish mission and the Roman church's experience of tension between Jewish and Gentile members. This situation elicits from the apostle a defense of God's covenant faithfulness in Romans that is based on his reinterpretation of Jewish narrative theology: God's covenant with Israel is fulfilled in God's Messiah, Jesus, who then transfers it to the church. Richard Hays detects common elements in the approaches of Keck and Wright, though he analyzes their essays separately. He proceeds to argue for a more nuanced view of Paul's covenantal thinking, a "post-Lutheran reading" of the righteousness of God, and a heightened appreciation of the role of the Old Testament in Romans.

Building on a proposal of Nils A. Dahl, Robert Jewett argues that the theology of the letter should be interpreted in relation to Paul's missional statements in 1:1–17 and 15:14–16:24. The apostle carefully employs language and rhetorical structures to define his vision of a tolerant and inclusive Christianity—in contrast to the intolerant viewpoint expressed by an interpolator in 16:17–20. In reply, Paul Sampley argues that Jewett exaggerates the centrality of the Spanish mission for interpreting Romans. He proposes that more vital to Paul is the "mission" of promoting unity of Jews and Christians in the Roman churches—the apostle invites the Romans to risk working for unity, just as he himself takes calculated risks in planning his final journey to Jerusalem.

Andrew Lincoln addresses the first four chapters of Romans as an indication that Paul's theological reflection moves, in the language of E. P. Sanders, from the solution the gospel provides to his diagnosis of the human plight. This movement of Paul's thought is in response to the situation of the Roman congregation, whose divided membership needs to understand the universality of that plight as it affects both Jew and Gentile. Jouette Bassler responds that Lincoln's reading of chaps. 1–4 relies more heavily on a rhetorical than on a theological analysis of the letter. Although she does not dispute all his conclusions, she offers an interpretation that attends to the function of two theological claims made in this earlier part of the letter which continue to structure the argument of the remaining chapters: the unchanging character of God's impartiality and the new revelation of God's righteousness in Paul's gospel.

Frank Thielman approaches Romans 5–8 with the perennial question of how those chapters relate to the preceding four and the following seven, since their focus apparently turns away from Israel and its scripture to the experience of the Christian life. He claims that Israel's history, the biblical picture of Israel's disobedience to the law, its punishment in the exile, and its eschatological restoration informs Paul's discussion of the new life in Christ. Charles Cousar raises questions about the influence of Israel's history in these chapters and proposes an alternative reading of Romans 5–8 that finds in its apocalyptic language and thought a critical key to its interpretation.

In her essay on Romans 9–11, Elizabeth Johnson argues that Paul's driving concern is to show the trustworthiness and integrity of God as the final object of faith, a concern fully in line with the earlier and subsequent chapters of the letter. She finds the primary tension in these chapters to be that between divine impartiality and God's special faithfulness to Israel. Douglas Moo answers her essay by contending that Christology and Israel's failure to respond to the gospel are more central to these chapters than she allows. Yet he agrees with her on the need to find a line of interpretation avoiding the extremes of a traditional "displacement" view of Israel, on the one hand, and a "bi-covenantal" model of salvation, on the other.

In his essay on "the rule of faith" in Romans 12:1–15:3, William Campbell argues that that rule requires Christians to be tolerant of each other's differences. In particular Paul is urging that Jewish Christians need not repudiate

Judaism and a Jewish life-style and, further, that Gentiles cannot reach the consummation of their salvation apart from the salvation of Jews. In his reply to Campbell's essay, Mark Reasoner argues that, after all, the "weak" and the "strong" are actual groups of Jewish and Gentile Christians in Rome respectively. He also maintains that "faith" takes on different shades of meaning in different parts of Romans, having, for example, a more cognitive sense in chap. 14 than in chap. 12. He also argues that Paul is more concerned than Campbell suggests to argue against Jewish presumption as well as Gentile pride.

The final contribution is a selected bibliography of studies of theology in Romans prepared by Robert Jewett.

The abbreviations used in this volume are taken from the *American Academy of Religion and Society of Biblical Literature Membership Directory and Handbook 1993*, 391–400. Unless otherwise noted, biblical translations are from the New Revised Standard Version (NRSV).

Contributors

Jouette M. Bassler
    Professor of New Testament
    Perkins School of Theology
    Southern Methodist University

William S. Campbell
    Director of Religious and Theological Studies
    Westhill College
    University of Birmingham

Charles B. Cousar
    Samuel A. Cartledge Professor of New Testament
    Columbia Theological Seminary

David M. Hay
    Joseph E. McCabe Professor of Religion
    Coe College

Richard B. Hays
    Professor of New Testament
    The Divinity School
    Duke University

Robert Jewett
    Harry R. Kendall Professor of New Testament Interpretation
    Garrett-Evangelical Divinity School

E. Elizabeth Johnson
    Associate Professor of New Testament
    New Brunswick Theological Seminary

Leander E. Keck
  Winkley Professor of Biblical Theology
  Yale University Divinity School

Andrew T. Lincoln
  Professor of New Testament
  Wycliffe College
  University of Toronto

Douglas Moo
  Professor of New Testament
  Trinity Evangelical Divinity Seminary

Mark Reasoner
  Assistant Professor of Biblical Studies
  Bethel College

J. Paul Sampley
  Professor of New Testament and Christian Origins
  Boston University

Frank Thielman
  Associate Professor of Divinity
  Beeson Divinity School
  Samford University

N. T. Wright
  Dean
  Lichfield Cathedral

Part I

Comprehensive Overviews

1 WHAT MAKES ROMANS TICK?

Leander E. Keck
Yale Divinity School

I. PRELIMINARY REMARKS

THE TITLE of this paper,[1] given with the invitation to prepare it, deserves comment. To begin, *what is asked for* is not simply to identify the letter's distinctive traits but to discover what gives this letter its remarkable power. It is not the passion that Paul infuses into his letters, for in Romans that is manifest only in chaps. 9–11. Indeed, apart from occasional touches, this letter is marked by a lofty, cerebral, dispassionate tone, noticeably different from the personal qualities in the rest of Paul's correspondence. The quest for what drives this letter pertains rather to its content.

The question is more appropriate for Romans than for the other letters because, on the whole, we think we know what makes *them* tick—Paul's engagement of the issues he perceived to be threatening the house-churches that his mission had called into being. Even if there remains considerable disagreement about the portrayals of those issues and their origins, at least we know what to look for. But after fifteen decades of intense scrutiny and bold assertions, the question, What makes *Romans* tick? has become even more urgent now that it has become *de rigueur* (in some quarters!) to repudiate the "Lutheran" lenses that, it is said, have kept us from seeing what Romans is really all about.[2] But recognizing that what energizes Romans is not the ques-

---

[1] The paper presented to the seminar has been edited generously but not changed substantially. Unfortunately, various other considerations, as well as the work of numerous colleagues, could not be adduced without expanding the text unduly.

[2] Francis Watson, for example, inaugurates his monograph by declaring roundly, "The Reformation tradition's approach to Paul is fundamentally wrong." He then devotes the initial chapter to a critique of "the Lutheran approach" (*Paul, Judaism and the Gentiles: A Sociological Approach* [SNTSMS 56; Cambridge: Cambridge University Press, 1986] chap. 1). For Watson's own view, see p. 21 below.

3

tion of how the guilty individual may find a gracious God does not automatically make either chaps. 9–11 or chaps. 14–15 the driving force of the whole letter. In other words, the question is wide open and the answer is more elusive than we may expect.[3]

It is useful, therefore, to note that *answering the question requires clarity* in two areas. First, in order to put the question properly, one must have a clear view of Romans as a whole. This implies examining assumptions and taking nothing for granted. Krister Stendahl's dictum is worth bearing in mind: "Our vision is often more obstructed by what we think we know than by our lack of knowledge."[4]

For example, as a literary phenomenon, Romans has a number of seams marking transitions to quite different material. It has three distinct units of discursive material (1:18–11:36; 12:1–13:14; 14:1–15:13) surrounded by customary epistolary matter (1:1–17; 15:14–33), followed by a chapter consisting primarily of greetings interrupted by a stern warning in 16:17–20. The transitions from one to the other are abrupt. Only at 1:18 is what follows explicitly connected with what preceded.[5] At 12:1, however, the οὖν ("therefore") evidently intends to link the two sections but does not succeed well in doing so, as the commentators' struggles to make the relation explicit show. At the remaining seams (14:1; 15:14; 16:1) we find even looser linkage, for the text relies on the multipurpose δέ ("and," "but") (at 16:1, D* F G m lack even this). In a newly found text, such loose transitions to blocks of different content, coupled with the lack of explicit cross-references, might well suggest that the text is composite. Considering such a possibility seriously would make answering our question considerably more complex.

Generally, in seeking what makes a text "work" effectively one assumes that it has a discernible coherence. Why do we assume this for Romans? It is, of course, a sound methodological principle to assume that what an author wrote makes sense and that our difficulties with it are at least as attributable to us (and our predecessors) as to the writer. Moreover, in Romans Paul himself reinforces this assumption by dictating a letter whose relentless argument is longer and more tightly woven than that in any of his other letters.[6] In other words, the argumentative character of Romans 1–11 may well have influ-

---

[3] See the essays in *The Romans Debate* (ed. Karl P. Donfried; rev. ed.; Peabody, MA: Hendrickson, 1991).

[4] Krister Stendahl, *Paul Among Jews and Gentiles and Other Essays* (Philadelphia: Fortress, 1976) 7.

[5] The γάρ ("for") in v. 18 is the fourth in a series beginning in v. 16; the ἀποκαλύπτεται ("revealed") in v. 18 repeats that of v. 17.

[6] Rom 1:16–11:36 requires slightly more than twenty-one pages of the Nestle text—as many as Hebrews 1–12, which, however, oscillates between argument and parenesis.

enced unduly our perception of, and expectations of, the whole letter as a coherent work. Indeed, Ernst Käsemann declared roundly, "Viewed as a whole, the Epistle . . . reveals a closely knit argument which is hidden only to those who do not exert enough effort over it."[7] This may well be the case. Yet this pronouncement contains the seeds of its own dissolution: if intense effort is required to see a closely knit argument, one wonders whether Paul constructed it or the exegete imposes it. It should also be noted that a closely knit argument is one thing, conceptual consonance another.

The second area where clarity is required concerns the tense of what we are looking for: What *makes* Romans tick or what *made* it tick? At issue is the extent to which we are determined to answer the question historically, to correlate it as closely as possible with the situation in which and for which Paul created the text in the first place.

Strictly speaking, the present tense ("makes") requires but minimal attention to historical considerations, including authorial intent, for one can study the text as a literary piece without requiring information about the contingent factors that elicited it. Focusing on what *makes* Romans tick does not require one to find an answer that was plausible in Paul's day or that fit Paul's purposes, for the key to the text lies not outside the text but within it. This approach acknowledges that what Paul produced may exceed what he intended to create or, for that matter, fall short of it. Moreover, this rather ahistorical way of answering the question need not account for, and perhaps resolve, the text's inner tensions by deleting one element as an intrusion, for it can appreciate them as part of the dynamic that actually helps to make the text "tick."

Putting the question in the past tense, however, makes it inevitable that Paul's purpose in sending precisely *this* letter to *Rome* comes to center stage, just as it leads unavoidably to a mirror reading of the text.[8] That, in turn, produces a range of reconstructions of Paul's situation that appears to be limited only by the imagination of researchers, as the history of Romans studies shows. The habits developed in studying the other Pauline letters not only cause one to see in almost every emphasis a response to an issue in Rome (or Jerusalem) but also invite one to see in Paul's use of traditions (Jewish as well as Jewish Christian) an unstated agenda—to show that he is a bona fide Jewish Christian, for example.

The dominance of the historical form of the question has made it virtually habitual to give a past-tense answer to the present-tense question. That is, it

---

[7] Ernst Käsemann, *Commentary on Romans* (Grand Rapids: Eerdmans, 1980) 324.

[8] Exemplified, e.g., in A. J. M. Wedderburn, *The Reasons for Romans* (Studies in the New Testament and Its World; Edinburgh: T. & T. Clark, 1988).

is commonly assumed not only that what made Romans tick is what makes it tick (thereby equating the two forms of the question) but also that the latter is legitimate only if it is identical to the former. Given the nature and content of the evidence, however, the historical mode may well have promised more than it can deliver convincingly. After 150 years there is no obvious reason to think that now, or tomorrow, we will discover exactly what made Romans tick when Paul dictated and the Romans read it.

The final preliminary remark concerns the scope of *this paper*. Since its aim is to facilitate a discussion of the question among colleagues, it is more concerned to identify issues and question assumptions than to "solve" problems. This design reflects the conviction that the epigram, whose origin I can no longer recall, is correct: "Our problem is solutions." The paper first calls attention to two limitations, not always duly acknowledged, on efforts to answer the question on strict historical grounds. Then in proposing an answer, it threads its way between the ahistorical and the rigorously historical approaches, though informed by both, before concluding with brief personal observations.

II. TWO LIMITS ON THE HISTORICAL ANSWER

The historical form of the question, What *made* Romans tick? can be answered in one of two ways, depending on critical judgments about the letter. (a) If Paul wrote the text we read, then we can assume that it is coherent and consistent,[9] that the letter's intended function in Rome will have shaped its form and content, and that both can be correlated with the apostle's life and thought as known apart from this letter. This should allow us to infer what he thought made it tick. (b) If, however, the text before us was produced not by Paul but by one or more editors using what Paul had written as well as additional material, then the text at hand will yield first of all what made Romans tick in the thinking of the last editor. Then discerning what in Paul's mind made it tick requires one to distinguish what Paul sent to Rome from what lies before us, and the answer to our question will be based on a somewhat shortened text. In other words, the first limitation on our ability to answer the question historically concerns the literary integrity of Romans.

---

[9] Romans sends conflicting signals: the letter is written in Paul's name only, yet it alone identifies the scribe Tertius (16:22). It is pointless to speculate on what he might have contributed to the text. Although E. Randolph Richards's monograph illumines the many uses of secretaries in Paul's day, he can but restate the problem: "In view of the diverse yet recognized and acceptable ways of using a secretary, there are far-reaching consequences on such issues as how completely 'Pauline' are the letters' thoughts, contents, argumentation, organization, style, or vocabulary" (*The Secretary in the Letters of Paul* [WUNT 2/42; Tübingen: Mohr (Siebeck), 1991] 201).

Whatever one's considered judgment about the integrity of the text might be, in detecting what made Paul's letter tick in his own situation one must cope also with a second factor: What did Paul not include in what he sent to Rome? In other words, what made it tick was his combination of what he argued and what he bypassed. The difficulty of accounting for Paul's silence is therefore the second limitation to be noted, albeit briefly.

The Literary Integrity of Romans

Most critics regard the question of the letter's literary integrity to have been settled once a judgment has been reached about chap. 16. What the mobile concluding benedictions and the various endings attest is abbreviation and adaptation of the letter for church use. Apart from ongoing debate about chap. 16 (as a whole or in part)[10] and possible glosses here and there,[11] the literary integrity is regarded as assured. But has scholarship accounted adequately for the data that prompted a minority of critics to question or deny the letter's integrity? Raising the issue briefly should show that the matter is not settled as firmly as widely thought.

If our Romans lacks integrity, it is either because it consists of disparate pieces that someone (including Paul)[12] assembled or because Paul's text was expanded significantly, or both.

A composite text? Romans 1–11, beginning at 1:18, consists of three distinct parts: 1:18–4:25; 5:1–8:39; and 9:1–11:36. Whereas the central part (chaps. 5–8) is clearly linked to the first by δικαιωθέντες οὖν ἐκ πίστεως ("therefore, since we are justified by faith"), no connection at all joins 9:1 to 8:39; chap. 9 begins afresh and appears to inaugurate a self-contained unit whose content is related to chaps. 1–4, so that the discussion of Christian existence and hope in chaps. 5–8 virtually interrupts a discussion of the meaning of Abraham (the pivotal figure in chap. 4) resumed at 9:1. Once we no longer take the even

---

[10] In his recent discussion, Joseph A. Fitzmyer himself has changed his view and now regards chap. 16 as an integral part of the letter (*Romans: A New Translation with Introduction and Commentary* [AB 33; New York: Doubleday, 1993] 55–67).

[11] See, e.g., Rudolf Bultmann, "Glossen in Römerbrief," in *Exegetica* (Tübingen: Mohr [Siebeck], 1967) 278–84; see also Leander E. Keck, "The Post-Pauline Interpretation of Jesus' Death in Rom. 5:6–7," in *Theologia Crucis-Signum Crucis: Festschrift für Erich Dinkler zum 70. Geburtstag* (ed. C. Andresen and G. Klein; Tübingen: Mohr [Siebeck], 1979) 237–48; as well as "Romans 15:4: An Interpolation?" in *Faith and History: Essays in Honor of Paul W. Meyer* (ed. Charles H. Cosgrove, John C. Carroll, and E. Elizabeth Johnson; Atlanta: Scholars Press, 1990) 125–36.

[12] It has been suggested from time to time that Paul himself expanded/adapted an earlier circular letter; see Fitzmyer, *Romans*, 55–56. See also n. 13 below.

flow of the text for granted, our curiosity seeks an explanation for this sequence of material with this divergent content.

Robin Scroggs has accounted for it by proposing that Paul himself combined two homilies so different that they could not have been created together: (a) chaps. 1–4 + 9–11 (probably an "actual text of a sermon Paul had preached to Jews") and (b) chaps. 5–8.[13] The former develops an argument, relies on scripture, uses little "explicit Christian language and content," and reinterprets Israel's existence from creation to the eschaton; the latter concentrates on the new life in Christ, has a "repetitive circular structure" characterized by refrain-like sentences at the end of each subsection, and cites scripture but twice (and differently). Whereas the compositional pattern of chaps. 5–8 is like that of 4 Maccabees, Paul's model for the longer homily is "the narration of *Heilsgeschichte* found in Jewish homiletic tradition."[14] So great is the difference between them that Scroggs can write, "everything that the first homily is, Rom 5–8 is not."[15] Even if Scroggs exaggerated the difference, one wonders why, and on what basis, Paul would have linked them.[16]

Jurji Kinoshita and Walter Schmithals not only factored the entire letter into its components but traced the Romans we know to the hand of an editor.[17] Kinoshita claims that someone combined three of Paul's writings: (a) chap. 16; (b) a two-part "Manual of Instruction on the Jewish Problems," the fruit of Paul's many debates with Jews (Part I: 2:1–5, 17–29; 3:1–20; 3:27–4:25; 5:12–21; 6:1–7:25; 9:1–11:36; Part II: 14:1–15:3), which Paul had been using and to which he added Part II (15:4–13) when he gave Phoebe a copy to take to Ephesus; (c) the "original Romans" (chap. 1; 2:6–16; 3:21–26; 5:1–11; chap. 8; chaps. 12–13; 15:14–33), "the crown sermon of his Gentile mission," sent before leaving for Jerusalem. Phoebe took a copy also of this "original

---

[13] Robin Scroggs, "Paul as Rhetorician: Two Homilies in Romans 1–11," in *Jews, Greeks, and Christians: Religious Cultures in Late Antiquity: Essays in Honour of William David Davies* (ed. Robert Hamerton-Kelly and Robin Scroggs; SJLA 21; Leiden: Brill, 1976) 271–98. C. H. Dodd not only regarded chaps. 9–11 as an earlier piece of Paul's writing but suggested why Paul used it: "to save a busy man's time and trouble in writing on the subject afresh" (*The Epistle of Paul to the Romans* [MNTC; New York: Harper, 1932] 150).

[14] Scroggs, "Paul as Rhetorician," 292.

[15] Ibid., 281.

[16] Although Halvor Moxnes writes appreciatively of Scroggs's work and supports it with his own observations, he does not explain the sequence either, but merely states that in chaps. 5–8 and 12–15 Paul addresses Christians whereas in chaps. 1–4 and 9–11 he is "directly involved in a dialogue with Jews—Christian or non-Christian," and is meeting them on common ground by using traditional formulations for God (*Theology in Conflict: Studies of Paul's Understanding of God in Romans* [NovTSup 53; Leiden: Brill, 1980] 28–30).

[17] Jurji Kinoshita, "Romans—Two Writings Combined: A New Interpretation of the Body of Romans," *NovT* 7 (1965) 258–77; Walter Schmithals, *Der Römerbrief als historisches Problem* (SNT 9; Gütersloh: Mohn, 1975).

Romans" to Ephesus as Paul's gift to that church, where, we may infer, our Romans was created. Why the editor did not simply juxtapose these documents, Kinoshita does not say.[18]

Kinoshita does, however, distinguish two quite distinct lines of thought, manifest in three areas: (a) The manual views πίστις ("faith") as faith in God, the way of justification, but the original Romans views it as God's and Christ's faithfulness to the sinful.[19] (b) The manual views Christ as the basis of a new humanity, but the original Romans emphasizes his redemptive death. (c) The original Romans emphasizes the Spirit as the driving force of the Christian life, but the manual mentions it only sporadically.

Accepting Kinoshita's proposal would simplify what Paul wrote to the Romans, for the dialectic (or tension) created by "the Jew first" theme would be drained away into its own thematic text for a different readership, and the remaining (allegedly original) Gentile-oriented Romans no longer requires us to reconstruct a Jewish Christian community in Rome. The price for this simplification is, however, too high; first, the one who wrestles with the knotty problem of Jews and Gentiles is not Paul but his unknown editor, for Paul himself now appeals to Gentiles without dealing with God's faithfulness to Israel; second, since both the manual and the original Romans embody Paul's prior teaching and preaching, this proposal implies that Paul had two gospels, one for Jews another for Gentiles.

Schmithals too finds three Pauline texts embedded in Romans but regards two of them as the letter to Rome.[20] He discovers in 15:28 an important clue: Paul's travel plans appear to be set, whereas in 1:8–13 they seem to be delayed. Inferring that both passages would not have been written at the same time, Schmithals identifies the passages that Paul would have written on each occasion. The result: Paul dispatched First Romans (my label for 1:1–4:25; 5:12–11:36; 15:8–13) from Ephesus when it appeared that the trip to Rome was delayed. Second Romans (12:1–21; 13:8–10; 14:1–15:4a, 7a, 5–6, 14–32; 16:21–23; 15:33) was sent when the voyage became possible. First Romans, having advocated a law-free gospel, actually necessitated Paul's counsel to "the strong" in Second Romans. The third letter (16:1–20) was sent to Ephesus. The editor/initial publisher of the Pauline corpus added 16:25–27 as well as 15:4b and perhaps 5:1a and inserted fragments of Paul's letter to Thessalonica (5:2–11 and 13:11–14) as well as a wholly non-Pauline piece (13:1–7).

Schmithals is probably the only student of Romans who believes all this. It

---

[18] Ibid., esp. 275.

[19] Kinoshita does not reckon with the possibility of rendering πίστις Χριστοῦ as "the faithfulness of Christ" instead of "faith in Christ" (3:22, 26 [Jesus]).

[20] Schmithals, *Römerbrief*, 210–11.

would be unfortunate, however, if the implausibility of this construction were to result in an overall refusal to consider seriously the question of the integrity of Romans. Not to be overlooked here, at any rate, is what Schmithals deleted from both letters—the characteristic Pauline eschatology and the uncharacteristic treatment of civil authorities in 13:1–7. These passages will be discussed below. Nor should one miss two consequences of detaching chap. 16: one must reconstruct the Roman situation, and Paul's knowledge of it, without the presence of his friends who could have informed the apostle. At the same time, the task is somewhat simplified because 16:17–20 is no longer a factor. The troublesome effect of this short passage will also concern us later.

Expanded by interpolations? Interpolations, especially if their content is at odds with the surrounding text and/or with what we take to be Pauline thought, can have a drastic effect on a historical answer to our question. At the same time, in light of tradition/redaction criticism, many of the phenomena adduced on behalf of Paul's use of already extant material can also be used to identify post-Pauline interpolations: awkward syntax or transitions, unusual vocabulary, and divergent context.[21] It is too simple to say that what Paul adopted (and perhaps adapted) fits the argument but interpolated material disturbs it, because the interpolator (like pre–redaction-critical interpreters!) thought that it did fit; and if Paul himself used existing material, he thought so too. Indeed, it might be profitable for a group dealing with Pauline theology to put high on its agenda a thorough examination of the criteria and method for distinguishing one from the other. Were such efforts to succeed, the results would be significant for the interpretation of Paul during the period when the Deutero-Paulines were being created and the corpus formed, as well as for the modern history of our discipline. In the meantime, it is instructive to note the possible consequences of regarding certain passages as interpolations.

Half a century ago, Robert Martyr Hawkins argued not only that interpolations are found throughout the corpus but also that in Romans they distorted rather effectively Paul's real thought.[22] The possibility that Paul used traditions never crossed Hawkins's horizon. Eschewing all footnotes, Hawkins simply traces conceptual tensions to interpolated material, so that in effect what Paul himself wrote became a *Grundschrift* for the Romans we read. As a result, the difference between the original Romans and ours is as deep as that

---

[21] See, e.g., Charles H. Talbert, "A Non-Pauline Fragment at Romans 3:24–26?" *JBL* 85 (1966) 287–96.

[22] Robert Martyr Hawkins, *The Rediscovery of the Historical Paul* (Nashville: Vanderbilt University Press, 1943) chap. 4.

produced by Marcion; only this time the culprit is triumphant Christian orthodoxy.

Nonetheless, Hawkins forces us to look again at the content of Romans in the light of Paul's purpose. Hawkins insists that in presenting his gospel to the Romans Paul needed to "be at his best"; being committed to preaching the crucified Christ, he would have avoided "all the dubious paths of subtle disputation so that his readers should not be bewildered." We expect "clarity, definiteness, the utmost simplicity, and above all an unwavering consistency . . . for if the trumpet gives forth an uncertain sound, how would the Romans know what Paul thought or preached?" But "subtle disputation" is just what we find in Romans! "So far as the clarification of Christian thought is concerned, and the unification of diverse groups in the early church, the dispatch of such an epistle as lies before us could be nothing but calamitous." But Paul "was not foolish enough to dispatch to Rome an epistle so ambiguous."[23]

In Romans 1–8 we find tensions between the desire to maintain Israel's privileged status and Paul's "clearly Hellenistic" gospel, which "rests squarely upon the central teaching of the mystery religions"; apocalyptic passages are to be rejected "because they modify or deny Paul's most basic conceptions," especially the presentness of salvation. Accordingly, in Rom 8:17–20 "we are the farthest from the mind of Paul," who was "conscious of present triumphs." All references to the future eternal life are suspect, as "sub-Pauline perversions," many having "a Johannine flavor."[24]

For Paul, 2:13 is axiomatic: "the doers of the law will be justified." For the real, undialectical Paul, there is no *simul justus*: "with Paul nothing can take the place of a real righteousness, which consists in an actual doing of the law. The only justification which he can recognize consists in being just."[25] It is slanderous "to make Paul's idea of justification a verdict 'not guilty' apart from the radical transformation of nature and conduct." Rather, by faith righteousness can be attained by all, even though the Jews had failed to do so by obeying the law. What Paul needs to make clear to the Romans is

> that this has always been the way God dealt with men, even under the covenant and the law, and . . . the nature of that faith through which we become righteous. It is an utter misrepresentation of Paul's basic position that . . . God will "justify" unrighteous men. His position is rather that

---

[23] Ibid., 62–64.

[24] Ibid., 105, 141, 115, 117, 114. Hawkins insists, "Too much stress is placed on the Jewishness of Paul. Jew he was, but he followed Judaism only so far as his insight and conscience would allow"—and that did not include the "hateful spirit" of Malachi, quoted at Rom 9:13 (p. 128).

[25] Ibid., 85.

through faith both Jews and Gentiles may become righteous so that the law can be fulfilled, as 8:4 says.[26]

Accordingly, 3:23–26 "has modified, if not utterly perverted, the basic connotation of every term employed," for it makes righteousness refer to God instead of people, and perverts faith by making it directed to Jesus' blood rather than God." Rom 4:5 (the gospel in the gospel, according to Käsemann) is not from Paul, for it makes Abraham an ungodly man; 4:17–22 expresses a non-Pauline view of faith: "believing what God says, especially if it is hard to believe. And the harder it is, the greater the faith."[27]

Just as Hawkins sees Paul's gospel as a simple, coherent whole, so he sees coherence in the interpolations; therefore, in Romans two theologies actually compete. The interpolations emphasize the universality of sin,[28] the impossibility of persons becoming righteous, justification of the ungodly on the basis of Jesus' substitutionary atonement and intercession,[29] the Christian life as virtually devoid of present triumph but a matter of hope, the interests of Israel, and the use of scripture. Romans 9–11 reworks what Paul wrote in order to reflect the interests of the Roman church.[30] Paul's own thinking about Israel was clear and consistent: it failed because it misunderstood the role of the law. Since this view was unacceptable in Rome, interpolators introduced two ideas: (a) Israel was not to blame; it was all God's fault; (b) God never intended to save more than a few—that is, predestination and the remnant. The allegory of the olive tree (11:17–24) is a "deliberate attempt to destroy Paul's entire argument that the Gentiles are the ones who have really exemplified God's purpose in the attainment of righteousness through faith and that the Jews must emulate them" if they are to attain it.[31] On this reading of Paul, the differences between Galatians and Romans result not from a shift in Paul's thinking or a change in readers but from the defensive interpolations made by the Jewish-minded Roman church. Even more than Kinoshita, Hawkins forces us to decide whether Paul's letter to Rome, like his gospel generally, was simple and straightforward, or complex and dialectical.

[26] Ibid., 90.

[27] Ibid., 91, 97–98.

[28] Hawkins accepts virtually none of Romans 5; Paul's view of sin is in 7:7–25 (ibid., 108–10).

[29] Hawkins notes that Christ's Session and Intercession "have at no place figured in Paul's discussion as to the possibility of attaining righteousness." Even if we credit the motif to Paul's use of tradition, we still do well to ponder Hawkins's claim that intercession "would be unnecessary for one who is more than victor" (ibid., 118).

[30] Hawkins claims that since there is no evidence in Paul's other letters that the fate of Israel was a "consuming interest of his," this discussion of Israel's rejection must reflect the concerns of the Roman church (ibid., 120).

[31] Ibid., 125, 126, 133–34.

The importance of deciding whether a passage contains Paul's tradition or is an interpolation is well illustrated at 1:3–4. John C. O'Neill's commentary not only regards these verses as part of a somewhat larger interpolation but also contends that our Romans has been expanded by interpolations throughout.[32] Of interest here is a major consequence of denying the integrity of 1:1–7:[33] the inclusion of the creedal statement would reveal nothing at all about Paul's strategy for dealing with the Roman situation, allegedly marked by tensions between Jewish and Gentile believers. Robert Jewett, on the other hand, sees in Paul's treatment of a creedal tradition significant signals pertaining to the rest of the letter as well as its desired effect in Rome. Jewett thinks Paul added both ἁγιωσύνης ("of holiness") to κατὰ πνεῦμα ("according to the Spirit") and ἐν δυνάμει ("in power") to υἱοῦ θεοῦ ("Son of God"). As a result, "'spirit of holiness' made clear that the divine power . . . entailed moral obligation . . . a theme developed at length in Romans 5–8," thereby preparing the reader "for a major emphasis of the letter." Although ἐν δυνάμει, like "concerning his son," corrects Jewish Christian adoptionism, "the most significant feature of all . . . is that Paul selects a credo that bears the marks of both 'the weak and the strong,' thereby showing his effort to be even handed" with Jewish and Gentile readers, and to find common ground.[34]

The truly pivotal passage, however, is the sharp warning against disturbers of the community in 16:17–20, sometimes regarded as an interpolation,[35] though

---

[32] John C. O'Neill, *Paul's Letter to the Romans* (Harmondsworth: Penguin, 1975). O'Neill not only calls attention to the unusual length of the salutation but notes, for example, that Paul makes "no further use of the specific terms of this particular creed in his subsequent argument"; that the text is "a grammatical monstrosity which no writer would have perpetrated"; that the creed is similar to those in Ignatius's letters to the Ephesians (18:2) and to the Smyrnaeans (1:1); that v. 6 violates the rule that salutations do not use the second person until the blessing (here, v. 7)—indeed, v. 6 assumes that the recipients have already been named, and seems to comment on "among all nations"; and that v. 7a is attested in four forms, indicating that editorial work has been done here.

[33] O'Neill notes that one manuscript (G) does not include 1:1b–5a, though oddly Nestle's apparatus ignores the omission. The passage is too long to have been dropped out accidentally. Thus, G attests an early form of the text, which originally may have read: "Paul, servant of Christ Jesus, by call Apostle to all Gentiles, on his behalf; to all at Rome who are by call saints; grace to you and peace from God our Father and the Lord Jesus Christ."

[34] Robert Jewett thinks that the confession had already been expanded in a Hellenistic/dualistic direction by the addition of κατὰ σάρκα ("according to the flesh") and κατὰ πνεῦμα ("according to the Spirit"). He provides an excellent history of the discussion ("Redaction and use of an Early Christian Confession in Romans 1:3–4," in *The Living Text* [ed. D. Groh and Robert Jewett; Lanham, MD: University Press of America, 1985] 117–20).

[35] O'Neill summarizes the reasons for regarding these verses as an interpolation (*Romans*, 258). Ernst Käsemann, who regards them as "a wild polemic," is inclined to see them as "a small independent letter to Ephesus" (presumably by Paul) (*Romans*, 419). Otto Pfleiderer thought of it as an interpolation made in the second century in order to have Paul condemn Gnostics

there is no manuscript evidence to indicate this. If it is genuine, it casts remarkable retrospective light on what made Romans tick, for it has far-ranging consequences for the way one views Paul's relation to Roman Christianity and the intended function of the letter in it. C. E. B. Cranfield, who accepts the genuineness of the passage, seems to sense this and resolutely tries to neutralize its difficulties.[36] P. S. Minear goes beyond Cranfield, for he identifies the disturbers with two of the five groups he detects—the weak and the strong who are condemning each other. Consequently, here Paul "condensed the pastoral polemic, which had absorbed his thought at least since 14:1, into a last warning, perhaps in his own hand." Indeed, although Satan does not appear elsewhere, not even in 5:12–21, Minear finds it "natural" that Paul would confront the readers with the alternative: God or Satan.[37]

Markku Kettunen goes farther still, making the passage important for the entire letter.[38] Because 1:8 and 15:14 show that Paul is "satisfied" with the readers' faith, Kettunen infers that as Paul was completing the letter he received information that their faith was in danger after all. Moreover, the troublemakers might be opponents he had already answered in chaps. 1–11; they surface in 3:8 and are similar to Paul's opponents in Galatians, 2 Corinthians 10–13, and Philippians 3. Because of their agitation in Rome, now both Paul's and the reader's faith is endangered.[39] Like Kettunen, Ulrich Wilckens's commentary sees the troublers as outsiders, traveling teachers like the judaizers of 2 Cor 11:13–15, whose imminent arrival in Rome was reported to Paul as he completed his letter.[40] Clearly, this imaginative, far-reaching reconstruction collapses if 16:17–20 is interpolated, as is probable.

Another key passage sometimes thought to be interpolated is 13:1–7. That

---

(*Primitive Christianity: Its Writings and Teachings in their Historical Connections* [New York: G. P. Putnam's Sons, 1906] 1. 247). K. Erbes thought Paul wrote it to the Roman church during his Roman imprisonment ("Zeit und Ziel der Grüsse Rom 16,3–15 und der Mitteilungen 2 Tim 4, 9–21," *ZNW* 10 [1909] 128–47, 195–218).

[36] C. E. B. Cranfield, *A Critical and Exegetical Commentary on the Epistle to the Romans* (2 vols.; ICC; Edinburgh: T. & T. Clark, 1975, 1979); Paul S. Minear, *The Obedience of Faith: The Purpose of Paul in the Epistle to the Romans* (SBT 2/19; Naperville, IL: Allenson, 1971) 27–29.

[37] Minear, *Obedience,* 27–29.

[38] Markku Kettunen, *Der Abfassungszweck des Römerbriefes* (Annales Academiae Scientiarum Fennicae; Helsinki: Suomalainen Tiedeakatemia, 1979).

[39] Ibid., 43–73.

[40] Ulrich Wilckens, *Der Brief an die Römer* (EKKNT 6; Cologne: Benziger, 1982). On the other hand, W. S. Campbell denies that there were judaizers in Rome, and gives seven reasons for this conclusion (*Paul's Gospel in an Intercultural Context: Jew and Gentile in the Letter to the Romans* [Studies in the Intercultural History of Christianity; Frankfurt/Bern/New York/Paris: Peter Lang, 1991] 169–70).

a persistent minority has asserted its secondary character is well known,[41] though there is no agreement about its alleged non-Pauline origin. Alexander Pallis saw it as an insertion made after 133 CE—after the second Jewish revolt prompted Christians to emphasize *their* loyalty. O'Neill regards the passage as a collection of eight injunctions which a Stoic had collected, perhaps long before, and which was inserted here because of the verbal similarity between 13:7 and 13:8. Schmithals sees no connection with the Roman situation and so regards it as a synagogue topos with an anti-apocalyptic thrust. James Kallas finds that the passage contradicts Paul at four points: it lacks the imminent expectation of the end and assumes that the church must make peace with the world; it uses ἐξουσία ("authority") in a non-Pauline way; it does not see this world under the control of demonic powers; and it contradicts Paul's view of suffering in this world. Winsome Munro views 13:1–7 as part of a "subjectionist stratum" that was interpolated (for reasons like those given by Pallis); this stratum is said to extend across the whole Pauline corpus and 1 Peter; Rom 1:19–2:1 and 14:1–15:13 are seen as part of it.[42]

Naturally, those who accept the genuineness of 13:1–7 try to relate it to the letter's content and setting. Oddly, although Käsemann regards it as "alien" material, he rejects the interpolation theory, and sees it as an *anti-Enthusiasmus* passage, a view that Schmithals (like others) finds unconvincing. Marcus Borg argues that it not only intends to thwart anti-Roman attitudes that Jewish agitations in Palestine elicited among Jewish Christians in Rome but that it "has an intimate connection to Romans as a whole." The jointly-written article by J. Friedrich, W. Pöhlmann, and P. Stuhlmacher also claims to detect exactly what motivated Paul to write it—the agitation in Rome against Nero's taxes (58 CE), a view Wilckens finds possible but lacking support in the text.[43] He himself concedes that he does not know what prompted Paul to include this topos—though it would have been particularly pertinent to the Jewish Christians who had recently returned to Rome. Although Minear thinks it would have been pertinent to "the strong" (thus approaching Käsemann's view), he

---

[41] The most extensive defense of this position is that by Ernst Barnikol, though rarely discussed ("Röm 13: Der nichtpaulinische Ursprung der absoluten Obrigkeitsbejahung von Römer 13,1–7," in *Studien zum Neuen Testament und zur Patristik* [Berlin: Akademie-Verlag, 1961] 65–133).

[42] Alexander Pallis, *To the Romans* (Liverpool: Liverpool Booksellers' Co., 1920); O'Neill, *Romans*, 207–10; Schmithals, *Römerbrief*, 191–97; James Kallas, "Romans XIII. 7: An Interpolation," *NTS* 11 (1964–65) 365–74; Winsome Munro, *Authority in Paul and Peter* (SNTSMS 45; Cambridge: Cambridge University Press, 1983) 79 (the entire stratum is given on p. 94).

[43] Marcus Borg, "A New Context for Romans XIII," *NTS* 19 (1972–73) 214; J. Friedrich, et al., "Zur historischen Situation und Intention von Röm 13,1–7," *ZTK* 73 (1976) 131–66.

also candidly admits he could not find "particular reasons in the Roman situation for Paul's inclusion of this teaching."[44] J. D. G. Dunn, on the other hand, infers from the position of the paragraph in chaps. 12–15 that the content "stands very much at the center" of Paul's concern, "since redefining the people of God" was the result of the argument in chaps. 1–11,[45] a view similar to Borg's. Were that the case, Paul would surely have made the connection clear. That 13:1–7 is a "specific example of what enactment" of his vision of a new people of God "with a mission to gather the nations unto God"[46] entails would surely have been news to Paul.

The purpose of raising the question of the literary integrity of Romans is not to launch a campaign on behalf of interpolations in order to simplify the letter but rather to post a warning to skaters on Romans Pond: Danger! Thin Ice. It is not evident that the warning will be heeded, however, for previous signs too have been ignored or taken down. Skaters, desiring to use the whole pond, do not relish having to cope with patches of thin ice. All too frequently the evidence that points to the possibility of an interpolation is ignored or explained away, sometimes ingeniously. This is particularly true of 13:1–7 and 16:17–20. Would it not be better to allow such questionable passages to function as the Deutero-Paulines in critical discussions—acknowledge that they belong to Pauline tradition while declining to create historical reconstructions and interpretations of Paul himself that rely heavily on them?

Perhaps the time is at hand to take up the question systematically, following the lead of Winsome Munro's inquiry (without accepting her results), to ascertain not only the range and strength of the evidence but also whether the allegedly interpolated material reflects a consistent perspective. Should that be the case, one would have a clearer picture of the alleged "Pauline school" as well.

The Silence of Romans

There is so much *in* Romans that requires attention that interpreters seldom do more than acknowledge in passing that certain elements deemed characteristic of Paul's thought are also absent from it. But we cannot answer satisfactorily the question of this paper until we take account of what is not

---

[44] Minear, *Obedience*, 88; so also Robert H. Stein, "The Argument of Romans 13:1–7," *NovT* 31 (1989) 327.

[45] J. D. G. Dunn also relies on a psychological reason for the abrupt transition at 13:1: Paul's "concern to take up this subject causes him to do so in a sudden and somewhat brusque way" (*Romans 9–16* [WBC 38b; Dallas: Word, 1988] 759).

[46] Jeffrey A. Crafton, "Paul's Rhetorical Vision and the Purpose of Romans: Toward a New Understanding," *NovT* 32 (1990) 336.

included as well. This becomes evident when we look at what is present or absent in relation to Paul's alleged aims in writing this letter.

First, if Paul were really rehearsing what he would say in Jerusalem, so to speak, it becomes difficult to account not only for what is in 12:1–15:13 but also for what these chapters do not contain. Admittedly, Jerusalem-centered antipathy toward Paul probably went beyond what Acts 21:20–21 has the elders tell Paul (actually, the reader). In any case, the more one thinks that in Romans 1–11 Paul effectively rebuts charges against his gospel and its effects,[47] the more difficult it becomes to see in the quite different chaps. 12–13 an equally relevant answer to the (supposed) charge that his "law-free gospel" destroys the ethos of Jewish existence.[48] Nor is it easy to see what Paul's Jerusalem concerns have to do with 14:1–15:13.[49] (The "apostolic decree," of which Paul allegedly was informed in Jerusalem [despite Acts 15:22–32] introduces a complexity that must be ignored here, even though it too deals with food taboos.) In other words, if Romans 12–15 too was part of what Paul was preparing to say in Jerusalem in order to make the collection for the poor acceptable, one can hardly avoid saying that he misread the situation, and so "laid the egg beside the nest." If one says that "Jerusalem" controlled Romans 1–11 but "Rome" determined chaps. 12–16, then the coherence of Romans is undermined, making the validity of our question problematic. That Jerusalem was on Paul's mind is undeniable; however, the claim that it shaped the letter to Rome is a remarkably apt instance of the proverbial red herring.

Second, if one holds that in writing Romans Paul addressed the multileveled tensions between Gentiles and (returned) Jewish Christians in Rome, then here too the silences of the letter pose questions that appear to defy reliable answers, beginning with the obvious one: in a letter that twice speaks of Paul's travel plans, why does he not once even allude to Jewish Christians' return to Rome (including Prisca and Aquila)? And, although one can regard chaps. 1–11 as the theological basis on which Paul's counsel in 14:1–15:13

---

[47] Halvor Moxnes, noting that in 2:23–25 Paul is as polemical against the Jews as they are against Paul in 3:8, finds the cause in 1 Thess 2:14–16: Jewish opposition to Paul's mission, which (for Paul) prevents God's promise from being fulfilled. Moreover, Paul fears that the unbelievers in Jerusalem (Rom 15:31) "may make his journey to Rome and subsequent mission to Spain impossible. . . . It is this *mission*, which started with *Jesus*, that is the center of the controversy between Paul and his opponents in Romans. . . . It is this 'apart from the law' that causes the charge that Paul slanders God with his preaching" (*Theology in Conflict*, 61–63; his italics). Wedderburn too emphasizes the defensive nature of chaps. 1–11; see n. 66 below.

[48] Jacob Jervell, the champion of the "Jerusalem hypothesis," virtually limits his discussion to chaps. 1–11 ("The Letter to Jerusalem," in *The Romans Debate*, ed. Donfried, 53–64).

[49] So too A. J. M. Wedderburn, "'Like Ever-Rolling Stream': Some Recent Commentaries on Romans," *SJT* 44 (1991) 371.

rests,[50] why do these chapters not follow 11:36? Indeed, precisely if dealing with the tensions in Rome drives the letter, it is far from obvious why doing so requires the relentless theological argument in chaps. 1–11. In fact, only in 15:7–13[51] does Paul really connect his counsel with chaps. 1–11; the counsel itself is quite intelligible—and its internal theological grounding adequate—without 15:7–13, or even without chaps. 1–11, whose themes are not explicitly cross-referenced in 14:1–15:13.

Above all, if the tensions between Gentiles and (returned) Jewish Christians in Rome are as serious and as threatening to Paul's plans for Spain as is alleged, why does he deal with them so allusively, so obliquely, when he himself says he has written "very boldly" (15:14)? Did he assume that 11:13–32 (his response to Gentile Christian theological arrogance regarding Israel's election), coupled with 14:1–15:13 (his critical support of the "strong" Gentile Christians in the divisive matters of days and diets) suffices to create a turnabout in which *ethnic*-based hostilities would be overcome? Moreover, what has the olive tree analogy to do with eating a chop?

If, on the other hand, he counts on the theological argument in 1:18–11:12 to overcome these animosities, why are these chapters almost totally bereft of any reference to the situation? Or is Minear right after all in seeing various parts of the letter addressed to particular groups at Rome? Nor is it obvious how, on the customary reconstruction, Paul can credit the Jews with a "zeal for God" (10:2) but regard those Jews who became Christian vegetarians as "weak in faith" since they abstain from eating meat "in honor of the Lord" (14:7). It is no less obscure why, if the (Jewish) "root" supports the (Gentile) graftee, it is the strong Gentile who is urged to "bear with the failings of the weak" (Jewish Christian). Does one not expect Paul to ask the scrupulous "root" to be patient with the freewheeling Gentile until the graft has "set"?

Further, if it is really harmony between Jewish and Gentile Christians in Rome that Paul is trying to achieve, why does the letter not come closer to the theology of Ephesians? Whatever accounts for the nonuse of ἐκκλησία ("church") (until chap. 16), why does the theme of unity not appear in connection with the sole reference to Christ's body (12:4–8), which talks about

---

[50] So, e.g., Wayne A. Meeks, "Judgment and the Brother: Romans 14:1–15:13," in *Tradition and Interpretation in the New Testament: Essays in Honor of E. Earle Ellis* (ed. Gerald F. Hawthorne and Otto Betz; Grand Rapids: Eerdmans, 1987) 290–300.

[51] See Leander E. Keck, "Christology, Soteriology, and the Praise of God (Romans 15:7–13)," in *The Conversation Continues: Studies in Paul and John in Honor of J. Louis Martyn* (ed. Robert T. Fortna and Beverly R. Gaventa; Nashville: Abingdon, 1990) 85–97. Hendrikus Boers goes farther, calling this passage "the explicitly paraenetic culmination of Paul's argument" (throughout the whole letter) ("The Problem of Jews and Gentiles in the Macro-Structure of Romans," *SEÅ* 47 [1982] 192–94).

the exercise of gifts instead? Did Paul think that the single phrase "individually members of one another" (compared with three verses about χαρίσματα (spiritual gifts) would be as effective in unifying the yet-unseen Christian community as virtually the whole of 1 Corinthians 12 in a church he knew well? Indeed, since Paul was in Cenchreae, it would have been easy enough to have Tertius get a copy of 1 Corinthians, summarize that chapter, and include *it!*

In the third place, the more one regards Romans as Paul's means of persuading the readers that, contrary to what they heard, his gospel is sufficiently consistent with "mainstream" Christianity that they need not hesitate to welcome him and then support him in Spain, the more baffling is the omission of so much Pauline theology. If by this letter Paul takes responsibility for what the Romans know of his thought, then he either failed to do justice to it (quite apart from Hawkins's ideas), or else Schweitzer got it backward in saying that justification is a "minor crater" in Paul's theology because in this self-introduction Paul presented precisely this theme in order to present the real Paul. In any case, if this letter was to be a self-introduction—a hypothesis Käsemann calls a "tempting" solution[52]—the themes missing from Romans deserve more reflection.

Remarkable is the total absence of the Lord's Supper. Are we to think that the tensions over food did not impinge on the eating of this supper too? Were the issues in Rome so different from those in Antioch (Galatians 2)? (Or did Paul not want to risk losing this battle too?) Would not the axiom of 1 Cor 10:17—one Lord, one body—apply to the Roman situation as well (however the issue that evoked it in Corinth was related to the problem at Rome)? And if Paul could emphasize baptismal participation in Christ's death (Rom 6:3–11), would it not have been easy at least to allude also to participatory eating and drinking (1 Cor 10:16)? And if Paul uses christological/soteriological traditions in chaps. 1 and 3 to show his solidarity with the larger church's tradition, why does he not reinforce this claim with an allusion to the tradition of the supper? If, on the other hand, he avoided it deliberately because for him the cup represented the "new covenant" (1 Cor 11:25)[53]—a theme that would have required chaps. 9–11 to have taken a different turn (especially the allegory of the olive tree)—then what does that say about his alleged need to present his thought accurately? The same question arises in connection

---

[52] Käsemann, *Romans*, 402.

[53] The absence of any reference to the eucharistic cup as the "new covenant" is especially intriguing if one agrees with N. T. Wright "that covenant theology is one of the main clues . . . for understanding Paul" (*The Climax of the Covenant: Christ and the Law in Pauline Theology* [Edinburgh: T. & T. Clark, 1991] xi).

with the complete absence of an explicit mention of the cross, save for the sole allusion in the neologism "co-crucified" (Rom 6:6). No less remarkable is the fact that although Paul's eschatological expectation is clearly "alive and well" in 13:11–12, he never mentions the parousia. Readers of the Pauline corpus can see in 8:18–25 various allusions to the future turning point when the eschatological redemption of body-selves will be part of the emancipation of creation, but Paul does not deem it necessary to associate this explicitly with the coming of the Lord. In short, readers of Romans are given no reason to think that the parousia was an important component of Paul's eschatology.

These observations are not of equal weight, to be sure; some of the difficulties are more easily accounted for than others. Their value is largely heuristic and self-critical: they remind us of the fragile character of the reconstructions which are said to provide the key to Romans.

Do these various silences disallow the view (a) that Paul had Jerusalem in mind when writing to Christians in Rome, (b) that he sought to deal with polarizations among them, or (c) that he wanted to present his construal of the gospel? Μὴ γένοιτο! ("By no means!") What they do suggest is that in the creation of this letter the role of these aims should not be overestimated, since they do not account for the entire letter, including what it does not contain. And that implies that their role in making Romans tick is limited.

III. A SEVENTH-INNING STRETCH

The resolutely historical-critical approach to our question, determined to read Romans as a letter thoroughly shaped by its historical context, appears to have placed us not so much on a cleared path toward the goal but rather in a labyrinth—"an intricate combination of passages in which it is difficult to find one's way or an exit."[54] If we are somewhat frustrated, it is less because of a serious flaw in the method than because we expected it to yield for Romans what it did for the other letters.[55]

The frustration generated by our question would be alleviated markedly by assimilating more rigorously two distinctions. First, "occasion" should be distinguished from "purpose" instead of regarding each as the obverse of the other. Concretely, the unique constellation of factors in Paul's situation, symbolized by Jerusalem, Rome, and Spain, undoubtedly did provide the occasion for Paul to write this letter. But there is no clear evidence that these factors, whether singly or in concert, determined Paul's actual purpose in writing or the specific content of what he did send to Rome. For example,

---

[54] *Random House Dictionary of the English Language* (New York: Random House, 1966).

[55] That the judgment expressed here is not too harsh can be confirmed by reading Wedderburn's review of recent commentaries; see n. 49.

the absence of clear evidence does not prevent Francis Watson from reading Romans in light of a well-defined purpose ascribed to Paul: "create a single Paulist congregation in Rome,"[56] which entails the complete withdrawal of Jewish Christians from the Jewish community; viewed sociologically, Paul's "theology" is really his (often contradictory) attempt to legitimate his sectarian view of the church.[57] Nonetheless, Romans is a "highly coherent piece of writing when considered from its social function."[58]

Second, content should be distinguished more sharply from both occasion and purpose and, in keeping with rhetorical considerations, be related more to its function within the text itself. For one thing, the function of what Paul says about a given subject is more easily tested and substantiated than correlations between content and either purpose (authorial intent) or occasion (historical reconstruction). This distinction is essential if one allows for the possibility that Paul relied on material he had developed before, and in other contexts. This would account for the existence of carefully crafted, relatively self-contained passages (such as 5:12–21) whose function can be discerned but whose situation-oriented pertinence eludes convincing recovery.[59]

IV. THE GAME CONTINUES

These reflections lead up to a remarkably simple conclusion: What *makes* Romans tick is neither Paul's situation nor even the letter's actual themes but the convictions that both generate these contents and allow them to be juxtaposed.[60] This conclusion does not require tenuous but interlocking judgments

---

[56] Watson, *Paul, Judaism and the Gentiles*, 97. Agreeing with Acts that Paul turned to the Gentiles after Jews rejected him, Watson also contends that Paul then decided to abandon much of the law in order to make the gospel more attractive to Gentiles; as a result his churches were completely separated from the synagogue (p. 38). Thus, earliest Christianity was a reform movement within Judaism, but in Paul's hands it became a sect. Naturally, "faith is incompatible with works because participation in the life of a Pauline Gentile Christian congregation is incompatible with continued membership of the Jewish community" (p. 134, italicized). For a critique, see W. S. Campbell, "Did Paul Advocate Separation from the Synagogue? A Reaction to Francis Watson: Paul, Judaism and the Gentiles: A Sociological Approach," *SJT* 41 (1988) 1–11. Campbell's own essays on Romans are published as *Paul's Gospel in an Intercultural Context*.

[57] According to Watson, in Paul's eyes Gentile Christians are members of "Israel" because it is the Jewish community that had separated itself from "Israel" (*Paul, Judaism and the Gentiles,* 172).

[58] Ibid., 173.

[59] The same can be said of 12:14–21 and 13:11–14 (or are we really to think that 13:13 was particularly relevant in Rome?), as well as 13:1–7, as noted above.

[60] What is in view here, freed from technical jargon, comports with how Boers defined the "macrostructure" or "deep structure": "That which determines and controls the choice of

about which passages are non-Pauline traditions quoted by Paul, older Pauline material reused by Paul, material freshly minted at Cenchreae, or subsequently interpolated. It also allows one to acknowledge, without pretending to know the unknowable, that Paul had his eye on Jerusalem, Rome, and Spain as he dictated to Tertius.

Occasion as Catalyst

Without the projected mission to Spain, there is no reason to think that Romans would have been written at all. Why Spain? The clear emphasis on Paul's vocation to Gentiles (1:5; 11:13; 15:16–18) implies that he regarded Spain as the place where he could fulfill his calling precisely because it was Gentile territory, having very few Jews.[61] Indeed, according to 11:13 Paul "glorified" (NRSV; RSV "magnify") his ministry among Gentiles as part of the divine economy according to which Israel would become "jealous" of the Gentiles. Precisely Spain would serve this purpose better than continued work in areas with significant Jewish populations, where his preaching elicited anything but jealousy—not to mention judaizers. In other words, Spain offered the opportunity for creating wholly Gentile churches.

That in going to Spain Paul would need various kinds of support from Rome, perhaps the Christian community nearest Spain, is understandable, though there is no way to ascertain whether the needs adduced in recent studies were also on Paul's list.[62] In any case, to gain support, two things were essential: a theological grounding that is persuasive in a community of both Jewish and Gentile Christians, and a lessening of the tensions that currently divided that community, lest he become another divisive factor there —which, in view of 3:8 and the presence of former associates, might already have been the case. The former need prompts chaps. 1–11, the latter chaps. 14–16; it is doubtful that any historical circumstances can be adduced as the

---

words and construction of the sentences" ("The Problem of Jews and Gentiles," 184 n. 1). Thus, Boers declares that "justification by faith . . . is not the point of the letter but the fundamental presupposition on which it is based" (p. 188). See also his stimulating *The Justification of the Gentiles: Paul's Letters to the Galatians and Romans* (Peabody, MA: Hendrickson, 1994).

[61] W. P. Bowers, having made a comprehensive survey of all available evidence, concludes that "a major Jewish presence in Spain" emerged only in the third century, and that its roots go back to the decades between the two Jewish Revolts in Palestine. "That there were Jewish communities in Spain prior to this is not supported by any evidence currently available" ("Jewish Communities in Spain in the Time of Paul the Apostle," *JTS* 26 [1975] 400).

[62] Crafton, e.g., says Paul needed "financial backing, letters of recommendation, and travel companions who could translate and make essential contacts" ("Paul's Rhetorical Vision," 327).

catalyst for chaps. 12–13; *we* can see their function in the text, but that is not historical motive.

It is one thing to reconstruct the catalysts that prompted Paul to write, another to account for what he wrote. There is no clear reason to think that the catalysts made the actual content inevitable (though mirror reading gives this impression). Paul might have written a quite different letter—one in which, for example, he said a good deal more about his distinctive vocation, reflected on his experience in the Aegean area, gave reasons for choosing Spain rather than Gaul, and correlated chaps. 14–15 with his view of the church as the Lord's body. The fact that he did not correlate what he had to say more explicitly with the Roman situation, or with his specific needs for the Spanish mission, strongly suggests that to understand what he did say we should not do so either. In other words, ample "space" must be allowed for the inner logic of his thought to assert itself.

If the two factors that energized Paul to write chaps. 1–11 and 14–16 were Spain and Rome, respectively, then the historical factor that unites them is Paul's construal of his apostleship, which lies beneath the surface of the whole text. It is this sense of identity, and what he takes to flow from it, that grounds the sovereign authority with which he writes, in effect inserting himself, uninvited, into the Roman situation in order to make possible his next mission.

Paul's apostleship manifests itself in the role he plays in the letter—primarily that of a teacher of the church. Whether by diatribe, by exposition of scripture,[63] or by wisdom-like instruction (in chaps. 9–11[64] no less than in chaps. 12–13), or by pastoral counsel, Paul presents himself as a teacher of the gospel and its theological substructure. It is not surprising, then, that what makes Romans Romans is its theology of the gospel.

The Gospel as God's Power

Although chaps. 9–11 are an integral part of chaps. 1–15,[65] 1:18–8:39 is a major section in which Paul states the gospel in such a way that its scope reaches from Eden to the eschaton, from "the fall" to the redemption of the

---

[63] Emphasized by Richard B. Hays, who writes that Romans "is most fruitfully understood when it is read as an intertextual conversation between Paul and the voice of Scripture" (*Echoes of Scripture in the Letters of Paul* [New Haven: Yale University Press, 1989] 35).

[64] See E. Elizabeth Johnson, *The Function of Apocalyptic and Wisdom Traditions in Romans 9–11* (SBLDS 109; Atlanta: Scholars Press, 1989).

[65] Though often argued on the basis of various verbal links, Boers has exhibited how these chapters are integral to the whole by listing the rhetorical questions in chaps. 1–11, all of which "concern the problem of the Jews and the law" ("The Problem of Jews and Gentiles," 186–87).

world. One of the functions of this section is to show why Paul, whom God has set apart for "the gospel of God," is both proudly confident (taking "not ashamed" as litotes[66]) in preaching it and an ὠφειλέτης ("debtor") to all persons: it is God's saving power for every human being, albeit to the Jew first. There is one gospel and only one, for all. If Paul cannot show how this is the case, there would be one gospel for Jews and one for the Gentiles. But if the gospel is God's power for salvation for *all* who believe, the one gospel must bring one solution to the one condition in which all find themselves. However important are the election of Israel, the promise to Abraham, the gift of the law, and the Davidic ancestry of God's Son, in no way do these exempt "the Jews" from solidarity with the Gentiles in the human condition.[67] So important is this parity in sin/salvation that Paul reasserts it in 11:32, just before the hymnic conclusion of chaps. 1–11. It is the *human* problem that the gospel addresses.

In making his case for the one gospel for everyone, Paul puts Gentiles and Jews in the same boat, yet without ignoring or canceling the unique situation for the Jew with a particular history. In fact, he must affirm it,[68] but in doing so he redefines it, thereby implying that the Jew has misread the meaning of his own existence. But what warrants such a sweeping redefinition? God's act in Christ as a truly eschatological event, one that by definition reconstructs everything not aligned rightly with the character and will of God. This is Paul's starting point.[69] E. P. Sanders rightly saw that Paul's thought moves from

---

[66] For a contrary view, see C. K. Barrett, "I am Not Ashamed of the Gospel," in *New Testament Essays* (London: SPCK, 1972) 116–43. Given the mirror reading on which Wedderburn's reconstruction depends, it is not surprising that he asserts that someone in Rome had in fact claimed that Paul "ought to be ashamed of his gospel" because it was discredited and disgraceful, in fact "unrighteous." Consequently, through chap. 11 Romans is a defense of his gospel (*Reasons for Romans*, 104, 112).

[67] So also Wedderburn, *Reasons for Romans*, 119–20. Like Jacob Jervell (*Imago Dei: Gen 1,26f im Spätjudentum, in der Gnosis und in der paulinischen Briefen* [Göttingen: Vandenhoeck & Ruprecht, 1960] 318), he noted that in 1:23 Paul uses LXX language about Israel and the golden calf to talk about the turn to idolatry—an association known already in Jewish traditions ("Adam in Paul's Letter to the Romans," in *Studia Biblica 1978* [JSNTSup 3; Sheffield: JSOT Press, 1980] 2. 413–30).

[68] Richard B. Hays put it well when he wrote of "Paul's tenacious integrity in holding to the proposition that unless the Law and the Prophets really bear witness to the gospel there is no gospel at all" (*Echoes of Scripture*, 64). J. C. Beker makes a similar point: "Paul's gospel is a gospel for the fulfillment of God's promise to Israel" (*Paul the Apostle: The Triumph of God in Life and Thought* [Philadelphia: Fortress, 1980] 87). This is not evident in 1 Thessalonians, however.

[69] So too Halvor Moxnes: "It was not Paul's intention to describe the gospel itself as the fulfillment of the promise. Rather it is the gospel itself which was this point of departure" (*Theology in Conflict*, 219).

solution to plight;[70] in Romans, however, the *argument* moves from plight to solution because Paul's rhetorical strategy calls for it.

Given the need to show that the gospel provides the definitive remedy for the universally shared human condition, it is inevitable that Paul emphasizes Adam; in fact, he unpacks the Adamic situation three times. His argument moves in spiral fashion, each time going deeper into the human condition, and each time finding the gospel the appropriate antidote.[71]

The first exposition (1:18–4:25) falls into two parts: an indictment of Gentile and Jew which reaches its climax in 3:19–20, followed by the good news of God's righteousness apart from law categorically, manifested in the πίστις Χριστοῦ ("faithfulness of Christ") and made salvific in the rectification of Jew and Gentile alike ἐκ/διὰ πίστεως ("through faith") (3:30). Paul puts Jew and Gentile on a par before God by expounding the shared human condition within a coherent linguistic field: righteousness (the right relation to God and the God-given norm), law (the obligatory norm that exposes that no one is in fact righteous), and justification (the rectification of the wrong relationship). Although Gentiles do not have Moses, they do acknowledge a norm of right and wrong, and have conscience as well; therefore, they are as indictable without Moses as Jews with him, and so are in need of the same rectification. Of this rectification apart from the law Abraham is both the prototype and the promise.

But the Adamic situation is deeper than being wrongly related to God and so needs more than a rectified relationship. Sin entails also participation in a domain marked by sin's enslaving power, whose consequence is death. Thus, the exposition of Adam in 5:12–21 prepares for 6:1–7:6, where Paul argues that freedom from this yoked tyranny of sin and death is through participation in an alternate domain—Christ's death and resurrection, which in the present manifests itself as "newness of life," whose outcome is eternal life.

Paul goes deeper still into the human condition as he returns (tacitly) to Adam in chap. 7. It is one thing to understand sin as a tyrant in whose domain one finds oneself subject to death, another to see it as an illegal alien resident who usurped control of the house, thereby compelling the enslaved self to do

---

[70] E. P. Sanders, *Paul and Palestinian Judaism: A Comparison of Patterns of Religion* (Philadelphia: Fortress, 1977) 442–43. In conversation, J. L. Martyn reminded me that Sanders is not the discoverer of this point, for Karl Barth had already insisted on it in his discussion of Christ and Adam. New Testament critics are not known for their readiness to learn from Barth, of course. N. T. Wright, on the other hand, contests Sanders's view, contending that Paul's thought moved from plight (the sorry state of Israel) to solution to a fresh analysis of plight (*Climax of the Covenant*, 260–62).

[71] See Wedderburn, "Adam in Romans," which builds on Morna Hooker's "Adam in Romans i," *NTS* 6 (1959–60) 297–306.

the opposite of what it intends, including obeying the law. The ultimate failure of the law, any law, is that it is ineffective against sin as a power resident in
the self. To deal with this wretched condition a superior power must displace
sin by becoming resident in self—the Spirit, as 8:1–17 makes clear. The inner
residence of the Spirit not only makes it possible for the δικαίωμα ("just
requirement") of the law to be fulfilled (8:4) but is a pledge of the redemption
of the body through which indwelling sin operated. And that will be nothing
less than the emancipation of all creation from the consequences of Adam.[72]

Despite the need to abbreviate here Paul's tightly woven argument, it
should be apparent that what makes Romans 1–8 tick is the inner logic of having to show how the gospel deals with the human condition on three
ever-deeper levels, each understood as a dimension of the Adamic condition:
the self's skewed relationship to God in which the norm (law) is the accuser,
the self in sin's domain where death rules before Moses arrived only to exac-
erbate the situation by specifying transgression, the self victimized by sin as a
resident power stronger than the law (thereby showing that the problem is not
the law itself). Unless Christ is the effective antidote to the Adamic situation,
there is no good news for anyone, not even for the Jew because Moses cannot
save from the consequences of Adam. Conversely, if the Adamic situation is
redeemed in Christ, then there is one gospel for all people, and it becomes
clear why Paul is obligated to go even to Spain.

In developing this theology, Paul is not writing a series of essays on sundry
loci but carefully crafting an argument, a discourse, which controls what he
thinks must be said and need not be said. Each statement has its role in the
immediate flow of argument toward its goal, whether or not it logically
squares with related assertions elsewhere. It is the inner logic of the gospel that
made this part of Romans tick—and keeps it ticking.

Just as the logic of the gospel for the human condition drives chaps. 1–8, so
the logic of God's commitment to Israel, despite Israel's history and current
response to the gospel, drives the argument in chaps. 9–11. Indeed, it is the
same logic, the same theology of the divine Nevertheless. The God who has
power to save all persons through the gospel (1:16) also has power to graft in
again the severed natural branches (11:23). Romans 9–11 is nothing other
than the application of the theology of chaps. 1–8 to the problem of Israel, its
history and destiny. Both parts are held together by a theology of God's righteousness (integrity) faithfully asserting itself salvifically through earthly discontinuities.

---

[72] This reading of Adam in Romans differs from that advanced by N. T. Wright, who argues
that "Paul's Adam–Christology is basically an Israel–christology"; indeed, "the last Adam is the
eschatological Israel, who will be raised from the dead as the vindicated people of God" (*Climax of the Covenant*, 29, 35).

The unexpressed theme that holds these eleven chapters together is the freedom of God to be self-consistently faithful in the face of the human history of faithlessness and its consequences for creation. Although Paul never explicitly writes of God's freedom, it pervades the argument. Only if God is free can God manifest divine righteousness apart from law, rectify the ungodly, give life to the dead, call into existence the nonexistent, send the Son to die for us while we were sinners, raise Christ from the dead and pledge resurrection to the baptized, choose Jacob over Esau, have mercy on whomever he will, make Gentiles into God's children, preserve a remnant in Paul's day as in Elijah's, harden Israel now and save it in the future. After "senseless minds were darkened," at the outset, such a God can no longer be inferred but must be revealed; the "riches and wisdom and knowledge . . . [and] judgments" of the inferred God are always searchable and knowable (11:33). It is no accident that Romans is a theocentric text.[73]

The Δικαίωμα of the Law

Given the absence of an explicit argument or line of reasoning that links the discrete parts of 12:1–15:13, the quest for what drives this section of Romans is pursued best by seeking its angle of vision. While there is no assurance that what we find would have been acknowledged as correct by Paul, we are not left entirely dependent on our imaginations.

Walter Wilson's dissertation has shown that the structure and argumentative strategy of Romans 12 follow those found in four Hellenistic Jewish sapiential discourses (Prov 3:11–35; Sir 6:18–37; Pseudo-Phocylides 70–96; *T. Naph.* 2:2–3:5)—namely, a programmatic statement (12:1–2), followed by descriptive (12:3–8) and prescriptive sections (12:9–21).[74] This observation suggests that a number of scattered details, when taken together, might point to a perspective that plausibly might underlie and unify chaps. 12–15.

First, the programmatic statement includes 12:2, which gives the goal of mental renewal as δοκιμάζειν ("test out," "discern") God's will, implying that it is not simply identical with obligations codified by law. At the same time, law can express it and point to it, because in 2:18 Paul describes the Jew as knowing God's will and as "approving" (δοκιμάζειν) what is excellent by being instructed in the law. Next, the prescriptive section (12:9–21) begins with a call to love, a theme expounded by 13:8–10, where love is the fulfill-

---

[73] This is why Moxnes's study of Romans, *Theology in Conflict*, rightly focuses on the function of Paul's God-language.

[74] Walter T. Wilson, *Love Without Pretense: Romans 12:9–21 and Hellenistic-Jewish Wisdom Literature* (WUNT 2/46; Tübingen: Mohr [Siebeck], 1991) chap. 3.

ment of the law. According to 8:4, what Christians are to "fulfill" by the indwelling Spirit[75] is not simply "law" but the δικαίωμα ("just requirement") of the law.[76] Moreover, when Paul compares and contrasts the consequences of Adam and Christ, he says that the gift that follows many transgressions leads to δικαίωμα (5:16). In other words, the δικαίωμα of the law is love. Third, since the obligation to love is the prescriptive adumbration of 12:2, it appears that beneath these varying formulations lies the unstated equation: will of God = δικαίωμα of the law = the obligation to love—an obligation pertaining to everyone, Jew and Gentile.

This inference is consonant with another set of data as well. According to 1:32, the plight of the Gentiles is marked by their approving the manifold forms of wickedness (spelled out in the foregoing vice list), despite their knowing the δικαίωμα of God—that doers of such deeds deserve death. In other words, knowing the δικαίωμα of God does not require one to be a Jew (or proselyte). This is supported by 2:25–29, where Paul identifies the real Jew as one whose heart has been circumcised by the Spirit (a non–gender-specific circumcision) and also insists that when the uncircumcised Gentile does in fact observe the δικαίωμα of the law, he is in effect a true Jew. In other words, δικαίωμα appears to be an umbrella term for what is right in God's eyes without being Moses-dependent, though Moses points to it. This too is consonant with the sapiential (i.e., not specifically Jewish but basically human) character of chap. 12, to which Wilson calls attention.[77]

These considerations, then, support the conclusion that the rubric under which Romans 12–15 can be put is the δικαίωμα νόμου θεοῦ ("just requirement of the law of God").[78]

V. CONCLUDING REMARKS

"What then shall we say to these things?" That the quest for what makes Romans tick is a futile exercise? Μὴ γένοιτο! ("By no means!") If this judgment is sound, a few personal observations may be in order.

[75] E. P. Sanders argues exactly the opposite: "not only is there no explicit distinction between the law of Rom 8:4 and the Mosaic law, the course of the argument requires them to be the same" (*Paul, the Law, and the Jewish People* [Philadelphia: Fortress, 1983] 98–99). See also p. 105: "Living in the Spirit results in obeying the law."

[76] Fitzmyer's commentary rightly notes that the passive πληρωθῆ ("be fulfilled") means that it is God "who brings about the fulfillment of the law through Christ and the Spirit."

[77] "The constituent literary forms of 12:9–21 are predominantly wisdom admonitions, organized under a common theme and combined with other gnomic and non-gnomic forms" (*Love Without Pretense*, 149).

[78] For a different view of δικαίωμα (viz., life), see Wright, *Climax of the Covenant*, 211–14.

To begin with, whoever formulated our question identified the right task, for without at least a provisional answer, one simply cannot penetrate this remarkable text. One reason that the answer to our question has proved to be elusive is that its tense factor ("makes"/"made") insinuates itself into the discussions repeatedly, and inevitably. Insofar as we hear the heartbeat of Romans, we hear it through sonar devices informed by historical criticism; yet few of us use an identical instrument, some relying on historical inference based on mirror reading, some on sociology; others use a different tool; moreover, few of us use the identical model of the same device. Above all, because our listenings reflect varying agendas and sensibilities, we not only hear Romans beat differently but inescapably listen for what matters to us, assuming that it mattered equally to Paul.

We must, of course, continue trying to discern what *made* Romans tick in the first place; for even though we can expect but limited success, the effort remains an essential check on our disposition to make it say what we want to hear. The effort to do so would be advanced if one distinguished two things more clearly: what Paul communicated to the Romans, and what he intended to accomplish by doing so. Intimately related though these questions are, distinguishing them allows Paul's thought to retain its own integrity, even if he had sent the letter to another church, where he might have expected it to exert a different influence. Some "space" must be made for his thought to be grasped and dealt with as a construal of reality whose truth claims must be heard and addressed. It would be ironic, to say the least, if we succeeded so well in fitting Romans into its unique first-century moment that the net effect would be to imprison it there instead of releasing it so it could be (mis)heard here.

Romans ticks because Paul did not allow his immediate situation to govern completely what he had to say, but allowed the inner logic of his gospel to assert itself even if that meant subjecting his first readers to a certain amount of theological overkill. And that, I suspect, is what made the letter tick loud enough that it was preserved despite Paul's even longer delay in arriving in Rome and the nonevent of the mission to Spain. And I also suspect that this is why we hear it still.

2 ROMANS AND THE THEOLOGY OF PAUL

N. T. Wright
Lichfield Cathedral

I. ON READING ROMANS THEOLOGICALLY

A JEWISH THEOLOGY for the Gentile world, and a welcome for Gentiles designed to make the Jewish world jealous. That, I suggest, is what Paul offered his Roman readers, and I suspect it puzzled them as much as it puzzles us, though perhaps in different ways. This paper addresses these puzzles by means of a theological reading of the letter; that is, a reading of the letter drawing out its main theological line of thought, and a summary of the theology that thus emerges, showing how, and perhaps why, it was deployed in this fashion. This, I take it, is my assigned topic; I have not forgotten rhetorical analysis, narrative criticism, historical setting, and so on, but I cannot give them full measure here.

Since this essay is part of an extended conversation, I shall use most of my space for exposition, not for annotation, which could of course proliferate *ad infinitum*. History of research is important in this subject, but must here be assumed, not elaborated.[1] Suffice it to say that different ways of reading

---

[1] Dialogue throughout could be carried on with the major recent commentaries of C. E. B. Cranfield, *A Critical and Exegetical Commentary on the Epistle to the Romans* (2 vols.; ICC; Edinburgh: T. & T. Clark, 1975, 1979); Ernst Käsemann, *Commentary on Romans* (trans. Geoffrey W. Bromiley; Grand Rapids: Eerdmans, 1980); Ulrich Wilckens, *Die Brief an die Römer* (3 vols.; EKKNT 6; Cologne: Benziger, 1982); and James D. G. Dunn, *Romans 1–8* and *Romans 9–16* (WBC 38a, 38b; Dallas: Word, 1988); the following monographs: Richard B. Hays, *Echoes of Scripture in the Letters of Paul* (New Haven/London: Yale University Press, 1989); Glenn N. Davies, *Faith and Obedience in Romans: A Study in Romans 1–4* (JSNTSup 39; Sheffield: JSOT Press, 1990); R. Neil Elliott, *The Rhetoric of Romans: Argumentative Constraint and Strategy and Paul's Dialogue with Judaism* (JSNTSup 45; Sheffield: JSOT Press, 1990); L. Ann Jervis, *The Purpose of Romans: A Comparative Letter Structure Investigation* (JSNTSup 55; Sheffield: JSOT Press, 1991); Bruce W. Longenecker, *Eschatology and the Covenant: A Comparison of 4 Ezra and Romans*

Romans usually reflect different understandings of Paul's whole theology and his place within a history-of-religions scheme, and the ways in which those two interact. The weight of the letter is deemed to fall where the interpreter's theology finds its *locus classicus:* for Albert Schweitzer, this was chaps. 5–8; for F. C. Baur, chaps. 9–11; for various Lutherans, chaps. 1–4; for Minear and others, chaps. 12–16. Sometimes a fresh reading of Romans has itself generated a new way of reading Paul as a whole; or, at least, the reading of Romans has played a vital role, interacting of course with other factors, in producing a totally new understanding. Ernst Käsemann, I think, provides an example of this. Ultimately, the best argument for any exegesis ought to be the overall and detailed sense it makes of the letter, the coherence it achieves. Solutions that leave the letter in bits all over the exegetical floor do not have the same compelling force, as hypotheses, as does a solution that offers a clear line of thought all through, without squashing or stifling the unique and distinctive contribution of the various parts.

But what do we mean by *theology* itself, in this context? Our many previous discussions have set a context in which I have developed the following broad scheme.[2] All societies, and subgroups within societies, have what may loosely be called a worldview, a set of assumptions about the way things are, which can be studied in terms of its four constituent elements: symbols, praxis, stories, and assumed questions and answers (the latter may be itemized: Who are we? Where are we? What's wrong? What's the solution?). These form the grid through which reality is perceived and experienced; they them-

---

1–11 (JSNTSup 57; Sheffield: Sheffield Academic Press, 1991); Douglas A. Campbell, *The Rhetoric of Righteousness in Romans 3.21–26* (JSNTSup 65; Sheffield: JSOT Press, 1992); and the wider discussions of Paul in E. P. Sanders, *Paul and Palestinian Judaism: A Comparison of Patterns of Religion* (Philadelphia: Fortress, 1977); *Paul, the Law, and the Jewish People* (Philadelphia: Fortress, 1983); and *Paul* (Past Masters; Oxford: Oxford University Press, 1991); J. Christiaan Beker, *Paul the Apostle: The Triumph of God in Life and Thought* (Philadelphia: Fortress, 1980); Heikki Räisänen, *Paul and the Law* (Philadelphia: Fortress, 1986); F. B. Watson, *Paul, Judaism and the Gentiles: A Sociological Approach* (SNTSMS 56; Cambridge: Cambridge University Press, 1986); Stephen Westerholm, *Israel's Law and the Church's Faith: Paul and His Recent Interpreters* (Grand Rapids: Eerdmans, 1988); James D. G. Dunn, *Jesus, Paul and the Law: Studies in Mark and Galatians* (London: SPCK, 1990); Alan F. Segal, *Paul the Convert: The Apostolate and Apostasy of Saul the Pharisee* (New Haven/London: Yale University Press, 1990); and of course many others. This dialogue must in most cases be inserted by the reader into the intertextual space left implicitly blank in what follows. At the same time, I shall try and achieve brevity here and there by reference to my own previous work, esp. *The Climax of the Covenant: Christ and the Law in Pauline Theology* (Edinburgh: T. & T. Clark, 1991).

    [2] See further Wright, *Climax of the Covenant,* chapter 1; and *Christian Origins and the Question of God: Vol. 1, The New Testament and the People of God* (Minneapolis: Fortress, 1992) chapter 5.

selves, like the foundations of a house, normally remain unexamined and indeed unnoticed. They generate ways of being in the world that emerge into the public gaze: on the one hand, *aims and intentions;* on the other hand, closely related to the first, sets of *basic and consequent beliefs.* These can be, and often are, discussed. Serious debate usually takes place at this level, not at the level of worldview, since then there would be no fixed point on which debaters could agree to stand. "Theology," as a topic to be studied or an activity to be engaged in, normally operates at this level of explicit discourse about basic and consequent beliefs. It concerns beliefs relating to a god, or gods, and the world. It is organically and dynamically related to the worldview. This is where so many of our problems of method have arisen. Explicit "theology" is out in the open, but if studied piecemeal it remains unintegrated. Some like it like that, preferring atomistic exegesis to question-begging a priori theological schemes. I can see why. I take it, nevertheless, that the present exercise must involve the tricky attempt to make inferences about Paul's worldview, and about the large-scale belief system he held; in other words, not simply to study Romans as a rag-bag of loci or topoi within Paul's hypothetical *Compendia* or *Summa,* but to show how the letter belongs within, and indeed acts as a window upon, Paul's symbolic world, his nonreflective praxis, his assumed narrative framework, and his fundamental answers to the key questions. In what follows I shall regularly distinguish between the actual argument of the letter, which has its own rhetorical force, and the wider worldview and belief system on which Paul draws. I shall refer to these two hypothetical entities, in Norman Petersen's terms, as the "poetic sequence" and the "narrative sequence" respectively.[3]

As an example of this abstract model, and as the necessary historical and theological background to Paul and Romans, we may take a broad description of Second Temple Judaism. I have elsewhere argued in detail both for the propriety of this exercise (alongside more atomistic treatments) and for the detail of the following rough sketch.[4]

The symbolic world of Judaism focused on temple, Torah, land, and racial identity. The assumed praxis brought these symbols to life in festivals and fasts, cult and sacrifice, domestic taboos and customs. The narrative framework which sustained symbol and praxis, and which can be seen in virtually all the writings we possess from the Second Temple period, had to do with the history of Israel; more specifically, with its state of continuing "exile" (though it

---

[3] Cf. Norman R. Petersen, *Rediscovering Paul: Philemon and the Sociology of Paul's Narrative World* (Philadelphia: Fortress, 1985).

[4] Wright, *The New Testament and the People of God,* part 3. Cf. E. P. Sanders, *Judaism: Practice and Belief, 63 BCE–66 CE* (Philadelphia: Trinity Press International, 1992).

had returned from Babylon, it remained under Gentile lordship, and the great promises of Isaiah and others remained unfulfilled) and the way(s) in which its god would intervene to deliver it as had happened in one of its foundation stories, that of the exodus.[5] Its fundamental answers to the worldview questions might have been: We are Israel, the true people of the creator god; we are in our land (and/or dispersed away from our land); our god has not yet fully restored us as one day he will; we therefore look for restoration, which will include the justice of our god being exercised over the pagan nations.

This worldview, which (I stress) concentrates on that which was assumed by a majority of Jews in the period, and which of course could be modified within different branches, generated a wide variety of aims and intentions on the one hand, and on the other a more or less settled core of theology. Many Jews aimed to keep their heads down and remain faithful to their god as best they could, in some cases by intensification of Torah. Others aimed to hasten the coming of restoration by political, and sometimes by military, action. As for theology, belief in the one true god remained basic (the creator god, hence the god of the whole world), as did belief in Israel's election by this one god (who can therefore be given a capital letter, "God"; the fact that scholarship uses this form unthinkingly has not been healthy for discussion of ancient theology). The *purpose* of this election is not so often noticed, but is, I suggest, vital. Israel's controlling stories sometimes ended simply with its own vindication, but more often than not they included the idea that its god, in vindicating it, would *thereby* act in relation to the whole world, whether in blessing or in judgment or both (e.g., Tobit 13–14). Israel's vocation had to do, in other words, with the creator's plan for the whole creation. God called Abraham to deal with the problem of Adam. This theme, marginalized in many contemporary discussions and some ancient ones, is central to (e.g.) Isaiah 40–55, and is visible also in the final redaction of the Pentateuch. Both, clearly, are passages on which Paul drew heavily.

Both, in particular, focus attention on *the righteousness of god.* Here I think the main thrust of Käsemann's point is established, that in Jewish literature the phrase refers to the creator god's own righteousness, not "a righteousness which comes from/avails with god." But Käsemann's subsidiary point (that the phrase formed a technical *and noncovenantal* term within Second Temple Judaism) is misleading. This divine righteousness always was, and remained throughout the relevant Jewish literature, the *covenant faithfulness* of god. The

---

[5] On the idea of continuing exile, see, e.g., Baruch; Tobit 13–14; CD; *1 Enoch* 85–90; and elsewhere, studied in, e.g., Odil Hannes Steck, *Israel und das gewaltsame Geschick der Propheten* (WMANT 23; Neukirchen-Vluyn: Neukirchener Verlag, 1967); idem, *Überlieferung und Zeitgeschichte in den Eliaerzählung* (Neukirchen-Vluyn: Neukirchener Verlag, 1968); and idem, *World and Environment* (Nashville: Abindgon, 1980 [1978]); and many other writers.

fact that, as Käsemann observed, this "righteousness" includes the idea of the justice of the creator being put into effect vis-à-vis the whole cosmos does not mean that the covenantal idea has been left behind. It should remind us that the covenantal idea itself *always included in principle* the belief that when the creator/covenant god acted on behalf of Israel, this would have a direct relation to the fate of the whole world, to the rooting out of evil and injustice from the whole creation.

Paul's Christian theological reflection begins, I suggest, from within exactly this matrix of thought, with the realization that *what the creator/covenant god was supposed to do for Israel at the end of history, this god had done for Jesus in the middle of history.* Jesus as an individual, instead of Israel as a whole, had been vindicated, raised from the dead, after suffering at the hands of the pagans; and this had happened in the middle of ongoing "exilic" history, not at its end. This by itself would have been enough, I think, to propel a Jewish thinker to the conclusion that Jesus had somehow borne Israel's destiny by himself, was somehow its representative. When we add to this the early Christian belief in Jesus' messiahship, and Paul's own exposition of this theme, there is every reason to suppose that Paul made exactly this connection, and indeed made it central to his whole theology. The creator/covenant god has brought his covenant purpose for Israel to fruition *in Israel's representative, the Messiah, Jesus.*[6] The task I see before us now is to show how the actual argument of Romans, the "poetic sequence" of the letter, relates to this underlying "narrative sequence," that is, the theological story of the creator's dealings with Israel and the world, now retold so as to focus on Christ and the Spirit.

II. THE POETIC SEQUENCE OF ROMANS:
INTRODUCTION

Resisting (of course) the temptation to treat Romans as Paul's systematic theology, it is vital that we consider the question of what Paul was actually arguing for. After going round and round this question for two decades, I find myself in the following position, each element of which is of course controversial but which, I think, makes sense in itself and in its exegetical outworkings.[7] The Roman church, initially consisting most likely of converted Jews and proselytes within the capital, had been heavily affected by Claudius's banishment of Jews in 49. Many of the Christians who were left would undoubt-

---

[6] On incorporative messiahship in Paul, see Wright, *Climax of the Covenant,* chapters 2, 3.

[7] On the debates, see above all *The Romans Debate* (ed. Karl P. Donfried; rev. ed.; Peabody, MA: Hendrikson, 1991 [1977]).

edly have been erstwhile godfearers or proselytes. Unlike the Galatian church, these Gentile Christians were not eager to keep the Jewish law, but would be inclined, not least from social pressures within pagan Rome, to distance themselves from it, and to use the opportunity of Claudius's decree to articulate their identity in non-Jewish terms. When the Jews returned to Rome in 54 upon Claudius's death, we may properly assume that the (Gentile) church leadership would not exactly be delirious with excitement. Even though, as we must stress, not all Jewish Christians were ardent Torah observers, and even though the church was most likely scattered in different small groups around the large city, internal tensions, reflecting at least in part a Jew–Gentile split, were inevitable.

But such internal tensions alone do not explain the letter that Paul actually wrote, any more than it is explained when treated as an abstract book of systematics. All the inventive mirror reading in the world has not yet produced a convincing account of Romans in terms purely of the internal problems of the church, except of course for chaps. 14–15. I suggest that the far more plausible setting for the bulk of the letter, and its theological thrust, is the tension that Paul can see as at least a possibility in relation to his *missionary strategy*. He intended to use Rome as his base of operations in the western Mediterranean, as he had used Antioch for the eastern Mediterranean. Antioch had, certainly on one occasion and possibly thereafter, virtually stabbed him in the back, undermining the theological foundation of his mission by insisting on the continuing separation of Jews and Gentiles within the Christian fellowship. The so-called Antioch incident of Galatians 2 reflects Paul's opposition to any sense that Jewish Christians are superior to Gentile Christians.

What Paul faced as a serious possibility in Rome was the mirror image of the problem he had met in Antioch. In making Rome his new base, there was always the danger, as the rise and popularity of Marcion in the next century was later to show, that local anti-Jewish sentiment would lead Gentile Christians not only to isolate Jews within the Christian fellowship but also to marginalize a mission that included Jews. Paul, therefore, wanted to insist that the gospel was "for the Jew first and also, equally, for the Greek."[8] How to do this without (a) reinstating exactly that Jewish superiority which he had resisted in Galatians, and (b) giving any opportunity for proto-Marcionism: that, I suggest, was the problem that called forth the letter we now have and explains the outline and the detail of its argument. The strategy that Paul adopted was that of expounding his own fresh understanding of the terms of the covenant, the original divine answer to the problem of Adam. What did the promises to

[8] For this emphasis in 1:16 (τε πρῶτον καί ["both first . . . and"]), see Cranfield, *Romans*, 1. 90–91.

Abraham and his family actually say and mean? How were they intended to work out in practice? The technical term for this whole theme is, of course, that which he announces programmatically in 1:17: in the gospel of Jesus, the Messiah, is revealed the *covenant faithfulness of god,* the δικαιοσύνη θεοῦ. What Paul needed, in order to address the problem of his new home church failing to understand his missionary strategy, was a large-scale map of the righteousness of god, on which he could locate the Romans' particular situation, and in the light of which he could address other issues, not least those tensions within the church itself which were, so to speak, the internal reflection of the tensions Paul saw within the church's external attitude.

The poetic sequence of Romans, therefore, consists of a major argument, as is now regularly recognized, running not just as far as chap. 8 but all the way to chap. 11. A good deal of this argument, like a good deal of this paper thus far, is a matter of setting up the terms of the discussion so that they can then be used quite directly when the real issue is confronted head on. Once the great argument is complete, Paul can turn to other matters in chaps. 12–16. These are not to be marginalized: 15:7–13, for instance, has a good claim to be considered the real summing-up of the entire letter, not merely of 14:1–15:6. But the division between chaps. 1–11 and 12–16 is clear enough to allow us to treat the two sections separately for our present purposes.

III. ROMANS 1–4

The sequence of thought in chaps. 1–11 follows a line that is thoroughly comprehensible within a Jewish covenantal scheme of thought, granted that the latter has been rethought in the light of the belief that its future hope has already in principle come true in the Messiah, Jesus, and is now being implemented by the Spirit.

The full force of the introduction (1:1–17) can best be seen when all else is clear, and will therefore be left until near the end. This introduction, though reaching a climax in 1:16–17, merges in fact directly into the first main section (note the repeated γάρ ["for"] in 1:16–18, continuing, with the occasional διότι ["since"] to v. 21). Paul's reason for coming to Rome, which grows out of his self-introduction (1:1–5) in terms of the divine plan, is that he is in the service of the divine covenant faithfulness; but, since the divine covenant with Israel always envisaged, and indeed was the intended solution to, the dark backdrop of human sin, Paul's own exposition of it must restate (and in doing so reshape) the problem that the covenant itself addresses. The standard Jewish critique of paganism (idolatry and immorality) is repeated, intensified, and turned back on to Israel itself (1:18–2:16; 2:17–29). This was pretty much standard practice in Jewish sectarianism, as is clear from the Dead Sea Scrolls. At this point Paul's worldview question, What's wrong? seems to require the answer: Not only are pagans idolatrous and immoral, but the people who were supposed to put the world to rights have themselves gone astray. In 2:17–24 Paul is not trying to prove that every individual Jew is immoral etc., but simply that, in view of the existence of *some* immorality within Israel, the *national* or racial boast cannot be sustained. Nor does Paul deny that Israel is called to be a light to those in darkness, and so forth; only that the present parlous state of Israel means that it is incapable of fulfilling that role.

In Israel's regular tellings of the world's story, such an exposé of paganism (and renegade Judaism) would of course be followed, logically and perhaps textually (i.e., in both the narrative sequence and the poetic sequence), by an account of the true people of the covenant god in and through whom the evil of the rest of the world would be undone. For Paul, whose critique of Israel is more biting still than that of the Essenes, a second-order problem has been raised. If the covenant was put in place to deal with evil in the world (this is the presupposition Paul shares with his imaginary opponent in 2:17–24), then the failure of the covenant people to *be* the light of the world means that the covenant itself seems to be under threat. This explains the questions of 3:1–8, which thus anticipate directly those of 9:6, 14, 17, and 11:1, 11. Israel was *entrusted* with the oracles of the creator god (3:2); that is, it was to be the messenger through whom the creator's saving purpose would be carried to the whole world. What is the covenant god to do about the failure of his covenant people (3:2) to be faithful, on their part, to this covenant? Somehow, this god must be faithful nonetheless; and, unless the covenant itself is to be dissolved (which would evoke a strong μὴ γένοιτο ["may it never happen"] from Paul) this means, logically, that there must somehow, after all, be an Israel that is faithful to the covenant, so that through this Israel the creator/covenant god can deal with the evil of the world, and with its consequences (i.e., wrath, as in 1:18ff.). What is provided in 3:21–31 is just such a solution. "The works of Torah," that is, those practices which mark Israel out from among the nations, cannot be the means of demarcating the true covenant people; they merely point up the fact of sin (3:20, looking back to 2:17–24 and on to 5:20 and 7:7–25). Instead, the covenant faithfulness of the creator of the world is revealed *through the faithfulness of Jesus, the Messiah,* for the benefit of all, Jew and Gentile alike, who believe.[9]

---

[9] I here presuppose, of course, one particular answer to the now notorious question of πίστις Χριστοῦ (faith "in" or "of" Christ). I think, actually, that the success of this way of reading this passage is the best argument in favor of the subjective genitive (faith "of" Christ) in some at least of the key passages.

Rom 3:21–31 then expounds this revelation of the divine covenant faithfulness. The central emphasis of this passage, I suggest, lies not on the human faith/faithfulness, which, in place of works-of-Torah, becomes the badge of covenant membership, but on the faithfulness of the Messiah, Jesus, as the means through which the covenant faithfulness of the creator is enacted.

The means of expounding this double theme is thoroughly Jewish. The supreme moment when the covenant god acted to deliver his people, because of the covenant promises, was the exodus. Paul alludes directly to this by saying that people are justified (that is, are reckoned to be within the people of god) "through the *redemption* that is in Christ Jesus." "Redemption," of course, evokes the slave-market metaphor, but this lies at the surface of the word's meaning. More fundamental by far, for a Jew, was the historical slave market of Egypt, from which Israel's god had liberated it. Now, Paul declares, there has been a new exodus, in which the same god has revealed the full depth of covenant faithfulness. The covenant was put into place to deal with evil, and that has been accomplished in Christ the ἱλαστήριον ("propitiation"). Just as regular Jewish discussions of the divine righteousness included the theme of the divine forbearance, so Paul's exposition here envisages the covenant god as waiting patiently, not punishing sin as it deserved (cf. 2:1–6). Alongside the fundamental covenantal meaning of the whole δικαιοσύνη θεοῦ complex, there is, of course, the second-order lawcourt metaphor, derived not least from the Hebrew Scriptures' image of the righteous judge: the judge must decide the case according to the law, must be impartial, must punish sin, and must vindicate the helpless. Rom 1:18–3:8 made it look as though the creator was faced with an impossible task: these various requirements are apparently mutually exclusive. Rom 3:24–26 claims that in Christ the apparently impossible has been achieved.

Two important results, one exegetical and one theological, follow from this. First, although I think it quite possible that in this passage Paul is drawing on earlier traditions, the main reason why that suggestion has been made in modern scholarship is to be ruled out. If there was a pre-Pauline Jewish-Christian topos about the covenant coming true in Christ, Paul is not opposing it. He is affirming it. The compressed nature of the passage owes more, I suggest, to the fact that Paul has imposed a self-denying ordinance at this point. The main thrust of the letter is not, in this sense, an exposition of the meaning of Jesus' death, of what we would call atonement theology. Paul is content to refer briefly to the achievement of the cross, and pass on.

Second, the divine "righteousness" (covenant faithfulness) is emphatically not the same as the "righteousness" that humans have when they are declared to be covenant members. That idea, despite its often invoking the "forensic" setting of the language, fails to understand what that forensic setting means. In the Hebrew lawcourt the judge does not give, bestow, impute, or impart *his own "righteousness"* to the defendant. That would imply that the *defendant* was deemed to have conducted the case impartially, in accordance with the law, to have punished sin and upheld the defenseless innocent ones. "Justification," of course, means nothing like that. "Righteousness" is not a quality or substance that can thus be passed or transferred from the judge to the defendant. The righteousness of the judge is the judge's own character, status, and activity, demonstrated in doing these various things. The "righteousness" of the defendants is the status they possess when the court has found in their favor. Nothing more, nothing less. When we translate these forensic categories back into their theological context, that of the covenant, the point remains fundamental: the divine covenant faithfulness is not the same as human covenant membership. The fact that the same word (δικαιοσύνη) is used for both ideas indicates their close reciprocal relationship, not their identity.[10]

The paragraph concludes (3:27–31) with a similarly brief account of the immediate result of the divine covenant faithfulness being revealed in this way. Specifically, it rules out a revelation according to the model expected within Judaism, that is, national vindication. The ethnic "boasting," of which Paul had spoken in 2:17–24, is eliminated, in a fashion that leaves two main pillars of Judaism undamaged. Monotheism and Torah, Paul claims, are enhanced, not undermined, in this paradoxical fulfillment of the divine righteousness. Rom 3:30 shows that the *Shema,* the basic Deuteronomic confession of faith which serves as a summary of Torah, is emphatically upheld when the one true god declares Jew and Gentile alike to be within his covenant family on the same terms.

Seen from this perspective, the place of Romans 4 in the argument is natural and completely coherent. It is not an "Old Testament proof" of "justification by faith," a mere prooftexting exercise resulting from Paul's ransacking of his mental concordance to produce occurrences of the roots δικαιοσύνη and πίστις ("faith") side by side. Within the poetic sequence of the letter, Paul moves on from the specific claims of 3:21–31 to the wider claim: all this has taken place precisely *in fulfillment of the covenant.* Genesis 15 was the chapter in which the creator god entered into covenant with Abram and promised him not only a large family but also that this family would be delivered in the exo-

[10] The case of Phil 3:9, often cited as if it were an example of "god's righteousness" seen as a human status, is not to the point; it is the status of covenant membership that is ἐκ θεοῦ, "*from god.*" 2 Cor 5:21, conversely, speaks of the apostles as being themselves the embodiment of the divine covenant faithfulness (cf. 2 Corinthians 3), not as having "god's righteousness" as their own status. On Rom 10:2–4, see below.

dus (Gen 15:13f.). If Paul's claim is to be made good, that in Jesus Christ the covenant has been fulfilled, it is vital that he should return to the fundamental covenantal passage and argue in detail for a meaning to the promises that has now come true in the death and resurrection of Jesus. In this case the focus is clear: Abraham is indeed the "father" of the covenant people of the creator god, but he is not the father "according to the flesh." He is the father of all, Gentile and Jew alike, who believe in the god who raised Jesus.

I therefore follow Richard Hays in reading 4:1: "What then shall we say? Have we found Abraham to be our forefather according to the flesh?" (Implied answer: No.)[11] But I diverge from his reading in terms of what this question *means*. Hays suggests that the "we" refers to Jews: "Do you think that we Jews have considered Abraham our forefather only according to the flesh?" I suggest, rather, that the whole of Romans 4 hinges on the question: Does this (i.e., 3:21–31) mean that we Christians, Jews and Gentiles alike, now discover that we are to be members of the fleshly family of Abraham? It is the question, in other words, of Galatians, which explains why there are so many echoes of that letter just here. Paul imagines that some Roman Christians will want to say: if you are right, and the covenant faithfulness and promises of Israel's god—yes, and the Torah itself—are fulfilled in Jesus, then you must be saying that Christians belong to the *physical,* fleshly family of Abraham. Romans 4 gains a new coherence, I think, when read as the answer to precisely this question. Verses 2–8: no, since "works of Torah" are clearly not involved as demarcating Abraham (or, for that matter, David) as god's covenant people. Verses 9–15: no, for Abraham was declared to be in the covenant when uncircumcised; after all, Torah was not involved in the process, and could not have been, since it would nullify the promises by calling down wrath. Verses 16–22, whose thesis, the real thrust of the chapter, is stated emphatically and cryptically in v. 16: "therefore by faith, so that according to grace, so that the promise might be valid for *all the family*, not only 'those of the Torah' but also those by the faith of Abraham, *who is the father of us all.*" We have not found Abraham to be our father "according to the flesh," but rather "according to grace"; the κατὰ χάριν ("according to grace") of 4:16 is the direct answer to the κατὰ σάρκα ("according to the flesh") of 4.1. Abraham's faith was in the life-giving god; 4:18–21 echoes 1:18–25, showing by implication how Abraham's faith is the genuinely human position, over against the Adamic refusal to give glory to the creator. This clears the way for the QED (*quod erat demonstrandum*) in 4:23–25: since "we," that is, Christians of all racial backgrounds, share this same faith, we will all, like Abraham, be

---

[11] Richard B. Hays, "'Have We Found Abraham to Be Our Forefather According to the Flesh?' A Reconsideration of Rom. 4:1," *NovT* 27 (1985) 76–98; idem, *Echoes of Scripture*, 54f.

reckoned as covenant members, on the basis of what the creator/covenant god has done in Jesus. Looking back to 3:21–31 (i.e., not merely echoing a randomly chosen pre-Pauline formula), Paul states that Jesus was given up "for our sins" and raised "for our justification." Sin has been dealt with on the cross (3:24–26); the resurrection of Jesus is the vindication for which Israel, the people of Abraham, had been waiting on the basis of the covenant promises; and now all those who belong to Jesus' people, who are characterized by faith in the god who raised him from the dead, are assured that the same divine verdict is pronounced over them, too.

This reading of Romans 4 suggests that the discussion of "works," "reward," "debt," and so forth in vv. 3–4 functions as a metaphor *within* the wider categories of "works of Torah" (i.e., badges of Jewish ethnic covenant membership). Rom 4:3–8 is sometimes cited as evidence that Paul did after all occasionally write as though he agreed with Martin Luther, as though (that is) the real issue he faced was the possibility of people trying to "earn" justification by "good works," by successful moral effort. The γάρ ("for") at the start of v. 2 suggests otherwise. The "justification by works" of which v. 2 speaks is clearly an explanation of something in v. 1; and v. 1, as we saw, raised the question not whether or not Abraham was a good moralist but whether those who are in Christ have become Abraham's family according to the flesh. I suggest, therefore, that the metaphor of "earning" by "working," which Paul exploits in vv. 3–8, is secondary, occurring to Paul's mind not because he is thinking about the propriety or otherwise of moral effort, but because he has been speaking of "works" in connection with "works of Torah" in the sense already outlined, and now sees a way of ramming the point home.

From this perspective we can see how, in Romans 1–4, Paul has set out the three tenses of justification. Justification is the *future* verdict in 2:1–16: there will come a day when the righteous creator will put the world to rights, and on that day some will be declared to be in the right, even though at the moment, within the poetic sequence of Romans, it is not exactly clear who will come into this category (2:7, 10, 14–16).[12] Justification is also the *past* verdict pronounced over Jesus in his resurrection: as the resurrection declared that Jesus was indeed god's son (1:4), so it declares in principle that he is the true Israel, the vindicated people of the creator. The famous doctrine of "justification by faith," as articulated in 3:27–30 and undergirded in 4:1–25, consists in the *present* justification (cf. 3:26, ἐν τῷ νῦν καίρῳ ["in the present time"]) in which the past verdict over Jesus is brought forward and applied to

---

[12] I agree with Cranfield (*Romans*) that 2:14–16 indicates the same category that appears in 2:26–29, that is, Gentile Christians. But I think that in 2:14ff. Paul leaves this deliberately vague for good rhetorical reasons.

those who have faith in the god who raised Jesus, and in which the future verdict is brought backwards with the same application and result (cf. 8:1: there
is therefore *now* no condemnation for those who are in Christ Jesus).

At the end of Romans 4, then, just as in principle at the end of chapter 2,
Paul has argued that the covenant people now consists of a group that is
demarcated not by the badges that signify Jewish ethnicity but by their
faith/faithfulness/belief in Jesus, himself the faithful one. More fundamentally, he has argued that the creator god has indeed been true to his covenant
with Abraham, in that in Jesus the Messiah the covenant faithfulness which
Israel should have offered, through which the dark world would have been
enlightened, has now been put into effect. The "oracles of god," entrusted to
Israel, have come true in Jesus.

IV. ROMANS SEEN FROM THE END OF CHAPTER 4

From here we gain one of the most important vantage points from which
to view the rest of the letter and its argument. It is not too difficult to see certain *theological* questions that need to be raised and that can in principle be
answered, from this standpoint. They can be itemized: (a) How can this verdict properly be announced over a people that is still not in fact completely
renewed and morally whole? (b) What does this then say about the divine purpose for Israel itself? (c) What are the implications for the church's life? It is
then (apparently) easy to see what happens: (a) is answered in chaps. 5–8, (b)
in chaps. 9–11, (c) in chaps. 12–16.

This is all very well; but does it do justice to the letter itself? The sequence
we have set out may in some respects correspond, in Petersen's terms, to the
narrative sequence which underlies the *poetic sequence* of the letter, though this
remains to be discussed. But the ease with which we draw up such lists
deceives us into thinking that we have thereby solved the problem of the
rhetorical needs of the letter, that we have automatically understood its *poetic
sequence*, as though it were after all simply an abstract theological treatise. If we
had lost chaps. 5–16, it is by no means clear that we would necessarily have
come up with such a list of topics as the right or appropriate way to continue
and complete the argument. And without a better understanding of these
rhetorical needs, and the way in which Paul has addressed them with this
actual letter, we are on dangerous ground in deducing a theological underlying narrative.

Here we must put together our awareness of what Romans 5–16 actually
contains with various possible hypotheses about the rhetorical needs. This
could take a lot of space, which we do not have; so I shall cut the corner and

suggest the hypothesis, and rhetorical strategy, of which I have gradually been convinced over the years. Paul's main purpose, I think, is to demonstrate to a largely Gentile Christian audience that (a) although it is true that the covenant promises, and the Torah itself, cannot now be read in terms of the validation of Jewish ethnic covenant membership, and that therefore (b) Jews who have not believed the gospel are therefore, for the moment at least, putting themselves outside covenant membership, (c) this does *not* mean that the Torah was a bad thing, or that the creator god has cut off Israel forever, so that the species "Jewish Christian" will shortly become extinct. Paul's strategy in arguing this, I suggest, is as follows:

(1) In chaps. 5–8 he shows that the full restoration of humankind, and of the cosmos, has in principle been achieved, and that those "in Christ" are the beneficiaries. This has come about because all the privileges of being the family of Abraham, the chosen people of the creator god, have been given to the Messiah, and to those who are "in him"; yet, at the same time, the Torah can be vindicated even in its negative task and function. This section is not an abstract exposition of "the result of justification"; if it were that, the detail of several passages, not least the crucial 7:1–8:11, would be inexplicable. Rather, it is the groundwork for the vital appeal that is to come in chaps. 9–11, which is later alluded to in the very revealing remark of 15:27: the Gentiles have come to share in the spiritual blessings of Israel, and therefore have a continuing obligation toward ethnic Jews. That this line of thought is present in chaps. 5–8 is strikingly confirmed when Paul, summing up the privileges of Israel in 9:4, produces a list of the blessings he has just ascribed to Christ and his worldwide people in chaps. 4–8: sonship (8), glory (5, 8), covenants (4, 8), lawgiving (7–8), worship (5:1–5; 8), promises (4), patriarchs (4). The Messiah himself (9:5) is the crowning blessing; and it is the Messiah himself who now belongs not merely to Israel according to the flesh, but also, and primarily, to the community of all who believe the gospel, Jew and Gentile alike.

(2) In chaps. 9–11 Paul uses the categories developed in chaps. 5–8 in order to expound the divine covenant faithfulness, the δικαιοσύνη θεοῦ. The purpose of this exposition, as suggested earlier, is to show that the divine intention was from the beginning that Israel according to the flesh should be cast away in order that the world might be redeemed. What has happened to Israel is not an accident (its god simply lost control of the situation, or changed his mind in mid-plan because of its recalcitrance), nor is it a sign that the covenant god has obliterated Jews from his purpose forever. Israel's rejection of the gospel and its "rejection" by the covenant god are to be seen, as the cross is to be seen, as the strange outworking of the divine plan to deal with the evil of the world; and, if that is so, Jews can and must be welcomed back into the covenant family at any time when they believe the gospel, and such a return

must be celebrated as a sign of resurrection. Here, I suggest, is the main rhetorical thrust of the whole letter. Rom 11:11–32, focused on vv. 18 and 25, states the point toward which Paul has been driving all along: you Gentile Christians in Rome will be tempted to boast over the Jews, but this temptation must be resisted. Yes, they have stumbled; yes, the Torah has been their undoing rather than their salvation; yes, the divine covenant faithfulness paradoxically involved them in being cast away so that the world might be reconciled (11:15). But all these things, so far from meaning that Gentile Christians are now the truest sort of covenant members, means rather that Gentile Christians owe the Jews an incalculable debt, cognate indeed with the debt they owe the Messiah himself, the Jew *par excellence* whose casting away meant reconciliation for the world. And that debt must be discharged in terms of a continuing mission to unbelieving Israel; indeed, the very Gentile mission itself has this as one of its sidelong purposes (11:13f.). Thus it is that the "gospel"— that is, the announcement about Jesus the Jewish Messiah and his death and resurrection—becomes the power of the creator god for the salvation of all who believe, the Jew first and also, equally, the Greek; thus it is that the covenant faithfulness of this god is revealed in this message, on the basis of, and for the benefit of, "faith" (1:16f.). This overview gives, I hope, the flavor of what is to come. We must now plunge into some details.

V. ROMANS 5–8

Chapter 5

As is often noted, 5:1–11 anticipates the conclusion of the whole section, 8:31–39. Its central thrust may be stated simply: if the creator god has acted in the death of Jesus on behalf of people who were then sinners, he will certainly act again at the last to deliver them, now that they are already his people. This draws into the center of Paul's focus the great theme of the *love* of this god. A moment's thought will reveal that this is every bit as much a *covenantal* theme as "righteousness"; indeed, it may be the case that Paul implicitly recognizes that δικαιοσύνη does not carry all the overtones of צְדָקָה ("righteousness"), and now moves into the realm of ἀγάπη ("love") in order to redress the balance. Not, I hasten to add, that he is simply working in the abstract; again, it is rather that the rhetorical needs of his argument demand that this aspect of the divine covenant faithfulness be brought out more strongly, without leaving the other behind.

If 5:1–11 gives a foretaste of the conclusion to the present argument in the end of chap. 8, so 5:1–5 contains the sum of chaps. 5–8 in a pair of tight-packed sentences. Indeed, 5:1–2 says it all even more compactly: being justified by faith (chaps. 1–4 summed up), we have peace with this god through our Lord Jesus Christ, through whom we have obtained access to the grace in which we presently stand (the cultic blessing previously associated with Israel's temple worship), and we rejoice in the hope of the divine glory (which Adam lost, 3:23; which is to be restored in Christ, 8:17–30). Already the great transfer has begun—the transfer according to which Israel's hope is made over to the Messiah and thence to his people. It was a characteristic claim of sectarian Jews that the glory of Adam would belong to them at the last.[13] Paul fastens on this hope as the ultimate restoration of genuine humanity which, anticipated in the resurrection of Jesus, will be given to all the Messiah's people. The Jew-plus-Gentile church has now inherited this supposedly Jewish privilege; Paul's stressing of it throughout this section is aimed both at showing Gentile Christians where their roots lie and, though perhaps not by means of this letter itself, "making my fellow Jews jealous and so saving some of them" (11:15).

The same is true, paradoxically, of 5:3–5, in which suffering itself is claimed as a sign of hope. The present suffering of the people of the true god, as they await their divine vindication, is also a Jewish theme now transferred, via the Messiah, to all his people. The hope that arises out of suffering is certain, because the love of god has been poured out in our hearts by the Spirit (5:5); not here, I think, the divine love for his people (Paul comes on to that in 5:6–10), but the love of the people for their god, as in 8:28, within the same sequence of thought (compare 1 Cor 2:9; 8:3). The *Shema* is at last fulfilled: in Christ and by the Spirit the creator/covenant god has created a people that, in return for redemption, will love him from the heart. The people defined as god's people by faith are the true covenant people, inheriting all the covenant blessings.

Chapter 5 thus unfolds, in characteristic Pauline fashion, from its tight initial statement of this *result* of justification (5:1–2), through a broader development (5:3–5), into a full statement of the position reached now in the epistle as a whole (5:6–11). This last draws out, in particular, the correlation between present justification, based on the death of Jesus, and the future verdict in which the justified people will be rescued from final wrath. The echoes awakened here include 2 Macc 7:37f.; 4 Macc 17:20–22: the death of Jesus has achieved what the martyrs (within those retellings of the story) had hoped to achieve, namely, the turning away of divine wrath from the people of god. The difference, of course, is that the community thereby rescued is not now the nation of Israel, but the Jew-plus-Gentile family as set out in 3:21–4:25.

---

[13] E.g., 1QS 4.22f.; CD 3.19f.; 1QH 17.14; 4QpPs37 3.1f.

And the result is that the boast that was disallowed to the nation of Israel (2:17–24) is restored to the people thus created: "we boast in god through our Lord Jesus Christ" (5:11). At every point in these eleven verses, that which is predicated of the true family of Abraham, those who are "justified by faith," is that which would have been seen as the privilege of Israel.

The great second paragraph of chap. 5 (vv. 12–21) can therefore at last tell the story of the world at its widest level. In Jewish retellings, Israel, or some subset of Israel, emerged as the people through whom the sin of Adam would finally be defeated. In Paul's retelling, as we might have anticipated on the basis of 3:21–4:25, it is in Christ, not in national Israel, that Adam's trespass is finally undone.

Two key modifications in the normal tellings of the story result from this. First, there is actually an imbalance between Adam and Christ: before Paul can move into the direct comparison (5:18–21), he must spell out the ways in which Christ does *more* than Adam (5:15–17). This is one of Paul's most complex passages, grammatically as well as theologically, but I think the right way through it is as follows. Israel's obedience/faithfulness should have been the means of undoing the problem of Adam, of humanity as a whole (2:17–24; 3:2f.); as we saw, the death of Christ (which is clearly the subject throughout this paragraph) functions as the true obedience/faithfulness of Israel through which this purpose is achieved. Rom 5:12–21 thus restates, in multiple and overlapping ways, what had been argued in 3:21–26. Christ has offered not merely Adam's obedience, but Israel's, the "obedience" that was to begin where the "many trespasses" of Adam left off (5:16). Christ, in other words, did not start where Adam started, but where Adam (and Israel) finished. Coming into the reign of death, he reinstated the divinely intended reign of human beings (5:17).

Second, the place of the Torah in the scheme is radically modified. Israel's normal tellings of the story would have included Torah as part of the means whereby Israel, defined as the people of the creator god, were enabled to escape the entail of Adam's sin and find themselves constituted as the true humanity. In Paul's summary, completely in line with 2:25–29; 3:20 and 4:14f., the law functions *to intensify the sin of Adam:* νόμος δὲ παρεισῆλθεν ἵνα πλεονάσῃ τὸ παράπτωμα ("the law came in on the side in order that the trespass might increase," 5:20). The story is now complete in Christ "apart from Torah" (3:21); the Torah functions *within* the critique of humanity as a whole, just as it had done in 2:17ff. within 1:18–3:20. This point is vital for understanding chap. 7 when we come to it in due course. Torah, instead of lifting up Israel to a level above the rest of the human race, simply throws a bright spotlight on the fact that Israel, too, is "in Adam," is "fleshly," is "sold under sin."

Is the Torah, then, to be cast off as useless, as a bad thing now happily got rid of? Μὴ γένοιτο ("May it never happen!"). "In the very place where sin abounded, grace also abounded." Here is the rhetorical argument of the letter in a nutshell. Yes, the Torah simply intensifies the sin of Adam in the people of Israel. No, this does not lead to Marcionism. How this is so is yet to be explained; it will take all of 7:1–8:11, and chaps. 9–11 as a whole, to do so. Paul, as ever, states cryptically that which he will later elaborate.

It seems to me that 5:12–21 thus functions *both* as the place where the "poetic sequence" of the letter is summed up *and* as the place where the underlying "narrative sequence" of Paul's theology finds its most fundamental statement. Taking the latter first, and looking forward to our later summary: the story of the creator and the creation, of the covenant purpose of salvation, of the strange twist that this purpose has apparently included, and of how that twist is finally resolved, are all here summed up. Taking the former (the "poetic" or rhetorical intention of this specific letter), it seems that Paul has deliberately summed up chaps. 5–8 in 5:1–11 in order that, by thus assuming for a moment the conclusion he will reach by the end of chap. 8, he can now offer this bird's eye view of the whole story. This will then enable him to develop specific aspects of the story in chaps. 6–8. His design at this stage is to give the (predominantly Gentile) Roman Christians exactly this perspective on the story of salvation, so that they may understand the positive purpose hidden within the apparently negative purpose of Torah and so may come to understand the positive divine purposes for the Jews at present hidden under the negative purpose of which the Roman Christians are at the moment somewhat too enthusiastically aware.

We should notice, most particularly, what Paul has achieved rhetorically and theologically at this point. Adam's story is the pagan story (1:18–32); and paganism, seen from the Jewish/Christian perspective, is the attempt to grasp at a form of human fulfillment, at a form of exploitation of the riches of the created world, without seeking to do so in the context of gratitude to the creator god, and so without proper responsibility. As a result, the end of the story is death; those who do not worship the life-giving god in whose image they are made come to share the corruption and decay of the present created order that they have worshiped instead. Paul's retelling of Adam's story, implicitly throughout Romans 1–4 and explicitly in 5:12–21, is therefore, as well as everything else, a way of saying: the true fulfillment you seek, the true human life, is to be found in Jesus Christ. He is the creator's means of rescuing and restoring, not simply of condemning, the world of humans and the wider creation. He is the way to recapture the lost glory (3:23). And he is this because he is the climax of the Jewish story. The glory is regained by the Jewish *route*, though not by the Jewish *means*. Adam's race, like Israel itself, has been in exile; Jesus has drawn that exile on to himself. In offering to the covenant god the obedience that should have characterized Israel (3:22; 5:15–17), he has become the means of Adam's rescue. Thus, to look ahead to the rest of chaps. 5–8, Jesus is the means of Adam's exodus (chap. 6); he is the means of Adam's Sinai, Pentecost (8:1–11); he is the means of Adam's entering at last upon his promised land (8:17ff.). All through, Paul is telling the Jewish story as the true-Adam story, in such a way as to undercut the stories both of paganism and of non-Christian Judaism. All that paganism itself had to offer, or sought to grasp, is relativized by the Jewish story, so that no pagan can boast; and all that non-Christian Judaism had to offer, or sought to grasp, is relativized by what Paul now tells as the true-Jewish story, so that no Jew can boast. The consonance of this conclusion with Rom 11:28–32 provides initial confirmation that it may be a thoroughly Pauline way of reading the text.

Chapter 6

From this perspective, we can see that chapter 6 is not a detached treatment of "the basis of Christian ethics," nor indeed simply a warding-off of the standard response that was made to Luther's gospel ("if we are justified by faith, not good deeds, shall we therefore not do good deeds?"). Rather, it is in effect the opposite question-and-answer to 4:1. If 3:21–31 could have been taken to imply that Christians were to be regarded as physical members of Abraham's family, 5:12–21 could be taken to imply that Christians were simply a new variety of pagans. If the Torah-defined people of god had been shown to be as Adamic as everybody else, does this not mean that one is simply left in the category of "sinners," confidently expecting that grace will come and find one there? Of course not, replies Paul: the people of god in Christ are marked out not by Torah but by the death and resurrection of Christ, which can be summarized, in the light of 3:21–5:21, as "righteousness" (6:16, 18, 19, 20) or, in the light of 5:12–21, as "obedience" (6:16). Resurrection, the great Jewish hope, has already happened; in other words, the entail of Adam's sin has already been broken, and those who are baptized have entered into the community of those for whom this was true, and can be "reckoned" as true, not by a supreme effort of moral will but by calculating what is in fact the case (that is the meaning of "reckon" in 6:11).

This has, of course, the force of a general moral appeal: no longer live like pagans, since you are no longer "in Adam." But the overall rhetorical purpose of the passage is much wider. The "sanctification" or holiness which Israel had thought was its in virtue of its election is now to be found in the risen Christ and in his people (6:19, 22). There can be no slide back into paganism, but it is not Torah that checks such a slide. It is the fact and meaning of baptism itself. Baptism has accomplished, graphically, the statement of present justification: the death and resurrection of Christ are brought forward into the present, and the verdict of the last day is truly anticipated. The "old human" (6:6), which seems to mean "the old Adamic identity," has been put to death. A new identity is given in Christ. Those who are thus "in Christ" (which I take to mean "belonging to the people of the Messiah") are to be regarded as those who have already died and been raised. In the context of first-century Judaism, this means that they are the eschatological people of the covenant god.

Torah has had nothing to do with their being defined in this way. Rom 6:14b ("Sin will not have dominion over you, *since you are not under Torah but under grace*") appears intrusive in the argument—until it is realized that the whole of chap. 6 stands under the rubric of 5:20–21. Paul is simply locating the church on the outline map of the divine purpose which he had sketched at that point. Torah, it there appeared, had been the divine instrument in confirming Israel under sin. Here, since (as the Roman church would have readily agreed) Christians are not under Torah, the rule of sin need have no dominion over them. Paul, in allowing this to stand, is of course letting the argument build up to the moment when he will need to mount his major defense of Torah, that is, in 7:7ff. At this stage he is stressing the general point that coming out from under Torah does *not* mean that one is therefore simply a pagan all over again, a "sinner" without the law (6:1f., 15; cf. Gal 2:17). This is the fundamental point from which he will argue, in chap. 11, his much more sharp-edged case, that one specific variety of pagan attitude, namely, anti-Judaism, has no place within the church.

Romans 7:1–8:11

If the material of chap. 6 is drawn from 5:12–21, the same is even more obviously true of 7:1–8:11. The way through the complex little argument of 7:1–4 is found by reading 5:20 in the light of 6:6 and 6:14f.: Torah binds "you" to Adam; Adam, the "old you," dies in baptism; "you" are therefore free to belong to another—namely, Christ—without Torah having anything to say about the matter. The problem, of course, is that the word "you" is made to do double duty; there is a "you" that is bound to Adam by means of Torah, so that this "you" cannot but bear fruit for death, and there is a "you" that is now set free from this bondage. For the full import of this to come out, we must remind ourselves again of how Israel would normally have told its own story. Adam's sin has infected the whole world; but (so Saul the Pharisee would have said) the creator god has given his Torah to Israel, so that Israel, married to this god—with the Torah as her marriage covenant—may be his people, his redeemed humanity. Putting this story beside Paul's, we see the following picture. Israel embraces the Torah as the divinely given covenant charter; but it also, in doing so, is embracing its covenant with Adam, and hence with sin and death.

This, to be sure, is complex. But such complexity cannot count as an argument against the exegesis, *for we meet the identical complexity in the rest of the chapter.* In 7:13–20 we find the double "you," only now in the first person instead of the second. And in 7:21–25 we find the double Torah: Torah, on the one hand, recognized as the god-given law; Torah, on the other hand, recognized as the bond with sin and death. The picture is the same as in 7:1–4.

What, then, is Paul saying by means of this highly rhetorical picture of Israel, Adam, and Torah? Seven things seem to me to emerge, all of immense importance for Pauline theology in general and that of Romans in particular.

First, as to the purpose and internal division of the passage. The chapter is a defense of Torah against any suggestion that it is identical with "sin" (7:7–12) or that by itself it was the ultimate cause of death (7:13–20). These are the most appropriate paragraph divisions (despite Nestle-Aland, and some other texts, which insert a paragraph break after v. 13), because of the clear question-and-answer format of 7:7, 12, 13, 20. One should translate 7:21a: "this, then, is what I find about Torah": vv. 21–25 are the conclusion to the argument, in which it becomes apparent that the Torah *bifurcates,* exactly as, by implication, in 7:1–4. The result is that Torah, the thing after which "I" strive when wanting to do what is right, *also* brings evil "close at hand" (7:21b). We should stress that νόμος means "Torah" throughout. Nothing is gained, and everything lost, by flattening it out into a general "principle"—as though Paul were not discussing Torah itself in every line of the passage. The same is true as we move into 8:1–7, where it becomes clear that the Torah is vindicated in and through the action of god in Christ and the Spirit.

Second, the flow of the argument from 7:7 on may be grasped by seeing it, in its two main sections, as the demonstration of what happens to Israel as a result of Torah. Rom 7:7–12 deals with the *arrival* of Torah as a one-time event; hence the aorist tenses. Rom 7:13–20 deals with the *continuing state* of Israel living under Torah; hence the present tenses. In each case what actually happens could be deduced from 5:20. In the first case, Israel, upon Torah's arrival, acts out the fall of Adam; hence the clear echoes of Genesis 3 in v. 11. In the second case, Israel, continuing to live with Torah, acts out the death of Adam. Whether or not it is true, as I have cautiously suggested elsewhere, that in 7:13–20 there are hints of the story of Cain,[14] it is clearly the case that the Israel that lives under Torah continues to carry about the mark of sin and death that results from being the child of Adam.

Third, the rhetorical "I" is best explained as an advance hint of the position Paul will take up in chaps. 9–11. It might have seemed all too easy for Paul to speak of "Israel" as though he himself were not personally involved, as though he had not himself lived in the position of which he here speaks. That would have been to play into the hands of the Roman church, ready to pick up any direct anti-Israel or anti-Torah argument and build their own construct upon it. Rather, he identifies himself with the Israel thus spoken of; this is his story, the sad tale of the αὐτὸς ἐγώ ("I myself"; compare 9:3). This does *not*, however, mean that it is what we would call "autobiography." As is often pointed out, Phil 3:6 pretty certainly rules out any suggestion that Romans 7 describes "what it felt like at the time." Rather, the passage is (as its derivation from chaps. 5 and 6 should make clear) a specifically *Christian* analysis of the plight of Israel under Torah.

Fourth, the frequently remarked parallel between 7:13–20 and passages in various pagan writers, describing the puzzle whereby virtuous persons finds themselves unable to accomplish the moral good that they approve with their minds (e.g., Epictetus, *Discourses* 2.26[15]), is perhaps best explained as follows. Paul's argument all along has been that Torah, in paradoxical contrast to its apparent intention, binds Israel to Adam, that is, to ordinary "sinful" pagan humanity. I suggest that in this passage, as a rhetorical flourish designed to appeal not least to a Roman audience that would have known this topos within pagan literature, Paul says, in effect: those who live under Torah have as their crowning achievement just this, that they come up to the level of— the puzzled pagan moralists. If this is the correct reading, it is actually not just a matter of a clever bit of rhetorical flourish, designed to put Torah adherents firmly in their place by showing that they do not in fact get beyond Epictetus, Ovid, or Aristotle himself. Rather, it also makes the point to the Roman ex-pagans, the point that prepares the way for 11:18, 25: Do not imagine that your pagan tradition makes you any more special than these noble Jews, who rightly embrace the Torah only to find that it becomes the unwitting vehicle of death. If they fail, the level to which they fall *back* is the level that, outside of the divine grace revealed in Christ, you yourselves would be proud to *attain* as the summit of your moral progress.

Fifth, Paul has so analyzed the failure of Israel and/or Torah that the solution to the problem lies close at hand. I have elsewhere shown that the refer-

[14] Wright, *Climax of the Covenant*, chapter 12.

[15] Cf. also 1.20.17, where Epictetus argues against the Epicureans, who say that "the good" resides "in my flesh" (cf. Rom 7:18).

ence to the sin-offering in 8:3 is exactly suited to the plight outlined in
7:13–20.[16] The sin-offering was designed to deal with sins that were committed either in ignorance or unwillingly; and that, Paul has said, is exactly the
sort of sin of which Israel is here guilty. As in 10:3, he claims Israel's ignorance
as part of the reason why it may now be rescued. It has not sinned "with a high
hand," deliberately going against the covenant plan of its god. On the contrary, it has honestly believed that it is following it to the letter. In the same
way, the failure of Torah does not lead to Marcionism. Torah remains "holy
and just and good" (7:12), even though it cannot give the life it promised
(7:10). When the creator god achieves, in Christ and by the Spirit, what Torah
by itself could not do, this functions as an affirmation, not a denial, of Torah
and its validity (8:1–11).[17]

Sixth, the underlying purpose of Torah, the reason why the covenant god
gave it in the first place, knowing that it would have these negative consequences, is here at last made clear, in a way that, like so much else in chap. 7,
points on directly to chaps. 9–11. This is what I have sometimes called "the
good side of the bad side of the law": instead of dividing the functions of
Torah up into negative and positive, as is sometimes done, it seems to me that,
within what is regarded as the "negative" side of Torah's work, Paul sees the
most positive role of all. This sixth point needs to be elaborated in a sequence
of moves, as follows:

(a) The covenant, we must remind ourselves, was put in place to deal with
the sin of the world. If Torah is the initial seal of the covenant, this must be its
ultimate purpose.

(b) Torah, Paul said in 5:20, came in *in order that* sin might abound. That is,
the divine purpose in the giving of Torah was in order to draw Adam's trespass to its full height precisely in Israel.

(c) This puzzling "in order that" is repeated and amplified in 7:13. Sin, *in
order that it might appear as sin,* worked death through the Torah, *in order that sin
might become exceedingly sinful.*

(d) I suggest that in all of this Paul sees the hidden divine purpose, in a manner not unlike that hinted at in 1 Cor 2:8, where the "rulers of this world"
did not realize what they were doing in crucifying the Lord of glory. God's
covenant purpose, it seems, is to draw the sin of all the world on to Israel, *in
order that it may be passed on to the Messiah and there dealt with once and for all.*
"Sin" is lured into doing its worst in Israel, in order that it may exhaust itself
in the killing of the representative Messiah, after which there is nothing more
that it can do. Rom 8:3f. is the great conclusion to this line of thought, pro-

---

[16] Wright, *Climax of the Covenant,* chapter 11.
[17] Ibid., chapter 10.

viding one of the most thoroughgoing statements of the achievements of Jesus' death anywhere in Paul. Torah could not of itself condemn sin in the flesh in such a way that it (sin) was fully dealt with. It could only heap up sin in the one place. Nor could Torah of itself give the life which, tantalizingly, it held out. In Christ the covenant god has done the former; in the Spirit this god has done the latter. The death of Jesus, according to 8:3, was the means whereby sin was condemned. (It is not strictly Pauline to say that *Jesus* was condemned; rather, *sin* was condemned *in his flesh.*) The resurrection of Jesus is the guarantee that the Spirit, by whom this was accomplished, will also raise to life all those who are in Christ (8:9–11).

(e) The apparently negative purpose of Torah, therefore, takes its place within what is essentially the most positive of purposes: the divine plan to deal with sin once and for all. This line of thought depends, of course, on the nexus between the Messiah and Israel: as Israel's representative, the Messiah takes on to himself the weight of heaped-up Adamic sin which Torah had left hanging over Israel's head. This, I suggest (at the level of the underlying narrative sequence of the letter), is the central significance which Paul here wishes to attach to Jesus' death. The "failure" of Israel is cognate with, and indeed designedly preparatory for, the crucifixion of the Messiah, without which, for Paul, there would be no covenant renewal (Gal 2:21).

(f) Israel's "failure," therefore, was part of the strange covenant plan of the creator god whereby this god intended to deal with the world's sin. This, I suggest (looking ahead once more to chaps. 9–11), is the theme that emerges at two crucial points: the "predestinarian" passages in 9:14–29, and the theme of Israel's casting away in 11:11–15. In the first of these, the "hardening" of ethnic Israel is seen as the strange means whereby the whole people of the creator god can be saved, just as Pharaoh's "hardening" was the necessary precondition for the exodus. In the second, Paul speaks of Israel's stumble as somehow instrumental in the salvation of the world. The two belong closely together, and both point to the eventual thrust of his argument to the Roman church: if *this* is why Israel has "stumbled"—so that you Gentiles can obtain the salvation won for you in the death of the Messiah—then you have no room to boast, and Israel has no reason to regard itself as forever cut off. Its stumble was necessary as part of the preparation for the crucifixion, both historically and theologically; now that this has been accomplished, Israel itself can once again be rescued, and indeed attain an honorable (and not a second-class) position within the renewed people of god. The gospel is "to the Jew *first,* and also equally to the Greek."

These six points about Rom 7:1–8:11 lead to a final, seventh, one. The action of the creator/covenant god in raising his people from the dead (8:11) is to be seen as the final great act of covenant renewal and vindication.

Resurrection is not, as it were, merely the glad human destiny for the members of a new religion that has left Judaism and Torah thankfully behind. In declaring that Israel's god will raise all those in Christ on the last day, Paul is explicitly transferring to this Jew-plus-Gentile family one of the greatest of all Jewish expectations.

Romans 8:12–39

All of this clears the way for 8:12–30, in which the themes of the letter so far are caught up and developed within a new argument: if the creator has thus dealt with the problem of Adam, this same god will thereby deal with the problem of all creation. In many first-century Jewish retellings of Israel's story, as in many subsequent Christian ones, this dimension of the covenant purpose was often forgotten; but Paul keeps it firmly in mind.

Before he can turn (in chaps. 9–11) to the specific issue he wishes to address to the Roman church, he must in this way show them that the entire covenant purpose is thus fulfilled in Christ and by the Spirit. The Christ-people are indeed the children of this god (8:12–17), inheriting the title ("son of god") Israel was given at the exodus; as a result, they are not to "go back to Egypt," but to go on through the present sufferings to the glory that is yet to come, the renewal of all creation, which will follow as a direct consequence of the resurrection of those in Christ (8:15, 17–25).[18] Here is the note of *hope* which has been sounded by implication so often since it was introduced in 5:2: hope for the renewal of all creation, in a great act of liberation for which the exodus from Egypt was simply an early type. As a result, all that Israel hoped for, all that it based its hope on, is true of those who are in Christ. Those he foreknew, he predestined; those he predestined, he called; those he called, he justified; those he justified, he also glorified. Likewise, all that paganism had to offer, in its deification of the created order, is shown up as a great parody of the true Christian understanding. The creation is not god, but it is designed to be flooded with god: the Spirit will liberate the whole creation. Underneath all this, of course, remains christology: the purpose was that the Messiah "might be the firstborn among many siblings" (8:29). Paul is careful not to say, or imply, that the privileges of Israel are simply "transferred to the church," even though, for him, the church means Jews-and-Gentiles-together-in-Christ. Rather, the destiny of Israel has devolved, entirely appropriately within the Jewish scheme, upon the Messiah. All that the new family inherit, they inherit in him.

---

[18] I am grateful to Sylvia Keesmaat for drawing my attention to aspects of the exodus imagery in this passage that I had not hitherto noticed.

Rom 8:31–39, like a musical coda, picks up the themes of the entire letter thus far and celebrates them in good rhetorical style. The divine love, which has been under the argument ever since 5:6–10, reemerges as the real major theme of the entire gospel message. This is covenant love, promised to Abraham and his family, a family now seen to be the worldwide people who benefit from Jesus' death. Since this love is precisely the creator's love, it remains sovereign even though the powers of earth and heaven may seem to be ranged against it. Since it is the love of the covenant god, it rests on his unbreakable promise. The language of the lawcourt and the language of the marriage contract thus merge (8:33–34, 35–39), with both of them now revealed as vital metaphorical aspects of the one more fundamental truth, which can be expressed both as δικαιοσύνη θεοῦ ("righteousness of god") and as ἀγάπη θεοῦ ("love of god"): the covenant faithfulness of the creator god, revealed in the death and resurrection of Jesus the Messiah and the gift of the Spirit.

I have stressed that much of Romans 5–8 must be understood, within the poetic/rhetorical sequence of the letter, as deliberate and explicit preparation for what is to come in chaps. 9–11. Paul is never, in this passage, simply celebrating the Christian hope (or whatever) for its own sake. The exhilaration of chap. 8, though clearly genuine and wholehearted in itself, is also at the same time a brilliant rhetorical device. The Roman readers, like any sensitive modern reader, could not but be swept up and carried along with the flow of Paul's discourse and its magnificent conclusion. Reading this passage (or, more likely to begin with, hearing it read), there could be no thought for them of lapsing back into the old paganism of 1:18–32. The glory of the genuine humanity, created in Christ and guaranteed finally by the Spirit, is here presented with the greatest literary and theological power. This is quite deliberate and prepares the way for the next section, totally different in mood and yet so intimately connected in theme. The stark contrast has nothing to do with different sections of the letter being loosely stitched together, or with a different theme inserted after a long lapse in dictation. The shift in mood is as much a feature of rhetorical skill as the sustained drama of chap. 8. As we have already seen, the underlying force of this whole section has been to say: all these blessings that you have, you have because the creator promised them to Israel, and has now given them, in Christ, to you. Therefore . . . what are we to say about Israel itself?

It is thus no denial of this poetic/rhetorical point to suggest that, in terms of the underlying narrative sequence, or theological story, of the letter, Romans 8 stands out as one of Paul's greatest, fullest, and most mature summaries of the gospel. Almost any Pauline topic that one might wish to discuss would lead to this chapter sooner or later. Just because we are rightly committed to reading it in context, we should not fail to notice as we do so the way in which it says, concisely, so many different things that Paul spells out in more detail elsewhere, and does so with a rhetorical force and flourish unparalleled even by Paul's own standards. We may suggest with some plausibility that we have here a sequence of argument and preaching which the apostle had used on many occasions, and which he adapted for its present purpose. If anything, it is Romans 8, not Romans 9–11, that gives us a hint of the sort of well-used sermon that Paul carried around in his head, or even (as C. H. Dodd suggested) in his knapsack.

VI. ROMANS 9–11

If we came "cold" to Romans 9–11, one of the first things that might strike us would be its story line.[19] Paul begins with Abraham, continues with Isaac and Jacob, moves on to Moses and the exodus, and by the end of chap. 9 has reached the prophets and their predictions of exile and restoration. Then, in 10:6f., he expounds that passage in Deuteronomy (chap. 30) which predicts the return from exile, and in 11:1ff. develops this in terms of the "remnant" idea, before reaching, toward the end of chap. 11, the great predictions of covenant renewal from Isaiah and Jeremiah. He narrates, in other words, the covenant history of Israel, in a way that, at least in outline, is parallel to many other great retellings of this story in Jewish literature.

This is already enough to alert us to a feature often ignored by scholars: that the whole passage is about the *covenant faithfulness of Israel's god*. Discussion of this cannot be limited to the occurrences of the phrase δικαιοσύνη θεοῦ (10:3 twice); when that phrase occurs in that context, its force is to sum up the whole argument so far. Israel was "ignorant of the righteousness of god"; that is, Israel did not understand or recognize what its god was doing within its history *in fulfillment of his covenant purposes*. Since Paul has already spoken of the divine righteousness being revealed in the death and resurrection of Jesus, it is therefore no surprise that this "ignorance" of Israel is directly correlated with its failure to believe the gospel, which is, of course, the material starting point of the whole section (9:1–5) as well as the focus of passages such as 9:30–33. The divine covenant purposes, it appears, are those that have been put into operation throughout the story. Israel's god has been narrowing it down to a point, choosing this son of Abraham and not that, choosing some of the wilderness generation and not others, making Israel, in fact, the vessel

---

[19] I have written in detail about these chapters in *Climax of the Covenant*, chapter 13. I am deliberately not attempting to summarize what I have said there, but to take a fresh run at the passage and see what emerges in the light of this paper so far.

of his wrath even as Pharaoh himself had been (9:21–23). This raises the question of the justice of such divine action (9:14, 17), which is, of course, the question of the δικαιοσύνη θεοῦ.

This, I suggest, is where the theme of 7:1–8:11 comes most strikingly to our aid. Paul is not talking about a double predestination of the Calvinist type. He is speaking of the way in which Israel's vocation to be the people of the creator god, including specifically its calling to be the "vessels of wrath," was the focal point of this god's plan to save the world. He can then sum up this theme in those often-puzzled-over phrases in chap. 11: "by their trespass, salvation has come to the Gentiles" (11:11); "their trespass means riches for the world, and their failure riches for the Gentiles" (11:12); "their casting away means the reconciliation of the world" (11:15); "you have received mercy because of their unbelief" (11:30); "they have disbelieved on account of your mercy" (11:31). This repeated emphasis is clearly a major theme of 11:11–32. It can scarcely be a new idea introduced at that point; it seems to refer to something already spelled out, which Paul there summarizes. I suggest that it all makes sense, in itself and within Romans in particular, if we envisage Paul's train of thought as running something like this:

(a) Israel's vocation to be the covenant people of the creator always envisaged that it would be the means of rescuing the whole world.

(b) This vocation could be, and was, distorted into the idea of Israel's privileged position over against the rest of the world, but in Christ this distortion has been shown up for what it is.

(c) The divine intention was, always, to deal with the evil of the world ("sin," personified as in chap. 7) by heaping it up into one place and there passing and executing sentence of judgment upon it.

(d) This "place" was always intended to be the Messiah himself.

(e) The necessary precondition for this judging of sin in the person of the Messiah was that Israel, the people of the Messiah, should itself become the place where sin was gathered together, in order that this burden might then be passed on to the Messiah alone.

(f) Israel was thus, as part of its covenant vocation, called to be the "vessels of wrath," the place where the wrath of the creator against the wickedness of the whole creation would be gathered together in order that it be dealt with.

(g) This was never intended to be a permanent condition. Israel was like a bomb disposal squad called to take the devastating device to a safe place to be detonated, and *then to leave it there*. If Israel clings to its status of privilege, refusing to give it up, it is like the members of a bomb squad who are so proud of their important mission that they become reluctant to leave the bomb behind.

(h) There can therefore be no covenant future for those Israelites who refuse to abandon their "own," that is, their ethnic, status of covenant membership

(10:3). Christ is the end of that road, the final goal of the covenant purpose which always intended to deal with sin and its effects (10:4, with all its deliberate ambiguities in play).

(i) But those who see, in Christ, the clue to what the creator/covenant god has righteously been doing in Israel's history, and who grasp this in faith—these Israelites can always regain their full covenant status, and when this happens it is to be a cause of great rejoicing within the community as a whole (11:11ff.).

This, I suggest, is perhaps the main underlying theme of chaps. 9–11, and it shows as well as anything else the close integration of the passage with the line of thought in the earlier parts of the letter. Building on the detailed analysis of the purpose and effect of Torah in chap. 7, Paul has told the covenant history of Israel in such a way as to bring out the strange truth of Israel's being cast away so that the world might be redeemed. This, I suggest, is simply in fact the writing into larger history of the truth of the cross. Israel is the Messiah's people according to the flesh (9:5); it has acted out on a grand scale what that means, namely, that it has become the place where sin has been drawn together in order to be dealt with. Beneath 9:5 lies 1:3f.: Jesus is the Davidic Messiah "according to the flesh." What is true of him was necessarily true also of his people "according to the flesh." This, I suggest, is at the heart of 9:6–10:21, and is the theological reason for the echoes of 5:10 in 11:15 (Christ's "casting away," like Israel's, means reconciliation; his new life, like that of Israel, means new life for others) and of 5:15–19 in 11:12 (Israel acts out Adam's παράπτωμα ["trespass"], just as in 7:7–12; it must then follow the Messiah through the Adamic death-in-the-flesh to new life).

But Paul has not told this story "in a vacuum." He has set out his material in such a way as to make the point that *the Gentile mission grows precisely out of this strange covenant purpose.* Rom 10:14–18, anticipated already in 9:24, 30, emphasizes that the apostolic mission to the nations and the incorporation of Gentiles within the covenant people of the creator god (9:30: "they have found 'righteousness,' even though they were not looking for it"), are the positive result of Israel's being "cast away." The inclusion of Gentiles is one of the features of the "return from exile" that takes place after Israel, the servant of the Lord, has borne the sins of the many. (Though Paul does not discuss Isaiah 52f. in these chapters, the occasional references such as 10:15 [Isa 52:7] and 10:16 [Isa 53:1] are, in my view, symptoms of a deep meditation on the whole passage as a major clue to the divine covenant purposes for Israel.) As a result, the rhetorical force of the entire exposition of the failure of Israel is not to give Gentile Christians a sense of smugness or self-satisfaction at their contrasting success, but to highlight and emphasize the fact that they owe the Israelites a huge debt of *gratitude.* This, of course, is precisely what Paul says in

15:27: the Gentiles have come to share in Israel's spiritual blessings, so it is right that they should reciprocate in terms of material blessings. It is also the theme that leads directly to the major thrust of 11:11–32, which ought now to be recognized as the rhetorical sharp edge of the whole letter. If I am right, the whole apparently negative emphasis of Romans 9 and 10 is to be read as an appeal for a sympathetic understanding, on the part of the Gentile church in Rome, of the plight of the Jews. Rom 9:1–5 and 10:1–2 are not merely personal intrusions into a devastating catalogue of Jewish failure. They are indications of the attitude Paul wishes his readers to adopt as they come to understand and appreciate the strange covenant plan whereby, for the sake of the world's salvation, Israel has stumbled over the stumbling-stone which had been placed in its path by its own covenant god (9:33). Paul, as in 7:7–25, sees "his flesh" in rebellion against the gospel (9:3; 11:14) and understands that rebellion in terms of the strange, but ultimately positive, saving plan of the covenant god, which will deal with Israel's unwilling and ignorant sin and so bring it, too, to salvation (8:3; 10:3).

The double movement of thought which comes together in 11:11–32 is therefore as follows. On the one hand, the Jews' "stumble," in accordance with the strange covenant plan, was part of the appointed means by which the Messiah would do his strange work of dealing with sin, and hence part of the means by which the world would be saved. Thus, the Gentile church in particular cannot look down on the Jews, but must recognize, as I have just argued, a great debt of gratitude. This builds exactly on chaps. 5–8, in which, as we saw, the privileges and blessings of being in Christ were so described as to make it clear that they were *Israel's* privileges, given to the Messiah and thence to all his people. On the other hand, the very fact of this transfer of privileges from Israel according to the flesh, to the Messiah, to the Jew-plus-Gentile church, means that Israel according to the flesh ought to be *jealous.* This is a major motif of chaps. 10–11, picked up by Paul in 10:19 from his favorite section of Deuteronomy (the covenantal passage in chaps. 30–32) and then developed in 11:14ff. Indeed, this motif only makes sense within the argument if the logic of the whole letter is more or less as I have described it. Gentiles have inherited Israel's blessings: this ought to make Gentile Christians grateful, and Jewish non-Christians jealous. What is more—since Paul is not, in chap. 11, addressing Jewish non-Christians, but still aiming rhetorically at Gentile Christians, as 11:13 makes clear—the prospect of this "jealousy" on the part of Jewish non-Christians ought, in turn, to heighten the Gentile Christians' awareness of the Jews' plight and of the appropriateness of Jews leaving their present state of "unbelief" and finding themselves to be valued and celebrated members of the one Jew-plus-Gentile family of Abraham

(3:30; 4:16f.; and now 11:23). The "olive tree" allegory is designed, I suggest, to make just this complex of points.[20]

What then of the "normal" reading of Romans 11, in which critical scholarship and fundamentalism have, for once, joined forces, suggesting that Paul here predicts a large-scale last-minute salvation of (more or less) all ethnic Jews? I have argued at length against this reading in *The Climax of the Covenant*,[21] and here wish to make two points only.

First, the rhetorical thrust of the passage seems to me clearly to have to do with Paul's missionary plans (cf. 10:14–18). His whole argument, I have suggested, is that the gospel is "for the Jew first and equally for the Greek." He is stressing, to a potentially anti-Jewish Roman church, that there can be no lapsing back into an inverted system of national privilege. He desires above all that the Roman church should understand his mission (for which he wanted Rome as his new base) in terms of the Jew-plus-Gentile strategy he intended to adopt, through which alone there could spring up the Jew-plus-Gentile church, through which alone the new, united humanity, about which Paul cared so passionately, could be evidenced.[22] The Roman church must not allow the latent, and sometimes visible, anti-Jewish sentiment in the proud pagan capital to infect them as Christians. The creator has not cut off his ancient people so that now there would only be a dwindling Jewish remnant, and soon a Gentiles-only church. The remnant is emphatically not a small minority clinging successfully to ethnic privilege but a remnant "chosen by grace" and hence not "by works [of Torah]" (11:5f.). If such a remnant exists, it can increase; Israel's god longs for it to increase; Paul's very Gentile mission is designed partly to help it increase, by the process of Israel's "jealousy" at seeing its own privileges being enjoyed by others. Paul's great hope, in writing Romans, is (negatively) to quash any potential Gentile-Christian arrogance against Israel, and (positively) to enlist the Roman church's enthusiastic and comprehending support for the fully-orbed missionary program which he intends to implement both in the capital itself and also around the western Mediterranean.

Second, the salvation of "all Israel" (11:26) does not refer to an event expected to take place at the "parousia." It has become customary to say, with E. P. Sanders, that Paul took the normal Jewish expectation and reversed it.

[20] Which explains some of its apparent peculiarities. Paul was not the only first-century writer to have an interesting time with horticultural metaphors; see also Epictetus, *Discourses*, 4.8.34–40. Compare too Ezekiel 17. Paul is not just using a "homely illustration," which could then be criticized if it does not work properly, but stands in a long prophetic/apocalyptic tradition of varied imagery.

[21] *Climax of the Covenant*, 246–51.

[22] Cf. Gal 3:25–29; Eph 2:11–22; 3:8–13 (usual caveats about authorship taken for granted).

Jewish "restoration eschatology" envisaged that Israel would be restored first, and that then the Gentiles would come to share the blessing. According to Sanders, Paul pragmatically reversed this order: now, it seemed, the Gentiles would come in first, and *then* Israel. What this reading ignores is that, for Paul, the restoration of Israel *had already happened* in the resurrection of Jesus, the representative Messiah. The texts he calls upon are the very ones that speak of Gentiles hearing the word of the Lord consequent upon the restoration of Israel. He evokes, in Rom 11:26b, not only Isa 59:20 but also, and perhaps more importantly, Isa 2:3 and/or Mic 4:2. When Zion is restored, the word of the Lord will flow from it to the nations: now, Zion has been restored in Jesus the Messiah, so that the word of salvation consists of Jesus himself, as Redeemer, coming *from* "Zion" to bless the nations. And the quotation from Jer 31:33 that appears in 11:27 is emphatically a prediction of the new covenant. Paul is not suggesting for a moment that Jews can enjoy a private covenantal blessing which still depends on a special, privileged, ethnic state. Rather, he is insisting that, within the renewed covenant now established in Christ and the Spirit, Jews are of course welcome alongside Gentiles. The καὶ οὕτως at the start of v. 26 does not mean "and *then*," but "and *so*," "and in this manner." This, Paul is saying, is how the covenant god will save his (polemically redefined) "all Israel." As a result of the Gentile mission, Israel will be brought to see "its" blessings, focused on its Messiah according to the flesh, now given freely to Gentiles; and Israel will want to come back and share in them itself.

Rhetorically, that is, in terms of the "poetic sequence" of the letter, Paul's main point is now made. He has told the story of the creator and the world as the story of the covenant god and his people, now understood in a new way on the basis of the death and resurrection of Jesus the Messiah. The message about this Messiah, as he said in 3:21, is the revelation-in-action of the covenant-faithfulness of this god: from this point of view, one can understand the plan according to which Abraham became the father of a worldwide covenant family, the plan according to which also Israel, after carrying out its fearful mission, can and must be invited to share in the blessings of covenant renewal. Gentile Christians, in Rome and elsewhere, cannot lapse into that anti-Judaism which refuses to see Jews as legitimate beneficiaries of the creator's action in Christ: the only story within which their own standing as Christians makes sense is precisely the Jewish story. They do not support the root; it supports them. Paul has placed the quite proper Gentile rejection of an ethnic-based people of god, the correct repudiation of Torah as the final charter of covenant membership, on to the larger plan of the divine covenant, in such a way as to undercut any possibility of Marcionism, of a rejection of Torah as less than god-given, of an anti-Judaism that would fit all too easily into the social pattern of pagan Rome and all too badly into a genuine covenantal understanding of the gospel. The sequence of thought of the letter so far is summed up in the "real" conclusion of its theological exposition (15:8f.):

> For I say that the Messiah became a servant to the circumcised, on behalf
> of the truthfulness of god, to confirm the promises to the patriarchs, and
> that the Gentiles might glorify the true god for mercy. (My translation.)

VII. CHAPTERS 12–16

Like many writers and lecturers on Romans, I have used up most of my space on chaps. 1–11 and have little left for the very important chapters that remain. I confidently expect, however, that, within the rhetorical setting of this paper itself, expectation and controversy will inevitably cluster around the first eleven chapters, rather than the last five, so that the imbalance, for all its risks, may correspond to the reality of our ongoing discussion. Something, nevertheless, must be said about the place of these chapters within the rhetorical design, the poetic sequence, of the letter itself.

Chapters 12–16, I think, turn from an argument that focuses on the *mission* of the church to an argument that focuses on its own internal *unity*. Having set out the covenant plan of the creator god, and having located the Roman (largely Gentile) church on that map, Paul can address both general and particular instructions to the church, the general preparing the way for the more particular. The appeal for unity-in-diversity in 12:5ff., following naturally from the appeal for the "presentation of the body" in 12:1, itself prepares the way for the more directed appeal of 14:1–15:13, where the main thrust of chaps. 12–16 undoubtedly lies. In the same way, the much-debated passage 13:1–7 makes a good deal of sense when read against the background of the Roman situation. If the Jews had been expelled from Rome within recent memory because of riots *impulsore Chresto* ("at the instigation of Chrestus"), the last thing the church needed was to live up to the bad reputation thus implicitly earned. The contemptuous references in Tacitus, Suetonius, and Pliny show only too well how Romans would naturally regard a cult like Christianity: a reputation for antisocial behavior was almost automatic, and the church should take care not to live up to it.[23] No pagan behavior was to infiltrate the church, who should live as the people of the daytime even though the night was for the moment still dark (13:8–14).

---

[23] Tacitus, *Annals* 15.44; Suetonius, *Claudius* 25.4; Pliny, *Letters* 10.97.

In this context, 14:1–15:13 makes its own clear point. If the riots referred to by Suetonius were indeed the result of problems within the Jewish community caused by some synagogues and/or individuals becoming Christian, and/or by Christian Jews coming from elsewhere to Rome and engaging in evangelism within the Jewish community, it was vital that the church itself should learn to live at peace along the "fault lines" that would most naturally develop. What Paul does, of course, is explicitly *not* to discuss these issues in terms of "Jewish Christians" and "Gentile Christians" but to line them up in terms borrowed from his (somewhat different) discussion in 1 Corinthians 8, where he had spoken of the "strong" and the "weak," both of which categories almost certainly included Gentile Christians, and both of which likewise may well have contained Jewish Christians. Paul refuses to reinforce a potential split by addressing different groups within the church in terms of their ethnic origins, but instead sorts out the issues as though they were simply a matter of private options.

This, of course, was in fact truer to life than some in the Roman church might have cared to admit. Paul himself was a "Jewish Christian" who took the "strong" viewpoint; presumably Prisca and Aquila (16:3) were too. And, underneath the whole argument specific to this particular setting, there runs constant reference to the narrative of the Messiah and his achievement, and a sense of overriding loyalty to him rather than to any other standard (14:4, 6, 8, 9, 14, 15, 18; 15:3–6; and above all 15:7–13). The covenant that the creator made with Abraham has been fulfilled in Christ, and a multiethnic people is the result; one must not, for the sake of human regulations, destroy this unique and climactic work of the creator god. Rom 14:1–15:13 is thus, like the rest of the letter, grounded in the basic christology of the gospel, the fundamental narrative sequence of Paul's thought.

With this appeal, Paul's theological task is over, and it remains to spell out the reasons for his coming to Rome (15:14–29), which we have already discussed. The request for prayer (15:30–33), the long list of greetings (16:1–16, 21–23), and the sharp extra warning (16:17–20) all make sense within this context. Even the closing greeting (16:25–27), sometimes regarded as secondary, seems to me at least a fitting conclusion. If we have grasped the subtlety and flexibility of Paul's thought in the epistle to date, excising such a passage looks suspiciously like straining out a gnat after swallowing a camel, taking revenge for the hard work of grappling with the rest of the text by dismissing a short passage that cannot, as it were, speak up for itself. In particular, there are a few hints in 16:25–27 which suggest that it belongs quite closely with the prologue to the letter, to which we must now return in concluding our study of the poetic sequence.

VIII. THE PROLOGUE (1:1–17)

With the letter as a whole now spread out before us, we may be able to understand more precisely why Paul wrote its introduction in the way that he did. He introduces himself in terms of the "gospel" by which his ministry is defined; and the "gospel" is not "justification by faith," not simply a message about how humans get saved, but the announcement of Jesus as the Son of god in emphatically Jewish categories (1:3–4). Paul may perfectly well be quoting an earlier formula, conceivably of his own earlier devising, but we should reject any attempt to marginalize 1:3–4 within his thought, or within the flow of the letter, on the grounds that it is too Jewish. It is precisely these categories (the Davidic and representative messiahship of Jesus, and his being marked out as Son of god through the resurrection) that are to dominate so much of the letter. It is this gospel of Jesus, representing Israel "according to the flesh," doing on its behalf and hence for the world what it had failed to do, that gives theological coherence to all that he is going to say.

The apostolic mission is the direct result of this proclamation (1:5–7). Its aim is "the obedience of faith"; "faith" is not, in Paul, starkly opposed to "moralism" in the way that, for contextual and polemical reasons, it came to be in later theological thinking. Though, of course, there is no sense of faith or obedience forming a human initiative which puts the creator under a debt; nor is there any idea that "faith" is not also, and does not lead further to, "obedience" in terms of 12:1, the glad offering of an entire human life to the service of the creator and covenant god in free response to mercy received.

Rom 1:8–15, leading naturally out of 1:6–7, then explains initially Paul's longing to come to Rome, anticipating the fuller statement in 15:14–29. This account of Paul's intention should not be split off from 1:16–17, even though it seems clear that those two verses form a short and pithy summary of the argument of the letter itself; in their context, they are offered as the explanation of why a visit to Rome, and by implication a mission that starts from Rome, are necessary developments of the apostolic mission.

Rom 1:16–17 then forms the statement of theme for the *poetic sequence* of the letter. Since Romans has often been seen as Paul's *Summa Theologica*, 1:16–17 is also often seen as the thematic statement for his whole theology, but this would be a mistake. In themselves, these verses refer back to the more fundamental entity of "the gospel," which, stated already in 1:3–4, is here presupposed. "The gospel"—that is, the Jewish message of a crucified and risen Messiah as the fulfillment of the covenant plan of the god of Abraham, Isaac, and Jacob—was of course multiple foolishness in the ancient world: not only a Jewish message, but such a bizarre one too! Yet, Paul declares, as in 1 Cor 1:18–2:5, it is within this strange and foolish gospel that there lies hidden the power of the creator god by which all humans, from whatever racial background, can be saved.

The reason why this gospel contains this power for these people is hidden in *the covenant faithfulness of the one god*. Here, in 1:17a, we can now see the theological dynamic of the entire letter, and with it the full meaning of δικαιοσύνη θεοῦ. The term is, and remains, based firmly in the covenant which was established with Abraham and with which Israel wrestled in succeeding generations, not least in the time between the Maccabees and Bar Kochba. But it always envisaged, at least as Paul sees it, not merely the divine faithfulness to ethnic Israel, but the choice of ethnic Israel as the ones who would bear the creator's saving purposes for the whole world. Here is the true thrust of Ernst Käsemann's point, that the divine righteousness has to do with the divine victory over the entire rebel cosmos; but this is achieved through the means that Käsemann never grasped, namely, the fact that in Jesus the Messiah the covenant purpose of the creator for Israel was finally fulfilled.

The covenant faithfulness of Israel-in-Christ, then, results in the revelation of the covenant faithfulness of the creator god. I therefore read ἐκ πίστεως ("from faith") in 1:17 in the light of 3:22, as referring to Christ's faithfulness, which in turn results in blessing for all those who are characterized by "faith" of the sort which will be further defined all through the letter. Hab 2:4 is drawn in, not as a proof text wrenched from its original context, but as a key passage dealing with the radical redefinition of the people of god through a time of turbulent crisis. In the midst of wrath and confusion about the covenant purposes of the one god, the prophet clung on to the saying that "the true covenant members would find life in their faith." Paul, in a time of even greater wrath, and even greater confusion about the covenant purposes of the same god, grasps the same point: covenant membership now has, as its worldwide badge, not those "works" which mark out Israel according to the flesh, but the faith which was Abraham's faith: belief in the god who justifies the ungodly, belief in the god who raises the dead.

IX. ROMANS AND PAULINE THEOLOGY

There is clearly no space for even an outline of the theological points that might be drawn out after this theological exegesis of Romans. But some concluding, somewhat unsystematic, observations may be made which will, I hope, sharpen issues for our continuing discussion.

First, a case has been made for seeing Paul not just as "a covenantal theologian," but as a very particular *sort* of covenantal theologian. He held on to the central Jewish doctrines of monotheism, election, and eschatology, seeing them all redefined in Christ and the Spirit. He rethought the entire world-view of ancient Judaism, not least his own former Pharisaism, without the slightest suggestion that in doing so he was selling out to, or borrowing indiscreetly from, the surrounding pagan environment. His theology and his place within the history of religions are characterized by his central belief that the creator god was also the covenant god, that the covenant with Israel was always intended as the means of setting the entire cosmos to rights, and that this intention had now in principle come true in Jesus and was being implemented by the Spirit.

Second, the reading of Paul's critique of Judaism which has been made popular by Sanders and others, in contrast to the "normal" Lutheran reading, has in principle been upheld by the details of theological exegesis. Paul's critique of Israel was aimed not at proto-Pelagianism or "moralism" but at ethnocentric covenantalism. What is not so often seen, though, is the way in which the theology of the cross, so dear to the hearts of Lutheran expositors as it is so close to the center of Paul, lies at the heart of this critique as much as it ever did in the old scheme. To read Paul in a post-Sanders fashion is not (as is sometimes suggested) to marginalize this central emphasis, but actually to give it its full measure.[24]

Third, however, Sanders's rereading has not, in my view, gone far enough. It still seems to assume, with the old model, that "justification" is a "transfer term" describing "how people get saved," and in consequence that Paul has actually pulled the Jewish theological language system out of shape. This is actually unnecessary, as is the continuing divide between "forensic" and "incorporative" readings of Paul's theology. Both of these latter categories are in fact outworkings of the central covenantal emphasis: once that is put firmly in the middle, all else falls into place around it, and the different metaphorical ideas that Paul evokes from time to time can find their proper places without getting in each other's way. "Justification" is not, for Paul, "how people enter the covenant," but the declaration that certain people are already within the covenant. It is the doctrine which says (cf. Gal 2:16–21 with Rom 14:1–15:13) that all those who believe the Christian gospel belong together at the same table. It is the basis for that unity of the church, across racial barriers, for which Paul fought so hard.

Fourth, we have seen all along that behind the *poetic sequence* of Romans, answering to the particular rhetorical needs of the situation Paul was addressing, there is a particular *narrative sequence* which shows, clearly enough, the overall shape of Paul's theology, and which, indeed, provides a window onto

---

[24] I have in mind, e.g., the polemic of Martin Hengel, *The Pre-Christian Paul* (Philadelphia: Trinity Press International, 1991) 85f.

the stories that characterized his entire worldview. The implicit narrative is the story of the creator and the creation; of the covenant with Abraham as the means of restoring creation and humans; of the paradoxical failure, and yet the paradoxical success, of this covenant purpose; of its fulfillment, both in failure and in success, in the death and resurrection of Jesus; of its implementation by the Spirit and through the apostolic mission; and of its final consummation in the renewal of all things. Romans is, perhaps, as good a text as any upon which to try out this two-level (or perhaps multilevel) way of reading Paul, and through which therefore to address our ongoing methodological issues concerning what sort of a thing "Pauline Theology" is, and how we might know when we have found it. Thus, it seems to me quite clear that Romans 5–8 is not the central thrust of Romans itself; but it may turn out to be one particular telling of the story which is at the center of Paul's narrative world. Likewise, Rom 1:3–4 is not the statement of the theme of Romans, but it is one particular statement of "the gospel" which, lying at the heart of his whole belief system, generated the specific argument of this letter, summed up proleptically in 1:16–17.

The proof of all these puddings will be in the eating. If I am right, or even partially right, Romans itself ought to gain in theological and situational coherence; and light ought to be shed on all the other letters, and on our various constructs about Paul's self-understanding and mission. This latter possibility is too vast to contemplate for the moment. I hope that this paper offers at least a step toward the former: in other words, that the text of the great letter itself can now be seen to hang together and to make both theological and situational sense, expressing exactly what Paul wanted it to express, addressing one particular context with one particular message, and at the same time drawing wholeheartedly on a consistent core, on a worldview and a belief system, in the midst of which Paul knew himself to be the servant of the Messiah, Jesus, called to be an apostle, and set apart for the gospel of the creator and covenant god.

3 ADAM, ISRAEL, CHRIST

The Question of Covenant in the Theology of Romans:
A Response to Leander E. Keck and N. T. Wright

Richard B. Hays
Duke Divinity School

LEANDER E. KECK and N. T. Wright have provided two richly nuanced approaches to understanding the theology of Paul's Letter to the Romans. On a first reading, these approaches—with their divergent methodologies—appear to produce fundamentally different accounts of the letter. I am persuaded, however, that a careful consideration of these essays will show that they share, at a deeper level, significant common ground. To be sure, the points of difference between them identify issues that may be fruitfully investigated in future work on Pauline theology; however, the common ground between Keck and Wright represents important territory gained by recent Pauline studies. In this essay I aim to name and claim that common territory so that, just as Paul hoped to bring the Roman Christians into unity so that he could use Rome as a staging base for further missionary work, so also these two substantial essays—despite their differences—can serve as a base for our further explorations of the shape of Paul's thought.

My working procedure will be as follows. First I shall describe several major *differences* between Keck and Wright, attending both to issues of method and to issues of substance. Then I shall attempt to identify the significant *agreements and convergences* in their accounts of Romans. Having carried through this comparison, I shall then respond to each writer individually, noting some of their distinctive contributions and highlighting certain features in their readings of Romans that seem problematical. Finally, I shall attempt to suggest some conclusions that emerge from reading these two essays in counterpoint and to highlight some unresolved questions that might form the agenda for further research on the theology of Romans.

I. KEY DIFFERENCES BETWEEN KECK AND WRIGHT

Questions of Method

The most immediately evident differences between Keck and Wright are located in the methodological assumptions and procedures that they bring to the task of interpreting Romans. I note four major ways in which their approaches stand apart.

(1) Wright presses hard to discover coherence; Keck probes for seams and tensions. According to Wright, the interpreter of Romans ought to aim for a coherent overall interpretation of the letter as it has come to us in canonical form: "Solutions that leave the letter in bits all over the exegetical floor do not have the same compelling force, as hypotheses, as does a solution that offers a clear line of thought all through, without squashing or stifling the unique and distinctive contribution of the various parts" (p. 31). Consequently, Wright labors mightily to render a reading that leaves no loose ends, organizing all of the letter's statements under the control of a master hypothesis so that "the text of the great letter itself can . . . be seen to hang together and make both theological and situational sense" (p. 67). Keck, on the other hand, devotes a major portion of his essay to problematizing the literary integrity of Romans (pp. 7–16). He sympathetically entertains various imaginative hypotheses that the text is a composite redactional product, and he declares his own preference for regarding certain difficult passages as interpolations, especially 13:1–7 and 16:17–20.[1] Such passages, he suggests, should be treated analogously to the Deutero-Pauline epistles and not relied on for interpretations of Paul's own thought (p. 16). Thus, while Wright eschews fragmentation, Keck eschews harmonization.

(2) Keck puzzles over silences in the letter; Wright fills them in. For Keck, various attempts to explain what Romans is about founder on Paul's stony silences (pp. 16–20). If the letter is an apology composed with an eye to Jewish Christians in Jerusalem, why does Paul neglect in 12:1–15:13 to deal directly with contested questions about circumcision and food laws? If the letter is directed at resolving local tensions between Gentile and Jewish Christians at Rome, why is the situation addressed so obliquely, if at all, in chaps. 1–11? If the letter is a fundamental statement of Paul's theology designed to win support for his mission to Spain, why are some major Pauline themes given so little atten-

---

[1] Keck has made similar arguments about other passages in Romans. See, e.g., "Romans 15:4: An Interpolation?" in *Faith and History: Essays in Honor of Paul W. Meyer* (ed. C. H. Cosgrove, J. T. Carroll, and E. E. Johnson; Atlanta: Scholars Press, 1990) 125–36.

tion in the letter (Lord's Supper, cross, parousia)? Wright, on the other hand, regards such silences either as signs of rhetorical art (e.g., Paul refuses in 14:1–15:13 to identify the issue as a point of contention between Jewish and Gentile Christians because he "refuses to reinforce a potential split by addressing different groups within the church in terms of their ethnic origins" [p. 63]) or as pointers to matters that required no explicit elaboration because they were so well known both to Paul and to his original readers.

(3) Wright correlates the details of the argument with the letter's historical occasion and purpose; Keck demurs. Wright sketches a scenario in which Romans addresses a particular crisis moment in Paul's missionary enterprise (pp. 34–36). In seeking to solicit support for his western mission, Paul was concerned to present his understanding of the gospel in a way that would combat "anti-Jewish sentiment" in the aftermath of the return of Jewish Christians to Rome following the death of Claudius in 54 CE, while at the same time opposing "any sense that Jewish Christians are superior to Gentile Christians" (p. 35). Keck, on the other hand, resists the effort to explain the letter in such specific situational terms: "given the nature and content of the evidence . . . the historical mode may well have promised more than it can deliver convincingly" (p. 6). The historical occasion—whatever it may have been—served as a "catalyst," but it cannot account for the actual content of the letter. "The fact that he [Paul] did not correlate what he had to say more explicitly with the Roman situation, or with his specific needs for the Spanish mission, strongly suggests that to understand what he did say we should not do so either" (p. 23).

(4) Wright interprets Romans deductively within a broad sketch of the symbolic world of Second Temple Judaism; Keck limits his interpretation to an inductive reading of evidence internal to the letter. Wright holds that all societies have a "worldview" which serves as "the grid through which reality is perceived and experienced" (p. 31). Such fundamental perspectives are usually unarticulated and unnoticed, but they form a matrix of thought that must be understood in order rightly to interpret any thinker. Paul, a first-century Jew, must be placed within the symbolic world of Second Temple Judaism, whose story can be broadly summarized—Wright contends—in a way valid for virtually all Jews of that historical period.[2] Wright's account of this story then pervasively shapes his reading of Romans. Keck, on the other hand, without denying the historical situatedness of Paul's thought, makes little appeal to other Jewish sources or to structures of thought not explicitly articulated in the text of

---

[2] Wright's detailed presentation of this Jewish worldview may be seen in his book *The New Testament and the People of God* (Minneapolis: Fortress, 1992) 145–338.

Romans. Thus, Wright runs the risk of superimposing an artificially constructed grid on Paul's thought, while Keck runs the risk of dehistoricizing Paul by isolating him from his native symbolic universe.

Questions of Substance

The differing approaches of Keck and Wright inevitably produce substantively different construals of the theology of Romans. Without going into matters of detail, the three most important differences may be highlighted as follows:

(1) Wright sees God's covenant with Israel at the heart of Paul's thought; Keck regards covenantal theology as displaced by Paul's fundamental concern for the salvation of all humanity. Wright's essay repeatedly sounds the themes of covenantal theology. Paul's "central belief" was that "the creator god was also the covenant god, that the covenant with Israel was always intended as the means of setting the entire cosmos to rights, and that this intention had now in principle come true in Jesus and was being implemented by the Spirit" (p. 66). Accordingly, Paul's programmatic expression δικαιοσύνη θεοῦ ("the righteousness of God") is to be interpreted as "the covenant faithfulness of the creator god" (p. 65). Keck, on the other hand, makes little use of the category of "covenant" in his analysis. Indeed, at one point, he even speculates (p. 19) that Paul may have avoided referring to the Lord's Supper in Romans precisely because the cup was understood to represent the "new covenant," a theme that would complicate his argument in chaps. 9–11. Although Keck does not deny the presence of covenant motifs in Romans, he finally regards the concept of covenant as too parochial and ethnocentric to do justice to the full scope of Paul's message: "However important are the election of Israel, the promise to Abraham, the gift of the law, and the Davidic ancestry of God's Son, in no way do these exempt 'the Jews' from solidarity with the Gentiles in the human condition. . . . It is the *human* problem that the gospel addresses" (p. 24, emphasis Keck's). Almost all the other theological differences between our two interpreters follow from this one fundamental divergence.

(2) Wright consistently interprets νόμος ("law") as a reference to Israel's Torah; Keck sometimes reads it, in accordance with Reformation tradition, as a generic reference to any sort of rule-governed structure of obligation. The difference becomes especially evident in a comparison of the two readings of Romans 7. Wright: "We should stress that νόμος means 'Torah' throughout. Nothing is gained, and everything lost, by flattening it out into a general 'principle'—as though Paul were not discussing Torah itself in every line of the passage" (p. 50). Keck: "The ultimate failure of the law, *any law,* is that it is ineffective against sin as a

power resident in the self" (p. 26, emphasis mine). Thus, Wright locates Romans 7 in the context of a specific debate about the role of Torah within the elect community after the death and resurrection of Jesus; Keck, on the other hand, reads the discussion as a generic phenomenological account of the human predicament.

(3) Wright interprets Jesus as Israel's representative, in whom God's covenant promise is fulfilled; Keck's account of Paul's christology makes no connection between Jesus and Israel. Fundamental to Wright's interpretation of the letter is his proposal that "the creator/covenant god has brought his covenant purpose for Israel to fruition *in Israel's representative, the Messiah, Jesus*" (p. 34, emphasis Wright's). The death of Christ functions as "the true obedience/faithfulness of Israel through which this purpose is achieved"; thus, "Christ has offered not merely Adam's obedience, but Israel's" (Wright, p. 46). Keck, on the other hand, simply declares that "Christ is the effective antidote to the Adamic situation" (p. 26), without making any reference to Israel as an intermediate term between Adam and Christ.

II. KEY AGREEMENTS BETWEEN KECK AND WRIGHT

Despite these major differences, Keck and Wright share more in common than might appear at first glance. Again, for the sake of clarity in the comparison, we shall attend first to matters of method, then to the areas of substantive theological agreement.

Questions of Method

(1) Both Keck and Wright hold that a study of the theology of Romans must investigate an implicit body of convictions that lie behind the explicit argument of the letter. Keck formulates the matter programmatically as follows: "What *makes* Romans tick is neither Paul's situation nor even the letter's actual themes but the convictions that both generate these contents and allow them to be juxtaposed" (p. 21, emphasis Keck's). Although Keck—unlike Wright—does not systematically set out a full account of these underlying convictions, he does point to at least one that he regards as fundamental to the theology of Romans. "The unexpressed theme that holds these eleven chapters [i.e., Romans 1–11] together is the freedom of God to be self-consistently faithful in the face of the human history of faithlessness and its consequences for creation. Although Paul never explicitly writes of God's freedom, it pervades the argument" (p. 27). Thus, the interpreter must distinguish between what Paul actually says in the letter and the unifying theology that undergirds his statements. Simi-

larly, Wright distinguishes between "the actual argument of the letter . . . and the wider worldview and belief system on which Paul draws" (p. 32). These different elements are described, borrowing terminology from Norman Petersen, as "the poetic sequence" of the letter and "the narrative sequence" of the theological story that underlies the text (p. 32). The task that Wright sets himself is to show how the letter's explicit argument ("poetic sequence") is related to the "narrative sequence" of Paul's symbolic world.

When Keck speaks of implicit convictions that "generate" the contents of Romans, he opens the door for hypotheses such as Wright's: perhaps an unexpressed story underlies the letter. The question remains, however, how fully Paul's underlying convictions may be reconstructed from parallel texts in the wider environment of first-century Judaism.

(2) Keck and Wright agree that a logic internal to the gospel drives the argument of the letter. In other words, the historical setting and purpose of the letter do not "explain" its content. "Romans ticks," Keck asserts, "because Paul did not allow his immediate situation to govern completely what he had to say, but allowed the inner logic of his gospel to assert itself even if that meant subjecting his first readers to a certain amount of theological overkill" (p. 29). Wright also can say, using very similar language, that a particular statement such as Rom 1:3–4 is "one particular statement of 'the gospel' which, lying at the heart of his whole belief-system, generated the specific argument of the letter, summed up proleptically in 1:16–17" (p. 67).

(3) Finally, despite Keck's methodological caution about constructing a reading of the letter on the basis of a theory about its historical setting and purpose, *Keck's actual account of the occasion for the letter tallies closely with Wright's.* Our authors agree that Paul is seeking support for his mission to Spain and that he must therefore provide "a theological grounding that is persuasive in a community of both Jewish and Gentile Christians" and that he must promote "a lessening of the tensions that divided that [the Roman] community" (Keck, p. 22). Keck's account is less specific than Wright's, but, as far as I can see, it is entirely consonant. This common perception of the situation that Paul is addressing allows the two readings to converge on a number of substantive issues, to which we now turn.

Questions of Substance

With regard to a number of central theological issues, Keck and Wright stand closely together in their reading of Romans. I shall enumerate only some of the most important points of concurrence.

(1) The universal scope of the gospel. As Keck formulates it, "Paul states the gospel in such a way that its scope reaches from Eden to the eschaton, from 'the fall' to the redemption of the world" (pp. 23–24). The gospel is therefore to be recognized as "God's saving power for every human being" (p. 24). Similarly, Wright, as we have seen, regards the gospel as the fulfillment of the goal to which the whole biblical story of election had pointed: the setting-right of the world under the sovereignty of its creator. Both Keck and Wright here stand in agreement with, if not directly under the influence of, Ernst Käsemann—though Wright's use of the category "covenant" to encompass the redemption of the whole world is foreign to Käsemann's interpretation. For Paul, the message of the gospel cannot be restricted merely to the religious conversion of believing individuals; it has to do with God's deliverance of the world from its "bondage to decay" (8:21).

(2) The centrality of the Adam-Christ typology. Both interpreters lay very heavy stress on the role of Adam in the theology of Romans. Keck (p. 25) explains Paul's preoccupation with Adam as a consequence of his radical diagnosis of the human predicament: "Given the need to show that the gospel provides the definitive remedy for the universally shared human condition, it is inevitable that Paul emphasizes Adam; in fact, he unpacks the Adam situation three times" (i.e., 1:18–3:20; 5:12–21; 7:7–25). Wright places even more weight on the figure of Adam. In 5:12–21, he contends, the theology of Romans emerges most clearly: "It seems to me that 5:12–21 thus functions *both* as the place where the 'poetic sequence' of the letter is summed up *and* as the place where the underlying 'narrative sequence' of Paul's theology finds its most fundamental statement" (p. 47). The extent to which Wright is willing to push this claim is illustrated by one sweeping paragraph in which he proposes that "Adam's story is the pagan story (1:18–32)" (p. 47) and that, throughout chaps 1–8, "Paul is telling the Jewish story as the true-Adam story" (p. 48):

> Adam's race, like Israel itself, has been in exile; Jesus has drawn that exile on to himself. In offering to the covenant god the obedience that should have characterized Israel . . . , he has become the means of Adam's rescue. . . . Jesus is the means of Adam's exodus (chap. 6); he is the means of Adam's Sinai, Pentecost (8:1–11); he is the means of Adam's entering at last upon his promised land (8:17ff.).

Here as elsewhere Wright's development of this theme is more lavish than Keck's; nonetheless, the two share the conviction that the argument of Romans 1–8 rests fundamentally on the typological antithesis between Christ and Adam, and that Romans 7 in particular should be read as an account of the Adamic situation.

(3) The faithfulness of God. Central to both presentations is the theme of God's unbreakable integrity and faithfulness. Wright, of course, more explicitly identifies this faithfulness as faithfulness to the covenant, but Keck also points to the fundamental place of the faithfulness motif in the theology of Romans. Romans 1–8 and 9–11 are held together, he suggests, "by a theology of God's righteousness (integrity) faithfully asserting itself salvifically through earthly discontinuities" (p. 26). God remains "self-consciously faithful" despite all human unfaithfulness, as Paul insists explicitly in 3:1–8. (In passing, one cannot help wondering how Keck understands such affirmations to be intelligible apart from the framework of a covenantal theology; *to what or whom* is God being faithful?) Wright, for his part, returns to this theme again and again, contending, for example, that in Romans 9–11 "the whole passage is about the *covenant faithfulness of Israel's god*" (p. 56). As Keck remarks, Romans is fundamentally "a theocentric text" (p. 27), focusing on the one secure center in a fallen world, the God from whose love nothing can separate us.

(4) The faithfulness of Jesus Christ. This point follows naturally from the previous one. Wright understands the divine covenant faithfulness to be "revealed *through the faithfulness of Jesus, the Messiah,* for the benefit of all, Jew and Gentile alike, who believe" (p. 37, emphasis Wright's). The central emphasis of the crucial passage Rom 3:21–31 lies, according to Wright, not on human faith in Jesus as a new "badge of covenant membership" (cf. J. D. G. Dunn), "but on the faithfulness of the Messiah, Jesus, as the means through which the covenant faithfulness of the creator is enacted" (p. 38). Keck places considerably less stress on this point, but at the pertinent point in his exposition (re: Rom 3:22) he also translates πίστις Χριστοῦ as "faithfulness of Christ" (p. 25). The result, for both interpreters, is that the theological focus in Romans lies not on the subjective experience of believers but on God's saving power through Christ's act *pro nobis* (cf. 5:8, 18–19).

(5) The elision of the parousia. Surprisingly, Keck declares that in Romans—despite eschatological passages such as 8:18–25 and 13:11–14—Paul "never mentions the parousia" (p. 20). Presumably this means that he agrees with Wright (p. 60) that 11:26–27 is not a reference to the future coming of the Lord. Keck does not, however, discuss the passage. It is not likely that he would endorse Wright's revisionary proposal that "for Paul, the restoration of Israel *had already happened* in the resurrection of Jesus, the representative Messiah" (p. 61). But how then does he understand Rom 11:26? In any case, neither author treats the future eschatological expectation as a major element in the theology of Romans. I shall return to reconsider this point below.

These brief observations should be sufficient to indicate how significantly Keck and Wright overlap in their theological readings of Romans. I turn now to raise a series of more specific responses to each of these interpreters individually.

III. RESPONSES TO KECK

Questions of Method

Leander Keck's essay is commendably cautious in its assessment of the explanatory value of historical hypotheses. We should not pretend to "know the unknowable" (p. 22), and we must recognize the limitations that the letter itself imposes upon our historical curiosity. This seems to me to be a wise caveat, reminiscent of Brevard Childs's suggestion that the canonical shaping of Romans permits it "to transcend the original concrete historical setting" and calls us to hear the letter as a broadly formulated proclamation of the gospel.[3]

All the more surprising, then, is Keck's decision to devote nearly half of his essay to summarizing a series of wildly speculative hypotheses concerning the literary disunity and prehistory of the text that has come down to us. Is it really profitable to rehash the idiosyncratic musings of Kinoshita, Schmithals, and Hawkins? Such theories belong in a museum of exegetical curiosities rather than in a serious discussion of the theological coherence of Romans. These hypotheses demonstrate nothing more than the inability of their authors to tolerate dialectical complexity. To be sure, Keck does not accept these speculations; he merely uses them as foils to illustrate the difficulty of tracing Paul's line of argument. The net effect, however, is to enhance our appreciation, by contrast, for Wright's sustained effort to read the text whole.

Keck's observations about the silences in Romans are well taken, but I wonder whether all of them are equally significant. The lack of reference to the cross does not seem particularly noteworthy in a letter that makes repeated references in other ways to the death of Jesus (e.g., 3:25; 4:24; 5:6–11; 6:3–11; 8:3; 8:34; 14:9, 15; 15:3). Apart from two clusters of references in 1 Corinthians 1–2 and Galatians 5–6, the specific terms "cross" and "crucify" are not common words in Paul (only one instance in 2 Corinthians; none in 1 Thessalonians). On the other hand, the omission of any reference to the Lord's

---

[3] Brevard S. Childs, *The New Testament as Canon* (Philadelphia: Fortress, 1984) 262. See also Richard B. Hays, *Echoes of Scripture in the Letters of Paul* (New Haven: Yale University Press, 1989) 35.

Supper is striking in light of the issues addressed explicitly in Romans 14–15. One wonders whether perhaps Paul was not able to assume any common tradition or practice of the Lord's Supper in the Roman house-church communities.

Questions of Substance

Keck affirms that "God's act in Christ as a truly eschatological event" necessarily calls for "a sweeping redefinition" of everything, including everything in Jewish history and tradition (p. 24). That, presumably, is why he shies away from "covenantal theology," which might be understood to posit too great a continuity between the past and the new life in Christ. Paul's "starting point," according to Keck, is God's act in Christ, not Israel's scripture or some set of preformed expectations established by the covenant promises. That is why Jews and Gentiles alike stand on the same ground, in the same relation to God through Christ.

As an account of the developing argument in Romans 1–8, this interpretation has many strengths, but one must ask a number of questions: How can Paul continue to insist that "the advantage of the Jew" is "much in every way" (3:1–2)? Why does he declare that his gospel supports rather than abolishes the law (3:31)? Why does he maintain so urgently that God has not abandoned his people? How do chaps. 9–11, along with the final recapitulation of the argument in 15:7–13, fit into Keck's construal? By focusing on chaps. 1–8 and stressing the radical eschatological newness of God's act in Christ, Keck moves chaps. 9–11 into the secondary position of being a special side issue to be resolved rather than being the central issue of the letter: "Romans 9–11 is nothing other than the application of the theology of chaps. 1–8 to the problem of Israel, its history and destiny" (p. 26). Here again Keck follows Käsemann. But if the problem of Israel represents merely one particular "application" of the more general theology of chaps. 1–8, why has Paul taken such pains from 1:16 onward to insist that the gospel is the power of God for salvation *to the Jew first* and also to the Greek? Why do all the rhetorical questions in the letter zero in on the status of Israel and the law? I would propose that the argument of Romans 1–11 has greater coherence and specificity than Keck's treatment would suggest. Its parts are held together not just by a common theology of God's integrity and faithfulness, but by a single line of argument about the distinctive form of God's faithfulness *to Israel*. Wright's analysis more adequately does justice to this dimension of the argument of Romans.

On the other hand, Keck's charting (p. 25) of the "spiral" pattern of the argument in Romans 1–8, dealing with the human condition on "three ever-deeper levels," is a helpful analysis that illuminates the progression of thought in the text without forcing it into an artificial grid. At this point, Keck's exposition seems to me to have the advantage over Wright's (see below).

One other point may be raised about Keck's emphasis on the redefinitional effect of God's act in Christ. If the Christ-event "reconstructs everything not aligned rightly with the character and will of God" (p. 24), should we pay more attention to Jesus himself—specifically in his death and resurrection—as a paradigm for the necessary restructuring, a paradigm that shows what the character and will of God looks like when embodied in human existence? This approach would perhaps help to integrate chap. 12 more fully into the discussion: the community's surrender of itself as a living sacrifice would parallel and reflect the action of Jesus in his death (cf. Phil 1:27–2:13). Furthermore, such an approach would also suggest that more attention should be given to the exposition of πίστις Ἰησοῦ Χριστοῦ ("faith of Jesus Christ") and to the role of christology in the theology of Romans. Keck touches on this issue but does not develop it in the essay in the present volume.[4]

Another question might be posed to Keck's interesting discussion of τὸ δικαίωμα τοῦ νόμου ("the just requirement of the law"). Keck argues that the phrase refers to "what is right in God's eyes without being Moses-dependent" (p. 28). How is this related to τέλος νόμου ("end of the law") in Rom 10:4? If, as I have argued elsewhere, τέλος means "goal" or "aim,"[5] and if Christ is the embodiment of the τέλος of the law, then the relation between 8:3–8 and 10:3–4 would be very close indeed. Christians in whom the δικαίωμα of the law is fulfilled and who therefore submit (ὑποτάσσεται) to the law of God (8:7) are set in contrast to those in Israel who do not recognize Christ as the τέλος νόμου and therefore do not submit (ὑπετάγησαν) to the righteousness of God (10:3–4). This is of course not a criticism of Keck's discussion but a proposal for further development along similar lines.

Finally, I would like to highlight and applaud Keck's concluding exhortation that our interpretation of the letter must make "space" for Paul's thought "to be grasped and dealt with as a construal of reality whose truth claims must be heard and addressed" (p. 29). It is good to be reminded, in the midst of an academic discussion, what is at stake in reading Romans. This is a text to be reckoned with: the reader who wrestles seriously with it will not be left unchanged. We should be grateful to Leander Keck for calling us—for whom the night is even farther gone than it was for Paul's first readers (cf. 13:11–12)—to hear the urgent "ticking" of Romans.

---

[4] See, however, L. E. Keck, "Jesus in Romans," *JBL* 108 (1989) 443–60.

[5] Hays, *Echoes,* 75–77.

IV. RESPONSES TO WRIGHT

Questions of Method

N. T. Wright's essay is a remarkable *tour de force,* consolidating the sprawling, untidy argument of Romans into a complex unity. Two methodological issues already noted in section I above loom large over Wright's undertaking: the role of Second Temple Judaism as a conceptual backdrop for the text and the question of the letter's overall coherence.[6] I shall comment briefly on each of these points in turn.

The first issue (the role of Judaism) has two distinguishable components. First, is it justifiable to construct a single symbolic/narrative grid that summarizes "how Israel would normally have told its own story" (p. 50)? Is it not necessary to acknowledge the varieties of Judaism in the first century? In fairness to Wright, the full argument for this synthetic procedure lies not in the present essay but in the much lengthier analysis found in his book *The New Testament and the People of God.*[7] Even there, however, one may question whether Wright's account of Judaism is sufficiently attentive to the sorts of Hellenistic Judaism that may have shaped Paul within the diaspora synagogue. As Luke Timothy Johnson protests in a recent review of *The New Testament and the People of God,* Wright's approach is in danger of pressing for "an artificial unification into a single story that he can term 'the authentic first-century Jewish worldview.'"[8] Second, even if one grants for the sake of argument the provisional validity of Wright's synthetic sketch, the question remains whether it is justifiable to read *Romans* within the apocalyptic and nationalistic framework thus described. Here a qualified answer must be given. On the one hand, some of the backdrop sketched by Wright is genuinely illuminating of Paul's argument; I would consider his account of δικαιοσύνη θεοῦ as God's covenant faithfulness to fall into this category. On the other hand, one sometimes has the impression that Wright's elaborate "set design" overwhelms the action "on stage" in the letter: for example, when Wright argues that Paul thought of the resurrection of Jesus as "the restoration of Israel" from a state

---

[6] One other minor methodological point may be noted in passing: Wright's adoption of the terms "poetic sequence" and "narrative sequence" (borrowed from Norman Petersen) is potentially confusing. As Petersen uses this terminology, "poetic sequence" refers to the way in which events are plotted in an actual particular telling of a story, as opposed to their logical absolute relation ("narrative sequence") on a time line. Since Wright is using the terms in a slightly different way, I think his point would be clearer if he would instead simply refer to the distinction between the letter's explicit *argument* and its underlying *belief system.*

[7] See n. 2 above.

[8] L. T. Johnson, *JBL* 113 (1994) 537, quoting Wright, *New Testament and People of God,* 149.

of exile (e.g., p. 61), one wonders whether the paradigmatic background sketch is controlling his exegesis inappropriately.

The second issue is closely related to the first. Is it possible or necessary to attribute to Paul's letter a comprehensive coherence? Must all the pieces fit into a single picture, like the bits of a jigsaw puzzle? Or is it possible that Romans might contain tangents and digressions not logically unified with its main line of argument? We may entertain this possibility even without recourse to Keck's theories of interpolation and secondary editorial activity. We need only suppose that Paul might have written a text that is less than fully integrated at the conceptual level. Anyone who listens to sermons—even very good sermons—over a period of time will be ready to credit this possibility, as will anyone who reads carefully through even the most scholarly essays. As Frank Kermode asks disarmingly, why does it require "a more strenuous effort to believe that a [text] lacks coherence than to believe that somehow, if we could only find out, it doesn't"?[9] Wright's effort to produce a reading that allows the letter to "hang together, . . . addressing one particular context with one particular message, . . . drawing wholeheartedly on a consistent core" (p. 67) is a bold thought experiment. (One is tempted to remark that Paul would have written a far more cohesive letter had he employed Tom, rather than Tertius, as his amanuensis.) Wright's attempt to press one particular construal of the letter's unity as far as it can possibly go has great heuristic value, for it forces us to explore both the possibilities and the limits of the explanatory scheme.[10] Wisdom may finally lie, however, on the side of Keck's more chastened acceptance that the coherence we seek may remain, at least in part, elusive.

Questions of Substance

Wright's essay is full of substantial and stimulating exegetical observations. It is impossible in this brief response to do justice to them all. I would spotlight for attention especially the following points.

(1) As already noted, the interpretation of δικαιοσύνη θεοῦ as God's covenant faithfulness (pp. 33–34, 38, 65–66) stands on firm exegetical ground.[11] As Wright recognizes, Paul subjects this traditional covenant lan-

---

[9] F. Kermode, *The Genesis of Secrecy: On the Interpretation of Narrative* (Cambridge, MA: Harvard University Press, 1979) 53.

[10] I note with interest Wright's acknowledgment (p. 67) that he might be only "partially right" in his comprehensive account of the logic of Romans. His point, of course, is that even if he is only partially right, some headway will still have been made in understanding the letter as a whole.

[11] See also my discussion of this matter in R. B. Hays, "Justification," *ABD* 3. 1129–33.

guage to significant hermeneutical transformation in light of the cross and resurrection, but the basic covenantal context of the language is crucial for
understanding the creative use that Paul makes of it.

(2) Wright's interpretation of Rom 4:1 is a helpful amendment of my own
earlier suggestion about how to understand this text.[12] Wright reads it as a
question asking whether the new Jewish and Gentile people of God (cf.
3:21–31) now find themselves to be members of the fleshly family of Abraham (p. 40). This makes excellent sense of the passage and also explains better than I had been able to do how 4:2–8 follows as a response to the rhetorical
question of 4:1 (see Wright, p. 40).

(3) Wright's reading of 5:5 as the fulfillment of the *Shema* is a fascinating
suggestion that deserves serious reflection: "The *Shema* is at last fulfilled: in
Christ and by the Spirit the creator/covenant god has created a people
that . . . will love him from the heart" (p. 45). Usually 5:8 is taken as a clear
indication that "the love of God" in 5:5, as in 8:39, must be a subjective genitive. Paul, however, is certainly capable of using language polyvalently, and,
as Wright notes, he can speak elsewhere of Christians as "those who love
God" (8:28). Wright's interpretation gives an excellent sense to 5:5 as the climax of the sequence of thought in 5:1–5.

(4) Wright's reading allows us to see clearly how 15:7–13 functions as "the
real summing up of the entire letter" (p. 36). The unification of Jews and Gentiles in the praise of God is the goal toward which the whole letter drives.

For the purposes of this response, however, it is perhaps less necessary to
praise Wright's exegetical work than to indicate some points at which I am
less than fully persuaded by his proposals, points where I think some critical
discussion is necessary.

(5) According to Wright, "Israel's obedience/faithfulness should have been
the means for undoing the problem of Adam," but Israel failed. Consequently,
"the death of Christ . . . functions as the true obedience/faithfulness of Israel
through which this purpose is achieved" (p. 46). I find this proposal theologically appealing—not least because it makes excellent sense of Paul's talk about
"the faithfulness of Jesus Christ" (3:22)—but I do not find it explicitly in the
text of Romans. Where does Paul ever say that Israel's obedience should have
remedied the problem of Adam or that "Christ has rendered not merely
Adam's obedience, but Israel's" (p. 46)? Such ideas must be read between the
lines of the text. Should we follow Wright in finding them there?

---

[12] R. B. Hays, "'Have We Found Abraham to Be Our Forefather According to the Flesh?'
A Reconsideration of Rom 4:1," *NovT* 27 (1985) 76–98.

(6) Wright's "bomb squad" theory of the atonement is explosive and dangerous in several ways. In his view, God designed "to draw the sin of all the world on to Israel" so that Israel in turn could pass it on to the Messiah, who "takes on to himself the weight of heaped-up Adamic sin which Torah had left hanging over Israel's head" (p. 53). Israel, however, by clinging to the law, which can only heap up sin, acts like "a bomb squad who are so proud of their important mission that they become reluctant to leave the bomb behind" (p. 57). Without doubt, Paul thinks that *Jesus* took upon himself the weight of the world's sin (8:3; cf. Gal 3:13 and 2 Cor 5:21). But where does Paul ever say that *Israel* was first supposed to draw all the sin of the world onto its own head so that it could be passed on to the Messiah? Wright's answer lies in his distinctive exegesis of Romans 7: the "I" who speaks there is both Adam and Israel, for Israel, having received the Torah, "acts out the fall of Adam" (p. 50). This "fall" of Israel is in accordance with the divine purpose to focus all sin on his covenant people so that covenant renewal can be brought about through the death of the Messiah who represents the people.

I find two difficulties with all of this: first, I am not yet persuaded by Wright's exegesis of Romans 7. If Paul is referring here to Israel, the people of God corporately, why does he not say so more explicitly? Why the simple and repeated first-person pronoun? Apart from the desire to produce a grand unified theology "behind" the letter, what factors *in the text* would suggest that Romans 7 should be interpreted in these terms? Again, Wright is having to read between the lines. The validity of his reading will have to be tested through continuing exegetical discussion of Romans 7. The second difficulty, however, is a more troubling one that has to do with the meaning of the text for us: the notion that it is *the Jewish people who somehow embody or absorb all the world's evil* could lead to some disturbing conclusions different from the ones that Paul draws in Romans 9–11. Certainly Wright does not intend any anti-Jewish implications, but his reading of Romans 7 is fraught with the potential for such inferences. In light of the ugly history of Christian anti-Judaism and in light of the fact that Paul never actually says what Wright's theory requires him to have meant, I would be persuaded only if Wright could offer considerably more exegetical evidence than he has produced so far.[13]

(7) One of the most curious features of Wright's reading of Romans 9–11 is that it places the "hardening" and "stumbling" of Israel *prior to* the death of Jesus: "[Israel's] stumble was necessary as part of the preparation for the cru-

---

[13] In *The Climax of the Covenant: Christ and the Law in Pauline Theology* (Minneapolis: Fortress, 1991), Wright offers what he himself calls "A Tendentious Sketch" of his reading of Romans 7 (pp. 196–200). This sketch is no more exegetically detailed than the interpretation of Romans 7 set forth in his essay in this volume.

cifixion, both historically and theologically; now that this has been accomplished, Israel itself can once again be rescued" (p. 53). But surely this misses Paul's main concern in Romans 9–11, which is that Israel has now fallen precisely because of their failure to believe the proclaimed good news of salvation through Jesus Christ. *The problem is not that Israel was sinful before the coming of Christ; rather, the problem is that they have been hardened against believing the gospel.* This is made most explicit in 10:14–21, especially in v. 16: "But not all have obeyed *the gospel.*" Paul is wrestling dialectically with a problem provoked specifically by widespread Jewish unresponsiveness to the early Christian mission. At this point, Wright's grand theory causes him—in my judgment—to overlook entirely what Paul is actually saying.

(8) Finally, Wright's treatment of Rom 11:26–27 should certainly demand careful scrutiny. The passage, on his reading, is not a prophecy of the parousia; rather it describes what has *already* occurred and is now occurring in the Christian mission: "Zion has been restored in Jesus the Messiah, so that the word of salvation consists of Jesus himself, as Redeemer, coming *from* 'Zion' to bless the nations" (p. 61). In favor of Wright's reading is the fact that it gives a reasonable account of the odd appearance of the preposition ἐκ ("from") in the quotation from Isa 59:20 ("The Redeemer will come *from* Zion"). No known manuscript of Isaiah cites the passage in this way. Wright is also correct in noting that "the quotation from Jer 31:33 that appears in 11:27 is emphatically a prediction of the new covenant." This too, would suggest that the taking away of Israel's sins might be understood as a present rather than a future event, since Paul elsewhere regards the new covenant as effectually inaugurated (2 Cor 3:6).

Wright's interpretation, however, fails to take into account the clear implication of 11:25b: "a hardening has come upon part of Israel *until the full number of the Gentiles has come in.*" Since Paul manifestly regards that condition as not yet met, it follows that the hardening remains upon Israel in the present and that the mysterious deliverance promised in vv. 26–27 remains a future hope rather than a present reality. Paul certainly would not say as unguardedly as Wright does, that "the restoration of Israel *had already happened* in the resurrection of Jesus" (p. 61). The resurrection of Jesus is for Paul "the first fruits of those who have died"; it retains always a proleptic character that is obscured in Wright's account. As Paul insists in 1 Cor 15:22–23, "for as all die in Adam, so all will be made alive in Christ. *But each in his own order:* Christ the first fruits, *then at his coming* (ἔπειτα . . . ἐν τῇ παρουσίᾳ αὐτοῦ) those who belong to Christ." The restoration of Israel, like the resurrection of the dead, remains a future hope for Paul.

Wright underestimates the extent to which Jewish rejection of the gospel is a puzzlement and a vexation for Paul, indeed a mystery. More justice must be done to Paul's sense of agony in this situation, his lingering hope that even unbelieving Israel will at last somehow be reclaimed by the mercy of God. The realized eschatology that Wright attributes to Paul in this passage is thoroughly out of keeping with the characteristic Pauline eschatological reservation, his insistence that "we hope for what we do not see" (8:25).

V. CONCLUSIONS: WHERE DO WE GO FROM HERE?

Having surveyed all too briefly the contributions of Keck and Wright, let us consider what ground has been gained and what direction future reflection on the theology of Romans should take. I would propose six conclusions:

(1) Future work must focus on the question of "covenant" in Paul's theology. This issue is crucial for any reconstruction of the theology of Romans, and Wright's essay has laid the challenge squarely before our group. Is his hypothesis to be accepted or not? How could it be confirmed or disconfirmed exegetically? It will be evident from my remarks throughout this paper that I regard Wright's fundamental intuition as correct: Romans is a defense of the covenant faithfulness of the God of Israel, despite—or, indeed, precisely through—that God's decision to embrace Gentiles apart from the law. The fundamental message of Romans is encapsulated in 15:8–9a: "For I tell you that Christ has become a servant of the uncircumcised on behalf of the truth of God in order that he might confirm the promises given to the patriarchs, and in order that the Gentiles might glorify God for his mercy."

(2) A corollary of the first point is that the gospel articulated in Romans addresses God's election and transformation of a *people,* not just individuals *coram Deo.* In other words, the theology of Romans deals with the formation of covenant community. (This helps explain, by the way, how chaps. 12–16 function as an integral part of the letter.)

(3) It should not be overlooked that Keck and Wright, by placing primary weight on *God's* faithfulness and *God's* initiative in acting to reclaim the world through Jesus Christ, have shifted theological emphasis away from the subjective experience and response of the individual believer. In this respect, their interpretations of the theology of Romans are both "post-Lutheran" (and post-Bultmannian) readings in a way that, say, J. D. G. Dunn's commentary is not. For both Keck and Wright, despite their differences, δικαιοσύνη θεοῦ ("God's righteousness") refers to the powerful self-consistent action of God to recover a fallen world and set it right. In my judgment, this theological con-

strual of Paul, building on a foundation that Ernst Käsemann laid, is fundamentally sound and must not be relinquished.

(4) Wright's use of "story" as a heuristic category for discussing the shape and logic of Pauline theology is a very important advance.[14] Even if Wright's effort to fit everything in the letter into one grand narrative structure is overly ambitious, the basic insight that Paul's thought moves within a story-shaped world is enormously helpful in our effort to see how various motifs in his thought are connected to one another and how he can hold ideas in tension with one another. The ongoing debate about the meaning of "the faith of/in Jesus Christ" finds its proper location in the context of our effort to understand the Pauline story of redemption.

(5) Both Keck and Wright—in these essays, at least—underplay the apocalyptic character of Paul's thought. The account of the theology of Romans given by these writers needs to be supplemented by the insights of J. Christiaan Beker.[15] Paul's theological reflection can be understood only as a theology for the time between the times, grappling with the vocation of a community suspended between resurrection and parousia, living in the present under the shadow of the death of Jesus while joyously awaiting the eschatological consummation of the hope for "redemption of our bodies" (8:23).

(6) Finally, I hope that no one will consider it special pleading if I call attention to Paul's use of the Old Testament as a particularly important theological issue in Romans that does not come clearly to the fore in the essays of Keck and Wright. Certainly Wright's emphasis on covenant presupposes the OT's promises as an interpretative matrix for the letter, but—perhaps because of the limitations imposed by the essay's scope—he does not reflect on the distinctive Pauline hermeneutical strategies and practices that allow him to appropriate the law and the prophets as witnesses to the gospel (3:21). For Romans, however, more than for any other Pauline letter, this hermeneutical process is

---

[14] For similar proposals, see R. B. Hays, *The Faith of Jesus Christ: The Narrative Substructure of Galatians 3:1–4:11* (SBLDS 56; Chico, CA: Scholars Press, 1983); idem, "Crucified with Christ: A Synthesis of the Theology of 1 and 2 Thessalonians, Philemon, Philippians, and Galatians," in *Pauline Theology, Volume I* (ed. J. Bassler; Minneapolis: Fortress, 1991) 227–46; N. R. Petersen, *Rediscovering Paul: Philemon and the Sociology of Paul's Narrative World* (Philadelphia: Fortress, 1985); S. E. Fowl, *The Story of Christ in the Ethics of Paul* (JSNTSup 36; Sheffield: JSOT Press, 1990); B. Witherington III, *Paul's Narrative Thought World: The Tapestry of Tragedy and Triumph* (Louisville: Westminster/John Knox, 1994).

[15] J. C. Beker, *Paul the Apostle: The Triumph of God in Life and Thought* (Philadelphia: Fortress, 1980).

somewhere near the heart of what makes the text tick.[16] Future investigations of the theology of Romans must pursue this matter more thoroughly. Indeed, I would suggest that the study of Paul's exegesis of scripture might offer us the only viable way to adjudicate the question of the role played by "covenant" in Pauline theology. Wright's thesis about the general significance of covenant in Second Temple Judaism raises some interesting possibilities for the interpretation of Romans, but the thesis will prove sustainable only if it can be shown in detail that Paul actually draws consistently on covenant language and exposits scripture in a way that highlights covenant themes. How does Paul's treatment of the scriptural texts handle the themes of continuity and discontinuity with Israel? Romans offers a rich trove of evidence to be explored on this question.

"Let us then pursue what makes for peace and mutual upbuilding" (14:19). Thus Paul exhorts the Romans. If the measure of our actions is to be the test of communal edification, then we should indeed be thankful for the work that Leander Keck and N. T. Wright have performed on our behalf. Our community of Pauline scholarship has been built up significantly by their insightful reflections on the theology of Romans; their readings, if we attend to them carefully, will make us all better readers of Paul's gospel.

---

[16] Cf. Hays, *Echoes*, 34–83.

Part II

Section-by-Section Explorations

4 ECUMENICAL THEOLOGY FOR THE SAKE OF MISSION

Romans 1:1-17 + 15:14-16:24

Robert Jewett
Garrett-Evangelical Theological Seminary

MY THESIS is that the theology of Romans should be understood in the light of Paul's missional purpose, which is stated in the introduction and reiterated in the conclusion of the letter. This approach builds on the foundation of Nils A. Dahl, who concluded that the "theology of Romans is closely tied to the Pauline mission with its historical and eschatological perspectives."[1] Paul presents himself in 1:1–6 as the representative of Christ, committed to preaching the gospel in Rome as a decisive center of a pluralistic world (1:13–15) and appealing for cooperation in the planning and support of the Spanish mission (15:22–29). This would complete the mission to the end of the Roman world, making possible the eschatological "offering of the Gentiles" (15:16) in fulfillment of the vision of Isaiah 66,[2] which would transform and sanctify the human race.[3] The conclusion of the formal proofs in Romans 15:7–13 contains six references to the Gentiles being converted by the gospel and lending their voices to the universal praise of God. The unification theme is particularly prominent in the citation of Psalm 117, "Praise the Lord, all you Gentiles, and let all the peoples praise him." All the peoples would include Jews as well as Gentiles, Greeks as well as barbarians. This echoes the theme

---

[1] Nils A. Dahl, "The Missionary Theology in the Epistle to the Romans," originally published in 1956 and reprinted in Dahl's *Studies in Paul: Theology for the Early Christian Mission* (Minneapolis: Augsburg, 1977) 88.

[2] See Roger D. Aus, "Paul's Travel Plans to Spain and the 'Full Number of the Gentiles' of Rom 11:25," *NovT* 21 (1979) 232–62.

[3] See James D. G. Dunn's comment on 15:16 in *Romans 9–16* (WBC 38b; Dallas: Word, 1988) 867: "And by speaking of the Gentiles as themselves the sacrifice, Gentiles who could not even approach the altar of sacrifice in the Temple, who were instinctively regarded by the typically devout Jew as outside the covenant, unclean, Paul confirms that for him the cultically defined barrier between peoples, between Jew and Gentile, had been broken through and left behind."

of "all the Gentiles" in 1:5, 13–14; 10:18; 11:25 as well as "all who believe" in 3:22, 30, producing a transformed human race that includes "all Israel" in 11:26 and simply "all" in 11:32. It is clear from these references that Paul is following an apocalyptic vision containing "a concrete utopian design"[4] of a transformed human race.

The peculiar cultural and linguistic conditions in Spain necessitated the unprecedented preparations implied by the writing of Romans.[5] The theological and parenetic arguments of the letter all serve this end, aiming at uniting the Roman house-churches so that such cooperation would be possible. Romans is a carefully designed, tactfully written appeal to the Roman house-churches to support Phoebe's patronage of the Spanish mission, which Paul planned to undertake after delivering the offering to Jerusalem. Romans should be understood as a document of missional diplomacy, which should be interpreted in the light of its intended impact on the audience in Rome and its ultimate goal of a world-transforming mission. Its thesis (1:16–17) concerning the gospel as "the power of God for salvation to all who have faith" implies that the restoration of divine righteousness will be achieved as the mission proposed in the letter is accomplished.

I would therefore like to show that, in contrast to the dominant tradition of theological interpretation, Romans provides a rationale for cooperative missionary praxis in a cross-cultural context rather than a program of ideological and cultural conformity. Paul's description of his missionary vocation and his use of shared confessional materials convey a sensitivity to cross-cultural issues. I will also suggest that, when one takes the interpolation of 16:17–20a into account, the canonical letter offers two antithetical modes of understanding the gospel of global transformation and pacification. The interpolation promotes righteousness through the enforcement of cultural and theological conformity, while the rest of the letter proclaims righteousness through a tolerant transformation of culturally diverse forms of faith. Unfortunately, the dominant tradition of theological interpretation has tended to understand the entire argument of Romans in the ideologically conforming spirit of 16:17–20a.

I

A brief treatment of the rhetoric of Romans will serve to frame the issue. While most commentators have avoided a discussion of the genre of the let-

---

[4] Dieter Georgi, *Theocracy in Paul's Praxis and Theology* (trans. D. E. Green; Minneapolis: Fortress, 1991) 82.

[5] See my study entitled "Paul, Phoebe, and the Spanish Mission," in *The Social World of Formative Christianity and Judaism: Essays in Tribute to Howard Clark Kee* (ed. P. Borgen et al.; Philadelphia: Fortress, 1988) 144–64.

ter, they have tacitly assumed it is either forensic or deliberative. Whether one views Romans as a forensic defense of the true gospel against misunderstandings and criticisms,[6] or as a protreptic letter in the deliberative genre designed to convert the Romans to Paul's point of view,[7] the evidence concerning cultural and theological diversity tends to be played down, and the spirit of 16:17–20 continues to hover over the discussion. The decisive breakthrough in my understanding of the issue was provided by Wilhelm Wuellner's analysis of the demonstrative genre of Romans.[8] In "Romans as an Ambassadorial Letter," I suggested that a narrowing of the demonstrative genre was warranted by the peculiar content and form of the letter.[9] Romans appears to be a fusion of the ambassadorial letter with several other subtypes that could fit either within the deliberative or the demonstrative genre: the philosophical diatribe, the parenetic letter, and the hortatory letter. The nature of the materials, the generalizing style of argumentation, and the relation between writer and audience point more strongly to the demonstrative alternative.

Here is a sketch of the disposition in the sections of Romans dealt with in this paper, using traditional rhetorical categories.[10] The *exordium* ("introduction") consists of 1:1–12, where Paul introduces himself to the divided Roman audience, stressing his apostolic vocation, defining his gospel in a preliminary way, and thanking God for their faith. He concludes with the main purpose of his letter, his forthcoming visit to Rome for the sake of the world mission. The narration section is found in 1:13–15, where Paul describes the background of his missionary project to visit Rome, which has thus far been frustrated. The letter then provides a formal thesis statement (1:16–17), where Paul states the major contention of the letter concerning the gospel as the powerful embodiment of the righteousness of God for an inclusive community of faith.

In the formal proofs of the letter (1:18–15:13), which are being covered by other colleagues, Paul argues that the righteousness of God, rightly understood, has transforming implications for the Roman churches and their par-

---

[6] See, e.g., Peter Stuhlmacher, "The Purpose of Romans," 236, and "The Theme of Romans," 333, in *The Romans Debate* (ed. Karl P. Donfried; rev. ed.; Peabody, MA: Hendrickson, 1991).

[7] See David E. Aune, "Romans as a *Logos Protreptikos*," in *The Romans Debate,* ed. Donfried, 278–96.

[8] Wilhelm Wuellner, "Paul's Rhetoric of Argumentation in Romans: An Alternative to the Donfried-Karris Debate Over Romans," first published in 1976 and reprinted in *The Romans Debate,* ed. Donfried, 128–46.

[9] Robert Jewett, "Romans as an Ambassadorial Letter," *Int* 36 (1982) 5–20.

[10] My preliminary assessment of the rhetorical disposition is available in "Following the Argument of Romans," *WW* 6 (1986) 382–89, which was revised and reprinted in *The Romans Debate,* ed. Donfried, 265–77.

ticipation in world mission. The proof consists of four major arguments, a confirmation of the thesis followed by three amplifications, each of which has an important bearing on the situation in the house- and tenement-churches and on the subject of the mission to Spain.

The peroration (15:14–16:27), to be discussed in this paper, consists of an appeal for the cooperation of the Roman congregations in missionary activities in Jerusalem, Rome, and Spain. With the elimination of the two interpolations—the warning against heretics in 16:17–20a and the concluding doxology in 16:25–27—this peroration is organized in five distinct sections: (a) the recapitulation of Paul's missionary calling and strategy (15:14–21); (b) the appeal for participation in Paul's present and future missionary plans (15:22–33); (c) the recommendation of Phoebe (16:1–2); (d) greetings and commendations between missionary leaders (16:3–16, 21–23); and (e) the epistolary benediction (16:20b).

The disposition of Romans reveals not only rhetorical skill and forethought but also the intent to find common ground between the ethnic factions in the Roman house- and tenement-churches.[11] The goal of the entire argument, in fact, is to sustain the ethos of global pacification through the gospel, as the climax of the theological and ethical argument in 15:7–13 reveals.[12] If one were to pose the traditional question, however, of the "high point" or "climax" of Romans, it is surely be found in the peroration in chaps. 15–16 rather than in one of the doctrinal themes of the earlier part of the letter. If the dynamics of ancient rhetoric are taken into account, the proofs of the earlier chapters of Romans are seen to have a practical purpose developed with powerful emotional appeals at the end of the discourse. This purpose was to elicit the cooperation of the Roman house- and tenement-churches in Paul's missionary activities, thus serving the ultimate purpose of divine righteousness in regaining control of a lost and disobedient world. Salvation is inextricably joined here with world transformation, theology with ethics. This theological and rhetorical purpose is visible from the opening verses of the letter.

II

The evidence concerning the situation in the Roman churches provides support for the thesis concerning the tolerant, ecumenical focus of the theology of the letter. In contrast to my earlier work on Romans in connection

[11] For a definitive analysis of the complex ethnic and theological diversity in the Roman congregation, see James C. Walters, *Ethnic Issues in Paul's Letter to the Romans: Changing Self-Definitions in Earliest Roman Christianity* (Valley Forge, PA: Trinity Press International, 1994) esp. 84–92.

[12] See Dahl, "Missionary Theology," 87.

with the anthropological terms, I have abandoned the assumption that chap. 16 was directed to the Ephesian church and thus was irrelevant for reconstructing the situation at Rome.[13] This led to an analysis of the evidence concerning Roman house- and tenement-churches in chap. 16 and to preliminary efforts at correlating that evidence with the argument in chaps. 14–15.[14] Building on the historical scenario developed by Wolfgang Wiefel and amplified by Peter Lampe, I assume that the letter reflects multiple congregations of differing cultural backgrounds that are interacting critically with each other and are resisting the return of some of the Jewish Christian refugees after the lapse of the Edict of Claudius around 54 CE.[15]

Paul's approach to this complicated situation of cultural and theological conflict is to seek common ground. The expansive exordium sets the tone for the entire letter. Calvin J. Roetzel draws a widely shared inference from these expansions that Paul desired to "establish the 'orthodoxy' of his gospel and the legitimacy of his apostleship" against suspicions that he was a "theological maverick" and an "interloper" in the Roman church.[16] I would suggest, in contrast, that the expansions are designed to find common ground with various Christian groups in Rome, eliciting their "intensity of adherence" to Paul's project.[17] Two themes in the opening verse, the "apostle" and the "gospel," are expanded and developed in reverse sequence, with the latter taking up vv. 2–4 and the former v. 5. The delay in taking up the issue of apostolicity is balanced out, as it were, by the initial threefold expansion in v. 1 concerning Paul's office as "slave of Christ Jesus," his being "called" to the

---

[13] See Robert Jewett, *Paul's Anthropological Terms: A Study of Their Use in Conflict Settings* (Leiden: Brill, 1971) 41–42. The studies that caused my reappraisal of chap. 16 are the following: Harry Gamble, Jr., *The Textual History of the Letter to the Romans: A Study in Textual and Literary Criticism* (Studies and Documents 42; Grand Rapids: Eerdmans, 1977); Kurt Aland, "Der Schluss und die ursprüngliche Gestalt des Römerbriefes," in *Neutestamentliche Entwürfe* (Munich: Kaiser, 1979) 284–350; and especially Wolf-Hennig Ollrog, "Die Abfassungsverhältnisse von Röm 16," in *Kirche: Festschrift für Günther Bornkamm zum 75. Geburtstag* (ed. D. Lührmann and G. Strecker; Tübingen: Mohr [Siebeck], 1980) 221–44.

[14] Robert Jewett, *Christian Tolerance: Paul's Message to the Modern Church* (Philadelphia: Westminster, 1982) 26–36, 121–47; see also the relevant sections of my popular commentary, *Romans* (Nashville: United Methodist Publishing House, 1988).

[15] Wolfgang Wiefel, "The Jewish Community in Ancient Rome and the Origins of Roman Christianity," the translation of a 1970 article in *The Romans Debate,* ed. Donfried, 85–101; Peter Lampe, *Die stadtrömischen Christen in den ersten beiden Jahrhunderten: Untersuchungen zur Sozialgeschichte* (WUNT 2/18; Tübingen: Mohr [Siebeck], 1987, 1989); idem, "The Roman Christians of Romans 16," in *The Romans Debate,* ed. Donfried, 216–30.

[16] Calvin J. Roetzel, *The Letters of Paul: Conversations in Context* (Atlanta: John Knox, 1975) 20.

[17] See A. B. du Toit, "Persuasion in Romans 1:1–17," *BZ* 33 (1989) 192–209, esp. 200.

apostolic task and being "set apart" by God to proclaim the gospel.[18] The expansion of the "gospel" motif begins with a claim of scriptural foundation in v. 2, which would have been shared by all of the Christian groups in Rome. Paul then moves to a creedal formula in vv. 3–4 that reflects both Jewish Christian and Gentile Christian concerns—to be analyzed in section III below. The elaboration of "apostle" recurs in v. 5 with an insistence on its derivation from Christ, its coordination with "grace," and its inclusive scope among "all the Gentiles."[19] And although Don B. Garlington takes it as a given that the phrase in this verse coined by Paul, "the obedience of faith," had a polemical and antithetical motivation in contrast to Jewish theology,[20] it appears more likely that it would have honored both Jewish Christian and Gentile Christian concerns in Rome. Particularly if the genitive construction "obedience of faith" is taken to be epexegetical or appositional, translated as "the obedience which consists in faith,"[21] the equivalence of these two terms is maintained. Since "obedience" was a favored concept for Jewish theology[22] and "faith" was a favorite shibboleth for Gentile Christians in Rome (14:1, 22, 23), the coordination of these two terms conveys an interest in finding common ground. There is not a hint of polemical intent in the wording of 1:5 or in its rhetorical echo of 15:18.

The situation in the Roman house- and tenement-churches may also explain the peculiar address of Romans in 1:6–7. Commentators have wondered why the letter was not addressed to the "church" or "churches" in Rome.[23] Further, there is no satisfactory explanation of the peculiar redun-

---

[18] See Johannes P. Louw, *A Semantic Discourse Analysis of Romans* (Pretoria: University of Pretoria, 1979) 1. 1.

[19] James D. G. Dunn observes that the stress on "all" is "significant, not only because it confirms the truly universal scope of God's gospel . . . , but also because it reminds us that Paul seriously contemplated this outreach being achieved within his own lifetime, as the last act before the end and the necessary preliminary to the salvation of Israel" (*Romans 1–8* [WBC 38a; Dallas: Word, 1988] 18).

[20] Don B. Garlington, *"The Obedience of Faith": A Pauline Phrase in Historical Context* (WUNT 38; Tübingen: Mohr [Siebeck], 1991) 1–4, 233; he derives from Otto Michel's commentary on Romans the assumption, typical of traditional European commentaries, that the formula is both antithetical and polemical.

[21] See Heinrich Schlier, *Der Römerbrief* (HTKNT; Freiburg: Herder, 1977) 29; C. E. B. Cranfield, *A Critical and Exegetical Commentary on the Epistle to the Romans* (2 vols.; ICC; Edinburgh: T. & T. Clark, 1975, 1979) 1. 66; also Joseph A. Fitzmyer, *Romans: A New Translation with Introduction and Commentary* (AB 33; New York: Doubleday, 1993) 237.

[22] See Garlington, *Obedience*, 11–13.

[23] For example, Otto Michel, *Der Brief an die Römer* (5th ed.; Göttingen: Vandenhoeck & Ruprecht, 1978) 77; Dieter Zeller, *Der Brief an die Römer* (Regensburg: Pustet, 1985) 37; Ulrich Wilckens, *Der Brief an die Römer* (EKKNT 6; Zurich: Benziger, 1978) 1. 68–69. The lack of the term "church" in the address of Romans plays a prominent role in Günther Klein's hypothe-

dancy of the address.[24] Rather than a concentrated focus as in the other Pauline letters, here we find three parallel phrases that describe the recipients:[25] (1) "the called of Jesus Christ"; (2) "to those in Rome beloved of God"; and (3) "the called saints."

True to the requirements of ambassadorial rhetoric, Paul had to address the Romans in such a way that each group felt included. Demonstrative rhetoric proceeds by generalizations; it seeks to make a broad and oblique case that includes a variety of particular manifestations. This, I think, is what guided Paul to the threefold address of Romans. He selected language that would be inclusive of two broad streams of the house- and tenement-churches and those leaders not yet incorporated in their membership.[26]

Let me begin with the most easily defined expression, the "called saints." The use of κλητοί ("called" or "chosen") in this context seems "almost titular," with similarity to the self-identification of the Essenes.[27] When the term "saints" is used as a description of Christian groups, it usually refers to Jewish Christians of a traditional type. This is specifically apparent in 15:25 and 31, where the term "saints" refers to the Palestinian Christians currently under the leadership of James and his associates.[28] In the Roman context, I think this address would include many of those banned under Claudius who had returned to Rome, some of whom were being discriminated against by the Gentile Christian majorities in the house- and tenement-churches. This title would certainly include the group calling itself "the saints" (16:15); it might also include the Christian cell centered among the slaves and freedmen of Aristobulus (16:10).[29] The group stereotyped as "weak" in Romans 14–15 may have overlapped with such "saints."[30] The expression would include those perceived to be "barbarian," to use the discriminatory term selected in 1:14 to depict those to whom Paul felt obligated. Those Jewish Christians

sis, "Paul's Purpose in Writing the Epistle to the Romans," in *The Romans Debate,* ed. Donfried, 29–43.

[24] See Ernst Käsemann's reference to the "plerophoric solemnity" in the address of Romans (*Commentary on Romans* [trans. G. W. Bromiley; Grand Rapids: Eerdmans, 1980] 15).

[25] See Fitzmyer, *Romans,* 238; Michel refers to these three titles as expressing "all the honors that are granted to them in Jesus Christ" (*Römer,* 77).

[26] The rejection of this inclusive approach as "improbable" by Schlier (*Römerbrief,* 31) is supported by an inadequate historical premise of a unified congregation in Rome.

[27] See Wilckens, *Römer,* 68 n. 39; and M. Newton, *The Concept of Purity at Qumran and in the Letters of Paul* (Cambridge: Cambridge University Press, 1983) 40.

[28] Garlington (*Obedience,* 239–41) overlooks the specific evidence within Romans to conclude, following Dunn, that the expression "called saints" refers to Gentile Christians.

[29] See Cranfield, *Romans,* 2. 791–92, for the likelihood that Aristobulus was the "grandson of Herod the Great and the brother of Agrippa I," whose church contained "a good many Jews."

[30] See Walters, *Ethnic Issues,* 87.

whose Jewish accent remained prominent and who did not have enough edu-
cation to be fully conversant with Greco-Roman culture would fall into this
category, which overlaps to some degree with the expression "uneducated"
in the same verse. The evidence from Harry Leon's magisterial study *The Jews
of Ancient Rome* would be relevant here, because he discovered that several
Jewish cemeteries contained a large proportion of virtually illiterate grave
inscriptions, indicating that some of the Jewish synagogues served recent
immigrants and a lower-class population with low educational standards.[31]
Some of the Christians included among the "called saints" would probably
come from such backgrounds.

The expression "the called of Jesus Christ" seems to refer to Christians of
predominantly Gentile background[32] who may have been using the term
"Jesus Christ" as the proper name of a cult patron rather than as a peculiar
messianic title. The Gentiles reflected in Rom 11:18, who boasted of being
elected to replace the Jewish branches in the divine olive tree of the chosen
people, would have felt themselves included with this expression. I think it
would have included at least three of the Christian cells evident in Romans
(16:3–5; 16:11; 16:14). Insofar as the term "strong" in chaps. 14–15 refers to
some Gentile Christians, it would roughly correlate with this expression
"called of Jesus Christ." Most scholars currently feel that such Gentile Christians formed the majority of the membership of the house- and tenement-
churches at the time of writing Romans, which is perhaps why Paul used this
title first in his address. The preferred half of the derogative antitheses used by
Paul in 1:14 would match this group in all probability: the "Greeks" and the
"educated." Hence, when Paul referred in Romans to "the Jews first and then
the Greeks," he was referring to these constellations of Christians, reversing
their competitive status.

The address that does not match the social groupings in Rome is "the
beloved of God." I think it is significant that Paul places this address between
the two others so that it serves as a unification formula. The wording is explicitly inclusive: "all those in Rome beloved of God."[33] This phrase suggests the
theological argument of the entire letter, namely, that God's love is non-
discriminating.[34] No person on earth, whether Greek or Jewish, deserves such
love, as 1:18–3:20 argues. But everyone receives such love in Christ, as

---

[31] Harry J. Leon, *The Jews of Ancient Rome* (Philadelphia: Jewish Publication Society, 1960).

[32] See Schlier, *Römerbrief*, 30; Cranfield, *Romans*, 1. 68.

[33] This nuance is overlooked by Garlington in *Obedience*, 241–42, who concentrates on the
background in Isaiah 42–44 and Psalm 108, arguing that Paul applies this "honorific title of
Israel" to the Christian church.

[34] See Jouette M. Bassler, *Divine Impartiality: Paul and a Theological Axiom* (SBLDS 59; Chico,
CA: Scholars Press, 1982) 164–70.

3:21–4:25 so eloquently shows. God is no respecter of persons, as Rom 2:11 insists; all have made themselves into God's enemies (5:10), but all are included in the sweep of divine love. The offering of salvation "to all who believe" is virtually a litany of the argument of Romans (1:16; 3:22; 4:11; 10:4). In this sense, the opening address of Romans sets the tone for the entire letter, offering the most inclusive program of ecumenical cooperation found in the New Testament. If this gospel is understood and internalized, Paul suggests, the splintered congregations of Rome would become united in cooperation while preserving their distinctiveness. They would also be enabled to participate in a credible manner in completing the mission to the end of the known world, symbolized by Spain. When this message is received in faith, the goal of history will be fulfilled and all the nations will praise God for God's mercy, as the climax of the formal argument in chap. 15 proclaims.

If the purpose of an epistolary opening is to establish the relation between the recipients of a letter and the writer who is unable because of distance to speak his message in person,[35] this expanded introduction draws the Roman Christians into a missionary dialogue concerning the relevance of Paul's gospel. Many of the themes of the subsequent argument come to initial expression here. The apostolic motif is developed in 1:8–15 in relation to Paul's forthcoming visit to Rome to promote a mission among the nations. The content of Paul's "gospel" is elaborated from 1:16 through 8:39 with particular reference to its consistency with "holy scriptures" and the centrality of "faith." The motifs of lordship, the confession of the "name," the conversion of the Gentiles, and the tension between the fleshly realm of Jesus' origin as a Jew and the spiritual realm of his reign over all humankind are elaborated in 9:1–11:26. The themes of holiness and sainthood are picked up in 12:1–13:14. The triumph of the gospel among the nations climaxes the argument from 14:1–15:13, and the connection between apostolicity and world mission is restated in 15:14–33 with language strongly reminiscent of that used in 1:1–7.

III

A crucial transformation of materials in an ecumenical direction is visible in the confession cited by Paul in Rom 1:3–4.[36] Paul's emendation and use of

---

[35] See Heikki Koskenniemi, *Studien zur Idee und Phraseologie des griechischen Briefes bis 400 n. Chr.* (Helsinki: Suomalainen Tiedeakatemia, 1956) 155–67.

[36] The following is a revision of my full-length study of the confession, "The Redaction and Use of an Early Christian Confession in Romans 1:3–4," in *The Living Bible Text: Essays in Honor of Ernest W. Saunders* (ed. D. E. Groh and R. Jewett; Lanham, MD: University Press of America, 1985) 99–122.

an early Christian confession embedded in these verses correlate closely with the theory of an audience divided by tensions between ethnic groups containing traditionalists and liberationists. Studies by Reginald Fuller, Heinrich Schlier, and Jürgen Becker suggest that this creed originated as an expression of Jewish Christian theology:[37]

1:3b τοῦ γενομένου ("born")
1:3c   ἐκ σπέρματος Δαυίδ ("of the seed of David")
1:4a τοῦ ὁρισθέντος υἱοῦ θεοῦ ("designated son of God")
1:4d   ἐξ ἀναστάσεως νεκρῶν ("from resurrection of the dead")

It is widely agreed that the motif of Davidic descent points in the direction of early Jewish Christianity.[38] Leslie C. Allen has shown that ὁρισθέντος ("designated") in 1:4 is derived from the royal decree language of Ps 2:7, with its closest analogues in the Aramaic section of Daniel. There is a strong likelihood that this component in the confession derived from "the Aramaic-speaking primitive church," so it should be interpreted in light of the interests of that group.[39]

At the core of the original confession, therefore, is the affirmation of Jesus as the traditional Davidic Messiah, who was adopted and enthroned as the Son of God on the basis of his resurrection. The popular Jewish expectation of a Son of David as found in *Pss. Sol.* 17:21 and elsewhere is reflected here, with the traditional expectation of national restoration, victory over the Gentile nations, and governance of the world.[40] The potentially chauvinistic element in the first line of the credo is not diminished by the second line, which affirms the divine appointment of Jesus as the heavenly Son of God. The adoptionist christology of primitive Palestinian Christianity surfaces in this formulation, consistent with the confessional materials in Acts 2:36 and 13:33.[41] But it

---

[37] Reginald H. Fuller, *The Foundations of New Testament Christology* (New York: Scribner, 1965) 165–67; Heinrich Schlier, "Eine Christologische Credo-Formel der römischen Gemeinde: Zu Röm 1.3f.," in *Neues Testament und Geschichte: Historisches Geschehen und Deutung im Neuen Testament: Oscar Cullmann zum 70. Geburtstag* (ed. H. Baltensweiler and B. Reicke; Tübingen: Mohr [Siebeck], 1972) 207–18; Jürgen Becker, *Auferstehung der Toten im Urchristentum* (Stuttgart: Katholisches Bibelwerk, 1976) 20–31.

[38] See A. J. B. Higgins, "The OT and Some Aspects of NT Christology," *CJT* 6 (1960) 200–202; Michel, *Römer*, 38; Christoph Burger, *Jesus als Davidssohn: Eine traditionsgeschichtliche Untersuchung* (FRLANT 98; Göttingen: Vandenhoeck & Ruprecht, 1970) 28; Wilckens, *Römer*, 1. 60.

[39] Leslie C. Allen, "The Old Testament Background of (προ-)ὁρίζειν in the New Testament," *NTS* 17 (1970–71) 104–8, esp. 104–5.

[40] Becker cites Ps 2:8 in this connection (*Auferstehung*, 29).

[41] See Käsemann, *Romans*, 12; Dunn correctly points out an anachronistic element in the adoptionist identification but fails to eliminate the problem by contending that "Paul would certainly see the earlier formula as congruent with his own Christology" (*Romans 1–8*, 14).

appears clear that no diminution of authority is intended by this primitive formulation: the Son of God is emphatically appointed as ruler of the world.[42] The precise implications of the phrase "from the resurrection of the dead" depend on whether one accepts Hans Lietzmann's suggestion that this is an aesthetically motivated abbreviation of a formula referring more precisely to Christ's resurrection.[43] In light of the compelling evidence that H.-W. Bartsch assembled to show that this reference to the general resurrection from the dead is typical of early Christian apocalyptic, there is no reason to provide a less-than-literal interpretation.[44] As Käsemann writes, "The hymnic tradition does not isolate Christ's resurrection, but views it in its cosmic function as the beginning of general resurrection."[45] At the somewhat primitive level of the original credo,[46] no distinction is made between Christ's resurrection and the dawn of the age of the general resurrection. Both are apparently associated as the inbreaking of the new age.[47] This leads to a significant conclusion: the original, Jewish Christian confession contained an emphasis on the apocalyptic hinge between the two ages even before the insertion of the clearly antithetical expressions, "according to the flesh/spirit."

Studies by Rudolf Bultmann, Eduard Schweizer, Eta Linnemann, and Michael Theobald,[48] suggest that the second, redacted level of the confession

[42] See Anton J. Fridrichsen, *The Apostle and His Message* (Uppsala: Lundequistska, 1947) 10: "In other words, through His resurrection from the dead, Jesus, formerly the Messiah of the Jews, has been enthroned as Lord and Saviour of the whole world."

[43] Hans Lietzmann, *An die Römer* (4th ed.; Tübingen: Mohr, 1933) 25.

[44] Hans-Werner Bartsch shows the close parallels to Acts 26:23; Matt 27:51–53; and 1 Cor 15:20 ("Zur vorpaulinischen Bekenntnisformel im Eingang des Römerbriefes," *TZ* 23 [1967] 330–35). Dunn ("Jesus," 56) follows this approach, citing a number of scholars including S. H. Hooke, "The Translation of Rom. i.4," *NTS* 9 (1962–63) 370–71. Jürgen Becker overlooks this evidence in concluding that Rom 1:4 refers exclusively to Jesus' individual resurrection (*Auferstehung*, 30–31).

[45] Käsemann, *Romans*, 12.

[46] Schlier speaks of "a certain archaic quality" in the wording of ἐξ ἀναστάσεως νεκρῶν ("Zu Röm 1,3f," 214).

[47] It therefore appears inappropriate to conclude with Ferdinand Hahn that the credo features "the de-eschatologization of the messianic office of Jesus" (*The Titles of Jesus in Christology: Their History in Early Christianity* [London: Lutterworth, 1969] 251). For a detailed critique on this point, see Philipp Vielhauer, "Ein Weg zur neutestamentlichen Christologie? Prüfung der Thesen Ferdinand Hahns," in *Aufsätze zum Neuen Testament* (Munich: Kaiser, 1965) 141–98, esp. 187.

[48] Rudolf Bultmann, *Theology of the New Testament* (trans. K. Grobel; London: SCM, 1965) 1. 49; the first written expression of Bultmann's analysis appeared in "Neueste Paulusforschung," *TRu* 8 (1936) 11; Eduard Schweizer, "Römer 1,3f. und der Gegensatz von Fleisch und Geist vor und bei Paulus," *EvT* 15 (1955) 563–71; reprinted in Schweizer's *Neotestamentica* (Zurich: Zwingli, 1963) 180–89; Eta Linnemann, "Tradition und Interpretation in Röm 1,3f," *EvT* 31 (1971) 264–75; Michael Theobald, "'Dem Juden zuerst und auch dem Heiden':

included the antithesis, "according to the flesh/spirit," which is underlined below:

1:3b   τοῦ γενομένου ("born")
1:3c   ἐκ σπέρματος Δαυίδ ("of the seed of David")
1:3d   <u>κατὰ σάρκα</u> ("according to flesh")
1:4a   τοῦ ὁρισθέντος υἱοῦ θεοῦ ("designated son of God")
1:4c   <u>κατὰ πνεῦμα</u> ("according to spirit")
1:4d   ἐξ ἀναστάσεως νεκρῶν ("from resurrection of the dead")

When the original confession was edited by the insertion of references to σάρξ ("flesh") and πνεῦμα ("spirit"), the implicit antithesis between the ages was developed in a radical direction. As Eduard Schweizer has pointed out, Hellenistic thought tended to conceive the flesh/spirit dualism in material terms, as counterposed realms of damnation/salvation.[49] Human destiny was thought to be determined by the realm to which one was subordinate. Bondage to the realm of the flesh could be overcome only by divine means. When flesh and spirit are combined with the preposition κατά ("according to"), the thought of being limited or dominated by a particular sphere is strongly implied.[50] The antithesis thus has a negative as well as a positive set of implications. On the negative side, there is a clear depreciation of the significance of the Davidic origin of the Messiah and all that it implied. The Christians who inserted this line probably stood close to the radicals refuted in Rom 11:11–25, who vaunted their superiority as divinely grafted branches that displaced the original Jewish branches of the olive tree. They appear to have shared the outlook of the Corinthian radicals who devalued the fleshly, historical Jesus (1 Cor 12:3; 15:44–46). Insofar as Jesus descended from the fleshly seed of David, this insertion implies, he was bound to a realm of material bondage that was opposed to the power of salvation.

The positive implication of the phrase κατὰ πνεῦμα ("according to spirit") is that the redemptive power of Christ derives from his spiritual authority rather than his Davidic origin. Divine sonship is here qualified in terms of spirit, which means that the ecstatic experiences of early Christians could be seen to derive directly from him. In place of the apocalyptic expectation of the dawn of the age of bodily resurrection, this phrase implies that the salvation brought by the Son of God is pneumatic and experiential. To belong to the sphere of the spirit was to be set free from bondage to the flesh, to partake

Die paulinische Auslegung der Glaubensformel Röm 1,3f.," in *Kontinuität und Einheit: Für Franz Mussner* (ed. P.-G. Müller and W. Stenger; Freiburg: Herder, 1981) 376–92.

[49] Eduard Schweizer, "πνεῦμα, πνευματικός," *TDNT* 6. 389–451, esp. 392; idem, "σάρξ," *TDNT* 7. 98–151, esp. 124.

[50] See Bultmann, *Theology*, 1. 236–37.

in a superior world of divine power. In short, the insertions of the phrases κατὰ σάρκα ("according to flesh") and κατὰ πνεῦμα ("according to spirit") move the credo unmistakably in the direction of Hellenistic dualism, with all its appeals, powers, and dangers.

The third level of the confession includes two Pauline insertions[51] and the epistolary framing of 1:3a and 1:4e,[52] resulting in the text as we find it in Romans 1:

1:3a	περὶ τοῦ υἱοῦ αὐτοῦ ("concerning his son")	
1:3b	τοῦ γενομένου ("born")	
1:3c	ἐκ σπέρματος Δαυίδ ("of the seed of David")	
1:3d	κατὰ σάρκα ("according to flesh")	
1:4a	τοῦ ὁρισθέντος υἱοῦ θεοῦ ("designated son of God")	
1:4b	ἐν δυνάμει ("in power")	
1:4c	κατὰ πνεῦμα ἁγιωσύνης ("according to spirit of holiness")	
1:4d	ἐξ ἀναστάσεως νεκρῶν ("from resurrection of the dead")	
1:4e	Ἰησοῦ Χριστοῦ τοῦ κυρίου ἡμῶν ("Jesus Christ our Lord")	

I believe that it was to contend with the dangers of the Hellenistic Christian redaction as well as of the original Jewish Christian wording of the credo that Paul inserted the phrase ἐν δυνάμει ("in power") and the modifying term ἁγιωσύνης ("of holiness").[53] Aside from the use in 1:4, the only two other New Testament uses of "holiness" are in Pauline passages where ethical obligations are being stressed. These passages provide an initial clue to Paul's intention here as well. In 1 Thess 3:13, the homiletic benediction that summarizes the argument of the first portion of the letter, the action of God is described as establishing "your hearts unblamable in holiness before our God and Father, at the coming of our Lord Jesus with all his saints." The specific reference of ἁγιωσύνη is developed in the succeeding section which argues for sexual fidelity (1 Thess 4:1–8). A similar context is visible in 2 Cor 7:1, which refers to cleansing of "every defilement of body and spirit" so that "holiness" might

---

[51] See Jewett, *Anthropological Terms*, 136–39; Schlier, "Zu Röm 1,3f," 207–18; and Klaus Wengst, *Christologische Formeln und Lieder der Urchristentum* (Gütersloh: Mohn, 1972) 112–17; Fitzmyer, *Romans*, 229–30.

[52] See James D. G. Dunn, "Jesus," 40–68, and *Romans 1–8*, 5–6 for the argument that Paul added only the framing to a pre-Pauline confession.

[53] See also the recent discussion by A. B. du Toit, "Romans 1,3–4 and the Gospel Tradition: A Reassessment of the Phrase κατὰ πνεῦμα ἁγιωσύνης," in *The Four Gospels 1992: Festschrift Frans Neirynck* (ed. F. van Segbroeck et al.; BETL 100; Louvain: Leuven University and Peeters, 1992) 1. 249–56.

be made "perfect in the fear of God." In both instances congregational tendencies toward libertinism motivated by freedom in the spirit are countered by the use of ἁγιωσύνη. One suspects a similar concern in Rom 1:4, because the belief in having transcended the realm of σάρξ ("flesh") by virtue of one's adherence to the realm of πνεῦμα ("spirit") easily led to libertinistic excesses. The qualification of spirit as the "spirit of holiness" made clear that the divine power celebrated in the confession entailed moral obligations. This is in fact a theme developed at length in Romans 5–8, which shows that the new life involves righteousness, a repudiation of fleshly passions, and walking "according to the spirit." Paul makes plain that the spirit given to Christian believers is the "holy spirit" (Rom 5:5) and that the law remains "holy" even for members of the new age (Rom 7:12). The key to the new ethic is giving oneself as a holy sacrifice for others (Rom 12:1). In this sense, the insertion of the term "holiness" prepares the reader for a major emphasis in the letter.

Paul's insertion of the phrase ἐν δυνάμει ("in power") appears to be a correction of the christology of the original confession. It counters the adoptionism of the original confession by asserting that Christ bore the "power" of God prior to the resurrection,[54] thus bringing the confession more nearly in line with Paul's typical interest in the doctrine of preexistent κύριος ("Lord").[55] But as the subsequent argument of Romans indicates, the interest in "power" is more than christological. The thesis of Romans is that the gospel about Christ is "the power of God for salvation" (Rom 1:16). Insofar as Romans serves the task of world mission, aiming to elicit support for proclaiming the gospel in Spain, the entire letter can be understood as elaborating this thesis. It is consistent that the benediction wrapping up the formal argument of Romans reiterates this theme: "May the God of hope fill you with all joy and peace in believing, so that *by the power* of the Holy Spirit you may abound in hope" (Rom 15:13; see also 15:19). To return to the context of the confession, the insertion of "in power" therefore reiterates a motif that was implicit in the Hellenistic Christian insertion of the flesh/spirit dualism: the power of God resides not in Davidic descent but in direct, divine appointment of Christ as Son of God, so that the proclamation of the gospel about him can be the powerful means by which the "righteousness of God" is restored.

It would be a mistake, however, to interpret Paul's citation of the credo merely on the basis of two relatively minor corrections. The introductory and

---

[54] See Schlier, "Zu Röm 1,3f," 210; Oscar Cullmann infers from the phrase "in power" that "Jesus is the 'Son of God' from the beginning" (*The Christology of the New Testament* [trans. S. C. Guthrie and C. A. M. Hall; Philadelphia: Westminster, 1959] 292).

[55] See Burger, *Jesus*, 31f.; Wengst, *Christologische Formeln*, 114.

concluding formulations need to be taken into account; and, above all, the fact that Paul selected a composite creed should be reflected upon in light of the purpose of the letter as a whole. The characteristic assumption of form and redaction criticism is that introductory and concluding formulas should be ascribed to redactors rather than to the original scope of cited material. That Rom 1:3b, περὶ τοῦ υἱοῦ αὐτοῦ ("concerning his son"), was probably not part of the original credo has been assumed in this study. Klaus Wengst has pointed out that if this line belonged to the credo, the reference to appointed sonship in v. 4 would lose its emphatic quality through anticipation and redundancy.[56] By introducing the credo with these words, however, Paul thwarts adoptionist inferences and qualifies the Davidic sonship by stressing that Jesus was the Son of God prior to his earthly appearance.[57] The line that Paul provided to close the confession, Ἰησοῦ Χριστοῦ τοῦ κυρίου ἡμῶν ("Jesus Christ our Lord"), employs distinctively Pauline language that differentiates it from the cited material.[58] These words explicitly state the lordship theme that we detected both in the insertion of ἐν δυνάμει ("in power") and ἁγιωσύνης ("of holiness"). The preexistent Son of God celebrated in the credo is to be seen as the Lord of the world, a theme closely related to the thesis concerning the revelation of the "righteousness of God" (1:16–17) and the anticipated acknowledgment by the nations (15:10–12). In Käsemann's words, "For Paul the kyrios is the representative of the God who claims the world and who with the church brings the new creation into the midst of the old world that is perishing."[59] With this introduction and conclusion, Paul effectively encloses the credo within the framework of his own theology.

The most significant feature of all, however, is that Paul selects a credo that bears the marks of several ethnically diverse branches of the early church. Despite the careful framing with typical Pauline language, and regardless of the correcting insertions, the prominent location of this creed indicates Paul's acceptance of a common faith and his effort to be evenhanded. He is willing to cite the Jewish Christian affirmation of Jesus as coming from the "seed of David," despite his opposition to Jewish zealotism (10:1–3) and pride (2:17–24). He is willing to accept the Hellenistic Christian dialectic of flesh versus spirit, despite his subsequent effort to insist on moral transformation (chaps. 6–8) and to counter the results of spiritual arrogance (14:1–15:7). Yet none of these points is scored overtly; the credo is cited with respect, edited

---

[56] Wengst, *Christologische Formeln*, 112; see also Käsemann, *Romans*, 10.

[57] See Stuhlmacher, "Probleme," 382; Dunn, "Jesus," 55–56.

[58] See Schlier, "Zu Röm 1,3f," 208; Käsemann, *Romans*, 13–14; Gijs Bouwman, *Paulus aan de romeinen: Een retorische analyse van Rom 1-8* (Abdij Averbode: Werkgroep voor levensverdieping, 1980) 128.

[59] Käsemann, *Romans*, 14.

with skill, and framed effectively in language that various branches of the early church would have understood. The overwhelming impression one has after reflecting on the implications of Paul's use of the credo is his irenic approach. He is obviously seeking to find common ground, which brings the confession into the context of Paul's ambassadorial strategy in the letter as a whole.

IV

The theological center of Romans, integrally related to the missional purpose of the letter, is to be found in the thesis statement of 1:16–17. That this passage contains the main theme of Romans is almost universally accepted among commentators.[60] A major debate in this regard is how much of the subsequent argument of Romans is dominated by this theme, whether the first five or eight chapters.[61] On rhetorical as well as thematic grounds, I contend that all of the material through 15:13 carries out this proposition and that the subsequent peroratio in 15:14–16:23 takes up its practical enactment. By identifying 1:16–17 as a thesis statement located in the rhetorically proper spot between the narration and the proofs, it is accorded its proper weight as the argumentative burden of the letter. It takes up the issue of Paul's intended missionary enterprise mentioned in 1:13–15 and sets forth a thesis that is confirmed in 1:18–4:25 and amplified in the subsequent three major sections of the letter. In view of the manner in which the theme in these two verses is elaborated and amplified in the argument of Romans, I prefer the term *propositio*, drawn from Quintilian (*Institutio Oratorio* 4.4.1–4.5.28) to the term *partitio*, used by Cicero to describe a multifaceted thesis statement that divides up the subsequent argument (*De inventione* 1.22.31–23.33). Despite the complexity of the argument, there is a single theme in Romans: the triumph of divine righteousness through the gospel of Jesus Christ.

The rhetorical form of 1:16–17 sustains its identification as the *propositio* of the entire subsequent discourse. As Johannes Weiss pointed out, there is a parallelism in 1:16b and 1:17a, with two symmetrical statements about the "power of God" and the "righteousness of God" respectively, each providing a definition of the preceding contention about Paul not being ashamed of "the gospel."[62] The reference to "all who have faith" in the first member is

---

[60] See the discussion by William S. Campbell, "A Theme for Romans?" in his study *Paul's Gospel in an Intercultural Context: Jew and Gentile in the Letter to the Romans* (Frankfurt: Lang, 1991) 161–63.

[61] See Ulrich Luz, "Zum Aufbau von Röm 1-8," *TZ* 25 (1969) 166.

[62] Johannes Weiss, "Beiträge zur Paulinischen Rhetorik," in *Theologische Studien: Herrn Professor D. Bernhard Weiss zu seinem 70 Geburtstage dargebracht* (ed. C. R. Gregory et al.; Göttingen: Vandenhoeck & Ruprecht, 1897) 212–13.

balanced by the reference "from faith to faith" in the second member.[63] The element of inclusivity detected in the introduction and narration of the letter is reiterated by the stress on "*all* who have faith," explicitly including the culturally distinct groups of Jews and Greeks. The entire statement is then sustained by the scriptural citation from Hab 2:4, which implies in this context that anyone, regardless of cultural background, can gain life and share in the restoration of righteousness by setting faith in Christ.

The much-debated phrase "the righteousness of God" needs to be understood within this missional context. As Käsemann showed on the basis of the apocalyptic background of 1:17, this phrase "speaks of the God who brings back the fallen world into the sphere of his legitimate claim."[64] It is the inclusive gospel of Christ, which equalizes the status of Greeks and barbarians, wise and uneducated, Jews and Gentiles, that offers new life to all on precisely the same terms. The early Christian mission is thus viewed as a decisive phase in the revelation of God's righteousness, restoring individuals, groups, and the creation itself. This is why the key term ἀποκαλύπτεται ("is revealed") is in the present tense. Dunn is on target in suggesting that "Paul's experience of evangelizing the Gentiles gives him firm confidence that in the gospel as the power of God to salvation such early converts are being given to see the righteousness of God actually happening, taking effect in their own conversion."[65] Paul's hope in writing this letter is that this inclusive and restorative righteousness will be allowed to heal the divisions within the Roman house- and tenement-churches and thus enable them to participate in the campaign to missionize to the end of the known world, as far as the Pillars of Hercules in Spain, thus contributing to the pacification of the world.

V

The inclusive righteousness of God explicated throughout Romans is countered by the bipolar stereotype of theological opponents in the interpolation of 16:17–20a. I follow John Knox, Walter Schmithals, John C. O'Neill, and W.-H. Ollrog in holding these verses to be non-Pauline.[66] These fierce

---

[63] Weiss observes: "Only through taking account of the symmetrical rhythm can the quite remarkable, hardly explainable, in fact impossible ἐκ πίστεως εἰς πίστιν ("from faith to faith") be justified" ("Beiträge," 213).

[64] Käsemann, *Romans*, 29.

[65] Dunn, *Romans 1–8*, 48.

[66] John Knox, "The Epistle to the Romans," in *The Interpreter's Bible* (Nashville: Abingdon, 1954) 664; the 1959 article by Walter Schmithals was reprinted in *Paul and the Gnostics* (trans. J. E. Steely; Nashville: Abingdon, 1972) 219–38; John C. O'Neill, *Paul's Letter to the Romans* (Harmondsworth: Penguin, 1975) 252, 258; Ollrog, "Die Abfassungsverhältnisse von Röm 16," 230–34; see also Käsemann, *Romans*, 419; and Jewett, *Christian Tolerance*, 18–22.

denunciations are out of place in chap. 16, breaking into the sequence of
friendly greetings that would otherwise be continuous from 16:16 to 16:21
and introducing new material not found in the preceding proofs of the letter.[67] Rhetorically speaking, such antiheretical polemic belongs not in the
peroratio of the letter but in the proofs. This paragraph would fit fairly well at
the end of chap. 15, and thus stand in a position parallel to the denunciations
of heretics in other Pauline letters (Phil 3:1–3, 17–21; 4:2–3; Gal 5:12; and 2
Cor 11:12–15).[68] These verses contain six *hapax legomena*[69] and at least eight
expressions used in a non-Pauline way;[70] the style of "wild polemic"[71] in this
section matches that of the Pastoral Epistles and Ignatius rather than the
authentic Pauline letters;[72] and the passage flatly contradicts the efforts visible

[67] O'Neill writes that the "tone is peremptory in the middle of a peaceful passage" (*Romans*,
258).

[68] There are exceptions to this pattern in 1 Cor 16:22 and Gal 6:11–13, but in both cases the
warnings recapitulate arguments from the proofs of the letter, which makes the material suit-
able for a peroration. In 1 Corinthians there is extensive discussion of the theme of love and of
church disunity prior to the statement of a curse on "those who do not love the Lord." In Galatians, the final, handwritten postscript reiterates material from the body of the letter rather than
developing than a fresh new polemic against a group never before appearing in the argument,
as is the case with Rom 16:17–20a.

[69] Ollrog lists ἐκκλίνειν ("to avoid")—used otherwise only in the Psalm citation in Rom
3:12), χρηστολογία ("smooth talk"), ἄκακος ("unsuspecting"), ἀφίκεσθαι ("to become
known"), συντριβεῖν ("to crush"), ἐν τάχει ("quickly"), and εὐλογία, the last of which is used
with the non-Pauline meaning "well-chosen words" ("Abfassungsverhältnisse," 230). See also
O'Neill, *Romans*, 258.

[70] O'Neill observes that the expression "our Lord Christ" is unparalleled and that σκάνδαλα
is used here in the plural for the only time in the Pauline letters (*Romans*, 258). See also Karl-
heinz Müller, *Anstoß und Gericht: Eine Studie zum jüdischen Hintergrund des paulinischen Skan-
dalon-Begriffs* (SANT 19; Munich: Kösel, 1969) 46–47. Ollrog notes that διδαχή is used in a
non-Pauline way as a summary of Christian doctrine ("Abfassungsverhältnisse," 230–31); and
that the opponents are identified as Satan in a way that matches the heretical polemics of later
Christianity. I noted in *Christian Tolerance* that the rationale of being "wise toward the good but
guileless toward the evil" in 16:19 "flatly contradicts Paul's earlier argument in Romans"; that
the blessing formula in 16:20 lacks the optative that is characteristic of other Pauline blessings;
and that "obedience" is used "in an absolute sense unparalleled elsewhere in Romans" because
it is unconnected with either faith or the gospel (pp. 20–22). On this latter point, see also Ollrog, "Abfassungsverhältnisse," 233. Finally, the expression "God of peace" requires the annihilation of enemies within the church and thus is used with the opposite definition as in Rom
15:33, which was consistent with the references to peace as reconciliation in Rom 5:1 and
14:17. See Käsemann, *Romans*, 418; Schlier, *Römerbrief*, 449–50; and Gerhard Delling, "Die
Bezeichnung 'Gott des Friedens' und ähnliche Wendungen in den Paulusbriefen," in *Jesus und
Paulus: Festschrift für Werner Georg Kümmel zum 70. Geburtstag* (ed. E. E. Ellis and E. Grässer;
Göttingen: Vandenhoeck & Ruprecht, 1975) 81.

[71] Käsemann, *Romans*, 419.

[72] See Ollrog, "Abfassungsverhältnisse," 231.

throughout the rest of Romans to find common ground between Christian groups of different cultural backgrounds and theological orientations.[73]

While many commentators attempt to smooth over or explain away the disparities between this section and the rest of the argument of Romans, I agree with John Ziesler's comment that it "could hardly be farther from the mutual acceptance of differences of 14[1-12] and 15[7]."[74] The difference in orientation from the rest of chap. 16 is even more striking. The theological and cultural implications of the greetings and their crucial role in the purpose of Romans have still not been fully credited in recent studies, despite the challenge posed by Terence Y. Mullins a quarter of a century ago.[75] The word ἀσπάζομαι ("greet") is repeated twenty-one times in chap. 16, more than in all the rest of the Pauline letters. Paul's selection of the second person plural imperative form, ἀσπάσασθε ("you should greet"), in 16:3–16 was surely intentional and should not be translated as "I send greetings to."[76] As Michel points out, "The ones being greeted are at the same time those whom the Roman congregation should grant recognition."[77] When one observes the random sequence of the requested greetings and the interweaving of established Christian cells (16:3–5, 10b, 11b, 14, 15) and isolated Christian leaders, it becomes clear that the recognition is to be mutual. In this context, to greet is to honor and welcome one another, probably with the hug, kiss, handshaking, or bowing that gave expression to greeting in the ancient world; the original meaning of the Greek term ἀσπάζομαι was to wrap one's arms around another.[78] As Hans Windisch observed, the Pauline command to greet one another "expresses and strengthens the bond of fellowship with those who are engaged in the same task and who serve the same Lord, i.e., with saints and brothers."[79]

---

[73] See Käsemann, *Romans*, 419; and Jewett, *Christian Tolerance*, 18–23.

[74] John Ziesler, *Paul's Letter to the Romans* (Philadelphia: Trinity Press International, 1989) 353.

[75] Terence Y. Mullins expressed disquiet at the traditional view of the bearing of the greetings on the relationship between Paul and his audience as well as on the significance of the greetings for the understanding of Paul's argument in the letter ("Greeting as a New Testament Form," *JBL* 87 [1968] 426): "The relationship between Paul and the congregation at Rome seems to be other than scholars have assumed, and no simple readjustment of our old notions is likely to bring it into focus. . . . something in our usual interpretation of Romans is wrong; and the way to straighten it out is to establish as much objective data as possible before using the evidence supplied by the contents of the letter."

[76] Barclay M. Newman and Eugene A. Nida, *A Translator's Handbook on Paul's Letter to the Romans* (Stuttgart: United Bible Societies, 1973) 291.

[77] Michel, *Römer*, 474.

[78] See Hans Windisch, "ἀσπάζομαι, κτλ," *TDNT* 1. 497.

[79] Ibid., 501.

The inclusivity of the greetings is in striking contrast to the discriminatory polemic against Christian opponents in 16:17–20a. In 16:4 "all the churches of the Gentiles" are said to give thanks for the work of the Jewish Christian Aquila and his Roman wife Prisca; in 16:16 all the members of the competitive house- and tenement-churches as well as the returning refugees in Rome are admonished to "greet one another with a holy kiss," which implies a deep level of unity and mutuality between all Christians in Rome.[80] Paul passes on greetings from "all the churches of Christ," the only time Paul presumes to speak so inclusively in the entire Pauline corpus. Given the missional focus of the letter, these greetings have an integral purpose of embodying the inclusive righteousness of God so that the essence of the gospel of impartial love can be passed on in a credible manner to the barbarians in Spain and to others at the limits of the known world.

The canonical letter therefore offers two antithetical approaches to mission that have echoed through later Christian history to the present day, providing an urgent agenda for critical theological reflection. On the one side there is the strategy of crushing Satan by avoiding relations with his agents and crushing them underfoot. Here the restoration of righteousness is achieved through the enforcement of cultural and theological conformity. Rom 16:17–20a sustains the movement visible through later Christian history toward a univocal and monocultural construal of theology.[81] In these verses the "God of peace" achieves peace through smashing enemies under the feet of orthodox devotees. In contrast, the letter as a whole follows a strategy of seeking peace between diverse cultural groups through transformed attitudes toward diversities. In this approach, righteousness is recovered through the tolerant transformation of culturally diverse forms of faith.

---

[80] See Stephen Benko, "The Kiss," in *Pagan Rome and the Early Christians* (Bloomington: Indiana University Press, 1984) 79–102; and Nicholas James Perella, *The Kiss: Sacred and Profane: An Interpretative History of Kiss Symbolism and Related Religio-Erotic Themes* (Berkeley: University of California Press, 1969) 12–17.

[81] See, for example, the reiteration of the construal of Rom 16:17–20 as requiring separation from other Christians by Martin H. Franzmann, "Exegesis on Romans 16:17ff.," *Concordia Journal* 7 (1981) 13–20, which accepts the separatist conclusions of Robert George Hoerber, *A Grammatical Study of Romans 16:17* (Milwaukee: Northwestern Publishing House, 1948).

5 ROMANS IN A DIFFERENT LIGHT

A Response to Robert Jewett

J. Paul Sampley
Boston University

IN RECENT DISCUSSIONS regarding the occasion and purpose of Romans, three points have emerged. (1) While there is widespread agreement that the letter is occasioned by some interplay between matters pertaining to Paul and his needs and matters relating more directly to the Roman congregations, the weight placed on either side of the equation is much disputed. (2) While more scholars affirm that the framing material in Romans (1:1–17; 15:14–16:24) gives adequate clues to the purpose and occasion of the letter, the interpretations based on those verses vary remarkably. (3) Any interpretation of the framing material has implications for the understanding of the intervening chapters and in a measure depends on one's view of those chapters; and one's interpretation of the intervening chapters affects the reading of the framing verses.

Robert Jewett joins the discussion on each of these fronts. On (1) *matters Pauline: matters Roman,* Jewett bids to reshape the terms of engagement. His emphasis on the importance of the Spanish mission moves it from its more traditional place as one item among many in *matters Pauline* to a spot of its own and having paramountcy in his interpretation. So Jewett's position may be represented in the following way: *matters Pauline: matters Roman: matters Spanish,* with the last controlling the understanding of the first two. Predictably, therefore, on (2), his interpretation of the framing material highlights Paul's missional intentions regarding Spain (15:22–29 and 16:1–2), which he sees intimated already in 1:1–17, esp. 1:13–15. It follows that, on (3), Paul's concerns for unity expressed within the intervening chapters are understood to facilitate Roman participation in Paul's Spanish mission. In Jewett's view, Paul labors to secure unity among the various groups in Rome "*so that*"[1] the mis-

---

[1] See below.

sion to Spain can be undertaken when he arrives after his Jerusalem detour; the Spanish mission depends on the Roman churches' discovery of unity in light of Paul's intervention.

In his thoughtful study of the framing material of Romans, Jewett has made a series of judgments that I first simply list, without prejudice. Then I will highlight some of Jewett's positions on which I take a different stand.

I. JEWETT'S JUDGMENTS

1. Romans 16 is authentic.[2]
2. Romans is written to several house-churches in the capital.[3]
3. The rhetorical categories *exordium, narratio, propositio, probatio,* and *peroratio* are applicable; the *exordium* "sets the tone for the entire letter" (p. 93).
4. Romans is a demonstrative letter.
5. The letter's overriding and pervasive purpose is missional ("in contrast to the dominant tradition of theological interpretation" [p. 90]).
6. The focus of that mission is Spain; the Pauline outreach to Spain depends on Roman support, which in turn depends on cooperation among previously contending Roman churches or groups within them.
7. The letter is an integrated whole, climaxing in 15:7–13. The letter has no "high point" or "center" prior to chap. 15; it is wrong to separate chaps. 12–15 from the rest of the letter (even though Jewett persists in using older categories to refer to "theological and parenetic arguments of the letter" [p. 90; cf. also p. 92]).
8. One can dismiss the claim that Paul's purpose in writing Romans is to "establish the 'orthodoxy' of his gospel and the legitimacy of his apostleship" (p. 93, quoting Calvin J. Roetzel).
9. One can successfully discern historical layers in the pre-Pauline creedal formulation in 1:3–4 and, like Paul Minear, identify contending groups at Rome with the layers. [4]
10. Rom 16:17-20a is inauthentic and alien not only to Paul but to the spirit of all of the rest of the letter.

---

[2] See *The Romans Debate* (ed. Karl P. Donfried; rev. ed.; Peabody, MA: Hendrickson, 1992) lxx.

[3] Ibid., lxix.

[4] Paul S. Minear, *The Obedience of Faith: The Purpose of Paul in the Epistle to the Romans* (SBT 2/19; London: SCM, 1971).

II. SOME POINTS OF DIFFERENCE

Spain and Mission

We can stipulate that Paul did project a mission to Spain, and we can readily suppose that the Spanish venture was driven by Paul's understanding of his call as apostle to the Gentiles. Likewise, we can stipulate that mission must be at the center of any interpretation of Romans. But our differences with Jewett are proportional in regard to Spain and definitional with respect to mission.

Spain

Twice Paul states that he wants to see the Romans on the way to Spain (15:24, 28). Whether Jewett's imaginative, speculative suggestions regarding Phoebe's role as advance agent and patron[5] of the Spanish mission are true or not we will surely never know; the Romans must have found out one way or another after her arrival.

Jewett goes too far, however. The mention of the Spanish mission, explicit only at the end of the letter, is taken by Jewett as the governing motif and purpose of the letter as a whole, in all its parts. Everything is taken, as the title of his essay suggests, "for the sake of mission" to Spain. Jewett depicts Romans as "appealing for cooperation in the planning . . . of the Spanish mission" (p. 89); Romans is an "appeal to the Roman house-churches to support Phoebe's patronage of the Spanish mission" (p. 90); Romans seeks "to elicit the cooperation of the Roman house- and tenement-churches in Paul's missionary activities" (p. 92); the letter prepares the Romans for "Paul's forthcoming visit . . . to promote a mission among the nations" (p. 97); and "insofar as Romans serves the task of world mission, *aiming to elicit support for proclaiming the gospel in Spain,* the entire letter can be understood as elaborating this thesis" (p. 102, emphasis added). By contrast, Jewett gives less attention to a Pauline concern for intra-Roman Christian relations and even then sometimes casts it as instrumental toward enabling what he calls "credible" participation in the mission beyond Rome (pp. 97, 108).

Whatever weight we might give the Spanish mission, we must note that in Paul's calculus, as reflected in the organization of his life, the Spanish mission, and indeed the situation among believers in Rome—all of it is subordinated to his determination to see the collection delivered at Jerusalem. And if 15:30–33 suggests that he (rightly?) anticipated personal hazard in his trip to

---

[5] See James C. Walters, "'Phoebe' and 'Junia(s)'—Rom. 16:1–2, 7," in *Essays on Women in Earliest Christianity* (ed. Carroll D. Osburn; Joplin, MO: College Press Publishing, 1993) 1. 167–90.

Jerusalem, then those verses should function as a perspective-keeper on Paul's determination to get to Rome and to Spain.

Further, Jewett supposes that Paul's projected mission to Spain necessitates unified churches in Rome. The healing of their divisions will "thus enable them to participate in the campaign to missionize to the end of the known world" (p. 105). Jewett never says why they must be unified before they can participate. Presumably Jewett's answer would require an elaboration and clarification of what he means when he says that unified the Roman believers "would also be enabled to participate *in a credible manner* in completing the mission" (p. 97, emphasis added; cf. the same phrase again on p. 108). In terms of logistics, as p. 89 asks us to think, Paul's needs from the Romans might include (a) finances, (b) contacts, and (c) translator(s). Is Roman divisiveness wasting resources? How would greater unity yield more support? Are contacts for hospitality in Spain less likely with contention among the churches? Could not Paul secure those contacts from the different Roman churches? How many translators might a Spanish mission need?

Mission

Jewett is right to insist that mission should be at the center of our interpretation of Romans, but his understanding of mission is so narrow as to minimize Paul's very work *with the Romans as mission.* Jewett's conception of Paul's mission focuses too much beyond Rome; it does not do justice to Paul's mission *in Rome.* Consider Jewett's statement that 1:16–17 "takes up the issue of Paul's *intended* missionary enterprise" (p. 104, emphasis added). Throughout most of the paper, Jewett represents Paul's missional focus as being *really* on Spain, and the impression emerges that Paul's interest in Roman unity is simply functional and instrumental toward the goal of having them take part in mission *beyond* Rome. The phrase "for the sake of mission" in the title of Jewett's paper reflects his view. So does his statement, set in the context of the special requirements of a Spanish mission: "The theological and parenetic arguments of the letter all serve this end, aiming at uniting the Roman house-churches *so that* such cooperation would be possible" (p. 90, emphasis added). The "practical purpose" toward which the letter as a whole was oriented "was to elicit the cooperation of the Roman house- and tenement-churches in Paul's missionary activities" (p. 92). Again: "Paul's hope in writing this letter is that this inclusive and restorative righteousness will be allowed to heal the divisions within the Roman house-churches and thus enable them to participate in the campaign to missionize to the end of the known world" (p. 105).

For Paul, mission is not just naming the gospel where it has not been named; mission includes calling, nurturing, instructing, chiding, warning, encouraging as many persons as possible before the end of time. This side of the parousia, mission is never finished; it is always being expanded as new believers are added, but it is never completed with any believers, longstanding ones or new ones or ones yet to be evangelized. For Paul, mission is always eschatological: it works against the time constraints of a divinely foreshortened time, and it anticipates that the missioners and the ones missionized will be weighed in the balance of God's judgment at the eschaton. A profound part of Paul's mission is the presenting of a unified body of believers at the parousia as a demonstration of his having run the race, of his having fulfilled his apostolic calling. Whenever division threatens a community (Corinth, for example) or a set of communities (Galatians, for example), Paul responds as if his mission were called into question, and his efforts focus on regaining unity. A dispute between two women leaders in one community prompts a Pauline epistolary response (Philippians). Schisms in the body of Christ are unthinkable to Paul; practically that usually means that unity is to be recovered on Pauline grounds and in terms of allegiance to him and his gospel, but unity around him and his gospel is the *sine qua non* for Paul. Failure of that unity discredits his whole mission.

If divisions and interpersonal strife always caught Paul's attention, how much more when that conflict struck at the issue of the relationship of Jews and Gentiles in the gospel! The relationship of Jews and Gentiles in Christ blazed like a comet across the career of the apostle Paul. No other issue compares to it in proportion or in duration. From that fateful day when Paul, ever the Jew, came to the conviction that the Gentiles, whom he was called to evangelize, did not have to become Jews in order to belong to the people of God, Paul could be sure that his life and mission would never be free from this issue. The trajectory of the comet can be observed by us from the Jerusalem conference (Gal 2:1–10), through the contretemps with Cephas at Antioch (Gal 2:11–21), through the problems with soliciting the collection (1 Cor 16:1–4; 2 Corinthians 8–9), through Paul's fateful decision to attend to the delivery of the collection in person (Rom 15:22–29), and the comet blazes most brilliantly as it enters the atmosphere of the stress among the Jewish and Gentile believers in the Roman house-churches.

And why shouldn't Paul consider himself the logical one to intervene in the Roman house-churches' struggles? First, he is by his calling apostle to the Gentiles; and perhaps by this late point in his career he may have come to think of himself as *the* apostle to the Gentiles, since passages in Galatians and 2 Corinthians suggest that he looked at rivals and their gospel with some condescension. Second, he has no doubt heard from some of his contacts in

Rome that it is precisely the Gentiles who, with Claudius's edict banishing the Jews from Rome, had gained ascendancy of leadership in the Roman churches, and who, when Claudius died and Jewish believers returned, precipitated the troubles by treating the former Jewish leaders with arrogance. Third, even though Paul had not been the founder of a single church in Rome, he may have come to think of himself as alone among those he deemed apostles in understanding what he was convinced was the truth of the gospel, namely, that in Christ there could not be a separate Gentile church without its Jewish roots. Well he might have come to such a conclusion since even Cephas, who played a significant role in the Jerusalem conference accord on this matter, showed in Antioch that he had not stuck by the agreement (Gal 2:11–21). Furthermore, Paul saw his own cohort, Barnabas, dissemble on the same issue (Gal 2:13). Fourth, Paul was convinced that at the parousia he, like everyone else, would have to stand judgment as to whether he had lived up to his calling, whether he had run in vain. Finally, for the last couple of years he had worked to gather the collection for the saints in Jerusalem, this proof offering that symbolized, as Rom 15:26–27 so clearly states it, that a genuine reciprocity ought to exist between Jewish believers and Gentile believers—and what he hears about Rome must strike Paul as a breakdown of that mutuality. Accordingly, the situation among Roman believers is a real-life challenge to Paul's mission and to his calling, and Paul, despite considerable liabilities and problems that we will detail below, engages the Roman churches' struggles in the only way accessible to him as he heads off to Jerusalem with the collection: he writes a lengthy letter. He writes a long letter in which he undertakes his mission *to the believers, Jewish and Gentile, in Rome,* announces, very much as in Philemon 22, a projected visit to them as a follow-up, and places this personal mission to them in the context of his broader mission that he projects Spainward.

It is in such a context that we should understand his important self-description of his apostolic purpose for which we use the term "mission," a word that was not available to him. In 15:18–21, Paul summarizes his completed work framed by Jerusalem and Illyricum in this statement: πεπληρωκέναι τὸ εὐαγγέλιον τοῦ Χριστοῦ (15:19), which is almost universally translated as something like "I have preached the gospel of Christ"—even though the verb is not εὐαγγελίζω but πληρόω. I appreciate former efforts to make sense out of what should most reasonably be translated "I have fulfilled the gospel of Christ," but I think that we are now in a position to understand why Paul states it as he does. His calling is not just to *preach* the gospel to the Gentiles, not just, for example, to carry the message to a city or a province or an area; that is indeed part of his calling, but it would inadequately reflect his broader sense of mission. Paul's "fulfilling the gospel" involves also the inculcating of new ways of walking within his churches, the healing of schisms within those communities, and the calling for growth and mutual upbuilding among the believers, wherever Gentiles are a part of the body of Christ. It is this spirit of responsibility for Gentile believers and for their comportment toward their brothers and sisters in the faith, whether they be Gentiles or Jews as the world would reckon matters, that causes Paul to intervene in the Roman house-church contentions about which he has undoubtedly learned a great deal through his many contacts in Rome (see chap. 16). In this light, his letter to the Romans is also a part of his total effort to "fulfill the gospel"—in this case his fulfilling the gospel requires him to urge upon believers who never heard him preach the gospel the call to a fuller and more unified life. So Romans is not merely or even primarily written "for the sake of mission"; *it is mission* at work!

To be sure, if his mission in Rome via this letter is successful, then avenues may be opened for Roman participation in the Spanish mission. We must be clear, however, that Paul has a mission *to and for* the Roman house-churches, and the bulk of his letter addresses that mission. Note well: Paul's desire is to get on to Rome and go to Spain. But something larger preempts Paul's plans and prompts the only direct personal request Paul makes of the Romans in the entire letter.[6] That something larger is his hope and prayer "that my service for Jerusalem may be acceptable to the saints" (15:31). If the mission to Spain is important to Paul, as it is, and if we are to take his fears for his personal safety at face value, then Spain and Rome and Paul's personal hopes *all* take a back seat to his determination to see this collection through to its completion. In Paul's delay, if not final absence, the letter to the Romans carries Paul's burden concerning the internal relationships among the splintered Romans and allows him to hope not to have run in vain either in Jerusalem or in Rome.

Unity and the Purpose of the Gospel

Jewett is right to see unity at the heart of Paul's understanding of the gospel, but Jewett's casting of Paul's purposes in Romans reflects only part of Romans—and even that reflection may be misunderstood. Jewett has a persistent, relatively similar set of phrases whereby he seeks to capture the purpose of the gospel: "transform and sanctify the human race" (p. 89), "world-transforming mission" (p. 90); "global transformation and pacification" (p. 90); "world mission" (pp. 91, 102); "global pacification" (p. 92); "a mission among the nations" (p. 97); and "the pacification of the world" (p. 105). Along the same line is Jewett's depiction of Romans' missional strat-

[6] Paul J. Achtemeier, *Romans* (Interpretation; Atlanta: John Knox, 1985) 229.

egy as "seeking peace . . . through transformed attitudes toward diversities" (p. 108) as if attitudinal adjustment were at the heart of the working of the gospel. The unity that *is* fundamental to the gospel is life-transforming harmony among believers, a concord achieved without the loss of personal and cultural distinctions; Romans dwells on accord and depreciates judgment because Paul is urging his audience to live up to their calling.

We should not confuse the unity that should pertain among believers with a program of pacification among all people everywhere. God's righteousness, which is being revealed in the world (1:17), is paralleled by God's wrath, which is also being revealed in the world (1:18). Paul holds that all believers, including those in Rome, have peace with God (5:1); all who do not respond with faith remain in darkness; sin is their lord; and destruction, not salvation, is their destiny (Phil 1:28). Throughout the Pauline corpus, the title "God of peace" is used only in contexts of proper comportment among the believers; it never appears in a context of God's relation to the world, to sin, and to sinners. God tolerates neither sin nor the one sinning if there is no response of faith. Jewett has taken the rhetoric of unity between Jew and Gentile in 1:18-15:13 and has tended to identify it as a world program of tolerance and unity. Rather, the gospel and its preaching tell hearers the story of God's unfolding purpose and inform them that they can be partakers in God's glorious restoration of creation; the same gospel implies a warning that failure to respond has awesome consequences.

Jewett's interpretation diminishes the apocalypticism of Romans (cf. p. 105)—and indeed of Paul's gospel. Where in Jewett's depiction is the claim that "the creation itself will be set free from its bondage to decay and obtain the glorious liberty of the children of God" (8:21 RSV)? Where is the eschatological "redemption of our bodies" (8:23)? Where is an adequate portrayal of God's wrath (1:18; 2:5, 8; 3:5; 5:9) and the last-times judgment? God's reclaiming of the cosmos will have deleterious consequences for all who stand outside the community of faith or oppose God.

The Address and Creedal Formulation

Again somewhat reminiscent of Paul Minear, Jewett spends considerable effort in a treatment of the address (pp. 94–97) and in a lamellated dissection of the creedal affirmation that is found in 1:3–4 (pp. 97–103).

Address

Jewett is surely right when he says that "the opening address . . . sets the tone for the entire letter," and if "the splintered congregations of Rome"

understood the gospel they "would become unified in cooperation while preserving their distinctiveness" (p. 97). The address is rightly understood as
inclusive and designed to provide common ground, though Jewett is quite
unconvincing when he says that the different terms ("saints," etc.) might
apply more to any one group than another so that, for example, "faith" could
be said to be "a favorite shibboleth for Gentile Christians in Rome" (p. 94)!

Creedal Formulation

Likewise, when Jewett concludes his analysis of the creedal formulation in
1:3–4, he succinctly declares what must really be rhetorically at the heart of
the matter: "He [Paul] is obviously seeking to find common ground" (p. 104).
Jewett's preceding analysis, in which he characterizes Paul as proceeding in an
"evenhanded" fashion (p. 103), claims that, with "correcting insertions"
(p. 103), Paul "thwarts adoptionist inferences and qualifies the Davidic sonship." Jewett imagines a Paul who, trimming a bit of sail here, applying a little rudder to starboard there, craftily sails through perilous straits which would
only fully and properly be charted by the folks who brought us Nicea and
Chalcedon. Jewett's detailed evaluation of the creed is rhetorically at cross-
purposes with Paul's need to establish his ethos equally with *all* segments of
the Roman churches, where far from siding with this or that faction on fine
points of christological probity (which only modern students of New Testament and of the history of Christian thought might claim to understand, any-
way) Paul must embrace as wide a set of traditions as possible so as to ground
his gospel and his apostleship within the traditions that might have nourished
each segment of the Roman believers, and which common ground might in
turn enable the Romans to embrace him and his service in the gospel to them.

Why Is Romans So Long?

Any thesis concerning the purpose or purposes of Romans must be tested
as to how well it accounts for 1:18–15:13. If one argues that evangelizing
Spain is the underlying purpose of the letter, then one must account for the
length and appropriateness of the intervening chapters. Jewett jettisons what
he calls "the dominant tradition of theological interpretation" of the bulk of
Romans (p. 90); Romans is not Paul's "last testament." Instead, he argues that
the bulk of Romans "provides a rationale for cooperative missionary praxis in
a cross-cultural context" (p. 90). While he is on sound ground in suggesting
that the time is over for reading Romans as a last testament of Paul's theology,
his alternative is once again premised on the narrow conception of a projected
mission to Spain. Therefore, in his view, 1:18–15:13 is devoted to Paul's expli-

cation of the "world-transforming" vision of the gospel, a position that is least adequate in integrating 12:1–15:6.

Any accounting for 1:18–15:13 must factor three considerations: (1) the writer's concerns, interests, and problems; (2) the recipients' concerns, interests, and problems; and (3) the dynamics of the interaction of writer and auditors. Anything less fails to take seriously the exigencies of communication and underestimates the rhetorical challenge.

The Writer's Concerns, Interests, and Problems

We noted above the central factor: Paul is apostle to Gentiles. From that apostleship follows his intervention in the Jewish–Gentile contention of the Roman churches and his hope to carry the message beyond Rome to Spain. He asks for their prayers as he leaves for Jerusalem with the collection.

The Recipients' Concerns, Interests, and Problems

When Jewett notes, almost in passing, that Romans must be situated "after the lapse of the Edict of Claudius around 54 CE" (p. 93; cf. p. 95), he alludes to the sociopolitical context in which Romans must be understood. Claudius's edict (49 CE; cf. Acts 18:2), by its expulsion of Jews from Rome, changed the face of Christianity in the capital city. By default, leadership passed from exiting Jewish believers to the Gentile believers, who were not forced to leave. The edict expired with Claudius (54 CE), and Jews, among them some Christians, returned to Rome. Christianity in Rome changed once again, though now previous leaders, Jews all, returned to find an established Gentile leadership in the house-churches. The resulting tensions are palpable in Paul's letter (which arrived in Rome approximately a year after the return of the Jewish believers)[7] with its warnings against judging, despising, boasting, haughtiness, and overestimation of self.

The Dynamics of the Interaction of Writer and Auditors

Jewett underestimates the rhetorical problems Paul faces in this letter. First, Paul writes as an outsider, with the undoubtedly important exceptions of the persons whom he names so prominently in chap. 16. Second, he is writing to churches that were founded by others, so he lacks the authority he normally presumes, the common ground represented by the repository of his own

---

[7] See James C. Walters, *Ethnic Issues in Paul's Letter to the Romans: Changing Self-Definitions in Earliest Roman Christianity* (Valley Forge, PA: Trinity Press International, 1994); he lays out the data for understanding the social and ethnic complexity of Rome and examines Paul's treatment of some of the ethnic problems in Romans.

preaching and teaching and the individual suasion upon which he so frequently and freely relied in his other letters. Third, the churches in Rome have a significant number of Jews among them; the other extant authentic letters address predominantly Gentile congregations, so our scholarly expertise in those letters does not prepare us to understand how he might relate to Jews in a letter. Fourth, not only is Paul relatively unknown to the churches in Rome; he is apostle to the Gentiles. Paul's desire to address "all God's beloved in Rome" (1:7) means that he must establish credibility not only with the believing Gentiles but also with the faithful Jews in Rome. And the most problematic consideration: fifth, *Paul has good grounds to suppose that all of the recipients in Rome, both Gentiles and Jews, will hear his letter with a hermeneutic of suspicion*—the Gentiles because they must wonder whether this person of whom they have heard plans now to move in on them and take over, and the Jews because they must wonder whether this person of whom they have heard preaches a gospel in discontinuity with their traditions and practices.

Establishment and maintenance of ethos. Before Paul can work effectively with the churches at Rome he must establish his credentials with a significant number of the readers/hearers in Rome. Each of the aforementioned five dynamics is a problem of ethos; Paul's success in engaging any of these issues depends on his favorably establishing his ethos in a way that convinces the hearers. As D. A. Russell so rightly says: "It [ethos] is not just an incidental, to be indicated by odd remarks here and there; it must be woven into the whole texture of the speech."[8] And the same is true in letters.

Because Jewett underestimates Paul's rhetorical problems in writing Romans and in gaining a hearing there, he misses some points and skews others. In the framing material Paul engages these rhetorical challenges and problems. As an outsider, writing to churches he never founded, Paul identifies himself as the sole author (in distinction from every other authentic letter), giving the longest and most detailed self-description in any of the salutations in the authentic letters (1:1–6). In other letters, Paul's commonplace mention of coauthors ties his work in to that of others in behalf of the gospel; in Romans such references appear only at the end of the document and, instead of being outsiders to the recipients' community, in Romans they are gen-

---

[8] D. A. Russell, *Greek Declamation* (Cambridge: Cambridge University Press, 1983) 72. In a chapter-long treatment entitled "Character and characters," Russell identifies the importance of ethos in three ways: (a) that the speaker must "project a sympathetic image of himself" as one who is "likeable and—even more important—trustworthy"; (b) that the speaker needed to know his hearers well enough to know what kinds of appeals might function positively with them; and (c) he had to represent the other "people appearing in his story" in a plausible way (p. 87). All of these features are manifest in Paul's letter.

uinely insiders. The persons named in chap. 16 make up for and probably function rhetorically much as the names Paul lists as coauthors in the other authentic letters; their last position in Romans may in fact have more rhetorical force than his normal practice. No doubt the persons listed in chap. 16 have briefed Paul on the problems in and among the Roman churches and provide positive leverage that will serve to reinforce Paul's efforts to establish his ethos through the letter.[9]

It is imperative that Paul establish common ground between himself and the Roman churches—this is *requisite to any and every other goal* he has in this letter. Toward that end, Paul employs three complementary tactics. (a) He relies heavily on pre- and para-Pauline Christian formulations that he may reasonably expect them to know (e.g., the traditional material in 1:3–4 and 3:24–25) and he quotes scripture at crucial points (e.g., Hab 2:4 in 1:17, Jewett's *propositio;* Isa 52:15 in Rom 15:21 as a justification for the Gentile mission). (b) He stresses Jewish matters and the continuity of his gospel with God's purposes and promises (the gospel of God's son is the very gospel "promised beforehand through his prophets in the holy scriptures" [1:1–2]; Jesus' Davidic lineage [1:3]; the righteousness of God, now manifest in Christ, was borne witness to by the law and the prophets [3:21]; Abraham is typologically presented as the faithful person and all subsequent believers are his children; Paul's own identification as a Jew is clear [three times he identifies kinsmen, 16:7, 11, 21; cf. 9:3]; Paul's mission among the Gentiles is called a "priestly service" [15:16] in the "offering of the Gentiles" [15:16, echoing the catena of quotations in 15:9–12]; Paul's claim of "the Jew first" precisely in the *propositio* and reiterated twice in 2:9–10; even the description of the Jerusalem collection as being for the "saints at Jerusalem" [15:26, 31] and the associated statement of the obligations of Gentiles to the Jerusalem saints [15:27; cf. the directly related claim that "all the churches of the Gentiles give thanks" to the Jewish couple, Prisca and Aquila, 16:4]). (c) Paul reassures the Romans that he does not expect to lord it over them or to take over (note Paul's opening *correctio* of 1:11–12 which aims to counter Roman fear that Paul expects to treat them as inferiors, and powerfully discards that form of relationship for one of mutual encouragement, reaffirmed by his declaration of noninterference in 15:20, and his wish to see them "on the way" (διαπορευόμενος) to Spain (15:24, 28).[10]

---

[9] Apart from Phoebe (16:1–2), the persons mentioned in chap. 16 are not persons whom Paul seeks to help become leaders (*pace* O. Michel, *Der Brief an die Römer* [Göttingen: Vandenhoeck & Ruprecht, 1966] 474; Jewett, p. 107); they are surely already leaders.

[10] That he wishes nevertheless to "preach the gospel" (1:5) is no violation of his noninterference clause because Paul does nothing if not preach the gospel wherever he is and whatever his circumstances—witness preaching to the Galatians while sick (Gal 4:13), to the Pretorian Guard and to Onesimus while in prison (Phil 1:13; Phlm 10).

Paul's strategy for integrating his purposes and the exigences of his readers. Here Paul has two important tactics: the first is comprehensive and sweeps across the body of the entire letter; the second occurs, as an object lesson, in a single pericope toward the end.

(1) Comprehensive strategy. In Romans we have Paul's apostolic intervention, pastoral in style, in an intramural, ethnically grounded struggle over leadership and position in the Roman house-churches. Romans is a sustained, cohesive, comprehensive address of the Roman factions in a quest for unity. There is no "doctrinal" section that provides what might be called a basis for appeal; *all of Romans is carefully crafted as an effort to heal the divisiveness among Roman believers.*[11] This means that all the sections of the letter, from 1:18 to 15:13, are designed to bear directly on the struggles among Roman believers. Rom 1:16–17, Jewett's *propositio*, is of course the "thesis statement" and does declare "the main theme" of the letter (p. 104). The material between these verses and the concluding frame (15:14ff.), every passage of it, is directed toward helping all of Paul's readers/hearers to recognize and affirm their unity in the powerful gospel of God. Rom 1:18–8:39 is not the doctrinal base from which Paul will subsequently build ethical implications. In 1:18–8:39, Paul's interest is not doctrine per se; rather his purpose is to establish the broadest possible ground upon which all of the Roman believers, no matter what their ethnic background, can see that they stand in common.[12]

The following sketch shows how each major division of the letter carries out this strategy.

Rom 1:18–4:25: All share the same story apart from faith; and all believers have Abraham as their father. Rom 1:18–4:25 elaborates two important parts of the story. This section's negative side of the argument is designed to remind the Roman believers, *both Jews and Gentiles,* that their pre-faith story was the same: each of them was subject to the power and rule of sin. Likewise, in the positive development of the argument, each of them, *whether Gentile or Jew,* was totally dependent on God's grace; they all became right with God and children of Abraham when they believed God as Abraham did. So 1:18–4:25 lays out a two-sided portrayal of how Roman Jews and Roman Gentiles, equally under the power of sin, were also equally dependent on God's grace in Jesus Christ for their resulting peace with God. Far from Paul's enunciating

---

[11] If Paul's apostolic effort at Rome enables widespread Roman participation in a Spanish mission, that is well and good.

[12] Note that Paul's capacity to survey the vastness of the common ground of all believers, whether Jewish or Gentile, contributes, at each stage, to the enhancement of his own ethos.

his doctrines[13] of sin, grace, and faith for their own sake, 1:18–4:25 is Paul's establishment and rehearsal—a genuine remembering afresh (cf. Rom 15:15)—of the common ground that he knows is shared equally by all of his Gentile and Jewish readers/hearers in Rome.

For the most part (contrast 2:1–5) the claims are made in a sweepingly inclusive way so that Paul is not misunderstood to be saying that the Roman believers' story is different from his or that of others who have come to faith.[14] As examples, consider "both Jews and Greeks, all are under sin" (3:9) and "for all have sinned and come short of God's glory" (3:23). That this is not some systematic declaration of Paul's full thought about sin is clear when we realize that the extended portrait of Abraham does not count him among those who have sinned and missed God's glory. The same must be said for the strange Gentiles—whom scholars sometimes hastily baptize into the faith in an effort to make them fit—in 2:14–16 who seem, absent both the law and Christ, to be portrayed positively by Paul. So Romans' argument about all being under the power of sin is a porous argument designed to call to mind for the Roman believers that—no matter their ethnic origins—they stand, equally delivered from the clutches of sin and equally on the common ground of faith through God's grace. That is also the reason for Paul's amplification of the common paternity that Abraham represents both to Jewish and to Gentile believers.

Romans 5–8: All share the same story from peace to parousia. Chapters 5–8 unfold for the readers/hearers the scope of God's design of which they are now a part. This section opens with the newly established peace with God (5:1), closes with the awesome apocalyptic picture of God's cosmic redemptive purposes (8:18–25, 28–30) wherein the lost glory of 3:23 is restored beyond compare, and, in the enclosed chapters, details some of the factors bearing on how believers are to comport themselves. This vast story is rehearsed—again, the recalling to mind of Rom 15:15—as the shared narrative of their present lives and ultimate destiny as God's children. All the Roman believers are called to see their own stories as a part of God's unfolding drama.[15] In the light we are suggesting, consider how the different factions

---

[13] It is reasonable to wonder how far the employment of such a term is appropriate in application to Paul.

[14] This is a pattern in Pauline rhetoric. In 1 Corinthians he did not single out the glossolalists for attack but put consideration of glossolalia into the larger context of the proper use of spiritual gifts (chaps. 12–14); so here he is careful not to suggest that there is something peculiar about the Roman believers' story.

[15] Chapter 8 presents an apocopated version of the large picture of chaps. 5–8, harking back, as it does, to the origin of faith in the Spirit's moving with believers' spirits to enable the first act of all new believers: viz., to cry out "Abba, Pater" to God (8:15; cf. Gal 4:6). The distinc-

of Roman believers might have heard Paul's question: "Who shall bring charges against God's elected ones? It is God who justifies; who is the one who condemns?" (8:33–34; cf. the echo in 14:4). As surely as no putative cosmic powers can shake one's standing in God's cosmic redemptive purposes, so no believer may dare to oppose God's other elected ones; when God justifies (cf. 5:9 as the established common story of all the Roman hearers), who dares condemn? How can believers in Rome condemn other believers there?

Romans 9–11: All have been affected by God's faithfulness and by God's freedom. Chapters 9–11 address some of the implications and assumptions underlying what Paul has said in the preceding chapters. The issues focus around the faithfulness and freedom of God: faithfulness because God's promises, gifts, and call are not subject to alteration (cf. 3:3–4); freedom because God's mercy and call may gain expression in ways that surprise people and that move creatively around and through human obduracy. This section continues Paul's pastoral effort to help the Romans understand how God's faithfulness and freedom have impacted them. Jewish believers have a fundamental primacy with respect to God's faithfulness; they are, after all, part of the root stock onto which these "wild branches" have been grafted and by which the tree is nourished (11:18; cf. 15:27). Likewise, Gentile believers, though they have been grafted onto God's tree, are there only because of faith; φόβος ("fear"), not ὑψηλός ("pride"), would be the more fitting response.

Romans 12:1–15:13: All must live in thankfulness to God and in loving acceptance and encouragement of each other. In 12:1–15:13 Paul calls upon the Roman believers, as children of God, to live their lives individually and collectively in such a way as to reflect their gratitude to God and their loving acceptance of one another. As has been widely recognized, this section addresses the contending parties in the Roman house-churches. We must look more carefully, however, at the "weak" and the "strong" here. In his paper, Jewett follows a scholarly tendency in Romans studies, to identify the weak and strong as representing two groups in Rome. Scholars often identify these groups with Jewish and Gentile believers. On p. 95, Jewett labels the weak as Jewish believers; on p. 96 the strong are (tentatively) called "Gentile Christians." To identify the weak and the strong in Romans 14–15 as two distinct groups, no matter what ethnic designations, is to misunderstand Paul's rhetorical purposes and skills. Consider this. What is the profile of the weak person? He is a vegetarian (14:2). But three verses later, who is the weak person? The one who thinks one day is better than another or the one who values all days the same? Paul

---

tiveness of believers is not eradicated at the start of faith. Jews will still say "Abba" and Gentiles will still call "Pater," but it is the same God upon whom they call from the same ground of faith.

never makes an identification, probably because his concern is to say that such distinctions are *adiaphora*[16] (indifferent matters) when the central matter is doing whatever one does with respect to the Lord. Likewise, what is the description of the strong? They are persons who can eat anything (14:2), though I suspect this is one of those places where a literal reading is not advised! Also, they are the ones who ought to carry the weaknesses of the unpowerful (τὰ ἀσθενήματα τῶν ἀδυνάτων; 15:1; cf. Gal 6:1–2). That is all we can find in Romans about the identification of the weak and the strong—surely not enough to profile them onto either extreme of what was in reality more probably a continuum.[17]

Look once again, then, at the rather vague formulation about evaluating days (14:5–6). We may expect that one of the contentious issues among Roman believers was actually the sabbath, but Paul never says so. Instead, consider his rhetorical strategy. In a stroke of the pen, Paul moved the confrontation onto neutral ground: to be sure most Jews must have reckoned the sabbath fundamental, but Gentiles in that time were also notorious for honoring special days. By the way Paul has cast it, the issue of honoring days is not simply a Jewish problem. Paul has adopted an "oblique approach" whereby no single group in Rome is put in the spotlight; likewise, therefore, no group's members would be in a position to nudge each other knowingly and condescendingly as Paul's discussion of sabbath-keeping was read. In fact, the same rhetorical strategy is present earlier in the text, when Paul artfully moves any discussion of keeping kosher—or not doing so—over onto neutral and mutually accessible grounds of vegetarianism-by-choice[18] versus the omnivorous life. Paul's approach cloaks the actually divisive practices of the different Roman groups under the garb of putative practices with which no group has an entrenched position. This rhetorical strategy of oblique approach enables all of the Roman believers to consider afresh, and without already established prejudices, the relative insignificance of diverse practices and moral decisions when compared with their common ground in the Lord. When Paul finally brings to the surface—even then for only one sentence—what indeed must

---

[16] For a more detailed study of *adiaphora* and their function in Paul's letters, see James L. Jaquette, "Paul, Epictetus, and Others on Indifference to Status," *CBQ* 56 (1994) 68–80.

[17] Jewett's paper joins an increasing body of scholarly work that shows how complex and variegated early Christian communities were in belief and practice, even in a single city, so that we can no longer speak of the believers in Rome as if they were all alike. If we now realize how diverse the believers in a single city may be, then surely the time has come to jettison the old sweeping generalizations like Jewett's about "primitive Palestinian Christianity" (p. 98).

[18] Here, Paul is not concerned with the socioeconomics of the time, namely, that the poor would likely have to eat vegetables; he casts it as a choice in light of one's measure of faith (Rom 12:3).

have been a contentious issue, viz., what is κοινός ("common," "impure," "unclean"), he has assiduously prepared a context within which it can be considered afresh and on different grounds by all the parties among the Roman believers.[19]

The discussion from 14:1 to 15:7 is framed within an *inclusio* that moves from the more specific entreaty to give welcome to the "one weak with respect to faith" (14:1) to the more inclusive "Therefore, welcome one another just as Christ has welcomed you, to the glory of God" (15:7). The thrice-repeated προσλαμβάνω, coming as it does in the climax of the letter's body, is an explicit call from Paul for the contending factions to come together. It is the perfect admonitory term to sum up Paul's purposes throughout the chapters within the framing material, meaning as it may "receive or accept in one's society, in(to) one's home or circle of acquaintances!"[20] Paul exhorts the Roman believers to reach across the barriers that their separate house-churches have come to represent. Paul's call is grounded in the most basic claim: "just as Christ has welcomed you" (15:7).

Another *inclusio* complements the one just noted and reaches back to the opening of chap. 2, thereby not only encircling *all the intervening chapters* found within the framing material but also confirming this unitary reading of Romans. In sum, the *inclusio* reminds the Roman hearers that there are no grounds for them to pass judgment on one another (2:1; 14:4, reasserted in 14:10 and 14:13).[21] Paul's cautions regarding "despising" or "disdaining" are so fully interwoven (14:3, 10) with the call for no judgment that two questions parallel each other: "But you, why do you judge your brother? And you, why do you despise your brother?" (14:10).[22] To despise or pass judgment on one whom God has welcomed (14:3) and who is therefore a brother or sister in faith is unthinkable to Paul—and he thinks it should be for the contending believers in Rome.

(2) An object Lesson: Paul and the collection for the saints in Jerusalem. We have paid too little attention to the rhetorically powerful parallels Paul invites the Romans to see between themselves and Paul and his collection. Literally the

---

[19] For the particulars on the rhetorical traditions and strategy employed by Paul in Romans 14:1–15:13, see my "The Weak and the Strong: Paul's Careful and Crafty Rhetorical Strategy in Romans 14:1-15:13," in *The Social World of the First Christians: Studies in Honor of Wayne A. Meeks* (ed. L. Michael White and O. Larry Yarbrough; Minneapolis: Fortress, 1994) 40–52.

[20] BAGD, 717.

[21] See Wayne A. Meeks, "Judgment and the Brother: Romans 14:1–15:3," in *Tradition and Interpretation in the New Testament: Essays in Honor of E. Earle Ellis* (ed. Gerald F. Hawthorne and Otto Betz; Grand Rapids: Eerdmans, 1987) 290–300.

[22] As the Lukan parable of the two sons with one father (Luke 15:11–32) artfully reintroduces the older brother to the younger by calling him "your brother," so Paul does here.

last item before the commendation of Phoebe and the greetings, Paul's singular direct personal request of the Romans encourages them to identify with him (15:30). See how dedicated to the unity of Jewish and Gentile believers he is! He is so convinced of the necessity of Jewish and Gentile believers' celebrating their life together in Christ that he places his life on the line. When they join with him in prayer that he may be delivered and that the collection, gathered from predominantly Gentile congregations, might be accepted by the predominantly Jewish Jerusalem Christians, thus affirming one people of God, can they fail to find themselves compelled not only to rethink their own relations but also to move toward unity? From Paul's perspective, the problems in Rome are directly parallel with the delivery of the collection: both raise the fundamental question whether the body of Christ can be divided along Jewish and Gentile lines. Paul's letter to the Romans and his personal delivery of the collection to Jerusalem are of one and the same piece. The latter is a primary key for understanding the former and underlines why Paul dared to write a reminder to them on some points (15:15). Paul's rhetorical finish to this part of the letter invites the Romans to stand in his shoes and risk working for unity, just as he is doing. This prepares us for a fresh look at Paul's earlier reference to Jerusalem in 15:19. Paul's retrospective regarding his work "in the power of signs and prodigies, in the power of the Spirit" traces his orbit "from Jerusalem in a circle to Illyricum" (15:19). As contested as the interpretations of these geographical references may be, the marking of Paul's ministry as "from Jerusalem" parallels what Paul says about Jerusalem in the context of the collection: "For if Gentiles have shared their [the Jerusalem saints'] spiritual things, they [Gentiles] ought to be of service to them in things material" (15:27).[23] The Jews do indeed have priority when considered from the perspective that "from them comes the Christ, according to the flesh" (9:5), because God will be true and faithful (3:3–4), and because "the gifts and the call of God are irrevocable" (11:29 RSV).[24] "From Jerusalem" is foremost

---

[23] These very positive references to πνευματικοῖς and σαρκικοῖς at the end of the letter recall the occurrences of κατὰ σάρκα and κατὰ πνεῦμα in 1:3–4 and suggest that Jewett's interpretation of the function of those phrases in the traditional creed need not be read in his proposed antithetical way. Indeed, they sound rather Pauline in his capacity to consider almost any situation, event, or person from different perspectives. On this Pauline tendency, see my *Walking Between the Times: Paul's Moral Reasoning* (Minneapolis: Fortress Press, 1991) 18–19.

[24] From what is adumbrated here, Jewett is wrong when he claims that "when Paul referred in Romans to 'the Jews first and then the Greeks,' he was referring to these constellations of Christians, reversing their competitive status" (p. 96). First, he errs in his translation, which fits Matthew better than Paul, suggesting as it does that the Jews' chance passes and an opening comes for the Gentiles. Second, Jewett errs in taking the sequence as a Pauline polemic against one of the contending groups in Rome (how unlikely a rhetorical maneuver in the passage which Jewett takes to be the *propositio*). Cf. my own treatment of the thrice-repeated phrase

a *theological* claim, not simply a geographical one. So Paul traces his own career "from Jerusalem," and the letter under study shows him headed there. The reference to Illyricum sketches Paul's circuit to the Adriatic Sea opposite Italy and therefore Rome.

Authenticity of 16:17–20a

As to the inauthenticity of 16:17–20a, Jewett finds that "the interpolation promotes righteousness through the enforcement of cultural and theological conformity" (p. 90), which he deems inconsistent with the remainder of Romans, which he asserts "proclaims righteousness through a tolerant transformation of culturally diverse forms of faith" (p. 90). In his own *inclusio,* Jewett makes a similar claim at the end of his paper: "The inclusive righteousness of God explicated throughout Romans is countered by the bipolar stereotype of theological opponents" (p. 105). For Jewett, the passage is a "warning against heretics" (p. 92), contains "fierce denunciations" (pp. 105–6) and "discriminatory polemic" (p. 108); its style is "wild polemic" (p. 106, quoting Ernst Käsemann). Whether Jewett is right about the inauthenticity of 16:17–20, we have already seen problems with his characterization of the remainder of Romans. Similarly, there are problems with his characterization of this passage. Not everything in the passage is alien to the rest of the letter and to the Paul we know from the other letters. Rom 16:19a again affirms Paul's celebration of the Roman believers (cf. 1:8, 12; 15:14; cf. the mention of obedience in 1:5). For 16:19b, compare 1 Cor 14:20, "Brothers, do not become children with respect to thinking, but be babies with respect to evil; become grownups with respect to thinking" (cf. Rom 12:21; 1 Thess 5:21–22). Jewett has made it more difficult to see that 16:20 is possible for Paul because Jewett has missed that it is "the God of peace" who is expected to "crush Satan under your feet," not believers (p. 108). Jewett reads it that the text advocates "a strategy of crushing Satan by avoiding relations with his agents and crushing them underfoot" which he takes to eventuate in "cultural and theological conformity" (p. 108). But just as the Roman government kept peace by crushing enemies, so the verse assumes that it is God who crushes Satan under the believers' feet. Compare this with 1 Cor 15:24–28, a passage whose content is similar and whose focus is likewise on the culminating purposes of God: "Then comes the end, when he delivers the kingdom to God the Father after destroying every rule and every authority and power.

"the Jew first also the Greek" (1:16; 2:9–10) in "Romans and Galatians: Comparison and Contrast," in *Understanding the Word: Essays in Honor of Bernhard W. Anderson* (ed. J.T. Butler et al.; JSOTSup 37; Sheffield: JSOT Press, 1985) 329–32.

For he must reign until he has put all his enemies under his feet. The last enemy to be destroyed is death. 'For God has put all things in subjection under his feet'" (1 Cor 15:24–27). "Dissensions" and those who create them (16:17)[25] are, after all, what Romans is about! Paul's admonition to welcome the one who is weak with respect to faith follows *with a warning* not to dispute over opinions (14:1). Is not 14:16—"Do not let someone blaspheme your [collective] good"—a call to vigilance? And we should remember that Paul has expressed his satisfaction with the Romans regarding their ability to "admonish, instruct" (νουθετέω)—the word also carries the semantic range "*warn*"—one another. Rhetorically, 16:17–20a bids fair to make Paul, as the author, one with the Romans, sharing their faith, and standing over against any who would stray from the understanding of the gospel Paul and the Romans hold in common. Paul is capable of sharp warnings near the ends of his letters (cf. 1 Cor 16:22 and Gal 6:12–17). Finally, the whole matter is resolved very readily in favor of authenticity if one adopts M. A. Seifrid's not-unrealistic interpretation that the passage is directed against particular Christian outsiders whom Paul fears would hope to insinuate themselves into the Roman churches (or church, as Seifrid puts it).[26]

We ought to acknowledge that Paul has a penchant for thinking that his perception of the gospel is the only correct one. Let us put it bluntly: Paul is not tolerant of deviations from his understanding of the gospel; neither is he tolerant of those who propound a different formulation. It is not insignificant that he uses expressions such as "my gospel" (Rom 2:16; cf. 2 Cor 4:3; 1 Thess 1:5) and "my God" (Rom 1:8; 1 Cor 1:4; 2 Cor 12:21; Phil 1:3; 4:19; Phlm 4; cf. 1 Thess 2:2; 3:9). His Galatians anathema on any who would preach "to you a gospel contrary to that which you received" from him (1:9; cf. 6:17) is neither a singular occurrence in his letters nor simply a contingent phenomenon of that letter (cf. 1 Cor 16:22). His commendations of exemplars are always of persons who walk as he does, who are in tune with "my ways in Christ" (1 Cor 4:17; cf. also Rom 16:1–2; 1 Cor 16:10, 18; 2 Cor 8:16; Phil 2:25; 1 Thess 3:2). Paul's characterizations of his Galatian opponents and the interlopers at Corinth further document his intolerance of deviation from his gospel and authority, even in the name of Christ.

In the light of all these considerations, there is no need to consider 16:17–20a inauthentic.

---

[25] In Galatians 5 dissension is listed as disqualifying for inheritance of the kingdom of God (5:19–21).

[26] M. A. Seifrid, *Justification by Faith: The Origin and Development of a Central Pauline Theme* (NovTSup 68; Leiden: Brill, 1992) 198–201.

Why Paul Said He Wrote—A Passage Not Examined by Jewett
(Rom 15:14–15)

Rom 15:14–15 should be considered as a primary index of Paul's purposes in the intervening chapters because it is Paul's own attempt to tell the Romans what he has intended. His address of them as ἀδελφοί μου affirms the common ground that, by this point in the letter, he hopes he has established with them (15:14): "I myself am convinced/confident, my brothers, that you yourselves[27] are filled with goodness, filled with all knowledge, and capable of instructing/admonishing/warning one another." Two clauses express Paul's view of the Romans' current status: they are full of goodness and wisdom, and they have the *potential* to instruct or admonish or warn[28] one another. The last clause, however, notes a capacity, a potentiality. In this sense the Roman believers, no matter how different they are in some ways, could benefit from each other exactly as Paul thought he and all the Romans might: "that we may be mutually encouraged by each other's faith, both yours and mine" (1:12).

Rom 15:15 must be seen as a key to understanding (a) in what spirit and (b) why he has written because there Paul *says how and why he wrote.* "Rather boldly" (τολμηροτέρως) he has written them; by saying this he acknowledges that his effectiveness is audaciously grounded on his having successfully established his ethos with the readers through what he has written. Paul has written them "on some points" (ἀπὸ μέρους) to help them "remember something again" (ἐπαναμιμνῄσκων; a recovering of memory or former clarity). What a gentle touch! He does not portray himself as one who in this letter has told them something they do not know; he has not disclosed a previously hidden perspective or imparted new information. His purpose in the preceding sections is to assist the Romans in recovering what they as people "filled with all knowledge" (15:14) will surely remember is true about themselves in the gospel. I take his boldness to be his assertive intervention in the disputes of the Roman believers and the preceding chapters to be his effort to help them realize their true unity in Christ. At least this much is clear, Paul's stated purpose in writing is to help the Romans recover something which they seem to have lost from their memory. That is a purpose quite different from getting them to the point where they can understand something *new* such as joining in Paul's efforts toward Spain.

[27] Note the double emphatics, about Paul and about them.

[28] The verb νουθετέω has this semantic range of meanings and, in light of Paul's own border-keeping in his comments to Philemon about his obligations to his new brother in Christ, Onesimus, as well as Paul's urgings of the Corinthians to expel the one "having his father's wife" in 1 Corinthians 5, we should not rule out Paul's sense that believers must sometimes warn one another of actions detrimental to the community of believers.

6 FROM WRATH TO JUSTIFICATION

*Tradition, Gospel, and Audience
in the Theology of Romans 1:18–4:25*

Andrew T. Lincoln
Wycliffe College, University of Toronto

I. ORIENTATION TO THE SHAPE AND MODE
OF THE ARGUMENT

TO SPEAK OF A MOVEMENT from wrath to justification, as does the title of this essay,[1] is misleading, if it is taken to represent how Paul's thought is presented in the letter as a whole. This would be to tear this section loose from its context in the letter and miss the obvious point that Paul has already stated the solution of justification by faith before he begins his depiction of the plight of human sinfulness under the wrath of God.[2] In terms of the rhetorical structure of the argument (following Robert Jewett[3]), the *propositio* has already been stated in 1:16, 17 and what follows is the *probatio*, of which 1:18–4:25 constitutes the initial *confirmatio*. This enables us to see that Paul's thought pattern is one that moves from solution to plight and then back to solution.

His claim is that he has a gospel in which the righteousness of God is revealed through faith for faith for all. Since this is his distinctive law-free gospel, Paul is required to demonstrate both that all (both Jews and Gentiles) need his gospel in order to be righteous before God and that the only way for both Jews and Gentiles to be righteous before God is by faith in Christ. He must show that apart from faith in Christ all are unrighteous. In particular, this

---

[1] An earlier, more comprehensive version of the essay with fuller interaction with the secondary literature is to be found in *Society of Biblical Literature 1993 Seminar Papers* (Atlanta: Scholars Press, 1993) 194–226.

[2] In this regard, the thought pattern of Romans as a whole is no different from what E. P. Sanders has claimed about Paul's thought in general; see *Paul and Palestinian Judaism: A Comparison of Patterns of Religion* (Philadelphia: Fortress, 1977) 442–43.

[3] R. Jewett, "Following the Argument of Romans," in *The Romans Debate* (ed. Karl P. Donfried; rev. ed.; Peabody, MA: Hendrickson, 1991) 278–96.

will entail showing that not only unbelieving Gentiles but also unbelieving Jews, whose membership in the covenant is marked by their circumcision and adherence to the law, are unrighteous. By definition, his gospel of righteousness by faith in Christ will not be able to allow for righteousness through membership in the covenant or through the law. This does not yet, however, state his task in the argument accurately enough, for there is a significant element in his thesis statement that has been omitted. The salvation mediated by his gospel comes to all, but it comes "to the Jew first and also to the Greek" (1:16), and so he must also demonstrate how within the universal scope of his gospel there somehow remains a Jewish priority. All of this reinforces the likelihood that, whatever previous understanding of the human plight was part of his Jewish heritage,[4] when he depicts that plight in relation to his presentation of his gospel in this letter, he will do so not only in the light of what he now believes to be the revealed solution but also in a way that will correspond to that solution.

When Paul in fact proceeds to do precisely this, a considerable amount of space is given to showing that unbelieving Jews are in the same position of desperate need as unbelieving Gentiles, and the argument is developed by employing viewpoints similar to those found in the Wisdom of Solomon and by beginning with what no Jew would dispute in order then to turn the tables on such a person before concluding with the backing of a catena of scriptural citations. The issues treated in 3:1–8 are those that would be raised by a Jew in response to what has been said. What advantage has the Jew? What are the implications for the faithfulness and righteousness of God? And is not morality undermined? Even when Paul returns to depict the solution more fully in the light of the plight he has portrayed, he in all probability adapts a Jewish Christian formulation of the gospel, is concerned to draw out the implications of this solution for the matters of boasting and law works, and appeals to traditional belief in the oneness of God to drive home his insistence on the universal scope of his gospel. At the same time, Paul feels the need to make clear that, although righteousness is not attained by law, this does not mean that the law is totally done away with or of no account. At various points he is at pains to assert that the law has to be seen as having a different function in God's righteous purposes (cf. 3:19, 20; 4:15), and above all claims that the law witnesses to his gospel (3:21) with its depiction of Abraham's faith as his chief example of this role (4:1–25).

The obvious and age-old question must be faced. Why does this argument appear to be shaped primarily for Jews or Jewish Christians? The rhetorical situation of the letter suggests some possible answers. Most important is Paul's

---

[4] On this, see F. Thielman, *From Plight to Solution: A Jewish Framework to Understanding Paul's View of the Law in Galatians and Romans* (NovTSup 61; Leiden: Brill, 1989).

perception of his audience. The apostle needs to demonstrate his thesis about
the gospel in dialogue with Roman Christians, whose support as a unified
community he wishes to gain for his proposed mission to Spain (cf.
15:22–33). He appears to conceive of these Christians as primarily Gentiles,
whose "obedience of faith" he also wishes to secure as part of his purpose in
writing. But there is an obstacle to be overcome if his wishes are to be fulfilled. As Paul understands their situation, harmony among the Christians in
Rome is threatened, because these Gentile Christians are experiencing tensions with Jewish Christians, whom Paul evidently also expects to be among
the recipients of the letter (cf. 1:5–7; 14:1–5; 15:7, 14–16).[5] This is, of course,
to espouse the view that such tensions are reflected in the exhortations of
14:1–15:13. The self-styled "strong in faith" appear to be *predominantly* the
Gentile Christian majority who have dubbed those who are *predominantly*
Jewish Christian the "weak in faith."[6] From their name for themselves it
appears that the Gentile Christians stressed their faith and the freedom it
engendered and despised those who considered it necessary, as part of their
obedience to God, to observe food laws and sabbaths and festivals. As a consequence of embracing the gospel they also appear to have adopted an arrogance about Jewish unbelief which may have inclined them to believe that any
purposes of God for ethnic Israel were now abrogated (see esp. 11:20, 25).
The Jewish Christian minority condemned the "strong" for what they viewed
as the latter's moral laxity and, quite naturally, would have associated the Gentile Christians' attitudes with Paul's law-free gospel. The disputes in Rome
would only have heightened any suspicions about Paul they already had from
reports about his distinctive formulation of the gospel and its implications.

But the writer's own setting also plays a role in this rhetorical situation.
What is plain from 15:22–33 is that Paul, the Jewish Christian who is apostle
to the Gentiles, is about to set off for Jerusalem with the collection. As is
revealed by his anxiety about whether this offering from the churches of his
Gentile mission will be accepted by the Jewish Christian Jerusalem church (cf.
15:30), he is being forced to reflect about the same basic issues of Jewish
Christian–Gentile Christian relationships current in Rome but to do so at the
level of his whole Gentile mission. In pondering the outcome of this critical
visit to Jerusalem, which would also affect his proposed visit to Rome and
beyond to Spain in the west, Paul would inevitably be reflecting on the con-

---

[5] N. Elliott is right in his emphasis on a primarily Gentile Christian audience, but he neglects
the Jewish Christian element, which he acknowledges to be there (*The Rhetoric of Romans: Argumentative Constraint and Strategy and Paul's Dialogue with Judaism* [JSOTSup 45; Sheffield: JSOT
Press, 1990] 69–104, esp. 95–96).

[6] The Gentile/Jew categories in 15:7–13, which constitutes the climax of the exhortations,
provide very strong support for this interpretation.

troversy and objections his gospel provoked among Jewish Christians. He senses that his reflections about the gospel in his immediate situation are precisely what the Roman Christians need to hear in their own circumstances. Sensing also that the troubles in Rome have been fueled by some distortions and misperceptions of his gospel caused in part by Gentile Christian attitudes and views that he would not want to own, Paul is anxious to speak for himself. He wants to be his own advocate for his distinctive gospel in the discussions with Jewish Christians and to address their objections and suspicions himself. Jewish Christians need to be won over if there is to be harmony in Rome and if its Christians are to provide the effective base for the next stage of his mission. So Paul takes the opportunity of rehearsing his gospel for the Roman Christians and of rehearsing it in a way he hopes will prove persuasive to Jewish Christians.

It should be noted that, in comparison with the direct address of Gentile Christians in 11:13ff., the attempt to persuade Jewish Christians is more indirect. Individual Jews among the recipients are not addressed. Instead, the diatribe style enables Paul to dialogue with an imagined conversation partner or questioner, who, though representative, is addressed in the singular in 2:1–5, 17–23, 25, 27 (the second person plural of 2:24 is part of a scriptural citation). Paul's imagined dialogue partner is portrayed initially as one who feels morally superior to the unrighteous pagans who have just been described, but the attitudes depicted, which are characteristic of Judaism, and the explicit address later in 2:17 suggest that such a person is a Jew.[7] The use of the diatribe indicates that Paul is not attacking those he considers opponents but rather setting out his teaching in a way designed to lead its recipients to the truth, sometimes by correcting pretensions and presumptions.[8] Yet it cannot be denied that in terms of the rhetorical situation in the letter, the addressees for whom this dialogue with a Jew would have particular force are Jewish Christians, for whom belief in Jesus as Messiah has been added to earlier beliefs about Israel's privileged covenant status and the necessity of observing the law and who object to the far more radical version of the gospel Paul is preaching in his mission to Gentiles.[9] "In the diatribe there is often little distance between the real audience and the fictitious interlocutor," and "the typical is addressed to the

---

[7] See also, e.g., F. B. Watson, *Paul, Judaism and the Gentiles: A Sociological Approach* (Cambridge: Cambridge University Press, 1986) 109–10; J. D. G. Dunn, *Romans 1–8* (WBC 38a; Dallas: Word, 1988) 78–80; *pace* S. K. Stowers, *The Diatribe and Paul's Letter to the Romans* (SBLDS 57; Chico, CA: Scholars Press, 1981) 112.

[8] See Stowers, *Diatribe*, esp. 75–78.

[9] The material in 1:18–4:25 functions rhetorically therefore more as a dialogue with Jewish Christians than as a "debate with Judaism"; see J. C. Beker, *Paul the Apostle: The Triumph of God in Life and Thought* (Philadelphia: Fortress, 1980) 83.

particular pedagogical needs of the audience."[10] This view is reinforced when it is noted that the attitude of the one addressed in 2:1 is that of passing judgment on others and this is precisely the characteristic of Jewish Christians in Rome according to the later parenesis.

The diatribe style is intended to enable Jewish Christians to see the force of Paul's arguments without being alienated personally. At the same time this letter is addressed to a primarily Gentile Christian audience, whose own understanding of that gospel will be both reinforced and corrected, as they see how Paul treats the very issues they are discussing and disputing with Jewish Christians. In this way the letter's rhetoric falls into the category of epideictic rhetoric. It is designed to persuade both sections of the audience to hold a particular viewpoint, which they partially share already—the Gentile Christians somewhat more than the Jewish Christians—but which Paul wants to see prevail and orient their future actions. We should not expect therefore that Paul will be totally evenhanded toward the two groups. As apostle to the Gentiles, he is not about to compromise the law-free gospel which he considers integral to his vocation.

Paul's mode of argument attempts to make clear that he remains the *Jewish* apostle to the Gentiles and that one does not need to renounce one's Jewish heritage in order to espouse his controversial gospel. He wants to show that the distinctive elements of his gospel are not only compatible with his Judaism but also provide the best possible way of reshaping the Jewish tradition—something that has become necessary because of the implications of what God has done in Christ. In the course of the argument in 1:18–4:25 he attempts to explain that the gospel of justification by faith for all sits comfortably within his Jewish heritage and its beliefs about the one Creator God and his just judgment, the scriptures, being children of Abraham, and God's will expressed in the law. His is not a gospel that undermines the righteousness of God in any way. Instead it takes that righteousness as a given and reinforces it. Already in his initial statement of the salvation offered in his gospel (1:17), Paul has hinted strongly that it is not a gospel that calls into question the righteousness of God by entailing that he has now turned his back on Israel. After all, it is "to the Jew first and also to the Greek." It asserts both that there is no distinction between Jew and Gentile and yet that there is still a priority for Israel. The paradox or contradiction (one's choice of terms depends heavily on one's sympathies with the argument and its presuppositions) does not await chaps. 9–11 but is embedded in the *propositio* and is repeated in 3:1, 2, 9. In terms of Paul's view of God, this is a paradox that lies at the heart of divine righteousness, involving on the one hand God's impartiality and on the other his faithful-

[10] Stowers, *Diatribe*, 99, 180.

ness.[11] Clearly, the most delicate and difficult of these issues surrounding the relation of the gospel to Judaism, both for Paul in his own understanding of the gospel as that has been shaped by conflict with both non-Christian and Christian Jews and for the audience in Rome, is the place of the law. That issue runs like an undercurrent through the main argument of these early chapters before Paul gives it more extended treatment later, particularly in chap. 7. So in the first four chapters, as throughout the letter, Paul proves himself an apologist for his gospel from within the Jewish tradition. He not only makes the claim that his is a gospel that is for the Jew first but also for the Greek, but he also rehearses the gospel in a way that is for the Jew first and also for the Greek.

II. HUMANITY'S NEED FOR PAUL'S GOSPEL OF RIGHTEOUSNESS BY FAITH (1:18–3:20)

Although Paul is convinced that, in Christ, God has acted decisively to rescue humanity and in this light depicts the sort of plight that required a rescue act of this particular nature, with the exception of what might appear to be an almost incidental reference in 2:16, the name of Christ is not mentioned in his discussion. He makes his case for humanity's universal plight from within the parameters of assumptions his Jewish Christian addressees would already have held as Jews.

It would seem reasonable to attempt to find an exegetically plausible reading of some of the less clear stages in the argument in the light of its clear final goal before either declaring the whole incoherent or resorting to reinterpreting the conclusion on the basis of a particular reading of one of the stages. Recognition of Paul's goals and tactics in 1:18–3:20 helps in accounting for the apparent contradictions in the actual argument pointed out by E. P. Sanders and H. Räisänen among others.[12] At certain points there are some rather optimistic assertions about Jews and Gentiles being able to do what the law requires and thereby gaining justification and life (see 2:7, 10, 13–15, 27), and in one place it is said only that some Jews have been unfaithful, not all (3:3). The deductions that Paul eventually draws in 3:9–20 that all people alike are sinful and that justification through the law is impossible appear therefore to be undermined. But in 2:7, 10 Paul is talking about the criterion of God's

[11] For discussion of these two elements as the theme of Romans, see W. S. Campbell, *Paul's Gospel in an Intercultural Context: Jew and Gentile in the Letter to the Romans* (Frankfurt: Peter Lang, 1991) 173–83.

[12] E. P. Sanders, *Paul, the Law, and the Jewish People* (Philadelphia: Fortress, 1983) 123–32; H. Räisänen, *Paul and the Law* (WUNT 29; Tübingen: Mohr [Siebeck], 1983) 99–108.

future judgment and spelling out clearly the Jewish assumption which he will
in fact subvert, and talk of law-fulfilling Gentiles (2:13–15, 27) is one of the
weapons used in the subversion. But when the situation of Gentiles themselves is directly in view, it is a different story and Paul is quite clear about their
need of his gospel because of their being under sin and God's wrath (1:18–32;
3:9). The talk of some Jews being unfaithful in 3:3 is best taken as part of a
diatribal question arising from Paul's previous discussion, particularly that of
2:17–24, and it is noticeable that Paul's reply in 3:4 moves back to universal
terminology: "although everyone is a liar." Having, as he believes, subverted
Jewish presumption from its own premises, Paul himself has no difficulty
coming to the conclusion in 3:9–20 that he has wished to reach all along,
namely, that apart from faith in Christ *all* Jews and *all* Gentiles are dominated
by sin and condemned by the law. While some opt for elements of incoherence, G. N. Davies attempts to produce coherence by denying that this is
Paul's conclusion. To support his reading of 2:6–16 in terms of righteous Jews
and Gentiles receiving salvation before the coming of Christ, he has to rein-
terpret the clear universal language of 3:9–12, 20 as simply a reference to "the
distributive presence of sinfulness . . . across the boundaries of Jew and
Gentile."[13]

Not only his formulation of the gospel in 1:17 but also the framework in
which he places his indictment of humanity's sinfulness indicate Paul's concern to show how seriously his gospel takes the matter of the righteousness of
God. As we shall see, his talk of God's righteousness cannot be divorced from
its forensic connotations as God's righteous judgment, so to begin by talking
about the wrath of God in 1:18 is not to introduce a totally unrelated topic.
God's righteousness has to be revealed in the gospel for faith, because, apart
from the gospel, when God's righteousness meets human unrighteousness, his
righteous judgment is revealed not as salvation but as wrath. That wrath is the
negative side of God's righteous judgment is indicated in the conclusion to
the first stage of the argument in 1:32, which speaks of τὸ δικαίωμα τοῦ θεοῦ,
"the just requirement of God." It is precisely because of God's righteousness,
Paul is claiming, that such a gospel as his is necessary, and in the next section
(see 2:3, 5) he attempts to demonstrate that it is not his gospel but Jewish
Christian objections to it which have not taken seriously enough this aspect
of God's righteousness. We should be clear then that the notion of "the righteousness of God" is itself a Jewish tradition or axiom. Paul will exploit its two

[13] See G. N. Davies, *Faith and Obedience in Romans: A Study of Romans 1–4* (JSNTSup 39;
Sheffield: JSOT Press, 1990), esp. 96. The earlier attractive presentation of a similar view by
K. R. Snodgrass ("Justification by Grace—to the Doers: An Analysis of the Place of Romans 2
in the Theology of Paul," *NTS* 32 [1986] 72–93) appears to founder at the same point by not
accounting adequately for the force of 3:9–18 as it leads into the conclusion of 3:19–20.

major aspects: the legal or forensic aspect, God's righteous judgment, as seen here with its negative consequence of wrath; and the relational aspect, God's faithfulness to the covenant in bestowing righteousness on humans, which will appear together with the forensic in 3:21–26.[14]

What is not sufficiently recognized, when attention is drawn to specific parallel texts in Wisdom,[15] is the way in which the themes of wisdom as a whole provide a most appropriate resource for Paul's discussion in Romans 1 and 2. After all, Paul wishes to deal with God's righteous judgment as it relates to humanity as a whole and to Jews, and this is precisely what can be found in Wisdom. It provides a discussion of the life and destiny of the righteous and the unrighteous and of God's righteous judgment on behalf of the righteous. This discussion is peppered with the concepts of wrath and mercy in the context of God's judgment on pagans and on Israel.[16] Again, God's righteousness involves his righteous judgment: "You are righteous and you order all things righteously, deeming it alien to your power to condemn anyone who does not deserve to be punished" (12:15; see also, e.g., 12:12, 13, 18). Occasionally Wisdom speaks of God's sovereignty in his universal mercy ("but you have mercy on all," 11:23; see also 12:16), but most characteristic is the frequent juxtaposition of and discrimination between pagans' and Israel's experience of God's judgment. Pagans, who are spoken of in terms of the ungodly and unrighteous, the foolish and futile, should have known God from his creation but have refused to do so, and instead their idolatry has led to fornication and a whole catalogue of vices. As a result they will be deservedly punished through the very things by which they sinned and will experience God's wrath. The righteous, however, who know God and are his holy people may experience his discipline as sons but can be assured of his mercy and kindness. Two instances of this characteristic juxtaposition can be cited: "although they were being disciplined in mercy, they knew how the ungodly were judged in wrath and tormented. You admonished and tested them as a father, but examined and condemned the ungodly as a severe king" (11:9, 10); "with what care you have judged your own sons, to whose fathers you have given oaths and covenants of good promises! So while chastening us, you scourge our enemies ten thousand times more, so that when we judge, we may meditate on your

---

[14] The recent tendency has been to play down the forensic aspect in favor of the aspect of either covenant faithfulness (see, e.g., Dunn, *Romans 1–8*, 41–42, 165–76) or simply salvation (see D. A. Campbell, *The Rhetoric of Righteousness in Romans 3:21–26* [JSNTSup 65; Sheffield: JSOT Press, 1992] 138–65).

[15] See the list of parallels in W. Sanday and A. C. Headlam, *The Epistle to the Romans* (Edinburgh: T. & T. Clark, 1902) 51–52.

[16] On the similar treatment of these topics in the *Psalms of Solomon*, see M. Seifrid, *Justification by Faith: The Origin and Development of a Central Pauline Theme* (Leiden: Brill, 1992) 117–33.

goodness, and when we are judged, we may expect mercy" (12:21, 22; see also 14:31 and 15:1; 16:1, 2; 16:4, 5; 16:9–11; 16:24; 18:19, 20; 18:25; and 19:1). As he writes Romans, Paul appears to be aware of Wisdom, and it is not difficult to see what he does with its treatment of God's righteous judgment. He is going to exploit the notion of the sovereignty of God in his mercy on all later in chaps. 9–11, but at this early stage in the letter he wants to show God's righteous judgment on all and does so by first reinforcing the sort of perspective on paganism found in Wisdom before subverting its theology by arguing that Jews are in fact in the very same position in regard to God's judgment and wrath.

Paul's initial purpose in reinforcing the typical Jewish indictment of the pagan world is to demonstrate that such pagans need his gospel because they are deservedly under God's wrath. Whatever positive aspects of their knowledge of God are mentioned only render them without excuse (1:20), demonstrating that their idolatry is not innocent ignorance but culpable refusal to acknowledge God. They know the truth (particularly about the Creator in relation to the creation) but suppress it in their unrighteousness (1:18). Paul's supporting assertions in 1:19–21 are strong ones. The invisible God is known through the visible creation. God has in fact made plain to people this knowledge of himself. So there is no problem, according to Paul, with the clarity of God's revelation; the problem is with the human response. Humanity has known God but has chosen not to respond appropriately by glorifying and giving thanks to its Creator. In similar fashion Wis 13:1–9 had indicted all people who were ignorant of God for being "unable from the good things that are seen to know the one who exists. . . . For from the greatness and beauty of created things comes a corresponding perception of their Creator." Yet this passage talks about such inability in terms of seeking God and its reason why people should not be pardoned is "if they had the power to know so much that they could investigate the world, how did they fail to find sooner the Lord of these things?" So Paul has intensified the indictment and made it more damning. In traditional categories, whereas Wisdom talks of a failure in natural theology, not having succeeded in reasoning from the creation to the Creator, Paul talks of a failure to respond to natural revelation, suppressing a knowledge of God that has already been given.

But the results of the failure are the same for both Paul and Wisdom—idolatry, fornication, and all kinds of evils which in themselves constitute a deserved punishment. In the words of Wisdom, "In return for their foolish and unrighteous thoughts, which led them astray to worship irrational serpents and worthless animals, you sent on them a multitude of irrational creatures to punish them, so that they might learn that one is punished by the very things by which one sins" (11:15, 16; see also 12:24–27). "For the devising of idols was the beginning of fornication and the invention of them the corruption of life" (14:12). For Paul too, Gentiles, who began with knowledge of God, end up with the futility and folly of idolatry (1:21–23), which has the further consequence of sexual impurity (1:24–27). Whereas in this area Wisdom stressed disordered marriages and adultery and mentioned the "exchange of natural sexual roles" (Wis 14:26)[17] in passing, Paul focuses more on what, with other moralists of the time, he sees as the choice of exchanging or giving up natural intercourse for unnatural and regards this as receiving the due penalty for error (1:27; cf. Wis 12:24–27; 14:30, 31). For him also a whole catalogue of "things that should not be done," which overlaps with Wisdom's in terms of murder, deceit, and faithlessness (cf. Wis 14:24, 25), follows from humanity's willful refusal to treat God as God (1:28–31). But Paul broadens out the catalogue to include "every kind of unrighteousness" and lists several more subtle sins than those in Wisdom, such as covetousness, envy, gossip, slander, haughtiness, boastfulness, and heartlessness.

There are also differences in the way Paul has formulated his indictment. He is concerned to stress again and again the root sin, which provokes God's judgment and from which all else follows. "They exchanged the glory of the immortal God for images" (1:23); "they exchanged the truth about God for a lie and worshiped and served the creature rather than the Creator" (1:25); and "they did not see fit to acknowledge God" (1:28). Following each of these charges is the refrain "God gave them up," indicating that Paul is not content only to declare that sin has its own consequences but is convinced that God's activity is to be discerned in those consequences, so that the revealing of God's wrath within this process consists in giving humans what they choose in all its consequences. Wisdom can assert that the ungodly recognize God when they are punished (12:27); they know that they sin (15:13) and why they are perishing (18:19). In the climax of his indictment Paul takes this further. Not only do the unrighteous know God; they also know his righteous judgment and recognize death as a deserved punishment for their deeds. Yet despite this, they not only continue in these deeds, which could simply indicate their bondage to a process that has gone beyond their control, but they also applaud others who practice such deeds, which leaves no doubt that they are willfully flouting and suppressing the ethical insight they have been given (1:32).

The diatribe style makes its first contribution to Paul's argument in 2:1–5. Paul's dialogue with his imaginary partner is designed to show why he holds that being made right with God through faith in Christ and not through law works is the gospel for all and not just for Gentiles and, as we have suggested, enables him indirectly to attempt to puncture presumption about Jewish priv-

---

[17] See D. Winston, *The Wisdom of Solomon* (New York: Doubleday, 1979) 280.

ilege still harbored by some of the Jewish Christians in Rome. He will attempt the same with Gentile Christian pride later in 11:17–25, employing the same notion of presuming on God's kindness.

Just as Paul has asserted that unrighteous pagans are under God's wrath (1:18) and without excuse (1:20), now he will say exactly the same about those who believe themselves able to judge such evil deeds from a privileged position. They too are deserving of wrath (2:5) and without excuse (2:1). They have no excuse, because, while they agree with the indictment Paul has made, they are doing the very same things and are thereby condemning themselves. The premise on which this argument depends for its effectiveness is that all people, including Jews, are tainted in some way by participation in the evils that have been described in 1:28–31 and that Paul's purpose in broadening and refining the list of vices mentioned can now be seen.[18] His interlocutor has no trouble in agreeing that God's judgment on the perpetrators of such vices is in accord with truth and is just (2:2). Such a person would echo the sentiments of Wis 12:12–15 that no one could plead as an advocate for the unrighteous before God, since God is righteous and his condemnation is just. But, according to Paul, to endorse such sentiments while sharing in the vices is to shut off all escape from experiencing the same judgment of God (2:3).

The dialogue partner's response might well be to appeal to God's kindness, and such an appeal would, as we have seen, correspond precisely to the attitude reflected in Wisdom. This has been the pattern in the past: "Therefore they were deservedly punished through such creatures. . . . Instead of this punishment you showed kindness to your people" (16:1, 2; see also 11:9) and continues to hold good: "the just penalty for those who sin . . . always pursues the transgression of the unrighteous. But you, our God, are kind and true, patient, and ruling all things in mercy. For even if we sin we are yours, knowing your power" (14:3–15:2),[19] so that there can be confidence that "while chastening us, you scourge our enemies ten thousand times more, so that when we judge, we may meditate on your goodness, and when we are judged we may expect mercy" (12:22). But Paul is ready to cut off this escape

[18] *Pace* B. W. Longenecker (*Eschatology and Covenant: A Comparison of 4 Ezra and Romans 1–11* [Sheffield: JSOT Press, 1991] 175–81), who argues that Paul's indictment is simply a rhetorical technique typical of ethical denunciation and polemic without any empirical correspondence. But this is not only to leave Paul without any real grounds for his conclusion in 3:9, 19, 20 but also to distort his use of the diatribe, which is pedagogical rather than polemical.

[19] To observe correctly that Wis 15:2 continues, "but we will not sin, because we know that you acknowledge us as yours," and to claim that this invalidates appeals to Wisdom as the background of 2:1–5 is to miss the point (*pace* Elliott, *Rhetoric*, 174–82). There is no dispute that Wisdom encourages Israel not to sin. The issue is what happens when Israel does sin, and here the evidence from Wisdom, not just 15:2, is clear. Israel, in contrast to the Gentiles, has a distinctive claim on God's mercy.

route also, and he does so by playing off against this attitude another aspect of traditional Jewish theology found in Wisdom. To presume on God's kindness in this way, he claims, is in fact to despise that kindness, because God's kindness has always been meant to lead to repentance. This challenge simply reminds the interlocutor of Wisdom's own teaching: "you overlook people's sins so that they might repent" (11:23). In regard to the unrighteous this is the case, "judging them little by little you gave them an opportunity to repent" (12:10; see also 12:20), and the same is true for the righteous: "you have filled your sons with good hope, because you give repentance for sins" (12:19). So, concludes Paul, to entertain any notion of leniency if one judges sin and yet participates in it oneself is to misunderstand drastically the purpose of God's kindness, to show a hard and impenitent heart, and thereby to store up wrath for oneself at the time of the revelation of God's righteous judgment (2:5). Whereas the characteristic attitude of Wisdom is to indulge Israel by pointing to God's kindness and asserting that, in contrast to the ungodly who experience God's wrath without mercy to the end, Israel tastes God's wrath only temporarily and that wrath does not continue to the end (cf. Wis 11:9; 16:4, 5; 18:25; 19:1), Paul asserts uncompromisingly that God's people who act unrighteously can expect to experience wrath on the day of God's wrath.

Paul brooks no compromise because he holds that the criterion on which God's righteous judgment is based is a person's deeds or works (2:6). To point to judgment on the basis of works is only to underline in a rigorous fashion another tenet embedded in Jewish thought. Paul cites the formulation found in LXX Ps 61:13 and Prov 24:12. Again this is a familiar theme in Hellenistic Judaism. "For mercy and wrath are with the Lord. . . . Great as his mercy, so also is his chastisement; he judges a person according to one's deeds . . . everyone receives in accordance with one's deeds" (Sir 16:11b–14). Twice Paul elaborates on this basis for judgment, making clear that seeking glory and immortality by the working of good will result in eternal life, while the working of evil in unrighteousness will have wrath and fury as its consequence (2:8–10). There ought to be no confusion at this point. Paul is talking about the principle of judgment. He does not have in view here whether anyone succeeds in gaining eternal life in accordance with this principle. Once that question is raised, however, his answer is overwhelmingly clear, not only in terms of the thrust of the overall argument in 1:18–3:20 but quite explicitly: "there is no one who is righteous . . . there is no one who seeks God . . . there is no one who does good" (3:10–12).[20]

Significantly, Paul adds to both the negative and the positive side of the sec-

---

[20] See also U. Wilckens, *Der Brief an die Römer* (EKKNT 6; Zurich: Benziger, 1978) 1. 130–31, 145–46, 174–75; D. J. Moo, *Romans 1-8* (Chicago: Moody, 1991) 139–41.

ond elaboration of the principle the phrase "the Jew first and also the Greek."
It is not, as might have been assumed on the basis of the theology of Wisdom,
the ungodly Greek who will be judged first and then the Jew on a more
lenient basis. Just as his gospel is for the Jew first and also the Greek, so Paul
insists that God's righteous judgment has the same priority. If anything, then,
the Jew with privileged knowledge should expect to be judged more rather
than less harshly. But again this is a priority within a basic equality, for what
Paul's dialogue partner needs to remember is that in his judgment "God shows
no partiality" (2:11). It comes as no surprise to realize that again Paul is for the
sake of his argument drawing on a classic depiction of Israel's God, which had
clear forensic connotations: "For the Lord your God is God of gods and Lord
of lords, the great God, mighty and awesome, who is not partial and takes no
bribes" (Deut 10:17; see also, e.g., 2 Chr 19:7; *Jub.* 5:16; 21:4; 30:16; 33:18;
Ps. Sol. 2:18). Again this axiom would also be familiar from Hellenistic
Judaism: "The Lord is judge, and with him there is no partiality" (Sir 35:12).
In the hands of Paul it moves beyond any more restricted application to the
orphan, the widow, and the stranger within Israel (cf. Deut 10:18, 19) and is
given a universal application, which both illuminates Paul's purpose in the
preceding discussion and serves as a thematic foundation for the ensuing elaboration of the argument.[21]

God's impartiality is linked with the principle Paul has already appealed to
in 2:6, namely, that his judgment is on the basis of works. This is why it will
be of no help to be judged by the law. It is not the hearers but the doers of the
law whom God deems righteous (2:13). Again this is a principle embedded
in the law itself. Paul does not pause to cite it here, but his key text to underline this principle is Lev 18:5, which he will employ later in 10:5. Instead he
underlines that there can be no assumption that having the law and doing the
law are identical by claiming that those who do not have the law can still do
the law, and he shows that God's impartiality is at work because there is a sense
in which these Gentiles will be judged on the same basis of works of the law
(2:14–16). The argument is this. The very fact that on occasion Gentiles are
by nature, without the benefit of knowledge of the law, able to do what the
law requires indicates that the work of the law is for them written in their
hearts.[22] This ethical awareness is further witnessed to by their conscience and

---

[21] See J. M. Bassler, *Divine Impartiality: Paul and a Theological Axiom* (SBLDS 59; Chico, CA:
Scholars Press, 1982) 121–70.

[22] The Gentiles in view are not Gentile Christians, *pace,* e.g., C. E. B. Cranfield, *A Critical
and Exegetical Commentary on the Epistle to the Romans* (2 vols.; ICC; Edinburgh: T. & T. Clark,
1975, 1979) 1. 155–56; Watson, *Paul,* 121; N. T. Wright, "Romans and the Theology of
Paul," in *Society of Biblical Literature 1992 Seminar Papers* (Atlanta: Scholars Press, 1992) 192 n.
12. See also Bassler, *Divine Impartiality,* 141–49; Moo, *Romans 1–8,* 144–47.

by their own accusatory or defensive thoughts and provides the law by which they will be judged by God. It is here that Paul adds "according to my gospel through Jesus Christ." The addition is not superfluous. It provides a timely reminder to his Jewish Christian dialogue partner of the point Paul has been making all along, namely, that it is precisely his gospel which takes the righteousness of God in the sense of his righteous judgment seriously and that it is because it takes it seriously that this gospel is necessary for all.

It should be noted that, so far, the main basis for any condemnation of Jews is the same as that for the condemnation of Gentiles—their sinful deeds, their failure to measure up to the standard of judgment according to works. They are not condemned in the first instance because of their views about their covenantal status. Such views obscure the proper evaluation of their sinful deeds, leading them to think that despite these deeds they will be protected from judgment.[23] From this perspective Paul can now drive home the distinction between having the law, with the accompanying attitudes of superiority about the privileges this bestows, and actually doing it. It is frequently observed that the challenges of 2:17–24 will not support the condemnation of all Jews found in 3:9. But this is to misunderstand Paul's argument. The foundation for the conclusion of 3:9 has already been laid in 2:1–16. His point here is a more limited one. By stating what cannot be disputed— that is, that some Jews, who know God's will in the law and are therefore in a position to provide teaching and enlightenment for others, in fact break central elements of the law such as the commandments about stealing and adultery—he is able to dispose of the notion that such a privileged position provides a safeguard against God's judgment.[24] Such breaches of the law by the very ones who boast in the law exemplify the distinction between having the law and doing it and lead to the ironic indictment that the God in whom they also boast (cf. 2:17) is dishonored (cf. 2:24, citing Isa 52:5 LXX).

The axioms of God's impartiality and the necessity of doing the law provide the basis for Paul's reply to the dialogue partner who might still be inclined to contend that if having the law is of no avail, then surely being circumcised and bearing the badge of belonging to God's elect people must count for something in terms of being right in God's eyes. Paul simply pushes the logic through. Circumcision unaccompanied by doing the law is the equivalent of uncircumcision, and if the uncircumcised keep the requirements of the law, this not only can be regarded as circumcision but also will be a condemnation of those who have the law and circumcision but do not keep the law. In making his point, Paul again draws on scriptural tradition—in fact, the

---

[23] *Pace* Longenecker, who makes ethnocentric covenantalism the sole ground for the condemnation of Jews (*Eschatology*, 174–95).

[24] See also Dunn, *Romans 1–8*, 113–14.

same passage from which the axiom of God's impartiality had been taken. Deut 10:16 talked of the circumcising of the foreskin of the heart (see also Jer 4:4), and this circumcision, which entails true obedience, is the one that counts. These insights produce finally a whole new perspective on who is a Jew. Since being a Jew is not a matter of external, physical identity markers but an inward matter of the heart, the implicit thought is that the way is also open for a Gentile to be considered a Jew.

The significance of Paul's bold case should not be passed over. By this stage of his argument, through the creative use of Jewish scriptural tradition, Paul has not only attempted to demonstrate to his interlocutor that there is nothing about being a Jew that exempts a person from the consequences of God's righteous judgment and therefore from the need for the gospel he propounds, but he has also asked his interlocutor to rethink radically all the basic categories he or she has been employing for self-identification. The progression from "if you call yourself a Jew" (2:17) to the notion of whom God considers a Jew, with its allusion to the Hebrew wordplay (2:29; cf. Gen 29:35; 49:8), underlines this. Without being asked to abandon it, Paul's Jewish Christian dialogue partners are being invited to transcend the ethnic identification—and the circumcision and possession of the law integral to this—in which they place such stock and to see themselves and Gentiles with new eyes as ultimately standing with the same possibilities before God. In this way the ground is being prepared for them to accept the proposition that Paul will put to them in chap. 4 that Gentile Christians can lay claim on the same basis as they themselves to having Abraham as their father.

In 3:1–8 Paul embarks on the balancing act of explaining that, although there is ultimately no distinction between Jew and Gentile before God, there do remain advantages to being a Jew. This section is vital for Paul's perceptions of Jewish Christian objections to his gospel but will have to be passed over, both for reasons of space and because Paul postpones any detailed reply to these objections until later in the letter. Chapters 9–11 take up the questions of vv. 1–7 and chap. 6 that of v. 8. Just as later Paul will make use of a catena of scriptural citations to drive home his exhortation (see 15:7–13), so in 3:9–20 a catena of passages, presented back to back with no linking phrases in 3:10–18, function to clinch the main thrust of his argument. The oracles of God (see 3:2) now serve to demonstrate human unrighteousness (3:9–20), which in turn is part of the demonstration of the necessity of Paul's gospel. Paul expresses his conclusion through a modification and reapplication of the words of Torah. Ps 13:1–3 LXX, which is taken up in 3:10–12, contained a repetition of the clause "there is no one who does good, not even one." Paul, however, changes the wording of the first occurrence to "there is no one who is righteous, not even one," thereby making it fit more exactly his purposes in the overall argument about attaining righteousness. Whatever were the possibilities left open by the discussion of the criterion of judgment in chap. 2, they are closed off by this first line of the citation, which summarizes the force of the whole catena of texts. It is not just that people have failed in their search for God, as Wis 13:6–9 put it, but "there is no one who seeks for God" (3:11). This contributes to the recognition that the criterion for a positive judgment that Paul has set out in 2:7, 10—doing good, while seeking glory and honor and immortality—remains unfulfilled. "There is no one who does good, not even one" (3:12). Not only is sin universal, but, as LXX Ps 5:10; 139:4; 9:28; Isa 59:7, 8; Ps 35:2 are then enlisted to show by synecdoche, it also affects all of human life—throat, tongue, lips, mouth, feet, and eyes. It may well be that the texts in 3:10-18 would not only have been recognized as scripture but in this particular combination would have been known as a traditional catena already in existence prior to Paul's use.[25] If this were so, the material could have functioned originally either as an indictment of fellow Jews who were considered apostate[26] or as an indictment of Israel's Gentile oppressors. Paul would then be deliberately applying this traditional catena to "all, both Jews and Greeks" (3:9) and in the process again including those who concurred with such an indictment of others in their own indictment.

He anticipates the objection that such texts refer only to the really wicked or those cut off from the covenant and claims that whatever the law says, no matter what the original context or referent,[27] it speaks to those who are "in the law," those who possess these oracles. The Jewish scriptures themselves are in this way made to provide the universal indictment of humanity, including those to whom the scriptures were entrusted—the Jews. The picture painted in 3:19b is again a forensic one. Because of the weight of the evidence against them, humans will have nothing to say in their own defense, "so that every mouth may be stopped, and the whole world may be held liable to God's judgment." The modification of Ps 142:2 LXX, particularly the addition of "by works of the law" before the psalm's wording, adds to this picture. In this way 3:20 provides an appropriate summing up of the whole section—a universal indictment of humanity but with special reference to Jews. In the light

---

[25] See esp. H.-J. van der Minde, *Schrift und Tradition bei Paulus: Ihre Bedeutung und Funktion in Römerbrief* (Munich: Schöningh, 1976) 54–58; L. E. Keck, "The Function of Rom 3:10-18: Observations and Suggestions," in *God's Christ and His People: Studies in Honour of Nils Alstrup Dahl* (ed. J. Jervell and W. A. Meeks; Oslo: Universitetsforlaget, 1977) 142–51.

[26] Cf. the similar material in CD 5:13–17.

[27] Davies provides a useful discussion of the original meaning and context of the citations but holds that Paul is simply using them to make the same point—that there is no righteousness among the wicked, be they Jew or Gentile (*Faith and Obedience*, 82–88, esp. 93). But this is hardly a point that would be under dispute or in need of spelling out.

of the preceding argument it appears highly likely that the mention of "works of the law" by which a person cannot be justified is to be related to the judgment according to works (2:8) and to the principle of doing (2:13). Even if the deeds by which one hopes to be justified are deeds laid down in the law, this fails to alter the universal indictment that no one passes the judgment, no one is righteous.[28] Indeed 3:20—ἐξ ἔργων νόμου οὐ δικαιωθήσεται πᾶσα σάρξ ("by deeds of the law no flesh will be justified")—asserts the reality that provides the counterpart to the principle of 2:13—οἱ ποιηταὶ νόμου δικαιωθήσονται ("the doers of the law will be justified"). For Paul the law serves only to show up a person's lack of righteousness, a person's sin (see also 7:7–25), and he has just employed the law in its wider sense to do precisely this (3:10–18).

III. RESTATEMENT OF PAUL'S GOSPEL OF RIGHTEOUSNESS BY FAITH AND ITS IMPLICATIONS (3:21–31)

Paul is now in a position to restate his gospel and to underline what his depiction of the plight has demonstrated, namely, that the solution offered by the gospel has to be quite apart from law. The solution indicates that a decisively new era in God's dealings with humanity has been inaugurated (cf. "but now . . ." in 3:21) and it is marked by the disclosure of his righteousness. As we have seen, Paul's talk of the righteousness of God takes up a Jewish and indeed scriptural tradition. His treatment here highlights three aspects. In 3:21, and earlier in 1:17, the focus is on God's righteousness as his saving activity whereby he shows his covenantal faithfulness, and in 3:22 it becomes clear that this activity is one that also bestows his righteousness on all who have faith in Christ, setting them in a right relationship with him. But God's saving activity cannot be divorced from the character of God himself. It is in accord with who he is as the righteous judge, and so it is not surprising that in 3:25 (cf. also 3:26), and earlier in 3:5, God's righteousness denotes his justice or right judgment. Paul holds that, in acting to provide righteousness by pardoning those who have been declared guilty by his judgment, God retains his own character of righteous judge.[29] In restating his solution in 3:21–26, the

---

[28] For the broad reference of ἐξ ἔργων νόμου ("by deeds of law"), see, e.g., Wilckens, *Der Brief an die Römer*, 1. 176–77; idem, "Was heisst bei Paulus: 'Aus Werken des Gesetzes wird kein Mensch gerecht'?" in *Rechtfertigung als Freiheit: Paulusstudien* (Neukirchen: Neukirchener Verlag, 1974) 77–109; Moo, *Romans 1–8*, 209–18; *contra* the narrow reference in terms of ethnic identity markers suggested by, e.g., Dunn (*Romans 1–8*, 153–55) and Longenecker (*Eschatology*, 200–202, 206–7).

[29] On this major topic, see the recent clear overview of the main issues by Moo, *Romans 1–8*, 65–70, 75–86. For a similar interpretation to that sketched above, see P. Stuhlmacher, "The

apostle stays with his picture of the lawcourt from 3:19 not only through his mention of righteousness with its forensic connotations but also through his assertion that, although righteousness cannot come through the law, both the law and the prophets act as *witnesses* to the righteousness of God which comes through faith in Jesus Christ.[30] In particular, the witness of the law will be provided through his treatment of Gen 15:6, while the witness of the prophets has already been adduced through the use of Hab 2:4 in the *propositio*.

In the new formulation of the solution offered in his gospel Paul may well make use of a Jewish Christian formulation about Christ's sacrificial death and its significance, which already contains a reference to God's righteousness.[31] He connects this formulation with his own emphasis on the justification achieved through Christ's death, adds his own stress on faith in v. 25, and rounds it off with a further statement about the significance of Christ's death for the issue of God's righteousness in v. 26. His rhetoric of persuasion for the Jewish Christian members of his audience is again at work. He takes a statement about Christ's sacrificial death and its relation to God's righteousness with which they would agree, makes it the basis for his own formulation of the role of Christ's death in the solution offered by his gospel, and then extends it a stage further in support of the aspect of his gospel about which they are suspicious. They already believe that God has set forth Christ through his life yielded up in violent death ("by his blood") as a sacrifice. They have also already related this sacrificial death to their past sins. Now Paul, in effect, invites his readers to apply this perspective on Christ's death and God's righteousness to the present and asserts that it is also because of Christ's sacrificial death that God, in justifying the one who has faith in Jesus remains righteous.

Apostle Paul's View of Righteousness," in *Reconciliation, Law, and Righteousness: Essays in Biblical Theology* (Philadelphia: Fortress, 1986) 68–93. In its scriptural roots, especially in Isaiah, the righteousness of God can be synonymous both with his righteous judgment (e.g., Isa 5:16; 33:5; 59:9; 59:14 LXX) and with the salvation he provides (Isa 46:13; 51:5; 51:8; 62:1 LXX), and it is made clear that this salvation is his judgment, the activity of the righteous judge (Isa 63:1; 33:22; 45:21 LXX).

[30] This is to agree with J. D. G. Dunn, "Once More, ΠΙΣΤΙΣ ΧΡΙΣΤΟΥ," in *Society of Biblical Literature 1991 Seminar Papers* (Atlanta, GA: Scholars Press, 1991) 730–44 on the force of the genitive construction in 3:22 and 3:26 rather than R. B. Hays, "ΠΙΣΤΙΣ and Pauline Christology: What is at Stake?" in *Society of Biblical Literature 1991 Seminar Papers* (Atlanta: Scholars Press, 1991) 714–29, or D. Campbell, *Rhetoric of Righteousness,* 58–69, 214–18.

[31] The most convincing version of this view holds that vv. 25–26a contain traditional material; see esp. K. Wengst, *Christologische Formeln und Lieder des Urchristentums* (Gütersloh: Mohn, 1972) 87–91; B. F. Meyer, "The Pre-Pauline Formula in Rom 3:25-26a," *NTS* 29 (1983) 198–208, though he takes "to show his righteousness" in v. 25 as a Pauline addition; also P. Stuhlmacher, "Recent Exegesis on Romans 3:24–26," in *Reconciliation, Law, and Righteousness: Essays in Biblical Theology* (Philadelphia: Fortress, 1986) 94–109, esp. 96. For arguments disputing the use of such a formulation, see D. Campbell, *Rhetoric of Righteousness,* 45–57.

Jewish Christians should be able to see that their objections to Paul's gospel are ill-founded. In proclaiming that Gentiles can be justified simply by means of faith in Jesus and that anyone who has faith in Christ can be set in a right relation with God without obeying the law, he is not abrogating the need for justice or casting aspersions on God's righteousness, because the claim of God's righteousness has been met by the atoning sacrifice God provided in Christ. In this way, Paul holds, God's righteousness, not only in the sense of his saving activity to restore the relationship humanity has ruptured but also in the sense of his righteous judgment, is indeed revealed in his gospel.

Paul's use of the Jewish Christian formulation also enables him to provide a statement of the solution offered in the gospel that matches his depiction of the plight. He has already made clear that just as the plight was universal—all have sinned, so the solution is universal—God's righteousness is available to all who believe in Jesus Christ; and there is no distinction between Jew and Gentile (3:22, 23). But he goes on to stress that the solution has come freely, generously, and undeservedly ("by his grace as a gift") and to show that in it each of the main elements of the plight is met. The three types of imagery employed for God's activity in Christ match the three main elements in the situation of human sinfulness. The imagery of the lawcourt predominates through the language of justification. God's righteousness is the power by which those unable to be justified on the criterion of works are set right with him and being set in a right relationship with God involves his judicial verdict of pardon. It is not that people are deemed innocent of the charges in the indictment against them. Their unrighteousness has been clearly depicted in Paul's argument. But he believes the righteous judge has acted ahead of time in history and in his grace has pronounced a pardon on those who have faith in Christ, so that their guilt can no longer be cited against them. God's justification of sinners is "through the redemption that is in Christ Jesus" (3:24). Here the imagery is from the slave market, but the concept of redemption also has scriptural roots in God's acts of liberating his people from slavery in Egypt (cf. Deut 7:8) and in Babylon (cf. Isa 51:11). In the plight depicted in 1:18–3:20 sin had a dual character. Humans were responsible for it; their rebellion against the Creator left them without excuse, guilty. But they also unleashed a situation they were unable to control; sin became a force to which they were in bondage, imprisoned under its power (3:9). The righteousness of God not only justifies but also emancipates, freeing people from this domination of sin. The third kind of imagery for the effects of Christ's death represents that death not only as an expiatory sacrifice, making amends for sin, but also as a propitiatory sacrifice, averting the wrath of God on account of sin.[32] Paul could not have made clearer that both

---

[32] The linguistic evidence favors this force for ἱλαστήριον, and it is the one most appropriate

Gentiles and Jews are deserving of God's condemnation and wrath (1:18; 2:5, 8). Now in the resolution provided by Paul's gospel the imagery of a propitiatory sacrifice makes explicit that in dealing with sin Christ's death also averts God's wrath, and in this formulation it is of course God himself who provides the means of dealing with his own wrath. In this way Paul's solution fits the plight he has depicted. Corresponding to the universal situation of guilt, bondage to sin, and condemnation under the wrath of God is a gospel of the righteousness of God, which is available universally to faith and which through Christ's death offers a free and undeserved pardon, liberates into a new life where the tyranny of sin is broken and righteous behavior becomes possible, and provides satisfaction of God's righteous wrath.

Taking up the diatribe form again, Paul now underscores two implications for his Jewish Christian readers. If works of the law cannot produce God's verdict of approval and instead justification is by faith apart from such works, then there is no point in any boasting of a relationship to God based on reliance on the law (3:27, 28). Paul then presses another reason on Jewish Christians for recognizing their equality and unity with Gentile Christians solely through faith in Christ. He appeals to their fundamental belief that God is one, a belief confessed in the *Shema* (see Deut 6:4).[33] Since there is only one God, Paul argues, this God has to be the God of both Jews and Gentiles. From the unity of his relation to all as the one God of all, Paul deduces a unity of principle in this God's saving activity on behalf of both groups. There are not two routes to justification—one involving faith and the law and the other simply involving faith. Instead, the unity of God's relation to both Jews and Gentiles is shown by his justifying the circumcised by faith and the uncircumcised through faith. Again Paul's claim is that so far from involving any abandoning of the basics of the Jewish heritage, his gospel of justification by faith is in fact more appropriate to the universal monotheism of Judaism than is any emphasis on the law. It is precisely its faith aspect that makes his gospel universal in scope and fitted for his world mission, because, unlike an emphasis on law, it places no ethnic limits on participation in a right relationship with the one God.

---

to the context; see, e.g., D. Hill, *Greek Words and Hebrew Meanings* (Cambridge: Cambridge University Press, 1967) 23–41; Cranfield, *Romans,* 1. 214–18. In the traditional formulation the term may well have had specific reference to the mercy seat as the place of propitiation (see, e.g., Stuhlmacher, "Recent Exegesis," 96–104; Meyer, "Pre-Pauline Formula," 206; Wilckens, *Der Brief an die Römer,* 1. 191–93), but as it now stands it is open also to the broader force of "means of propitiation" (see also Dunn, *Romans 1–8,* 171).

[33] See esp. N. A. Dahl, *Studies in Paul* (Minneapolis: Augsburg, 1977) 178–91; H. Moxnes, *Theology in Conflict: Studies of Paul's Understanding of God in Romans* (NovTSup 53; Leiden: Brill, 1986) 78–80.

IV. ABRAHAM AS THE LAW'S WITNESS TO PAUL'S GOSPEL
OF RIGHTEOUSNESS BY FAITH (4:1–25)

Both of the main preceding points from 3:27–31 are taken up in Paul's treatment of Abraham in 4:1–25. There is also an immediate link with the preceding argument, however, through 3:31. To the objection of Jewish Christians that his formulation about justification means the abrogation of the law, Paul replies that, far from this being the case, he upholds the law—and he substantiates this claim by calling on Abraham as his witness from the law (cf. 3:21). He realizes that he is entering disputed territory and that the view of Abraham as the father of the Jews who showed his faithfulness by keeping the commandments and thus being reckoned as righteous could well be used against him. So Paul attempts to secure Abraham for his own position. In so doing, he appears to believe that he is upholding the law in the sense that, when it is read in the light of his gospel, the law can be seen to support that gospel's emphasis on faith. After all, it is the law (Gen 15:6) that says of the patriarch, "Abraham believed God and it was reckoned to him as righteousness," and Paul proceeds to provide a reading of the law in the light of justification by faith. His extended midrashic treatment of this passage allows us to see most clearly what we have been observing all along, namely, the way in which Paul employs tradition familiar to his Jewish Christian readers—here scriptural tradition—in the service of his rehearsal of the gospel for both Jewish and Gentile Christians in Rome.[34]

If the widespread Jewish understanding of Abraham were right (cf. 1 Macc 2:51, 52: "Remember the works of the fathers, which they did in their generations. . . . Was not Abraham found faithful when tested, and it was reckoned to him as righteousness?"; see also Sir 44:19–21; CD 3:2; Pr Man 8) and Abraham was justified by works, he would have a cause for boasting. But the preceding demonstration that justification has to be through faith by grace as a gift has ruled this out as a possible stance before God. The question "For what does the Scripture say?" introduces Paul's reading of the law, which puts Abraham's relation to God in a different perspective. The fact that the key text he cites, Gen 15:6, does not talk of works but only mentions faith in Abraham's being reckoned righteous enables Paul to press the point that in the case of Abraham there can be no thought of a justification owed him on the basis of a successful performance according to the criterion of judgment according

---

[34] I have reflected on Paul's imaginative correlation between scripture, his gospel, and the situation in Rome in an earlier discussion of Romans 4 in "Abraham Goes to Rome: Paul's Treatment of Abraham in Romans 4," in *Worship, Theology and Ministry in the Early Church: Essays in Honor of Ralph P. Martin* (ed. M. J. Wilkins and T. Paige; Sheffield: JSOT Press, 1992) 163–79, esp. 176–79.

to works (4:4; cf. 2:6, 10). By describing the object of faith as "the one who justifies the ungodly" (4:5), Paul is using language that would confirm the fears of those who believed with some scriptural support (see Exod 23:7 LXX: "you will not justify the ungodly") that his gospel undermines the righteousness of God. But he has already attempted to deal with this objection in drawing out the significance of Christ's propitiatory death (3:25, 26). The formulation of 4:5 also by implication places Abraham among the ungodly (cf. 1:18), who deserve only God's wrath and therefore have to receive justification as a gift.[35] So Paul's reflections on the Genesis text not only show Abraham to be a representative of the principles of the apostle's gospel but also open up for Jewish Christians a perception of Abraham, their forefather according to the flesh, and, by extension, themselves as being in exactly the same position as Gentile Christians in regard to receiving justification.

Paul goes on to claim in vv. 9–12 that the psalm's pronouncement of blessing on the one to whom God reckons righteousness apart from works does not apply just to Jews, as his Jewish Christian readers might well have supposed. It is the Abraham story that enables him to make his point. This time he draws attention to the sequence in the Genesis narrative whereby the statement of Gen 15:6 comes before the account of Abraham's circumcision in Genesis 17. So, when Abraham was reckoned righteous by faith, he was uncircumcised (4:9, 10). Again at this point Abraham was in precisely the same position as the Gentile Christian, and the Genesis story demonstrates that circumcision is irrelevant to a person's being reckoned righteous by God by means of faith. Abraham's circumcision can be described, therefore, not in the traditional way as a sign of the covenant but as a sign that was the seal of the righteousness he already had by faith (4:11a). Taking the argument a stage further, Paul can now claim that God's purpose in this sequence in the Abraham story was that Abraham's fatherhood should not be restricted to those who are circumcised or who become circumcised as proselytes but should embrace those, who like Abraham himself in Genesis 15, are uncircumcised but have faith. He is to be seen as the father of both uncircumcised believers and circumcised believers, Gentile Christians and Jewish Christians (4:11b, 12).

In 2:17–29 Paul had claimed that neither reliance on the law nor an appeal to circumcision could provide any safeguard in the light of God's impartial judgment. Now his treatment of Abraham reverses the order of topics and attempts to show that neither circumcision nor the law has any role in being reckoned righteous. He makes the point about the law in 4:13–15 by reading the Abraham story in the light of his own contrast between promise and faith

---

[35] See also Wilckens, *Der Brief an die Römer*, 1. 263; Dunn, *Romans 1–8*, 205.

on the one hand and law on the other. What Abraham believed when he was reckoned righteous was God's promise that he would have innumerable descendants (cf. Gen 15:5). So, Paul argues, building on his previous point, the promise, now extended to inheriting the world (cf. Sir 44:21), did not come through the law; it was believed by Abraham before the law, which was anticipated in the requirement of circumcision, was given. Jewish Christians need to see the law in a new light. So far from its providing a safeguard against God's righteous judgment, as they thought, the situation is quite the reverse: the law in fact brings about God's wrath, it contributes to the universal condemnation depicted in 1:18–3:20, because where there is law, sin becomes conscious violation of the law and all the more deserving of judgment (see also 5:13, 20). Paul now asserts that if there is to be any guarantee about inheriting the promise, the whole process has to depend on faith, because only in that way is the principle of grace rather than of law and performance (with their inevitable transgression and failure) brought fully into play (4:16a). The conclusion about Abraham's fatherhood from 4:11, 12 can now be restated in terms of law rather than circumcision (4:16b).

By now it has become clear that Paul wishes his Jewish Christian readers to reconsider any view of Abraham as simply "our forefather according to the flesh" and to entertain the notion of accepting Gentile believers as equally children of Abraham solely on the basis of their faith.[36] Previously they would have perceived Abraham primarily as the great dividing point in the history of humanity. Before Abraham there was the history of the nations, but with him began God's particularism in choosing out one nation. But now Paul has made Abraham the great rallying point for all who believe, whether Jews or Gentiles.[37] Gentile Christians, hearing Paul's midrash designed primarily to persuade Jewish Christians of his gospel, are therefore at the same time being invited to see themselves as part of a larger family which can trace its ancestry back to Abraham. They cannot write off Israel's past as of no account. The blessings in which they participate are blessings promised to Abraham and his descendants. As Paul will remind them later in 15:8, their faith in Christ is faith in the one who has confirmed God's promises to the patriarchs.

For Paul, sharing Abraham's justifying faith makes Jewish Christians and Gentile Christians equal members of the one family. Yet, as we have noted, the exhortations of 14:1–15:13 reflect a setting in which faith and its implica-

---

[36] See also P. Minear, *The Obedience of Faith: The Purpose of Paul in the Epistle to the Romans* (London: SCM, 1971) 53, 55.

[37] See A. Nygren, *Commentary on Romans* (Philadelphia: Muhlenberg, 1949) 175; he does not, however, apply this insight to the situation of the readers.

tions had become a divisive issue. The "strong" and the "weak" were despising and judging one another on the basis of their different interpretations of faith. Paul's treatment of Abraham should have provided a demonstration that justifying faith is grounds for unity rather than division in the Christian community. Both groups have Abraham as their father and inherit the promises, because they are reckoned righteous before God and accepted by him on the same basis—faith.

In a key insight for the relation between Abraham and the gospel, Paul points out that, in believing the promise that God would make him the father of many nations, Abraham had to believe in a God who gives life to the dead. It was this kind of faith that was reckoned to him as righteousness (4:17b–22). With Gen 17:15–21 and 18:9–15 in view, Paul can talk of Abraham displaying the strong faith that looked at the apparent impossibilities of his situation and yet still trusted completely in God to bring life (Isaac) out of death (his own body as good as dead and the deadness of Sarah's womb; cf. 4:19). Further, in a key insight for the relation between Abraham and the readers, when the apostle describes the quality of Abraham's faith in 4:19, 20, he does so in precisely the terms that are being used in the conflict in Rome: "he did not weaken in faith . . . but he grew strong in faith." In the later parenesis Paul will speak of "we, the strong" (15:1) and will underline his persuasion that nothing is unclean in itself (cf. 14:14, 20). So, in his depiction of Abraham, Paul signals clearly ahead of time where he stands theologically in the debate in Rome. Abraham does not merely exemplify the Pauline gospel as one who is righteous by faith; he is portrayed in such a way as to be aligned with the strong in faith. In his strong faith he is described as displaying the qualities that Paul will later stress as essential in the situation in Rome. He is said not to have doubted (cf. 14:23) and to have been "fully convinced" (cf. 14:5).

Was it not enough that Paul should have asked Jewish Christians to give up their exclusive claim to be Abraham's descendants and to share him as father with Gentile Christians? Depicting Abraham as one of the strong in faith is one way of showing that his distinctive gospel was "to the Jew first, and also the Greek," but does it not add insult to injury? Whatever his readers' response may have been, seen from Paul's point of view, this rhetorical move can still be considered part of his tactics of persuasion. After all, at this stage in the letter he is rehearsing his own perspective on justification by faith and its consequences, knowing this to be controversial. Later in the parenesis, for the sake of harmony in the community, he will not insist on all its ramifications being accepted and will argue that love and mutual acceptance are more important than being right. But at this point in the argument he would also like to convince the Jewish Christian minority that his interpretation of the gospel is right. He has already asked it to rethink radically the issues of law, circumcision, and ethnic identity in 2:17–29. He hopes it will already have been persuaded to think of Abraham in his way as one who was justified by faith. So it is not surprising that he allows his full position to emerge in his midrash on the Abraham story and talks of Abraham as strong in faith. If Jewish Christians can be drawn into reading the Abraham story in Paul's way, they might just be coaxed into seeing not only the basic gospel message but all the issues differently. For, on this reading, to treat all foods as clean and all days as holy need not be thought of as forsaking their election and becoming apostate but as emulating the strength of faith of father Abraham.

Paul's interpretation of Abraham's faith obviously reinforces the views of Gentile Christians at this stage of his argument. But giving them a sense of their own solidarity with Abraham prepares them in two ways for what is to come. By showing them that justification and strong faith are found first in Abraham, Paul provides a needed reminder that the gospel in which they believe is "to the Jew first." And when Paul in the parenesis asks them to change their attitude and make concessions to Jewish Christians, this portrait of Abraham will have been one of the means of helping them to realize that the request comes from one who clearly shares their basic perspective on faith.

It is with Abraham that Paul introduces for the first time in the letter the theme of hope or confident assurance that will prove significant in the later argument (see 5:1–11; 8:18–39). Abraham is said to have "against hope, in hope believed." Paul will complete his parenesis about mutual acceptance with the aid of scripture citations, and this, he says, is in order that "by the encouragement of the scriptures we might have hope" (15:4). His prayer wish which forms the climax is "May the God of hope fill you with all joy and peace in believing, so that by the power of the Holy Spirit you may abound in hope" (15:13). Just as Abraham's hopeful belief that he would be the father of many nations impelled him to positive action in the present despite the obstacles, so Paul holds that it is the faith that abounds in the hope of the salvation in which Jew and Gentile are one and equal that will provide the motivation for both groups in Rome to accept one another and worship together in unity and equality despite all obstacles.

This strong and hopeful faith in the creator God and his life-giving power is what was reckoned to Abraham as righteousness (4:22), and this is why, says Paul, as he now makes explicit the correlation that has been at work throughout his midrash, Gen 15:6 was written not only for Abraham but also for Christian believers in the same God who raised Jesus from the dead. Significantly for his attempt to persuade Jewish Christians, in 4:25 Paul's formulation of the gospel, in the light of which he has been reading the Abraham story, employs Jewish Christian traditional material, which interpreted Jesus' death and resurrection on the basis of Isaiah 53.[38] He wants his audience to see Abraham as a type of Christian believers, whose justification is through belief in Christ's resurrection, whereby Christ's vindication in the reversal of the condemnation of death, to which "he was handed over because of our transgressions," also becomes theirs. What is readily apparent from Paul's typological pattern of thinking is that he holds that being placed in a right relationship with God is like Isaac's being born despite Abraham's being as good as dead and despite the death of Sarah's womb. It involves a radical intervention on God's part to rescue humanity from its situation of death and bring it into the realm of life. This is an appropriate note on which to end our sketch of the development of Paul's argument in 1:18–4:25, since it reminds us that in the letter as a whole justification by faith and the enjoyment of eschatological life go hand in hand.

V. PAUL'S GOSPEL AND THE THEOLOGICAL ARGUMENT OF ROMANS 1:18–4:25

The theocentric focus of Paul's argument has frequently been noted,[39] and this section of the letter begins with God, a God active in wrath in a world in revolt, and ends with God, a God at work for human justification in the resurrection and death of "Jesus our Lord." The God who is the source of Paul's gospel (see 1:1) is clearly Israel's God, the God of scripture, the God of Abraham, but as such he is also the God of all human beings. Crucial to Paul's argument is that the creator God is related to all his creatures and remains in relation to them even when they fail to acknowledge him. His saving righteousness in the gospel takes place, therefore, not in a vacuum created by his absence nor simply in the context of human sinfulness but in the context of his own judging righteousness, his wrath. That the disclosure of God's righteousness is at the heart of the solution offered by the gospel (3:21) underlines that for Paul God is the gospel's source but also his activity is its content. Paul's argument reveals that he is at pains to demonstrate that his gospel in no way impugns the righteousness of God in the sense either of his faithfulness or his moral integrity. But his formulation goes further and involves the claim that in fact it is in his gospel that God's righteousness is most fully displayed. The God who is the righteous judge, impartial in his judgment of both Jews and Gentiles, is shown in Paul's gospel to be the one God who justifies both Jews and Gentiles in the same way—on the basis of Christ's sacrificial death and by

---

[38] See, e.g., Wengst, *Christologische Formeln*, 101–3; van der Minde, *Schrift und Tradition*, 89–99; Wilckens, *Der Brief an die Römer*, 1. 279–80.

[39] See esp. Moxnes, *Theology in Conflict*.

means of faith—and who in doing so remains righteous in his judgment and faithful to his promise, in particular his promise to Abraham.

What enables Paul to make such a claim for his gospel in relation to God is, of course, his eschatological conviction that the divine righteousness has now been decisively disclosed in the death and resurrection of Christ. For Paul, it is through these events that humans encounter God's saving power, have their sins atoned for in a way that deals with God's wrath, and are liberated from the power of sin. He is also convinced that through these events God has been at work in history inaugurating a new era by effecting justification ahead of the eschaton for those who have faith in Christ, both Gentiles and Jews, and that this makes everything else, including the law as a means of achieving righteousness, part of an old era characterized by unrighteousness, the power of sin and the wrath of God.

The formulation of the gospel in 1:16, 17, the forensic motifs throughout 1:18–3:20, the repetition of the language of justification in 3:21–31 and the content of the Abraham midrash make justification by faith the dominant soteriological metaphor in these early chapters. Although the gospel is rehearsed for the Roman Christians in a context of Jewish Christian–Gentile Christian tensions, the importance attached to its formulation in terms of a right relationship with God by faith indicates that this concept is more than a mere *Kampfeslehre* against judaizers.[40] It is integral to the universal scope of the gospel Paul believes himself called to proclaim as the apostle to the Gentiles. Appreciation of it is essential for both Jewish Christians and Gentile Christians if they are to see themselves as one and equal before God and if they are to live together as those who can jointly claim Abraham as their father. In his modification of the Jewish Christian tradition in 3:24–26 Paul underscores that justification is by God's grace as a gift and through faith. This makes clear that the new status of both Jews and Gentiles in the one people of God comes freely and undeservedly to them as those who were liable to God's righteous judgment and that all the credit for such a status belongs to the divine initiative and accomplishment.

Although the depictions of humanity's plight and that plight's resolution are mutually illuminating, it is the logic Paul believes to be inherent in his gospel that has led to the depiction of a universal plight in the first place. His efforts at theological persuasion derive from his eschatological conviction that in the gospel about the death and resurrection of Christ the power of God is decisively at work. His Abraham midrash indicates that he sees God bringing life out of death and, in particular, raising Jesus from the dead as integral to justification (4:17–25). The righteousness of God revealed in his gospel is this life-

---

[40] On its indispensability for Paul's gospel, see now Seifrid, *Justification*, esp. 182–270.

giving power at work. So Paul holds that through his gospel and its proclamation both the righteousness and the life of the end-time are being brought into the present. On the basis of its christological content, Paul is confident then that this powerful justifying and life-giving gospel is the fulfillment of scriptural tradition and meets supremely human needs. Such confidence lies behind the way in which in this letter his gospel is paramount in shaping his thought and in interpreting both the particular traditions he employs and the specific needs of his audience.

What emerges distinctively in Romans, and in a way that suggests it is not merely part of the contingent argument of the letter, although it certainly fits the rhetorical situation, is that Paul believes that in both the old and the new situation there is a priority in God's dealings with Israel. Paul's gospel itself is for all, but for the Jew first. The gospel of righteousness through faith in Christ and apart from the law or works of the law makes for a paradoxical faithfulness of God to his promises to Israel. Rom 1:18–4:25 with its stress on the impartiality of the divine righteousness in both its judgmental and its saving aspects, just as much as the discussion of Rom 9:1–10:21, prepares the ground for the revelation of 11:25–32 about the unexpected way God will remain faithful to his election of Israel. It helps to remove any notions of presumption about that election and to make clear that God will be faithful in a free and sovereign way—not because Israel as an ethnic entity can make binding claims on him but because in his mercy he will choose to have Israel recognize its Messiah.

The early chapters of Romans show Paul forging a theology based on his gospel through creative interpretation of Jewish and Jewish Christian tradition. He exposes the scriptural roots integral to the nature of his gospel, but at the same time his employment of such scriptural notions as God's righteous judgment, his impartiality and his oneness, judgment on the basis of works and circumcision as a matter of the heart, his interaction with Wisdom in 1:18–2:5, his use of the collection of citations in 3:10–18, and his extended midrash in 4:1–25 show him to be not only an exegetical theologian but also a critical biblical theologian, reading, adapting, and correcting scripture in the form of the Septuagint in the light of the gospel and in the light of his own and his readers' situation. It is no accident that scripture features so prominently in these chapters. Nor is it surprising that Paul should incorporate and adapt Jewish Christian formulations of the gospel at crucial points in his argument in 3:25, 26 and 4:25 (cf. already 1:3, 4). Both phenomena are integral to the pastoral and apologetic purposes of Paul in this letter. His stress on their unity and equality in sin and in experiencing justification by faith is what both groups in his audience need to hear. But, as we have seen, although it also has force for the Gentile Christians, the formulation of the argument in 1:18–

4:25 is designed to persuade the Jewish Christian minority. Hence the choice of subject matter and method of argument and the dominance of interaction with Jewish and Jewish Christian tradition.

At this early stage in the argument, it is primarily the Jewish Christians whom Paul is asking to make the changes in their thinking and attitude. His critique of the views they may hold is therefore balanced within this section not only by the affirmation of Jewish priority but also by the continuities he attempts to draw between his position and both Jewish and Jewish Christian traditions. It is also worth remembering that the position in which Jewish Christians find themselves in relation to Paul's argument in this part of the letter is the position Gentile Christians will be in later in chaps. 9–11. After being able to agree with Paul about God having been true to his purposes in his bringing a new people out of Jew and Gentile, about Christ being the end of the law, and about Israel being a disobedient people, they then have the tables turned on them and their own presumption is attacked. At that stage Jewish Christians, having seen that Paul's gospel does mean abandoning any superior or judgmental attitudes stemming from their belief in Israel's election, will be told more explicitly that acceptance of Gentile Christians does not mean acceptance of God having abandoned his purposes for Israel.[41]

In the interaction between Paul's gospel and tradition, both scriptural and Jewish Christian, there is interplay and mutual illumination. The tradition supplies concepts and semantic possibilities within which his gospel can be expressed, most notably the righteousness of God and sacrificial terminology in 3:21–26 and the formulations about the death and resurrection of Christ in 4:25. The Jewish Christian formulations are woven into Paul's overall pattern of thought in the correspondences between plight and solution and between Abraham's belief and Christian belief. But in the end tradition is clearly subordinate to gospel. Whether being exploited to show the universal sinfulness of humanity that is the presupposition for Paul's gospel or modified to demonstrate how God can remain righteous in providing justification for faith or reworked to portray Abraham as having justifying and strong faith independent of circumcision and the law, tradition is in the service of Paul's gospel. Clearly, it is important for Paul to find confirmation of his gospel in scripture and to claim that authentic justifying faith existed before the coming of Christ in the case of Abraham (and David). Yet equally clearly it is beside Paul's point in these chapters to attempt to extrapolate from his argument the outlines of

---

[41] C. H. Cosgrove has rightly and forcefully pressed the issue of the likely success of such tactics in regard to Jewish Christians ("The Justification of the Other: An Interpretation of Rom 1:18–4:25," in *Society of Biblical Literature 1992 Seminar Papers* [Atlanta: Scholars Press, 1992] 613–34, esp. 616, 631).

a theology of saving faith before or outside of Christ.[42] Paul's dominant way of thinking from solution to plight, from the new as a whole to the old as a whole, means that however crucial such an issue might be to the concerns of biblical theology, it is simply not his interest in Rom 1:18–4:25.

This essay has traced three main coordinates in the theology of Rom 1:18–4:25—tradition, which provides most of the symbol system within which the argument takes place; gospel, which supplies the convictions by which the symbols are realigned and reshaped; and audience, whose needs influence the argument but are interpreted in the light of the gospel. In the letter as a whole it is because Paul conceives of the gospel as for all, both Jews and Gentiles—but for the Jew first—that he can be even-handed in his rebuking of the pride on both sides. In this first part of the letter it is because of his particular conception of the gospel, deriving from his call to Gentile mission, that he pulls no punches in dealing with the obstacles in Jewish Christian thinking to their acceptance of his gospel, asks for a radical reassessment of some of their cherished views, and even depicts Abraham as one who has seen the full implications of justification by faith. Thus, in regard to Paul's theology in Rom 1:18–4:25, it can be said that tradition, gospel, and audience abide, these three; and the greatest of these is gospel.

[42] *Pace* Davies, *Faith and Obedience,* passim.

7 CENTERING THE ARGUMENT

A Response to Andrew T. Lincoln

Jouette M. Bassler
Perkins School of Theology

THE SUBTITLE of Andrew Lincoln's paper, "Tradition, Gospel, and Audience in the Theology of Romans 1:18–4:25," promises a wide-ranging investigation of this portion of the letter, and indeed he does provide one. He shows how the gospel informs and empowers Paul's argument, and he is attentive to Paul's creative use of traditions, both Jewish and Christian, in forging that argument. But Lincoln's real interest emerges, I think, when he poses the question, "Why does this argument [addressed, it would seem, to a primarily Gentile church] appear to be shaped primarily for Jews or Jewish Christians?" (p. 131). It is concern for the letter's audience, for its rhetorical situation, and for the way Paul has shaped his argument to address this situation that provides the heart and driving force of Lincoln's paper.

I. UNPACKING PAUL'S INTENT

Lincoln's question about the audience elicits a discussion of the occasion and purpose of the letter, which Lincoln defines in terms of Paul's desire to gain the support of the Roman church for his proposed mission to Spain. This goal was being threatened, however, by tensions that existed between the Jewish and Gentile Christians in that city. As Lincoln reconstructs the situation, these tensions had been fueled by misconceptions of Paul's gospel caused by "Gentile Christian attitudes and views that he [Paul] would not want to own." Paul wants to "speak for himself" in this letter and rehearse his gospel for the Roman Christians (p. 133). In doing so he can address the objections and suspicions of the Jewish Christians and at the same time reinforce, but also correct where necessary, the understanding of the Gentile Christians. Thus, in 1:18–4:25, Paul presents his law-free gospel, but he does so in a way calcu-

160

lated to show Jewish Christians "that one does not need to renounce one's Jewish heritage in order to espouse his controversial gospel" (p. 134). He hopes in this way to unify the community and to solidify its support for his Spanish mission.

Having discerned Paul's rhetorical goals, Lincoln undertakes an analysis of the argument of 1:18–4:25, paying careful attention to Paul's tactics in framing his argument as he does. The following sketch makes no attempt to summarize all aspects of Lincoln's analysis. It seeks only to highlight the rhetorical interests that guide it.

In Rom 1:18–3:20, Paul makes creative use of Jewish traditions both to subvert Jewish presumption and to counter the Jewish-Christian complaint that the gospel does not take seriously enough the forensic aspect of God's righteousness. The diatribe, employed frequently in this section of the letter, allows him to instruct the Jewish Christians without directly attacking them. Throughout this section, though, and working always within the parameters of Jewish-Christian assumptions, Paul is preparing them to accept the radical proposition of chap. 4 that Gentile Christians can also claim Abraham as their ancestor.

Lincoln's analysis of the restatement of the gospel in 3:21–31 highlights the way various aspects of God's righteousness are presented, but he also shows how Paul's rhetoric of persuasion is still at work. From the way Paul presents the gospel here, says Lincoln, Jewish Christians should be able to see that their objections to it are ill founded. They should also see how their own fundamental belief, summarized in the *Shema,* presses them toward recognizing Gentile Christians as their equals.

Paul presents Rom 4:1–25 as a direct response to Jewish Christian objections that his gospel means abrogation of the law. As he has done earlier, Paul uses traditions familiar to the Jewish Christians to address these objections. It is clear, says Lincoln, that Paul wants his Jewish Christian readers to "entertain the notion of accepting Gentile believers as equally children of Abraham," but he also wants Gentile Christian readers to be reminded that they are "part of a larger family which can trace its ancestry back to Abraham" (p. 152). This two-pronged message, which presents faith as the basis for unity rather than division, is directed toward the divisive situation in Rome. Lincoln notes, however, that Abraham's faith is described as "strong," signaling well in advance of his treatment of the subject Paul's approval of the theological position of the strong in Rome (14:14, 20; 15:1).

Though this tacit approval of the "strong" in chap. 4 might seem counterproductive to his rhetorical goal of persuading the Jewish Christians, the "weak in faith," to accept his gospel, Lincoln argues that it makes good rhetorical sense. Paul had to come clean on his position. And though he later argues for love and mutual acceptance, it could not hurt to provide an argument for embracing the position of the strong to the Jewish Christians. At the same time, the argument will have a salubrious impact on Gentile Christian readers: it cultivates their good will before Paul asks them to make concessions to their Jewish Christian brothers and sisters.

After his description of the development of the argument in 1:18–4:25 and the way it serves Paul's rhetorical goals, Lincoln reviews in the last seven pages of his paper the theological aspects of that argument: its theocentric focus on God's righteousness, its eschatological underpinnings, its dominant soteriological metaphor (justification by faith), and its emphasis on the priority of Israel in God's dealings with the world. Even here, though, Lincoln never loses sight of the pastoral and apologetic purposes that drive the construction of the argument.

II. RHETORIC OR THEOLOGY:
A QUESTION OF FOCUS

It is difficult to fault Lincoln's rhetorical analysis of Rom 1:18–4:25. He builds on a plausible reconstruction of the audience for whom Paul was writing and consistently keeps this audience in mind as he analyzes the argument of these chapters. At every turn Lincoln assesses Paul's strategy and the likely impact of the argument on the two hostile factions in Rome. We do not learn from this paper how Lincoln would define Paul's rhetorical goals in chaps. 5–8 or 9–11—a somewhat more challenging proposition—but that lies beyond his assigned task. On the other hand, we do learn a lot about what Paul "feels," "senses," "wishes," and "hopes." With these verbs Lincoln goes beyond explaining how the argument works and explores as well how Paul's mind worked as he constructed his argument. That seems a risky business, but it may be an inevitable aspect of any analysis of rhetorical intent. The real problem is that as a contribution to a group intent on studying the *theology* of the Pauline letters, Lincoln's paper seems to provide a view through the wrong end of a telescope. Instead of bringing the object of our attention into closer focus, this essentially rhetorical analysis causes it to recede even farther away.

There has been, of course, considerable debate about the appropriate object of the Pauline Theology Group's attention.[1] It seems clear from the last section of Lincoln's paper that he equates the theology of this portion of the let-

---

[1] See my summary of the debate in "Paul's Theology: Whence and Whither?" in *Pauline Theology, Volume II: 1 & 2 Corinthians* (ed. David M. Hay; Minneapolis: Fortress, 1993) 3–17; and Steven J. Kraftchick's helpful response, "Seeking a More Fluid Model" (pp. 18–34 of the same volume).

ter with its theological argument and the theological convictions that inform that argument. Yet the bulk of his paper was concerned not with the way theological convictions have driven the argument, but with the way rhetorical concerns have. It is striking, for example, how rarely Lincoln draws chaps. 5–11 into his discussion, even though theological concepts introduced in the first four chapters—sin, law, faith, faithfulness, righteousness—are developed further there. Instead his analysis of 1:18–4:25 really turns on correlations with chaps. 14–15, where, in his view, the rhetorical occasion of the letter is defined. Leander Keck, however, in his essay in this volume, warns us against an over-reliance on factors whose role can neither be demonstrated nor disproved.[2] Instead, he says, "'occasion' should be distinguished from 'purpose' instead of regarding each as the obverse of the other."[3] Indeed, the content needs to be "related more to its function within the text itself" rather than related to the letter's putative occasion and purpose.[4] Thus, we need to turn the telescope around and focus on the theological convictions that dominate this section of the letter and examine how they have directed the shaping of the argument.

In approaching the task in this way, I am assuming the general correctness of Victor Furnish's proposal concerning how a study of the theology in a letter should proceed. He suggests six steps, the first four of which are relevant to this paper: (1) examination of each of the letter's theological discourses within its literary and situational contexts; (2) analysis of the argument of each passage; (3) identification of the key theological conceptions of each passage; (4) consideration of how these conceptions have informed the overall contents and argument of the letter.[5] Lincoln's study has addressed the first and second steps, though his analysis of the argument (step 2) was more interested in rhetorical issues than with the theological argument per se. He does give some attention to the third step in the final section of the paper, but it functions almost as an appendix to his paper. More attention needs to be given to identifying the theological concepts that actually control the argument, to showing *how* they control the argument, and to documenting their continuing influence in the rest of the letter (step 4). In what follows, then, I do not

---

[2] Keck, "What Makes Romans Tick?" 20.

[3] Ibid.

[4] Ibid., 21.

[5] Victor P. Furnish, "Theology in 1 Corinthians," in *Pauline Theology II,* 63. The final steps that Furnish recommends are (5) consideration of theological statements found in nonexpository passages, and (6) formulation of some generalizations about the theological orientation of the letter as a whole. Since Lincoln's paper and this one as well are concerned with the theology of only a portion of a letter, these steps addressing the whole are not relevant.

intend to dispute the results of Lincoln's rhetorical analysis of Rom 1:18–4:25 but to refocus attention on some *theological* aspects of that passage.

III. IMPARTIALITY IN ROMANS: TRACING A THEOLOGICAL CONCEPT

Though 1:18–4:25 defines the first main section of the argument of Romans, it contains several discrete subdivisions. Rom 1:18–2:28 defines humanity's need for Paul's gospel, while 3:1–20 presents objections to that argument and a brief and partial response to these objections. Rom 3:21–26 is the restatement of Paul's gospel of righteousness by faith (cf. 1:16–17), while 3:27–4:25 presents objections to the argument and a lengthy response to these objections in the form of a midrash on the Abraham narrative. Thus, theological expositions are followed by objections and responses to the objections. To identify the theological convictions that control the argument here, we need to focus first of all on the primary expositions.

Rom 1:18–2:29 contains an abundance of theological conceptions—God's attributes of wrath, power, immortality, kindness, forbearance, patience; God's role as Eternal Creator, Righteous Judge, Reader of Hearts—but the argument centers and turns on the concept of the impartiality of God (2:11).[6] This concept sums up the judicial aspect of divine righteousness emphasized in 1:18–4:25, that is, recompense in strict accordance with works and without regard for group distinctions. In this portion of the argument Paul ignores the law, God's special revelation of God's will to Israel. With the emphatic application of God's impartial justice "to the Jew first and also the Greek" (2:9–10), however, he is forced to define this impartiality in terms of both law and covenant. Thus in 2:12–29 Paul shows how God's impartial justice manifests itself in the face of the competing claim of God's election of Israel, which culminated in the giving of the law.

Paul opens the argument with a general statement of impartial justice, framed now in terms of "doing the law" (v. 13), and then applies this principle first to the Gentiles, "who do not possess the law," and then to the Jews, "who rely on the law." Possession of the law, he argues, provides no automatic advantage to Jews, nor are Gentiles at a disadvantage because they do not possess the written law. Both can know God's will and both must obey it. By the time Paul has defined true circumcision in terms of obedience to the law (which, he has just argued, is possible for both Jews and Gentiles), he has radicalized divine judgment to the point that all distinctions between Jews and

---

[6] In what follows I am summarizing the argument I presented more fully in *Divine Impartiality: Paul and a Theological Axiom* (SBLDS 59; Chico, CA: Scholars Press, 1982) 121–70.

Gentiles have been eliminated. The basic objection that the imaginary interlocutor raises in 3:1–9 is directed to the challenge this concept of impartiality poses to Jewish election, but Paul remains firm in his insistence that there is no advantage to the Jew.

This opening argument, which focuses on the impartiality of God's juridical righteousness, serves several functions in the letter. It establishes the universal need for God's saving righteousness and anticipates a key feature of that righteousness: it, too, is available without distinction to all (3:22b). At the end of his brief exposition of the gospel (3:21–26), Paul again manipulates an imaginary interlocutor to draw out the significant features of his argument. These turn on the implications of *impartial* grace: "What becomes of boasting?" "Is God the God of Jews only?" "Do we overthrow the law (the mark of Israel's distinctive relationship with God) by this faith?"

When Paul presents the example of Abraham to provide support for his gospel, he emphasizes not only that the way of faith is grounded in the law but also, and more specifically, that the impartiality that ignores the distinction between Jews and Gentiles was already anticipated there. Thus, when Abraham received circumcision as a sign of the righteousness he had acquired earlier by faith, *God's purpose was* to make him the common ancestor of two groups of people, not just one (4:11–12, 16, 18).

The issue of God's impartiality emerges again strongly in the argument in chaps. 9–11, where Paul explores the dynamic tension between this concept and the equally firm concept of God's faithfulness to Israel.[7] It also guides Paul's treatment of the relationship between the "strong" and the "weak" in chaps. 14–15. Though these two groups are never explicitly identified with Gentiles and Jews, Paul, in dealing with the problem, follows rather closely his earlier argument concerning God's impartiality toward the two ethnic groups. The strong and weak are, for example, sharply distinguished by the external form of their piety (i.e., diet and holy days) as were the Jews and Gentiles. In neither case is it necessary for these differences to be removed (2:9–10, 12–13, 25–29). In chap. 14 Paul argues as before that both are accepted by God with their distinguishing features (14:1–4), and when they stand before God in judgment, these external features will not privilege one group or disadvantage the other. What matters will be the individual's internal disposition, whether defined as a renewed mind (12:1; 14:5), an attitude of thanksgiving (14:6) or trust (4:16–22), or a circumcised heart (2:29).

In these final chapters, though, Paul draws a social corollary to this divine

---

[7] The role of divine impartiality in this section of the letter is nicely presented in E. Elizabeth Johnson's essay, "Romans 9–11: The Faithfulness and Impartiality of God," found on pp. 211–39 of this volume. I will not repeat it here.

impartiality: the "strong" and the "weak" should accept each other without regard for their external differences (14:1, 3, 13; 15:1, 5–6). Just as God's impartial judgment is not swayed by external matters, so Christians are to refrain from judging each other on external matters (14:13). Just as God makes no distinction between Jews and Gentiles (3:22), no distinction between strong and weak is to be made within the community.[8]

God's impartiality thus emerges as a central theological concept, not simply in 1:18–4:25, but throughout major portions of the letter. Paul develops the message of God's impartiality in judgment in 1:18–3:20 in order to prepare for his message of grace, which, in this letter, is presented as *impartial grace*. But that is not the end of the matter. Later in the letter Paul argues that God's impartiality does not compromise God's faithfulness to Israel, and in the final chapters he urges the factions in Rome to model their behavior toward each other on God's impartial acceptance of them.

IV. GOD'S RIGHTEOUSNESS IS REVEALED

In the second major expositional section, a different aspect of God's righteousness is introduced. Picking up the theme of Rom 1:17, Paul speaks of the *revelation* of the righteousness of God. God's righteousness, says Paul, is eschatologically and definitively revealed through the death of Christ, when it is seen as an act of atonement for sins. Paul does not mention here the means of Jesus' death (cf. 1 Cor 1:23; Gal 3:1), nor does he really place the emphasis on what the atonement accomplishes for those who believe. This is, of course, mentioned in 3:24–25, developed in 5:1–11, and is a mainstay of Paul's thought, but the weight of Paul's argument in this section is found in its framing emphasis on the revelation that occurs in and through the death of Jesus.

Three times in this passage Paul uses the language of revelation to describe the effect of Jesus' death. In 3:25–26 the message is clear though the wording of some phrases is awkward: God put Christ Jesus forward as a sacrifice of atonement in order to show (εἰς ἔνδειξιν) God's righteousness.[9] Then, repeating for emphasis and clarification, Paul says that this was to show (πρὸς

---

[8] I am less certain now than I was when I wrote *Divine Impartiality* that Paul's treatment of the strong and weak in Romans is a generalization of his earlier exhortation to the Corinthians (see pp. 163-65 of that volume). Lincoln and others who see evidence here of an actual problem in Rome are probably correct, though how much that problem has influenced the content of the letter remains debatable.

[9] The questions concerning the meaning of διὰ πίστεως (Whose faith? Human faith? God's faithfulness? Jesus' faithfulness?) and its awkward position in the sentence, though important, do not concern us here.

τὴν ἔνδειξιν) that God is righteous. The opening statement is more difficult to assess because Paul has left out a crucial verb in 3:22: δικαιοσύνη δὲ θεοῦ διὰ πίστεως Ἰησοῦ Χριστοῦ. Lincoln, by supplying the verb "come," highlights the gift aspect of righteousness and translates the clause as "the righteousness of God which comes through faith in Jesus Christ" (p. 147). It is, however, God's own active righteousness that Paul has in mind here,[10] and the parallelism between the opening and closing statements of this section suggests that Paul is clarifying how that righteousness has now been revealed. It is revealed apart from the law and prophets and—as vv. 25–26 make clear—through the faith of Jesus Christ.[11]

Paul's emphasis on the language of disclosure commends the interpretation of πίστις Ἰησοῦ Χριστοῦ as faith *of* Jesus, for, as Richard Hays points out, it is difficult to see how our faith *in* Jesus would disclose God's eschatological justice.[12] Jesus' own faithfulness, his obedient surrender to his death on the cross, is, however, the counterpart to God's putting him forward as a sacrifice of atonement. God's act would be meaningless without Jesus' faithful obedience, so together—and only together—these two acts reveal God's righteousness.

What is revealed about God's righteousness through this atoning death? Lincoln says that the atonement reveals God's justice (p. 146; see also p. 148).[13] This is certainly the implication of v. 26, but justice is not the whole of it. In v. 25, which is probably a pre-Pauline formulation but one that Paul embraces, the atonement reveals that God's justice does not preclude forbearance. This divine forbearance had always been available, but only as an opportunity (unrealized, in Paul's view) for human repentance (2:4). Now this forbearance takes on an active quality, for God provides through the atonement a means to make it productive. The significant thing about this is that this still conforms to and confirms God's righteousness.

In Rom 5:8 Paul again describes Jesus' death as an atoning act ("while we still were sinners Christ died *for us*"), but here this serves to demonstrate (συνιστάναι) more than God's active forbearance. It demonstrates God's reconciling love, and God's righteousness is revealed as inclusive of God's love.[14]

---

[10] See, e.g., Ulrich Wilckens, *Der Brief an die Römer (Röm 1-5)* (EKKNT 6/1; 2d ed.; Zurich: Benziger, 1987) 187. J. D. G. Dunn concurs, and translates the verbless clause, "God's righteousness comes to expression through faith in Christ" (*Romans 1-8* [WBC 38a; Dallas: Word, 1988] 167).

[11] See also Richard B. Hays, "ΠΙΣΤΙΣ and Pauline Christology: What Is at Stake?" in *Society of Biblical Literature 1991 Seminar Papers* (Atlanta: Scholars Press, 1991) 720.

[12] Ibid., 721.

[13] Hays concurs: "Romans 3 is a defense of God's justice" (ibid.).

[14] Such love is, of course, impartially available to Jews and Gentiles and thus is not to be confused with God's election love for Israel (see, e.g., Deut 10:14–18).

This point is made briefly but powerfully in 8:31–39: in a description of the final judgment where God's justice prevails (cf. 3:5–6), Paul says, "[God] who did not withhold his own Son, but gave him up for all of us, will he not with him also give us everything else? . . . I am convinced that . . . [nothing] will be able to separate us from the love of God in Christ Jesus our Lord." This then becomes the theological position from which Paul tackles the difficult question of Israel's disbelief in chaps. 9–11.[15] As he works out there the "dynamic equilibrium between God's impartiality and faithfulness,"[16] two aspects of God's righteousness, the mediating role of mercy and compassion wins the day (9:13–18; 10:12, 21; 11:28–32). Likewise, the exhortations of chaps. 12–13 focus on love for one another (12:9–21; 13:8–10), so that God's self-disclosure in the atonement establishes a model for human behavior.

In Rom 3:21–26 Paul is concerned not simply to demonstrate how God's justice is revealed by the atonement but also to show how God's forbearance is actively promoted by it. As the argument of the letter evolves, this active promotion of forbearance is seen as the mark of God's love. For those who are "in Christ," love and forbearance will prevail at the final judgment, but not at the expense of righteousness. These qualities will also prevail in God's response to Israel's faithlessness, and a similar love and forbearance must prevail within the church itself.

V. CONCLUSION

Lincoln is surely right to insist that Paul's rhetorical purposes have shaped his argument in Romans, but I am not as confident as he is that we can recover Paul's purpose with enough certainty to rest an interpretation on it. Just as surely, though, the theological conceptions that Paul introduces in 1:18–4:25 had a shaping power of their own, and we are able to identify these concepts in the passage and show how they inform the argument of the letter. The concrete situation in Rome may recede somewhat from view, but the letter's distinctive theological arguments come more clearly into focus.

---

[15] See Johnson, "Romans 9-11," 222.
[16] Ibid.

8 THE STORY OF ISRAEL AND THE THEOLOGY OF ROMANS 5-8

Frank Thielman
Beeson Divinity School, Samford University

ONE OF THE CLASSIC PROBLEMS in the interpretation of Romans lies in deciding how the second major section of the letter is related to the rest of Paul's argument. The problem is not that the great theme of righteousness is missing nor that there are insufficient logical links between this section and the others.[1] The problem, simply stated, is that Israel and its scriptures seem to recede from view. Chapters 1–4 and 9–11 engage in vigorous dialogue with Israel: Paul speaks directly to "the Jew" or to "Israel" and quotes scripture fifty-three times.[2] Chapters 5–8, however, never mention Israel; the term "Jew" never appears; the subject is Christ rather than God; and Paul's biblical quotations shrink to two.[3] The discontinuity seems less drastic if chap. 5 is placed with chaps. 1–4 and if chap. 7 is taken as a digression in defense of the

---

[1] In chaps. 5–8 Paul uses "righteousness" (δικαιοσύνη) eight times, "justify" (δικαιόω) six times, "righteous" (δίκαιος) and "righteous requirement" (δικαίωμα) three times each, and "acquittal" (δικαίωσις) once. At the beginning of the section, the connective "therefore" (οὖν, 5:1) as well as the reappearance of the concepts of boasting (5:2–3, 11), Christ's death for the ungodly (5:6–8), justification by Christ's blood (5:9a), and salvation from God's wrath (5:9b) connect chaps. 5–8 with chaps. 1–4. At the other end, Paul's question in 8:33, "Who will bring charges against the elect [people] of God?" points forward to the discussion in chaps. 9–11.

[2] Paul uses the term "Jew" nine times in chaps. 1–4 and twice in 9–11. "Israel" is the term of choice in chaps. 9–11, where it appears eleven times. Paul quotes scripture twenty-one times in chaps. 1–4 and thirty-two times in chaps. 9–11. See Robin Scroggs, "Paul as Rhetorician: Two Homilies in Romans 1–11," in *Jews, Greeks, and Christians: Religious Cultures in Late Antiquity: Essays in Honor of William David Davies* (ed. Robert Hamerton-Kelly and Robin Scroggs; SJLA 21; Leiden: Brill, 1976) 278.

[3] On the *theo*logical orientation of chaps. 1–4 and 9–11 and the *christo*logical orientation of chaps. 5–8, see Scroggs, "Paul as Rhetorician," 276–77; and Halvor Moxnes, *Theology in Conflict: Studies in Paul's Understanding of God in Romans* (NovTSup 53; Leiden: Brill, 1980) 29–30.

Mosaic Law and as therefore connected thematically with chaps. 1–5; but chaps. 6 and 8 still stand apart, and the thematic connections between 5:1–11 and 8:1–39 go unexplained.[4]

Suggestions about how to solve the problem are manifold. Prior to 1980, when chaps. 1–8 were widely thought to contain the theological substance of the letter, the problem appeared less acute. Those who believed Romans to be a theological compendium viewed Paul's argument in these chapters as a progression from justification in chaps. 1–4(5) to sanctification in chaps. 5(6)–8. Far from posing a problem, Romans 5–8 contained a necessary exposition of an important step in the *ordo salutis*.[5] The *religionsgeschichtliche Schule* responded to this interpretation with the claim that in chaps. 1–5 Paul was thinking primarily as a Jew since he was in dialogue with other Jews but that in chaps. 6–8 Paul's real position emerged, a position derived from Hellenistic concepts.[6] Even Albert Schweitzer, who was uncomfortable with both interpretive trends, believed that Paul's initial line of reasoning in chaps. 3–5 only represented a rhetorically necessary concession to traditional ways of thinking and that it gave way in 6:1–8:1 to the real center of Paul's thought, "the mystical doctrine of redemption through the being-in-Christ."[7] For virtually everyone the crucial evolution from justification to sanctification, from "fighting doctrine" to "Christian conception," or from "subsidiary" to "main crater" had already taken place by the end of chap. 8. In a rare moment of

[4] For these thematic connections, which seem decisive in favor of placing all of chap. 5 with chaps. 6–8, see N. A. Dahl, "Two Notes on Romans 5," *ST* 5 (1952) 37–38.

[5] Among the reformers, John Calvin believed that chap. 5 made the argument of chaps. 1–4 on "the righteousness of faith" clearer by giving illustrations for it and that in chap. 6 Paul moved to a discussion of sanctification. See his essay "The Theme of the Epistle of Paul to the Romans," in *The Epistles of Paul to the Romans and to the Thessalonians* (Grand Rapids: Eerdmans, 1960) 7. Among more recent commentators see Charles Hodge's *A Commentary on Romans* (1835, rev. 1864; Edinburgh: Banner of Truth Trust, 1972) 10–11, 191. The scheme has continued to influence commentators in this century. See R. C. H. Lenski, *The Interpretation of St. Paul's Epistle to the Romans* (Columbus, OH: Wartburg, 1945) 89, 330, 387; and M.-J. Lagrange, *Épître aux Romains* (3d ed.; Paris: Lecoffre, 1922) 99. C. E. B. Cranfield argues that chaps. 6–8 explore "the meaning of the believer's sanctification" (*The Epistle to the Romans* [2 vols.; ICC; Edinburgh: T. & T. Clark, 1975, 1979] 1. 295–96), although he does not believe that Paul's argument is therefore complete at the end of chap. 8 (2. 445–47).

[6] See, e.g., Otto Pfleiderer, *Das Urchristentum, seine Schriften und Lehren, in geschichtlichem Zusammenhang* (Berlin: Georg Reimer, 1887) 117–27, 258–59 (esp. the note to p. 259).

[7] Albert Schweitzer, *The Mysticism of Paul the Apostle* (New York: Henry Holt, 1931) 212–26, esp. 213 and 225–26. E. P. Sanders argues similarly that Paul adopts a traditional description of the human plight in Romans 1–3 for rhetorical reasons but that Paul's real convictions about the human plight appear in Romans 6 (*Paul and Palestinian Judaism: A Comparison of Patterns of Religion* [Philadelphia, Fortress: 1977] 497–502).

agreement among all parties, the embarrassment posed by Paul's return to Israel in chaps. 9–11 was considered a small price to pay for the organizational and evolutionary beauty of these diverse schemes.[8]

Most recent interpreters, however, believe that this way of reading Romans is artificial. Chapters 9–11, they claim, cannot be an appendix to Paul's argument, for the dialogue with Israel in chaps. 1–4 is incomplete without them. The question of how God can be righteous and yet define the covenant so that the Gentile condemns the Jew (2:27) reaches a certain urgency at the end of chap. 4 and is resolved only in chaps. 9–11.[9] The problem posed by the interposition of chaps. 5–8 between 1–4 and 9–11, therefore, has become especially important in recent years.

Occasionally someone takes the dilemma by the horns and argues boldly that chaps. 5–8 are an independent composition, which either Paul or someone else dropped into the epistle at this point for reasons about which we can, at this distance, only speculate.[10] Most recent interpreters, however, opt for less drastic measures. James D. G. Dunn believes that chaps. 1–4 state the gospel and that chaps. 6–8 and 9–11 apply the gospel in two different situations—chaps. 6–8 to the individual and chaps. 9–11 to national Israel.[11] Chapter 5 serves as a bridge between the statement of the gospel in chaps. 1–4 and these two applications of the gospel in chaps. 6–8 and 9–11 respectively.[12] Ulrich Wilckens, similarly, argues that two urgent issues have emerged from chaps. 1–5: whether Paul has destroyed the basis for ethics with his claim that one is justified by faith apart from works of the law and whether Paul has cast a shadow of doubt over God's faithfulness to Israel by his polemic against their confidence in the law. Chapters 6–8 are directed to the first issue, says Wilckens, and chaps. 9–11 to the second.[13] For both interpreters, therefore, the reason Paul's dialogue with Israel recedes from view in chaps. 6–8 is that Paul has intentionally set it aside to deal

---

[8] See the comments of J. Christiaan Beker, *Paul the Apostle: The Triumph of God in Life and Thought* (Philadelphia: Fortress, 1980) 68–69.

[9] See, e.g., Cranfield, *Romans*, 2. 445–46; Ulrich Wilckens, *Der Brief an die Römer* (EKKNT 6; 2 vols.; Cologne: Benziger, 1980) 2. 181–83; Paul Achtemeier, *Romans* (Atlanta: John Knox, 1985) 153–54; James D. G. Dunn, *Romans 9–16* (WBC 38b; Dallas: Word, 1988) 519–20; and John Ziesler, *Paul's Letter to the Romans* (Philadelphia: Trinity Press International, 1989) 233–34.

[10] Scroggs makes the classic case in "Paul as Rhetorician," 272–98.

[11] James D. G. Dunn, *Romans 1–8* (WBC 38a; Dallas: Word, 1988) 242–44. Chapter 8, in Dunn's view, begins the transition from concern with the individual believer to concern with God's cosmic purposes when, in vv. 14–15, Paul refers to the eschatologically oriented concept of adoption (see pp. 243 and 458–59).

[12] Ibid., *Romans 1–8*, 243.

[13] Wilckens, *Der Brief an die Römer*, 2. 3–5, 181–82.

with the moral conduct of the individual and plans to return to it after he finishes the business at hand.[14]

Nearly all of these explanations of the structure of Romans make valid points. Paul's argument *does* advance from a discussion, in Cranfield's terms, of "the revelation of the righteousness which is from God by faith alone" to an examination of "the life promised for those who are righteous by faith."[15] Paul's language *does* take on a tone appropriate to the individual in chaps. 5–8, as the predominance of first person verbs indicates. Paul's concept of dying and rising with Christ *is* difficult to explain in biblical and Jewish terms, unlike his sacrificial language in 3:21–26. Nevertheless, many interpreters of Romans have too readily assumed that the content of chaps. 5–8 has little to do with the history of Israel.[16] It is true that Paul's explicit citations of the Bible grind nearly to a halt; that Paul shifts from the third person to the first in 4:24; and that "the history of Israel," so prominent in the discussion in chaps. 1–4, is less obvious to readers removed by twenty centuries from Paul's context. But the biblical story of Israel is still present, guiding the discussion and defining its terms. We do not see it as clearly because we do not appreciate how important the story of Israel was within the "symbolic universe" of first-century Jews.

I. THE STORY OF ISRAEL AND THE SYMBOLIC UNIVERSE OF FIRST-CENTURY JUDAISM

In their book *The Social Construction of Reality*, Peter L. Berger and Thomas Luckmann argue that societies overcome the dark, marginal experiences that threaten their existence by recourse to a "symbolic universe." This collection of symbols explains terrifying occurrences by asserting a theory of reality that interprets these experiences in familiar terms and therefore renders them

[14] Somewhere between the solutions of Scroggs on one hand and Dunn and Wilckens on the other lie those of Bent Noack, "Current and Backwater in the Epistle to the Romans," *ST* 19 (1965) 154–66; Moxnes, *Theology in Conflict*, 29; and Franz J. Leenhardt, *The Epistle to the Romans: A Commentary* (Cleveland, OH: World, 1961) 24. Noack believes that 1:1–7; 3:9–20, 27–31; 4:1–25; and 9:1–11:36 form the "current" of the letter; 5:1–8:39 the backwater. Moxnes contends that in chaps. 1–4 and 9–11 Paul addresses Jews whereas in chaps. 5–8 he addresses Christians. Leenhardt believes that Paul moves from a statement of the gospel in theological terms to a discussion of its anthropological ramifications. On the significance of the problem together with a survey of some solutions to it, see L. E. Keck, "What Makes Romans Tick?" pp. 7–10 in this volume.

[15] See Cranfield's outline of chaps. 5–8 in *Romans*, 1. xi.

[16] See Scroggs, "Paul as Rhetorician," 281.

harmless to the society's cohesiveness. Dreams, for example, might cause members of a technologically oriented society to wonder whether the dream world or the world of wakefulness is "real." In response, the scientific community explains dreams by means of sophisticated psychological theories. These theories pull the marginal, and sometimes disquieting, experience of dreaming into the ambit of a wider view of reality by explaining dreams in the language of waking reality. Science assures the dreaming person that "reality" resides in the world one experiences during waking hours, not in the dream world one experiences when asleep, and so forestalls a threat to the way the technological society perceives reality. In other similar ways the symbolic universe of science prevents both threatening experiences in everyday life and unusual catastrophes from paralyzing the society it serves.[17]

The most significant "marginal" experience of Jews during Paul's time was the Roman domination of Judea and the scattering of the people of God throughout the world to live under the rule of various foreign powers. This experience seemed to threaten Israel's very election, the most important of the various convictions that held the nation together. As a result, most people looked to the "symbolic universe" which the biblical history of Israel supplied to pull this disturbing enigma into the boundaries of the society's view of reality. In the midst of this ongoing national crisis, the Bible's account of Israel's history provided assurance that, in allowing Israel to suffer, God was only acting within the stipulations of the Sinai covenant. The biblical story of Israel also gave Jews confidence that in spite of Israel's present suffering, their election was still certain and their future bright.[18]

[17] Peter Berger and Thomas Luckmann, *The Social Construction of Reality: A Treatise in the Sociology of Knowledge* (New York: Doubleday, 1966) 92–104. A society's "symbolic universe," as Berger and Luckmann define it, bears some similarity to N. T. Wright's description of a society's "worldview" and to Howard Clark Kee's reference to a society's "life-world." See N. T. Wright, *The New Testament and the People of God* (Minneapolis: Fortress, 1992) 123 n. 5; and Howard Clark Kee, *Knowing the Truth: A Sociological Approach to New Testament Interpretation* (Minneapolis: Fortress, 1989) 105.

[18] According to Berger and Luckmann, a society's stories form part of its assumed or "pre-theoretical" knowledge and therefore play an important role in shaping its view of reality (*Social Construction of Reality,* 65). Members of the Pauline Theology Group have tacitly confirmed this insight when they have found narrative useful in describing Paul's theology. Richard B. Hays argues that a story beginning with Abraham's obedient faith and ending with Jesus' παρουσία ("appearance") is the map on which Paul plots and directs the progress of his communities ("Crucified with Christ: A Synthesis of the Theology of 1 and 2 Thessalonians, Philemon, Philippians, and Galatians," in *Society of Biblical Literature 1988 Seminar Papers* [ed. David J. Lull; Atlanta: Scholars Press, 1988] 318–35). N. T. Wright believes that the place Paul assigns the Messiah in the story of Israel is critical for understanding Paul's theology (*The Climax of the Covenant: Christ and the Law in Pauline Theology* [Edinburgh: T. & T. Clark, 1991]).

The elements of the story are simple and appear frequently in the scriptures, especially in the so-called Deuteronomic History and in the prophets. God made a covenant with Israel at Sinai which required them to obey his commands (Exod 19:1–24:18; Deut 4:13; 5:1–30:20). The covenant stipulated that blessing would come to Israel if they obeyed and detailed various curses if they disobeyed (Lev 26:3–46; Deut 28:1–30:20; cf. Isa 1:19–20). Although Israel's history had, with a few exceptions, been marked by disobedience and curse rather than obedience and blessing, God remained faithful to the relationship he had established with his people and promised that one day he would give them obedient hearts and restore their fortunes.[19]

This interpretation of Israel's history, moreover, was widespread within the Judaism of antiquity. At least from the composition of Deuteronomy, and particularly during the centuries surrounding Paul, ancient Jews appealed to this account of Israel's story in order to explain their suffering. The story is such an important part of the thinking of the author of Tobit, for example, that his tale not only assumes its truth on the national level but raises and answers an important question about it at the individual level: What happens to pious individuals who seem to suffer rather than experience blessing because of their piety?[20] The author of Judith, likewise, registers horror at the thought that

---

In light of such efforts, Jouette Bassler sounds a note of caution about the usefulness of ferreting out Paul's narrative assumptions in order to describe Paul's theology ("Paul's Theology: Whence and Whither? A Synthesis [of sorts] of the Theology of Philemon, 1 Thessalonians, Philippians, Galatians, and 1 Corinthians," in *Society of Biblical Literature 1989 Seminar Papers* [ed. David J. Lull; Atlanta: Scholars Press, 1989] 412–23). Kee, however, provides a sound rationale for including within any description of a New Testament writer's theology an account of the basic assumptions of his social world (*Knowing the Truth,* 70–106).

[19] The following list is representative: Deut 29:19–30:10; 31:16–32:43; 1 Kgs 8:23–53; 2 Chr 6:14–32; Ezra 9:6–15; Neh 9:6–37; Isa 2:2–22; 30:19–33; 42:24–25; 48:18–19; Jer 3:15–18; 4:4; 11:1–13; 22:8–9; 29:10–14; 30:1–33:26; Ezek 5:6; 11:5–21; 16:1–63; 20:5–44; 22:3–23:49; 34:11–31; 36:2–37:28; 39:23–29; Dan 9:4–27. The theology of the Deuteronomic History is the subject of intense debate. A persuasive case for the perspective presented here appears in J. Gordon McConville, *Grace in the End: A Study in Deuteronomic Theology* (Grand Rapids: Zondervan, 1993) 123–39.

[20] Tob 3:3–5 laments Israel's sin and its consequent exile in terms which show that the biblical story of Israel forms part of the author's symbolic universe. The tale itself, moreover, focuses on two Israelites who, although careful to observe the law, suffer severe hardship. With this complication the author seems to be posing the question of how God can be just and allow the righteous to suffer, in seeming violation of the promises in Deuteronomy. The problem is neatly solved by the story's end, however, when both protagonists recover health and happiness through the intervention of God's messenger. G. W. E. Nickelsburg comments that Tobit's outlook is close to Job's, with one major difference: "Whereas the book of Job confines its treatment to an individual, the fate of the nation is of great concern to the author of Tobit" (*Jewish Literature between the Bible and the Mishnah* [London: SCM, 1981] 33).

God's people might once again compromise with Gentile ways and suffer the covenant's curses (Jdt 5:17–21; 8:18–19). Jason of Cyrene's epitomizer tells the story of Israel's oppression and rescue from the Seleucids in order to show that those who keep God's law are victorious and those who break it inevitably suffer defeat.[21] The confessions in Dan 9:4–19; Neh 9:6–37; Bar 1:15–3:8; and Pr Azr 3–22, since they were probably used liturgically, demonstrate that this understanding of Israel's history was common not simply among the sophisticated and literate but among all who recited the synagogue's liturgy.[22]

The best illustration of the importance of this motif during Paul's era, however, comes from Josephus. In the *Jewish War* Josephus appeals to the biblical story of Israel again and again to make sense of his people's suffering during and after the great war with Rome. Just as God had used Nebuchadnezzar to punish his people for their sins, he claims, so God is now using Vespasian and Titus to chasten his people for their sins once again (4.370; 5.368; 6.215, 411; cf. *Ant.* 10.139). The destruction of Herod's temple, therefore, stands in parallel to the destruction of Solomon's temple, a correlation strikingly confirmed for Josephus by his belief that the dates on which the two temples burned corresponded exactly (6.250, 268).[23] The history of sin against God's law which had culminated in the burning of the first temple had continued in Josephus's time with the excesses of the Jewish insurrectionists and had once again culminated in the temple's destruction.

In his later work, *The Antiquities of the Jews,* Josephus elevated the principle of divine retribution, so clearly articulated in the biblical story of Israel, to a description of the way God deals with all people. The principal lesson that the reader of his work should learn, says Josephus, is that

> people who conform to the will of God, and do not venture to transgress laws that have been excellently laid down, prosper in all things beyond

[21] The law-abiding Judas and his army succeed against great odds (2 Macc 8:24–36), whereas hellenizers (4:16–17), Israelite idolaters (12:39–42), and errant high priests (13:7–8) suffer and die because of their sins. In addition, the righteous acknowledge that when they have suffered in the past, God has been mercifully chastening them only so that they will not sin more seriously and receive worse punishment (6:12–17; 7:18, 32–33; cf. 10:4).

[22] On the prayer in Nehemiah, see Leon J. Liebreich, "The Impact of Nehemiah 9:5–37 on the Liturgy of the Synagogue," *HUCA* 32 (1961) 227–37. Bar 1:15–3:8 occurs within a liturgical setting and was probably used liturgically after the composition of Baruch. It is modeled on the prayer in Daniel. The popularity of the story of Israel as it is told in Deuteronomy 28–32 among average diaspora Jews of the third century CE is clear from the grave inscriptions that Paul R. Trebilco cites in *Jewish Communities in Asia Minor* (SNTSMS 69; Cambridge: Cambridge University Press, 1991) 60–69.

[23] In his famous speech before the walls of Jerusalem, Josephus takes the correspondence between these two events in Israel's history even further when he compares himself to Jeremiah. See *J.W.* 5.391–94.

belief, and for their reward are offered by God felicity; whereas, in proportion as they depart from the strict observance of these laws, things (else)
practicable become impracticable, and whatever imaginary good thing
they strive to do ends in irretrievable disasters. (1.14)[24]

Although the work runs to twenty volumes in length, Josephus never loses
sight of this purpose. From the account of the flood in Genesis (*Ant.* 1.72) to
the burning of the temple during the war with Rome (20.166), Josephus
points out at every opportunity that God blesses those, whether individuals or
nations, who keep his laws and punishes all who stray from them. As we might
expect, the theme is especially prominent in Josephus's paraphrase of
Deuteronomy and the historical books, but he often makes it more explicit
than it appears in scripture and on occasion plants it in his sources when he
finds it missing from them.[25]

The Deuteronomic interpretation of Israel's story, then, was an important element in the symbolic universe of ancient Judaism and was especially
important during Israel's two tragic centuries on either side of Paul's career.[26]
If we attempt to enter this symbolic universe and read Romans 5–8 in light of
it, not only does the connection between these chapters and Romans 1–4 and
9–11 become clear, but the interpreter assumes a better position for resolving
some of the classic exegetical difficulties within these chapters as well.

II. THE FUNCTION OF THE STORY OF ISRAEL
IN THE ARGUMENT OF ROMANS 5–8

Most interpreters of Romans agree that, whatever the exact boundary of
the letter's second major section, the purpose of that section is to describe the
new, eschatological era of life to which those justified by faith have obtained
access.[27] It is seldom recognized, however, that Paul draws the language and

---

[24] This is a slightly altered version of the translation of H. St. J. Thackeray, *Josephus* (9 vols.;
LCL; Cambridge, MA: Harvard University Press, 1926–65) 4. 9.

[25] See, e.g., Josephus's retelling of Israel's encounter with the Midianite women in Num
25:1–9 (*Ant.* 4.131–55) and his paraphrase of Judas's short speech to his troops prior to battle
with Gorgias in 1 Macc 3:58–60 (*Ant.* 12.302–4).

[26] See Odil Hannes Steck, *Israel und das gewaltsame Geschick der Propheten: Untersuchungen zur
Überlieferung des deuteronomistischen Geschichtsbildes im Alten Testament, Spätjudentum und Urchris-
tentum* (WMANT 23; Neukirchen-Vluyn: Neukirchener Verlag, 1967); David P. Moessner,
Lord of the Banquet: The Literary and Theological Significance of the Lukan Travel Narrative (Min-
neapolis: Fortress, 1989) 82–91; Wright, *Climax of the Covenant*, 140–41; and James M. Scott,
"The Restoration of Israel," in *The Dictionary of Paul and His Letters* (Downers Grove, IL: Inter-
Varsity, 1993) 796–805.

[27] Dahl argues persuasively that the new section begins with 5:1 ("Two Notes on Romans
5," 37–40). Ernst Käsemann has reservations about Dahl's analysis but nevertheless believes that

the theological symbols he uses to accomplish this purpose in large measure from the biblical story of Israel's disobedience to the law given at Sinai, Israel's punishment in the exile for that disobedience, and Israel's eschatological restoration.[28] The deliberateness with which Paul recalls this story in chaps. 5–8 appears most clearly in the first and last chapters of the section, but allusions to it are probably present in the middle two chapters as well.

The Story of Israel in Romans 5 and 8

Nils A. Dahl demonstrated the close thematic relationship between 5:1–11 and 8:1–39.[29] Justification, hope, eschatological glory, patience in suffering, the love of God, the Spirit of God, and the death of Christ all appear in these two sections. The similarity is so striking that Dahl could describe chaps. 6 and 7 as digressions that Paul used to anticipate misunderstandings of his negative statement about the law in 5:20. In 8:1, says Dahl, Paul "finds his way back to the general themes of 5:1–11."[30] Although Dahl did not say so, one of those themes is that the people of God, newly defined on the basis of faith, are the recipients of God's promises through the prophets to restore Israel's fortunes and make a new covenant with them.

Chapter 5

Chapter 5 consists of two parts, the first of which (vv. 1–11) is commonly recognized as both transitional and introductory. It both sums up the themes of 1:18–4:25 and introduces the new emphases of 5:12–8:39. The second part of chap. 5 (vv. 12–21) lays the foundation for 6:1–8:39 by exploring the theological significance of the concepts of "life" and "death." These two concepts, as carefully defined in 5:12–21, become the chief subject of the chapters

---

the primary dividing line between sections comes at the end of chap. 4 (*Commentary on Romans* [Grand Rapids: Eerdmans, 1980]). See also Karl Barth, *A Shorter Commentary on Romans* (Richmond: John Knox, 1959) 55; Anders Nygren, *Commentary on Romans* (Philadelphia: Muhlenberg, 1949) 187–89; Cranfield, *Romans*, 1. 252–54, who notes the recurrence throughout chaps. 5–8 of the phrase "through Jesus Christ our Lord"; and Ziesler, *Romans*, 134–35. Lagrange (*Romains*, 99), Wilckens (*Römer*, 286–88), and Dunn (*Romans 1–8*, 242–44) believe that the new section begins at 6:1. Paul Achtemeier divides the argument at 4:23 (*Romans*, 89–95). On the importance of the term "life" in these chapters, see Nygren, *Romans*, 188; and Cranfield, *Romans*, 1. 254 n. 1. On the importance of the death–life antithesis, see Dunn, *Romans 1–8*, 301–3.

[28] Dunn's commentary is an exception. It consistently points out the biblical and covenantal significance of Paul's language.

[29] Dahl, "Two Notes on Romans 5," 37–42.

[30] Ibid., 41.

that follow.[31] This much is commonly observed. Less frequently recognized, however, is the role the biblical story of Israel plays in both parts of chap. 5, and especially in Paul's efforts in 5:12–21 to define the principal terms of his subsequent argument.

5:1–11. Paul begins 5:1–11 by describing the new era which believers have entered as a period of righteousness (5:1, 9), peace (5:1), the outpouring of God's love into believers' hearts through the Holy Spirit (5:5), and reconciliation (5:10–11). Paul's use of these terms together and his use of them to characterize the eschatological hope of God's people recall the biblical hope that God's wrath toward a disobedient Israel would one day cease and that the people of God would receive the covenantal promises of blessing. Paul's concern to echo this biblical motif becomes clear when his language and the context in which it occurs are compared to prophetic descriptions of the restored Israel.

Isaiah, Jeremiah, and Ezekiel frequently speak of the period of Israel's restoration as a time of peace characterized by the presence of a new spirit, the remaking of Israel's heart, and the reign of righteousness. Isaiah and Jeremiah depict the period of Israel's disobedience to the covenant as a time when "peace" is absent from Israel (Isa 59:8; Jer 8:11, 15). Not surprisingly, then, in Isaiah and Ezekiel, during the time of restoration God will establish a "covenant of peace" with his people (Isa 54:10; Ezek 34:25; 37:26), and, according to Isaiah, peace will reign during that time because of the presence of righteousness (Isa 32:17–18; 60:17). During this period, God will pour out his spirit on the anointed king (Isa 11:1), on the servant who proclaims the good news of Israel's restoration (Isa 61:1), and on the whole people (Ezek 37:1–14; 39:29).[32] This new spirit, moreover, will re-create Israel's heart to make it "new" (Ezek 11:19; 18:31; 36:26).[33]

Nowhere does the similarity between Paul's language in 5:1–11 and the

---

[31] The statistics on the use of terms related to "death" and "life" in the undisputed Pauline epistles show this clearly. In these letters Paul uses the term "die" (ἀποθνήσκω) a total of 42 times: 23 in Romans, of which 17 are in Romans 5–8. The case is similar with "death" (θάνατος): Paul uses it a total of 45 times: 22 in Romans, of which 21 are in chaps. 5–8. "Life" (ζωή) appears 25 times: 14 in Romans, of which 12 are in chaps. 5–8; and "live" (ζῶ) a total of 51 times: 23 in Romans, of which 12 are in chaps. 5–8. If we shape these figures into percentages, 45 percent of the references to "death" in the undisputed letters and 32 percent of the references to "life" occur in Romans 5–8. These are impressive figures for such a narrow slice of the Pauline corpus.

[32] At Ezek 39:29, the LXX has "And I will no longer turn my face away from them since I have poured out my *wrath* upon the house of Israel, says the Lord."

[33] In 11:19 the MT reads "one heart" and the LXX, "another heart." The Aramaic targums and the Peshitta, however, have "new heart."

biblical interpretation of Israel's history appear stronger, however, than in Isa 32:15–17. Here the prophet says that Israel's punishment will continue

> until a spirit from on high is poured out (יְעָרֶה; LXX ἐπέλθῃ) upon us and the wilderness becomes a fruitful field, and the fruitful field is deemed a forest. Then justice will dwell in the wilderness, and righteousness (צְדָקָה; LXX τὰ ἔργα τῆς δικαιοσύνης) will be peace (שָׁלוֹם; LXX εἰρήνη) and the result of righteousness (צְדָקָה; LXX δικαιοσύνη) quietness and trust forever (NRSV).

The outpouring of God's spirit, the presence of righteousness, and the combination of righteousness with peace are used to describe the eschatological period of hope in much the way that Paul uses these concepts to describe the same period in Rom 5:1–5. Although the resemblance is not so close that we can speak of direct dependence, it is close enough to show that Paul conceived of the eschatological period to which believers now had access as the final chapter in the biblical story of Israel.[34]

5:12–21. Paul has briefly mentioned the key terms "life" and "death" already in 5:1–11 (v. 10; cf. vv. 6–8), but in 5:12–21 he explores the theological significance of these terms at length in order to define them carefully for the subsequent argument.[35] He does this through referring to the role that death and life play in three interlocking stories—the story of Adam, the story of Christ, and the story of Israel. The first two stories claim most of the scholarly attention given to this passage, but the story of Israel is as important for Paul's purposes in 5:12–21 as the other two. Both rhetorical and theological considerations demonstrate this.

Israel's story first appears in 5:13–14, where Paul interrupts his comparison of Adam and Christ with the statement that although sin is only "reckoned" in the presence of law, death nevertheless reigned over those who had not sinned against a specific command. The rhetorical usefulness of placing this statement at this position in the argument is not entirely clear. Paul's point, after all, is simply that even people who did not violate a specific command of

---

[34] The remarkable parallels between Paul's language in 5:1–11 and the language of the opening prayer in the first introductory letter to 2 Maccabees increase the likelihood that Paul's use of the terms "peace," "heart," and "reconciliation" alludes to the prophetic promises of Israel's restoration. In 2 Macc 1:2–6, as in Rom 5:1–11, the suffering of God's people is in focus (v. 5b), and the expected time of restoration is described using precisely these terms (vv. 3–5).

[35] By mentioning death and life in 5:6–10 Paul is following his usual custom of introducing at the end of one section the key terms he will use in the next. On this feature of Paul's discourse in Romans, see Nils Alstrup Dahl, *Studies in Paul: Theology for the Early Christian Mission* (Minneapolis: Augsburg, 1977) 82–83.

God, as Adam had, nevertheless sinned and so were subject to death.[36] All Paul
needed to say in order to make this point was that "death reigned . . . even
over those who had not sinned in the likeness of the transgression of Adam"
(5:14). But Paul is determined, even at the cost of clouding his immediate
argument, to point out the similarity between what happened in Adam's case
and what happened in Israel's: "For until the law sin was in the world, but sin
is not reckoned when there is no law; nevertheless, death reigned from Adam
until Moses" (5:13–14a).[37] Paul's discourse, therefore, runs ahead of his argument to reveal an important basic assumption: Israel had violated the covenant
that God established with them at Sinai and so had received the penalty of
death, which, according to that covenant, all such violators would suffer.[38]
Although mention of the law of Moses obfuscated Paul's argument by delay-
ing the conclusion to his statement in 5:12 until 5:18b, the story of Israel's
violation of the covenant at Sinai was so close to the surface of Paul's thinking at this point in his discourse that, almost in the manner of a Freudian slip,
it broke through.

In 5:20–21 the story of Israel's violation of the covenant with God at Sinai
again comes to the surface, but, unlike its appearance in 5:13–14, here it is
well integrated into the flow of Paul's discourse. After drawing his comparison between Adam and Christ to a close in 5:19, Paul moves to another stage
of salvation history, the period of the law's intrusion, to draw a similar comparison between what happened when the law was given to Israel at Sinai and
what happened in Christ. At first Paul's reference to the giving of the law
looks like a relatively unimportant appendix to an argument he had made previously and more impressively in 5:12–19 by reference to Adam.[39] Much of
5:12–19, however, is devoted to a series of caveats and clarifications designed
to prevent the reader from taking the similarity between Adam and Christ too
far (5:13–18a). Once these are removed, Paul's statements about the parallels
between Adam and Christ in 5:12, 18b–19 turn out to be nearly as simple as
the comparison between Israel and Christ in 5:20–21. In 5:12 and 18b–19
Paul says that the disobedience of Adam sent many on a downward spiral

[36] Cranfield, *Romans*, 1. 282.

[37] For the translation of ἀλλά as "nevertheless" in 5:14, see BAGD, s.v., 2.

[38] J. Paul Sampley comments insightfully that in certain passages Paul opens a window onto
his theology by revealing his "primary assumptions." These, Sampley says, are important
moments in Paul's letters, for they reveal the basic terms of his theological thinking. See "From
Text to Thought World: The Route to Paul's Ways," in *Pauline Theology I: Thessalonians,
Philippians, Galatians, Philemon* (ed. Jouette M. Bassler; Minneapolis: Fortress, 1991) 12. See
also Kee, *Knowing the Truth*, 103.

[39] Thus Käsemann regards 5:20–21 as a "digression" which "unexpectedly . . . returns to the
question put in v. 13" (*Romans*, 158).

toward death and that the obedience of Christ has, in a similar but opposite way, rectified this situation. In 5:20–21 Paul says that the law given to Israel increased sin by defining it more specifically and that in a similar but opposite way God caused grace to increase "through Jesus Christ our Lord."[40] The fundamental point of Paul's discussion in 5:12–21, then, is that Christ is God's answer to the disasters created by Adam's sin and Israel's violation of the covenant, and the story of Israel's failure to keep the terms of the covenant is parallel to, and on an equal footing with, the story of Adam's failure in this argument.

The conclusion to which these rhetorical observations have led is confirmed by an examination of the theological function of Israel's story in 5:12–21. The theme that holds Romans 5–8 together as a discrete section of Paul's total argument is how God has brought life out of death "through Jesus Christ our Lord." It cannot be denied that this movement from death to life is described in terms that take much of their meaning from the story of Adam's fall, with its result of death for all, and the story of Christ's death and resurrection, with its result of life for all. Paul's language of death and life in 5:12–21 and therefore his use of these concepts elsewhere in the section, however, are also indebted to the story of Israel. Paul uses this third story in 5:12–21 to emphasize the depth of the human plight: Adam began the process of disobedience (5:12a); all humanity followed his lead (5:12b, 18a, 19a); and the situation grew worse with the coming of the law and Israel's disobedience to it (5:20). The result has been "death" for all (5:21a), a result that is remedied by the gift of life "through Jesus Christ our Lord" (5:21b).

Paul can assume a connection between violation of the law in Israel and death in 5:20–21, however, only because he shares with his readers a symbolic universe that includes the biblical story of Israel. A prominent part of the story as it is preserved both in the scriptures and in the literature of Paul's day is Israel's toil under the penalty of death, which Israel received for violating the covenant. In Deut 30:15–20 (LXX) Moses places life (ζωή) and death (θάνατος) before Israel: life if they obey the commandments that Moses has spelled out, and death if they change their heart (καρδία) and worship other gods. "Life" is used figuratively to refer to numerous descendants and length of days in the land of promise (30:15, 20; cf. Deut 4:1; 32:47); "death" conversely means destruction and exile (28:15–29:29). Ezekiel picks up this

---

[40] The adverb "where" (οὗ) of 5:20b probably refers to Israel as the place where sin increased; see Cranfield, *Romans*, 1. 293; and Wright, *Climax of the Covenant*, 39–40, 196. Wright believes that "where" also refers to Christ, who, as the Messiah, represented Israel. Sin was concentrated not only onto Israel, therefore, but onto their Messiah, who was then able to "condemn sin in the flesh" (8:3).

theme in his effort to persuade the exilic community that their present suffering is a result of their violation of the Sinaitic covenant (18:1–32; 20:11, 21, 25; 33:10–20) and is designed to lead to their repentance, cleansing, and restoration (20:40–49; 33:29). The prayer of confession in Nehemiah 9 similarly laments Israel's repeated disobedience to God's "ordinances, by the observance of which a person shall live" (9:29).

The reason why the story of Adam, the story of Christ, and the story of Israel are linked together in 5:12–21 now becomes clear. All three protagonists experienced death at the hands of sin, but only two of the three—Israel and Christ—experience life at the hands of God: Christ by means of the resurrection and Israel by means of their eschatological restoration. Israel, then, is the middle term between Adam and Christ, the two great representatives of death and life. God's people form the historical stage on which the consequences of the actions of these two metahistorical figures are played out: like Adam, postexilic Israel had experienced "death" as the penalty for violating God's commandments, and, like Christ, the eschatological people of God would experience the covenant's blessing of life. The stories of Adam and Christ give theological depth to the critical terms "death" and "life," and the story of Israel contributes to the definition of these terms as well. Wherever these two terms appear in chaps. 5–8, therefore, part of their meaning comes from the story of Israel's death in the exile and God's promise to restore his people to life.

Chapter 8

When we move from chap. 5 to chap. 8, we find that the story of Israel remains a prominent feature of Paul's argument. Paul again uses the complex of terms so popular among the prophets in describing Israel's restoration to refer to the eschatological era that believers have entered. "Spirit" reappears, as do "peace," "righteousness," "heart," and, of course, "life." Much more frequent in chap. 8 than in chap. 5, however, are references to the law. Having shown in chap. 7 that the law was good and should have been obeyed, Paul now advances the thesis that the eschatological era is one in which "the requirement of the law" is fulfilled in believers (8:4) who, because of the Spirit, are able to submit to it (8:7–9). "For the mind of the flesh is death," he says, "but the mind of the Spirit is life and peace, because the mind of the flesh is at enmity with God, for it does not submit to God's law, nor is it able to do so" (8:6–7). Paul alludes here to the blessings and curses of Deuteronomy 28 and Leviticus 26 to say that the time of warfare and death because of Israel's disobedience to the covenant of life and peace (cf. Mal 2:5) is over, and that the time of God's favor has come.

The allusions to those passages continue in Paul's assertion that God has rescued believers from slavery and fear a few sentences later (8:15). Paul recalls the description of Israel's exile in Deut 28:64–68, where Moses says that if Israel is disobedient to the law the Lord will scatter them among the nations (28:64), where they will have a "trembling heart, failing eyes, and languishing spirit" (28:65). There, we read, Israel will live lives of dread and will sell themselves into slavery (28:66–68). God has rescued the believing community from this plight, Paul tells the Romans, "for you have not received a spirit of slavery again with its consequence of fear but you have received a Spirit of adoption by which we cry, 'Abba, Father!'" (8:15; cf. v. 23).[41] In light of (γάρ, 8:15) this rescue from the plight into which disobedience has plunged God's people, Paul is able to call believers "children of God" (8:14), a term Deuteronomy uses of God's covenant people (Deut 14:1) and Hosea of their eschatological restoration (Hos 1:10).[42]

He is also able, in light of this, to end the chapter and this whole section of his argument with a series of rhetorical denials that the kind of suffering the biblical story of Israel describes as punishment for violation of the law will be able to separate the believer from the love of God demonstrated eschatologically through the sacrifice of Christ (8:32, 35a). The description of this suffering in 8:35b is drawn largely from the portraits of the suffering of God's disobedient people painted in Deuteronomy 28 and Leviticus 26. Deut 28:53, 55, and 57 link together "tribulation" (θλίψις) and "distress" (στενοχωρία) to describe the terrors of famine which will come to Israel if they disobey the law.[43] A few verses earlier Deut 28:48 links "nakedness" (γυμνότης) and "famine" (λιμός) to describe the terrors of military defeat which will come to Israel as a result of disobedience. Lev 26:25 and 33 use "sword" (μαχαίρα) in

---

[41] James M. Scott has demonstrated that Jews of Paul's era understood 2 Sam 7:14a as a reference to God's "adoption" of his people in the period of eschatological restoration (*Adoption as Sons of God: An Exegetical Investigation into the Background of ΥΙΟΘΕΣΙΑ in the Pauline Corpus* [WUNT 2/48; Tübingen: Mohr (Siebeck), 1992] 96–117). This understanding of the term, Scott argues (pp. 221–66), informs Paul's use of it in 8:15 and 23.

[42] Dunn, *Romans 1–8*, 451. In 9:26 Paul will use the phrase "children of God" again but this time in a direct quotation of Hos 1:10, which refers specifically to Gentile believers as part of God's eschatologically restored people. Believing Jews are also included according to the quotation of Isa 10:22 in 9:27. On this, see Richard B. Hays, *Echoes of Scripture in the Letters of Paul* (New Haven: Yale University Press, 1989) 66–68.

[43] Paul links these words together in 2:9 also. See Dunn, *Romans 1–8*, 88. In 2:9, as in Deuteronomy, the words indicate the punishment that comes "to every person who does evil, the Jew first and also the Greek." Even the idea that the curses of the law apply to Gentiles is anticipated in Deuteronomy. See, e.g., Deut 8:19–20. If the list of tribulations in 8:35 is indebted to Stoic ideas, as Lagrange believes (*Romains*, 218, following Rudolf Bultmann), Paul has nevertheless given it a biblical shape.

a similar way. The suffering that Paul and other believers experience as the people of God, therefore, is strangely analogous to the suffering that the disobedient and unrestored Israel experienced because of their sins. Paul can assert in a rhetorical question that suffering cannot separate the believing community from the love of Christ; but that it is present at all during the period of eschatological restoration is puzzling.

Perhaps this is why Paul chose in 8:35 to summarize his list of evils with a quotation from Psalm 44 (LXX 43). This Psalm is probably postexilic (43:12–15) and laments Israel's defeat and suffering at the hands of their enemies during a period when many in the nation believed that they had learned the lesson of disobedience and had diligently tried to keep the law. The experience of suffering within this context, then, retains an enigmatic quality:

> All these things have come upon us; but we have neither forgotten you nor
> dealt unrighteously with your covenant. Our hearts have not turned back
> to the former things and you have turned the paths of our lives (τριβοὺς
> ἡμῶν) aside from your way. (43:19–20 LXX)

The Psalm recognizes the tension that exists when a restored Israel, whose covenant relationship with God is unbroken, nevertheless suffers. It is precisely this kind of tension that Paul describes when he summarizes the puzzling suffering of the believing community in the words of this Psalm: "For your sake we are being killed all day long; we are accounted as sheep for the slaughter" (8:36; cf. Ps 43:23 LXX).

Summary

To those who shared Paul's symbolic universe, therefore, the language that the apostle used to describe the movement of the believing community from death to life in Romans 5 and 8 would have resounded with echoes from the story of Israel's disobedience to the law, subsequent suffering, and eventual restoration. In 5:12–21 Paul refers to the story explicitly and uses it as part of the theological foundation for his discussion of death and life. In 5:1–11 and 8:1–39 Paul uses many of the same terms that the Bible uses to describe Israel's restoration, uses them in contexts similar to the biblical ones, and often links them together in ways reminiscent of their use in the prophets. He even explains the problem of a righteous but suffering community in the words of a Psalm whose subject is the tension that a restored Israel experienced when, despite their restoration to piety, they suffered. Neither Israel nor its scriptures, therefore, have receded from view in Romans 5 and 8. Although explicit references are rare, the story of Israel is still present, filling Paul's language with theological significance and providing Paul's symbols with a theological context.

The Story of Israel in Romans 6 and 7

Echoes of Israel's story do not resound as loudly in chaps. 6 and 7, and investigation must proceed cautiously to avoid the exegetical disease that Samuel Sandmel has famously described as "parallelomania."[44] There are, however, two encouraging indications that the attempt to find the story of Israel in these chapters is not a symptom of that plague. First, we have already seen that these chapters are bounded on either side by clear allusions to the story of Israel. Paul was thinking in these terms as he wrote chaps. 5–8, therefore, and so we may reasonably expect allusions to the story of Israel in chaps. 6 and 7. Second, if the story of Israel forms the context of Paul's argument, then several difficult texts become easier to understand. We can safely assume that if parallels to Israel's story help to explain problems as difficult as the meaning of 6:17, Paul's abruptness at 7:1, and the antecedent of the "I" in 7:7–25, then we are in the presence not of parallelomania but of its cure.[45]

Chapter 6

To Jews steeped in the Deuteronomic perspective on Israel's history and committed to the premise that what happened to God's people happened through God's foreordination, Paul's claim that the law caused sin and its penalty of death to increase (5:20) may have been less shocking than interpreters commonly suppose. More shocking, perhaps, was Paul's assertion that God's wrath had been removed, peace had come, and reconciliation had taken place not when his chastened people were praying prayers such as the one in Nehemiah 9 but while they were still impious sinners (5:6–8, 20). Would this not mean that "we should remain in sin in order that grace might abound?"

Paul tackles this question first in 6:1–11 by speaking of the believer's death with Christ and then in 6:12–23 by using the metaphor of slavery. Echoes of the story of Israel in 6:1–11 are attenuated at best, but in 6:12–23 they resound more clearly. They begin with Paul's provocative statement that sin cannot rule over believers because they are "not under law but under grace" (6:14) and the repetition of the question at issue, "What therefore? Should we sin because we are not under law but under grace?" (6:15). The phrase "under

---

[44] "That extravagance among scholars which first overdoes the supposed similarity in passages and then proceeds to describe source and derivation as if implying literary connection flowing in an inevitable or predetermined direction" (Samuel Sandmel, "Parallelomania," *JBL* 81 [1962] 1). The antidote may be found in Hays, *Echoes*, 29–32.

[45] Hays writes that if, *inter alia*, the proposed echo renders a reading of a passage that is consistent with other themes in Paul and makes sense within its immediate context, then it is probably not a product of the reader's imagination (*Echoes*, 30–31).

law" in these two verses has been the subject of much debate, but the simplest explanation of it makes its meaning here consistent with the meaning of 5:13–14 and 5:20–21, the two passages in which Paul last referred to the law.[46] There, as we have seen, he traces the history of sin into the period of Moses. During that time, sin became worse because Israel violated the now unambiguously expressed will of God and experienced the penalty of death as a result. If this reading is correct, then "under law" in 6:15 refers to existence under the penalty of death—the curse of the law—which according to the biblical interpretation of Israel's history, came to Israel as a result of their disobedience.[47] By claiming that believers are no longer "under law" Paul is simply saying that they no longer live in the era during which, according to the biblical account of Israel's history, the law pronounced its curse of death upon the disobedient.[48]

This means in turn that Paul's comparison of the believer to a slave in 6:15-23 may also be indebted to the story of Israel. Usually the metaphor is interpreted within the context of the common Greco-Roman institution of slavery, and that is probably the primary context from which Paul's metaphor draws its power.[49] We should not forget, however, that the biblical portrait of God as redeemer, a portrait which Paul reflects in this letter (3:24; 8:23), depends for its forcefulness on the assumption that Israel was enslaved either to foreign nations (Deut 7:8; 9:26; Isa 41:14; 43:1, 14; 52:3; 54:5) or to sin (Ps 130:7–8; Isa 44:22). The connection between Israel's enslavement to foreign nations and its sin, moreover, was clear to postexilic biblical writers. The great prayers of confession in Ezra 9 and Nehemiah 9 both use the imagery of slavery to describe the suffering into which Israel's violation of the law had led them. After confessing that from ancient days Israel had been handed over to captivity for their sins, Ezra comments:

> But now for a brief moment favor has been shown by the Lord our God, who has left us a remnant, and given us a stake in his holy place, in order that he may brighten our eyes and grant us a little sustenance in our slav-

[46] On the connection between "under law" (ὑπὸ νόμον) in 6:14 and "the law slipped in so that the trespass might increase" (νόμος δὲ παρεισῆλθεν, ἵνα πλεονάσῃ τὸ παράπτωμα) in 5:20a, see Lagrange, *Romains*, 154; Nygren, *Romans*, 248; Dunn, *Romans 1–8*, 339; and Ziesler, *Romans*, 165.

[47] See Cranfield, *Romans*, 1. 320.

[48] *Contra* Dunn (*Romans 1–8*, 340), who believes that Paul refers to the "social function of the law" here, and Barrett (*Romans*, 129), who believes that the phrase refers to "the upward striving of human religion and morality."

[49] See Dale B. Martin, *Slavery as Salvation: The Metaphor of Slavery in Pauline Christianity* (New Haven: Yale University Press, 1990) 61–62; he does, however, recognize biblical influence on Paul's use of the metaphor.

ery. For we are slaves; yet our God has not forsaken us in our slavery. (Ezra 9:8–9 NRSV)

Nehemiah, similarly, summarizes the history of Israel's disobedience to the law and then describes the result this way: "Here we are, slaves to this day—slaves in the land that you gave to our ancestors to enjoy its fruit and its good gifts" (Neh 9:36 NRSV). Josephus's paraphrase of Deuteronomy shows us, moreover, that this concept was still alive during Paul's time. Josephus summarizes the message of Deuteronomy in a speech of Moses which emphasizes blessing for obedience to the law and suffering for neglect of it. Moses warns the people that the wealth they are about to inherit by conquering Canaan should not lead them to neglect their covenant with God,

> For, should ye be carried away by it into a contempt and disdain for virtue, ye will lose even that favor which ye have found of God; and, having made him your enemy, ye will forfeit that land, which ye are to win, beaten in arms and deprived of it by future generations with the grossest ignominy, and, dispersed throughout the habitable world, ye will fill every land and sea with your servitude (ἐμπλήσετε καὶ γῆν καὶ θαλάσσαν τῆς αὐτῶν δουλείας, *Ant.* 4.190).[50]

If this imagery lies behind Paul's use of the word here, then he is reminding his readers that they have been delivered from the bondage of "death" in which Israel labored because of their disobedience and subsequent punishment under the curse of the law (6:14–15) and have now become slaves of obedience with the result that they stand in a new covenant relationship with God (ὑπακοῆς εἰς δικαιοσύνην, 6:16). They have entered the period of restoration, when, according to Isaiah, "righteousness" (צְדָקָה; LXX δικαιοσύνη) will be the "taskmaster" (נֹגֵשׂ; LXX ἐπίσκοπος) of God's people (60:17; cf. Rom 6:18–23).

The new covenant relationship, Paul next says, is marked by obedience from the heart to the type of teaching the Romans received. The controversy surrounding these words is notorious,[51] but a measure of clarity can be

---

[50] This is Thackeray's translation in *Josephus* 4. 567.

[51] Some believe that the words are not Paul's own but an interpolation (e.g., Rudolf Bultmann, "Glossen im Römerbrief," in *Exegetica* [Tübingen: Mohr (Siebeck), 1967] 278–84; and Victor Paul Furnish, *Theology and Ethics in Paul* [Nashville: Abingdon, 1968] 196–98). Others believe that Paul is simply being inconsistent in denying the validity of law as an ethical guide and then introducing a new law (C. H. Dodd, *The Epistle of Paul to the Romans* [London: Collins, 1959] 117; John Knox, "The Epistle to the Romans," in *The Interpreter's Bible* [12 vols.; Nashville: Abingdon, 1954] 9. 483–84). Still others believe that Paul speaks not of the handing on of a fixed moral code in these verses but of obedience to "the way of life demanded by the gospel" (Cranfield, *Romans*, 1. 324) or of commitment to "something like a baptismal creed" (Käsemann, *Romans*, 181).

brought to Paul's language by recognizing that here too Paul is using imagery drawn from the biblical story of Israel's turbulent relationship with their God. The words "obedient from the heart" recall the language of Deut 30:14 (LXX), where the commandments are said to be easy to do (ποιέω) because they are in the Israelites' heart, and 30:17, where the Israelites are warned not to change their hearts so that they do not obey (εἰσακούω) the commandments.[52] Paul's choice of words in v. 17 also resembles the language of Jer 38:33–34 (LXX), which not only promises a new heart to the covenant people but indicates that the teaching of God will be so indelibly written on their hearts that they will not need to teach it to one another. Ezek 11:19–21 and 36:26–27 likewise speak of a time when God will give to Israel a new heart of flesh after plucking out their heart of stone, with the result that Israel will obey God's precepts and commands. The story of Israel's disobedience together with the hope that God would one day correct their disobedience, therefore, seems to be the context within nearest reach for understanding what Paul means in this otherwise enigmatic verse.

The same is true of v. 19.[53] Here Paul uses a series of terms which recall the biblical language of sanctity prominent in both the law and the prophets.[54] Paul tells his readers:

> For just as you presented your members as slaves to impurity (ἀκαθαρσίᾳ) and lawlessness (ἀνομίᾳ) for the purpose of lawlessness (εἰς τὴν ἀνομίαν), so now present your members as slaves to righteousness for the purpose of sanctification (εἰς τὴν ἁγιασμόν).

The terms "impurity" (ἀκαθαρσία), "lawlessness" (ἀνομία), and "sanctification" (ἁγιασμός) recall one of the primary functions of Israel's covenant with God—the separation of Israel from other people as a "priestly kingdom and a holy nation" (Exod 19:6).[55] Ἀκαθαρσία is used in the Septuagint not only to

---

[52] On the meaning of this passage, see the perceptive comments of McConville, *Grace in the End*, 137–38.

[53] Verse 18 repeats the substance of v. 16, and so what was said in connection with v. 16 is true of v. 18 as well.

[54] For God's desire that Israel should be holy, see particularly Lev 11:44–45; 15:31; 18:1–5, 24; 19:2; 20:24–26; and 22:32. For the hope that God would one day restore Israel's violated sanctity, see Ezek 20:33–44; 22:15; 36:25, 29, 33; 37:23, 28. For the literary connections between Ezekiel and Leviticus, see in particular Ezek 18:5–9 and the analysis in Walther Zimmerli, *Ezekiel 1: A Commentary on the Book of the Prophet Ezekiel, Chapters 1–24* (Hermeneia; Philadelphia: Fortress, 1979) 379–82.

[55] James Barr has spoken eloquently and correctly about the fallacy of isolating particular Old Testament words and then claiming that when New Testament writers use them they import into the words some special biblical significance (*The Semantics of Biblical Language* [Oxford: Oxford University Press, 1961] 263–82). He concedes, however, that "some words become

indicate the kind of ritual impurity that every Israelite contracted but also to refer to the conduct of those who lived outside the law, whether Gentiles (1 Esdr 1:49; 2 Esdr 9:11) or disobedient Israelites. Ezekiel especially uses the term to describe the flagrant violation of the laws of sanctity which led Israel to experience the curses of the covenant and from which God would eventually deliver his people.[56] If Paul's use of the story of Israel in chaps. 5–8 is as prominent as we have argued above, then this word refers not simply to "immorality" but to immorality as a violation of the sanctity God requires of his people. The same can be said of ἀνομία, which, like ἀκαθαρσία, was frequently used simply to mean wickedness but which, by the Hasmonean period, had become a special term for both Gentiles and Jews, who, by their violation of the laws of Israel's sanctity, had placed themselves outside Israel's covenant.[57]

Paul intends to say, however, that his readers have moved from outside to inside the circle of blessing created by God's restoration of the covenant with his people. Now, he says, they must present their members as slaves to righteousness "for the purpose of sanctification" (εἰς ἁγιασμόν). The word ἁγιασμός ("sanctification") is used infrequently in the Septuagint and is not used to refer specifically to the people of God, but, when it is used, it refers to the special nature of that which is unique to the people of God, whether God himself (Sir 17:10; 2 Macc 14:36), the temple (3 Macc 2:18), or the sacrifices (Sir 7:31; 2 Macc 2:17). Far more importantly, it participates in the semantic field of the term ἅγιος ("holy"), which in the Septuagint is the adjective of choice for describing the distinctiveness of God's people.[58]

In 6:19, then, Paul wants to remind his readers that they have crossed the boundary of sanctity from "impurity" and "lawlessness" to "sanctification." This change in status means that they are in a right covenant relationship with God (6:16, 18, 19) and that they have moved from existence under the curse of death (6:21, 23), which the law pronounces on all who are unclean, lawless, and unholy, to existence under the blessing of life (6:22–23), which the law promises to all those who live within the ambit of God's covenant.

In summary, if we read Paul's references to the law in 6:14–15 through the lens of his reference to it in 5:20, and if we then take 6:14–15 as a clue to the

---

specialized" and that, when this happens, the significance of these words in one context may be transported to another. It is this kind of specialization that the words "impurity," "lawlessness," and "sanctification" possess.

[56] See Ezek 9:9; 22:15; 24:11; 36:17, 25, 29; 39:24; cf. Mic 2:10 and Lam 1:9.

[57] See 1 Macc 3:5–6; 7:5; 9:23, 58, 69; 11:25; and the comments in Dunn, *Romans 1–8*, lxix–lxx, 206, and 346–47.

[58] See, e.g., Exod 19:6; Deut 7:6; 26:19; Jer 2:2–3; Leviticus 17–26; Isa 4:3; 1 Macc 10:39, 44; and Wis 18:9.

conceptual world in which Paul is thinking as he constructs his argument in 6:12–23, enigmatic texts appear less strange and we begin to appreciate how deeply indebted the structure of Paul's theology is to the biblical story of Israel: Paul believed his Roman readers to be the purified and restored Israel for which Ezekiel and others had hoped.

Chapter 7

If this understanding of 6:12–23 is correct, then Paul's facile movement into the topic of the law in 7:1–6 should seem less surprising than it usually does to interpreters. Many believe that apart from his brief references to the law in 5:20 and 6:14–15, Paul has concentrated on other matters in chaps. 5 and 6. It then comes as a surprise that Paul introduces his lengthy discussion of the law in 7:1–25 with the phrase, "Or do you not know?" (ἀγνοεῖτε), a phrase which implies that

> if the people addressed really know—the assumption is that they surely must—the truth which is about to be stated (in every case a ὅτι [because] clause follows), then they ought to recognize the truth, or agree with the sentiment, expressed or implicit in something that has been said already (*usually immediately before the formula is introduced*).[59]

Because of their belief that the law has not been central to Paul's argument in chaps. 5–6, however, most commentators are obligated to argue that in 7:1 Paul has not followed his usual custom but has instead used the phrase "Or do you not know?" to refer all the way back to his statement about the law in 6:14b.[60] If, on the other hand, the story of Israel's violation of the law, punishment, and restoration has defined the terms of Paul's discussion in 6:12–23, then 7:1 looks perfectly natural.

If Paul's mention of the law in 7:1 should occasion less surprise than it usually does, however, what he says about the law in 7:1–6, should probably occasion more. After hinting in 6:17 that the new covenant of Jeremiah 31(38):31–34 with its heart-inscribed law has been fulfilled in those who believe in Jesus Christ, Paul now says unequivocally that we "have no more to do with" the law (7:2, 6; BAGD s.v. καταργέω). Like the husband in Paul's illustration, we "have died to the law through the body of Christ," and so, like the wife, we are free "to belong to another" (7:4). It is not easy to reconcile Paul's positive and negative statements about the law in this letter, but if the story of Israel's

[59] Cranfield, *Romans*, 1. 332, my emphasis.
[60] Lagrange (*Romains*, 160), Dodd (*Romans*, 119), and Cranfield (*Romans*, 1. 332) all comment on the abruptness with which Paul introduces the law into the discussion at 7:1.

disobedience and restoration is as prominent in chaps. 5–6 as the argument above indicates, then at least here Paul seems to say in a more complete way what he has already said in 6:14–15—that the eschatological community of believers no longer labors under the curse of the Mosaic Law but is subject to a new "law," which Paul identifies with the new covenant of the Spirit and of peace about which the prophets so frequently speak. This seems to be Paul's meaning in 7:6 when he says that "we have been set free from the law, having died to that by which we used to be suppressed, so that we serve in the newness of the Spirit and not in the oldness of the letter."[61]

Such an interpretation of the prophetic passages about God's establishment of a new covenant was not, of course, the typically Jewish one. Jews, whether Christians or not, would probably have understood the prophets to be predicting a restoration of the eternally valid Mosaic covenant. In light of this, Paul must address the objection that he has, in a circuitous way, argued that the law is not good. Just as at the end of chap. 5 Paul had placed a new twist on the old story of Israel and had been compelled to warn against misunderstanding as a result, so here Paul faces a new misunderstanding and produces a lengthy argument against it. Using the same rhetorical signal that he used in 6:1 ("What, then, shall we say?"), Paul in 7:7 addresses the question, Is the law sin?

Paul's basic answer to the question in 7:7–13 is clear enough: the law, far from being sin, is exonerated from blame because sin took advantage of the law to cause "me" to disobey God. The fault lies with sin, therefore, and not with the holy, righteous, and good law. The details of Paul's argument, however, particularly the identity of the infamous "I" and the period of time to which the secondary tenses in the passage point, are matters of hot dispute.

It has become increasingly popular for interpreters to see the story of Adam, already recounted in 5:12–21, behind the "I" and the past tenses of 7:7–12. Since W. G. Kümmel's revolutionary work, most interpreters have been willing to view the "I" in Romans 7 as figurative rather than as a straightforward reference to Paul himself,[62] and with the door open to a figurative interpretation, Adam has seemed to many to be the most likely candidate for the reality behind the figure. "I was once alive apart from the law" (7:9) appears to be a statement that only a figurative Adam could make, and a reference to Genesis 3 would certainly clarify more sharply than any other context the statement that "sin . . . deceived me" (7:11). Observations such as these eventually

---

[61] Wright, perhaps correctly, does not speak of a "new law" in this context but of a "new covenant, whose boundary-marker is Christ and Spirit and not Torah" (*Climax of the Covenant,* 196–97, 203). We do not fundamentally disagree on this point. I am simply taking 8:2 as permission to use the term "law" of the new covenant.

[62] W. G. Kümmel, *Römer 7 und die Bekehrung des Paulus* (UNT 17; Leipzig: Hinrichs, 1929).

led to Ernst Käsemann's famous pronouncement that "there is nothing in the passage which does not fit Adam, and everything fits Adam alone."[63]

This statement is, however, more rhetorically effective than exegetically sound. There are, after all, several aspects of the passage that do not fit Adam alone and at least one that does not fit him at all. Paul's fivefold use of the words "command" (ἐντολή) and "law" (νόμος) and his quotation of the tenth commandment (7:7) can hardly be described as fitting Adam alone, since the Bible uses them not in connection with Adam but with Israel.[64] Moreover, as Douglas Moo points out, most interpreters of Romans agree that 7:7–12 is an excursus in defense of the law, made necessary by Paul's negative statements about the law in 3:20; 4:15; 5:13; 5:20; 6:14–15; and especially 7:1–6. That law, however, is clearly distinguished in 5:13–14 from the commandment given to Adam. Having distinguished between the period of Adam, an intervening period in which there was no law, and the period after the law came, Paul would now be veiling his argument with confusion if he suddenly used the word "law" to refer to the period of Adam.[65]

In addition to these considerations, one aspect of the passage seems inexplicably inappropriate if the "I" refers exclusively to Adam: Paul says that the commandment's purpose was life (ἡ ἐντολὴ ἡ εἰς ζωήν, 7:10), and yet the purpose of the commandment given to Adam is nowhere connected with life. The penalty for not obeying the commandment is, of course, death according to Gen 3:19, but it would be faulty logic to say that the penalty expresses the opposite of the commandment's purpose. Gen 3:22 says that Adam had to be expelled from the garden because he had gained divine knowledge and might eat of the tree of life and live forever, but it is difficult to see how this could express the purpose of the command not to eat of the first tree.[66] The most obvious context for the statement that the purpose of the commandment was life, then, is once again the story of Israel. At Israel's initiation into the covenant, God told his people that he intended the commandments to bring "life" (Deut 6:24; 30:15–20; Lev 18:5), and this claim became Israel's settled conviction (Prov 6:23; Ezek 20:11, 21; Sir 17:11; 45:5; Bar 3:9).[67] Nevertheless, as we have seen, many Jews believed that Israel had not yet

---

[63] Käsemann, *Romans*, 196. Others who see Adam in the passage include S. Lyonnet ("L'histoire du salut selon le chapitre vii de l'épître aux Romains," *Bib* 43 [1962] 117–51), Cranfield (*Romans*, 1. 344), Dunn (*Romans 1–8*, 399–403), and Ziesler (*Romans*, 182).

[64] Josephus (*Ant.* 1.43) uses ἐντολή of God's "command" to Adam, but the Bible does not use the word in this way.

[65] Douglas J. Moo, "Israel and Paul in Romans 7.7–12," *NTS* 32 (1986) 124.

[66] *Contra* Dunn, *Romans 1–8*, 384.

[67] For several of these references I am indebted to Dunn, *Romans 1–8*, 384.

attained life because they had disobeyed the covenant, and many awaited the restoration of Israel when the life promised in the covenant would be theirs.

Some elements of 7:7–13, then, fit Adam and others fit Israel. The most sensible explanation for this is that Paul has mingled elements of both stories in this passage.[68] We have already seen that in chap. 5 Paul viewed the story of Israel as the existential outworking and heightening of the experience of the primal Adam and that the two stories were theologically intertwined. Both violated a specific precept (5:13–14), and Israel's sin caused the sin that Adam had initiated to increase (5:20).[69] If this understanding of chap. 5 is correct, then, it seems natural for Paul in chap. 7 to combine elements of both stories in order to exonerate the command of God from blame for the plight of humanity in general and of Israel in particular.

Beginning with 7:13, however, allusions to Adam seem to be replaced with references to an individual's struggle to keep the law, and discussion of the passage has tended to focus on who this individual is. Does Paul speak of himself, of unbelievers generally, or of believers? If of himself, does he speak as an unbeliever or as a believer?[70] In the tangle of attempts to sort out the best answers to these questions, the correlation between what Paul says in 7:13 and in 5:20 is seldom noticed.[71] In 5:20 Paul has identified Israel as the place where sin, because of the giving of the law, increased. In 7:13 Paul uses the first person singular to make much the same statement: "sin, in order that it might be revealed as sin, worked death in me through what was good, in order that through the commandment sin might become exceedingly sinful." Whoever the "I" of 7:13–25 is, he or she functions in a way similar to Israel in Paul's previous argument.

The possibility that the story of Israel lies beneath the struggle of the "I" in 7:13–25 is strengthened, moreover, by the broad similarity between this passage and the prayers of confession in Ezra 9:5–15; Neh 9:6–37; Dan 9:4–19; and Bar 1:15–3:8. Just as Rom 7:13–25 is marked by an anguished awareness of the individual's tendency to disobey the Mosaic Law, so the primary characteristic of these prayers is anguish over national Israel's repeated disobedience to the law in spite of God's continuing faithfulness to his people. Ezra is grieved that after the great iniquity of his ancestors, and the great mercy of

---

[68] See also Wright, *Climax of the Covenant*, 227.

[69] See ibid., 196.

[70] The alternatives are presented and discussed by Cranfield with characteristic thoroughness (*Romans*, 1. 344–47).

[71] N. T. Wright is a prominent exception (*Climax of the Covenant*, 197–98; idem, "Romans and the Theology of Paul," in *Society of Biblical Literature 1992 Seminar Papers* [ed. Eugene H. Lovering; Atlanta: Scholars Press, 1992] 200).

God in spite of that iniquity, once again he and his people have violated the Mosaic covenant and intermarried with the people of the land. He is so moved by this lack of concern for the covenant that as he prays he not only weeps but throws himself on the ground before the temple (10:1). The prayer in Nehemiah focuses similarly on Israel's repeated violation of the law in spite of God's merciful patience in withholding punishment (9:16–17, 18, 26, 28–30). Daniel says that Israel has sinned, acted wickedly, turned aside from God's commandments, and refused to listen to God's prophets (9:4–5); and Baruch confesses that "from the day when the Lord led our fathers out of Egypt even until this day we have been disobedient to the Lord our God and careless to disobey his voice" (1:19). Although all of these prayers are in the first person plural rather than the first person singular, Daniel and Baruch recognize the role of the individual in the sins they confess. Daniel describes his prayer as a confession of "my sin and the sin of my people Israel," and Baruch twice attributes the sins of the nation to the evil intentions of each person's heart (1:22; 2:8).[72]

The similarity between Rom 7:13–25 and these passages does not reach to the level of specific details; nor is there any biblical precedent for Paul's bifurcation of the law and of the self in this passage. But the anguish of the confession and the origin of that anguish in continued disobedience to the law open the possibility that as he wrote Paul was thinking not simply of himself but of his people and of the biblical story of their disobedience.

III. CONCLUSIONS

If the story of Israel is as important to the argument of Romans 5–8 as this essay suggests, then the tension that many interpreters have found between these four chapters and chaps. 1–4 and 9–11 begins to relax.[73] Because Paul argues in chaps. 5–8 that the believing community stands in continuity with the story of Israel as it appears in Leviticus, Deuteronomy, the historical books, and the prophets, these chapters are as important as chap. 4 for supporting Paul's claim that faith establishes rather than nullifies the law (3:31). By his appropriation of the language that these writings use to describe the restoration of Israel, Paul implies that the believing community of Jews and

---

[72] Bar 1:22 says, "each of us has followed the intent of our own wicked hearts" (ᾠχόμεθα ἕκαστος ἐν διανοίᾳ καρδίας αὐτοῦ τῆς πονηρᾶς), and 2:8, "and we have not entreated the face of the Lord in order to turn back, each one, from the intentions of our evil hearts" (καὶ οὐκ ἐδεήθημεν τοῦ προσώπου κυρίου τοῦ ἀποστρέψαι ἕκαστον ἀπὸ τῶν νοημάτων τῆς καρδίας αὐτῶν τῆς πονηρᾶς).

[73] See also Wright, *Climax of the Covenant*, 194–95.

Gentiles in Rome has become the protagonist in the last chapter of Israel's story as it is told in the Bible.

This assumption, however, creates a theological tension that grows in intensity throughout Romans 5–8 until it reaches the boiling point at the end of the section in the rhetorical question "Who will bring charges against the elect of God?" (8:33). How could Paul claim that the ethnically mixed community of believers in Rome were God's elect—the restored Israel—when so many circumcised Jews still lived, in the words of 2 Maccabees, "in the time of evil" (2 Macc 1:5)?[74] Paul's reply to this critical difficulty comes, of course, in chaps. 9–11. The presence of the story of Israel in chaps. 5–8 means, therefore, that Paul's argument is neither complete at the end of chap. 8 as a previous generation of scholarship thought nor, as more recent treatments of Romans sometimes imply, that Israel dives beneath the text at 4:25 to resurface only at 9:1.

The presence of the story of Israel in Romans 5–8 also means that these chapters are as concerned with the people of God as they are with the individual. Although they certainly use the first person and therefore take on a more personal tone than chaps. 1–4 and 9–11, the interpreter should not reduce them only to a discussion of the implications of justification for the individual believer. By using biblical language for the restoration of God's people, they constantly situate the individual within the wider community. This is true even of chap. 7, where, as we have seen, the first person singular reflects a corporate as well as an individual struggle.[75]

The biblical story of Israel, therefore, forms a pivotal part of the theology of Romans 5–8. Even in these chaps., where Israel never appears by name and Paul quotes scripture only rarely, Paul's theology takes a biblical shape. All of this is substantial evidence that Paul's symbolic universe was Israel's symbolic universe and that any adequate description of Paul's theology must understand the symbols of that universe as well.

---

[74] This phrase (ἐν καιρῷ πονηρῷ) may refer to life in the diaspora and therefore under the curse of the broken covenant. See the comments of Solomon Zeitlin in *The Second Book of Maccabees* (ed. Solomon Zeitlin; New York: Harper, 1954) 100–101.

[75] Cf. Isa 61:10–11, where the prophet uses the first person singular to describe the restored community.

9 CONTINUITY AND DISCONTINUITY: REFLECTIONS ON ROMANS 5-8

(In Conversation with Frank Thielman)

Charles B. Cousar
Columbia Theological Seminary

IN HIS APPRECIATIVE REVIEW of J. Christiaan Beker's *Paul the Apostle*, J. Louis Martyn notes that Beker has discovered in Paul a kind of marriage between apocalyptic and salvation history, and Martyn wonders if the marriage is more arranged by Beker than discovered in Paul.[1] One has the feeling that many of the differences surfacing in the papers and discussions of the Pauline Theology Group often boil down to whether such a marriage is possible, and if so, which marital partner succeeds in changing the other. In many ways, the discussion is reminiscent, *mutatis mutandis*, of Ernst Käsemann's response to the essay of Krister Stendahl "The Apostle Paul and the Introspective Conscience of the West" and Stendahl's rebuttal.[2]

The issue is not whether Paul draws on the language and texts of the Old Testament (that is a given) but whether there is a discernible line of continuity between Israel's story in the past and the death and resurrection of Christ or whether the apocalyptic character of God's disclosure in Christ precipitates an irreparable rupture in the story that makes any smooth notion of continuity difficult to discern. In the latter case, the inbreaking new age is seen as a radical alternative to the old, rather than its sequel.[3]

Frank Thielman's carefully crafted paper on Romans 5–8 clearly comes down on the side of continuity. The problem he addresses is why Israel and its scriptures apparently recede from view in Romans 5–8, why the term "Jew" ('Ιουδαῖος) never appears, why the biblical quotations shrink to two, and why

---

[1] J. Louis Martyn, *WW* 2 (1982) 196.

[2] Ernst Käsemann, *Perspectives on Paul* (Philadelphia: Fortress, 1971) 60–78. Stendahl's essay was originally published in 1963. Both the essay and his rebuttal of Käsemann can be found in *Paul Among Jews and Gentiles and Other Essays* (Philadelphia: Fortress, 1976) 78–96, 129–133.

[3] Leander E. Keck, "Paul as Thinker," *Int* 47 (1993) 27–38.

the subject becomes Christ rather than God. If a dialogue with Israel has been initiated in chaps. 1–4 and is continued in chaps. 9–11, then how are chaps. 5–8 to be read? Is it really the case, as Robin Scroggs argues, that this section "has nothing to do with the meaning of the history of Israel"?[4]

Thielman's thesis is that the story of Israel functions as a critical ingredient in the symbolic universe of first-century Judaism, and if modern readers can enter that universe and appreciate the way Jewish writers employ the basic elements of the story to interpret their own plight under Roman domination and dispersion, then they can see also in Romans 5–8 how Paul recalls the story and how it shapes his message. Though he rarely cites biblical texts, Paul nevertheless appropriates the language of Israel's story as it appears in Leviticus, Deuteronomy, the historical books, and the prophets to affirm that his Roman readers are the purified and restored Israel. The accounts of Israel's persistent failure to keep the covenantal commitments, the punishment received in the exile for its disobedience, and its anticipated restoration provide the theological foundation for Paul's argument throughout Romans 5–8.

My purpose in this paper is to respond to Thielman's argument and to propose another perspective on Romans 5–8, one which is not without its own problems. In the conclusion, I offer a proposal about the function of discontinuity in the message of Romans.

I. A RESPONSE TO THIELMAN'S READING OF ROMANS 5–8

First, a hunch about the problem posed in Thielman's paper—the apparent lack of overt attention to Israel and its scriptures in Romans 5–8. Clearly Romans is concerned with the faithfulness of God in regard to promises made and thus invites attention both when texts of the Old Testament are cited and the language of the Old Testament is prominent and when such texts are rare and the language distant. It is worth pondering why in Romans 5–8 the latter rather than the former is true.

Yet other commentators (as Thielman notes) observe the apparent omissions in Romans 5–8 and find them not so puzzling. The omissions are attributed to the topics and complex style of Paul's argument, an argument that, while orderly, hardly moves in a smooth, linear fashion. Theses are introduced and immediately elaborated or delayed for a later stage in the argument; conclu-

---

[4] Robin Scroggs, "Paul as Rhetorician: Two Homilies in Romans 1–11," in *Jews, Greeks, and Christians: Religious Cultures in Late Antiquity: Essays in Honor of William David Davies* (ed. Robert Hamerton-Kelly and Robin Scroggs; SJLA 21; Leiden: Brill, 1976) 281.

sions are drawn that either raise further questions or warrant further clarification; charges are reported that are only finally answered later in the letter.

A recognition of how Paul's argument develops throughout the letter makes the absence of Israel and its scriptures in Romans 5–8 a slightly less urgent matter. The chapters are not disconnected from the rest of the letter. Paul appropriately elaborates the character of the gospel in relation to his purposes in writing and in doing so prepares for the "mystery" to be revealed in chaps. 9–11. His lack of specific references to Israel and his skimpy use of the Old Testament in chaps. 5–8 seem not so unusual.

Second, a demur about terms in Thielman's paper. I find the phrase "the restored Israel" (p. 178) and the notion of the Roman readers as "the purified and restored Israel" (p. 190) confusing and highly problematic. I take it that when Paul writes in 11:26 of the eschatological salvation of "all Israel" he means his "kindred according to the flesh" (9:3). Thus it is difficult prior to that moment to speak of the church as Israel restored. Nowhere in the letter are the Roman readers explicitly addressed as "Israel," and it would seem highly unusual in a document that in some sense carries on a discussion with and about Judaism to wrench the very name away from implied conversation partners.[5]

Third, another demur about terms. At least twice in the paper reference is made to "the Deuteronomic interpretation of Israel's story" (pp. 174, 176), which then is used synonymously with "the biblical story of Israel." For Thielman the phrases are shorthand for Israel's failure to keep the covenant requirements, the punishment received from God for disobedience particularly in the exile, and the promise that one day God would give Israel a new spirit of obedience and restore its fortunes. Old Testament scholars, however, are not at all unanimous on the details of the so-called Deuteronomistic pattern. Some play down or even eliminate from the scheme any hope of the eschatological deliverance of Israel. Others emphasize the repeated sending of messengers to Israel, who are then rejected or ignored, a characteristic feature of those texts that help to construct the symbolic universe of first-century Judaism. Interestingly, one ingredient widely recognized in the Deuteronomistic pattern is the decisive call for Israel to repent, something totally missing from Romans 5–8.[6]

---

[5] See Keck's sharp judgment: "Paul shows no interest whatever in the restoration of Israel's past independence or glory, and his 'Christ' is no longer a messianic liberator" ("Paul as Thinker," 31). The problem with the term "restoration" is that it implies a return to a *status quo*, something far from Paul's argument.

[6] See the convenient *Forschungsbericht* of the term "Deuteronomistic History" in *ABD* 2. 160–68.

Is the expression "the Deuteronomic interpretation of Israel's story" an accurate or helpful one to use in connection with Romans 5–8? It may fit Luke-Acts, where there are rehearsals of Israel's refusal to hear the prophets and repeated demands for repentance, and where Jesus is depicted as a prophet like Moses.[7] It seems, however, a strange phrase to use in relation to a section whose only two Old Testament citations come from Exodus (20:17 in Rom 7:7) and Psalms (44:22 in Rom 8:36), that says nothing about repentance, that emphasizes the universal scope of Christ's death in rectifying the Adamic situation (5:12–21), and where suffering is taken not as punishment for disobedience but as a necessary dimension of life in Christ (8:17).[8]

Fourth, with regard to 5:12–21, Thielman makes the point that the story of Israel takes a prominent place alongside the stories of Adam and Christ. In 5:13–14 Paul's purpose in mentioning the law is to call attention to the similarity between Adam's disobedience and Israel's violation of the covenant. Even at the cost of obfuscating his (i.e., Paul's) argument, "the story of Israel's violation of the covenant at Sinai was so close to the surface of Paul's thinking at this point in his discourse that, almost in the manner of a Freudian slip, it broke through" (p. 180).

The issue in 5:13–14, however, is not Israel's sin (which, apart from its participation in the "all," is not even hinted at), but how people between the time of Adam and Moses, who had no command to violate (as Adam had and Moses had) nevertheless shared Adam's plight. Though unreckoned, sin was in the world, and because of it all people died. Even without the presence of a command and without the culpability of an Adam or a Moses, the reign of death prevailed as a consequence of Adam's disobedience.[9]

In 5:20 law is mentioned again, and the point is that its intrusion into the human predicament did nothing to help. It made matters worse rather than better. It must have been a jolt to the portion of the Roman readers who were

---

[7] See David P. Moessner, *Lord of the Banquet: The Literary and Theological Significance of the Lukan Travel Narrative* (Minneapolis: Fortress, 1989).

[8] I confess to some misgivings with Thielman's methodology throughout the paper, in which he establishes a particular understanding of Jewish history in the symbolic universe of first-century Judaism and then determines that particular words used by Paul cohere with and reflect this understanding of history. It seems to imply an image of a monolithic Judaism. Furthermore, if we had access to the whole scope of such a symbolic universe, it would be much larger than the Deuteronomistic interpretation, and terms Thielman labels as "specialized" (see n. 58) would likely cease to be so.

[9] As Paul Achtemeier points out, Rom 5:13–14 answers an implied question: Must there be a command to break in order for sin to happen? Could it be that sin in fact is not universal because those between Adam and Moses had no law? (*Romans* [Interpretation; Atlanta: John Knox, 1985] 97).

Jewish to hear that "law came in, with the result that the trespass multiplied." That the law should have such a negative result (or purpose, depending on how the ἵνα ["in order that"] is taken) was hardly a part of the Jewish readers' symbolic universe. As James D. G. Dunn rightly comments, "For Paul to put the law, God's good gift to Israel, so emphatically on the wrong side of the division between the epochs, must have seemed like the blackest treachery to many of his countrymen, including Jews at Rome who were hearing his exposition of the gospel for the first time."[10] Rather than solving or even improving the Adamic predicament, the law simply became a tool for sin's dominion. If Israel's story is implied in 5:20, it is in terms of the law's inability to cope with sin—a spin on the law that most Jewish interpreters would be hard pressed to accept.

Fifth, in considering Romans 8, one of the key points Thielman makes in support of the prominence of Israel's story in Paul's argument concerns the language for suffering in 8:35b. It is drawn, he argues, largely from Old Testament descriptions of the suffering of Israel for its disobedience. Furthermore, the citation of Psalm 44 (LXX 43) becomes instructive for Paul. In the postexilic psalm Israel puzzles over its calamitous situation when many in the nation cannot reconcile their prolonged suffering with their diligence in keeping the law. "It is precisely this kind of tension which Paul describes when he summarizes the puzzling suffering of the believing community in the words of this psalm" (p. 184).

But is Paul in Romans 8 really puzzling over why the believing community suffers? Hardly. Verses 1–17b describe the Spirit as God's power to do what the law is incapable of doing—to bring freedom from the law of sin and death (8:2), to give life to mortal bodies (8:11), to effect the adoption of humans as children of God (8:14–16), and to make them heirs of God and joint heirs with Christ (8:17). But this somewhat triumphalistic section is brought to a close with the sobering caveat—"if, in fact, we suffer with him so that we may also be glorified with him" (8:17c).[11] Why the believing community suffers is no riddle for Paul: the community suffers because it is united with the crucified Christ in a world not yet redeemed.

On the one hand, the community's sufferings are not unique. It shares in the painful groans of a creation that longs for redemption. Instead of exempting the believing community from suffering, the Spirit in fact intensifies its sense of unfulfilledness (8:23) and turns even its praying into "inarticulate

---

[10] James D. G. Dunn, *Romans 1–8* (WBC 38a; Waco: Word, 1988) 299.

[11] Whether the εἴπερ is to be translated "if" (a condition not yet fulfilled) or "since" (a condition fulfilled) is not critical to our argument. See Dunn, *Romans 1–8*, 456.

groans" (NEB, στεναγμοῖς ἀλαλήτοις). It lives in solidarity with creation and its suffering, and it lives by hoping in something unseen.

On the other hand, the sufferings of the Christian community are distinct. From the common anguish of the creation, Paul turns to the peculiar hope of the predestined, called, elect community in 8:28–39. In 8:35b he simply rehearses the particular incidents of suffering listed elsewhere in his own catalogues of hardship; only now they are descriptive of the community's situation.[12] Union with the crucified Christ inevitably places the community in a vulnerable spot, subject to the hostility of the unredeemed world. Rather than puzzling over such suffering, Paul writes of the incomparable love of God in Christ that sustains the community in the midst of its trials. The citation from Psalm 44 (in 8:36), originating in a psalm of anguished lament, "now universalized as an apocalyptic truism that God's faithful are always exposed to violent death, becomes Scripture's own reminder that tribulation is a sure mark of belonging to God."[13]

There is no question that the language of the Old Testament can be found in the argument of Romans 5–8—Adam, the many references to the Mosaic Law, citations from the Decalogue (7:7) and from Psalm 44 (8:36), a possible allusion to Abraham's offering of Isaac (8:32), among others. The references are not perfunctory or a mere strategy in Paul's appeal to his readers, and it is to Thielman's credit that he takes them seriously. But do these add up to a continuous story of Israel "guiding the discussion and defining its terms" (p. 172)? I think not.

II. AN ALTERNATIVE READING OF ROMANS 5–8

Any interpretation of these critical chapters of Romans must account for the logical movement of the argument and the contribution the section makes to the larger message of the letter. My intention here can only be to hint at the progression of the major units of the text and to highlight some of the distinguishing points scored.

(1) As is often noted, Rom 5:1–11 serves as a transitional unit. "Therefore, having been justified by faith" (5:1a) recapitulates the thrust of the previous

---

[12] The most obvious overtones to be heard in the language of 8:35b are from other Pauline texts rather than from Deuteronomy 28 and Leviticus 26. See 1 Cor 4:9–13; 2 Cor 4:8–12; 6:4–10; 11:23–29; 12:10. Every one of the seven terms used in 8:35b, with the exception of "sword," occurs in one or more of Paul's catalogues of hardships.

[13] Paul W. Meyer, "Romans," *HBC*, 1154.

section and facilitates the movement of the discussion in new directions.[14] The section itself is framed by the uses of the verb "boast" (καυχάομαι) in 5:2 and 11, giving the affirmations a doxological character.[15] In the first subsection (5:1–5), God's love provides the grounds for hope, even in the face of suffering; in the second subsection (5:6–8), the extraordinary nature of Christ's death is the supreme expression of God's love; in the third subsection (5:9–11), the justification and reconciliation experienced in the present are reasons for confidence in the day of final judgment.

Two dimensions of 5:1–11 warrant special consideration. First, the particular way in which Christ's death is depicted is striking. It is an unforeseen and unparalleled event that occurs as a surprise. There is no preparation for it, no contingency that makes it provisional, no call to repentance to activate its results. It is a happening of unconditional grace. The phrase κατὰ καιρόν (v. 6) carries eschatological significance, but Käsemann, following the preferred rendering of Bauer-Arndt-Gingrich, is probably correct in translating it "then, at that time," rather than "at the right time."[16] The point of the text seems to be that according to all human reckoning the event occurred unexpectedly, at the most inopportune moment.

Moreover, when Paul attempts to draw comparisons to the deaths of other heroic figures in v. 7, perhaps martyrs of the Maccabean revolt, the parallels do not fit.[17] The death of Christ for weak, ungodly sinners is both unanticipated and incomparable. It does not neatly fit into any preconceived categories.

Second, at the beginning of the section attention is directed to the future. Not only do we now have peace with God, but "we boast in our hope of sharing the glory of God." The very reality humanity has lacked (3:23) becomes the object of confident anticipation. This in turn makes possible a positive attitude toward the sufferings of the present time. Rather than being the occasion for puzzlement or lament, afflictions are understood as the necessary part of the experience of grace. Then at the end of the section (5:9–11), the theme

---

[14] Nils A. Dahl is certainly correct in calling attention to the parallels between 5:1–11 and 8:1–39 ("Two Notes on Romans 5," ST 5 [1952] 37–42). The earlier section states the themes and the latter section elucidates them.

[15] The parallelism between Rom 5:1–2 and 5:11 is also evident in the repeated phrases "through our Lord Jesus Christ, through whom we . . . ." The verses function as an *inclusio* to the section.

[16] Ernst Käsemann, *Commentary on Romans* (Grand Rapids: Eerdmans, 1980) 137.

[17] The difficulties of Rom 5:7 lead Keck to conclude that 5:6–7 represents a post-Pauline interpolation ("The Post-Pauline Interpretation of Jesus' Death in Romans 5:6–7," in *Theologia Crucis–Signum Crucis: Festschrift für Erich Dinkler zum 70. Geburtstag* [ed. C. Andresen and G. Klein; Tübingen: Mohr (Siebeck), 1979] 237–48).

of the future is still very much in view. In rhetorically parallel expressions ("much more surely"), readers are given warrant not to fear the eschatological judgment. Christ's death will deliver them from the divine wrath and will assure salvation, thus establishing the grounds for boasting.

Paul's bifocal vision in 5:1–11—one focal length oriented to the death of Christ and the other to the final salvation—shapes the understanding of the present. The trials facing believers are a part of the current eschatological situation. Something astounding has taken place in Jesus' death that has decisive consequences for the end of the age, but until then both the old and new ages coexist. Readers face tribulations in hope, even exulting in them, not out of a sick masochism, but because they are sure that the present is not the end of the story.[18]

(2) The "therefore" (διὰ τοῦτο) of 5:12 indicates that the section 5:12–21 is a development of 5:1–11, addressing the question of how weak, ungodly sinners can have such confidence in the day of judgment. The answer is, as Achtemeier puts it, "Christ got us out of the mess that Adam got us into. What Adam did, Christ undid; where Adam failed, Christ succeeded."[19]

But of course Adam and Christ are more than individuals; they incorporate in themselves all people. Each is the progenitor and prototype of all humanity. Through the one person death spreads to all people; through the other person life comes to all. The one figure dominates the other. Obedience triumphs over disobedience; grace triumphs over sin; life triumphs over death.

Two observations about this section. First, the apocalyptic two-age scheme of 5:1–11 is even more prominent in 5:12–21. Adam and Christ personify the old and the new in strikingly antithetical ways—the one marked by sin, death, disobedience, and condemnation; the other by grace, life, obedience, and justification.

Second, a feature of the apocalyptic structure is the world-embracing character of both Adam and Christ.[20] The act each performs (disobedience and obedience) determines the destiny not of a few but of the whole of humanity. Nothing is said about Christ's having made life "potentially" available to

---

[18] In light of the eschatological structure of the passage, one can perhaps assume that the "sufferings" spoken of in Rom 5:3 are a part of the apocalyptic woes of the last days. It is interesting that Paul does not say here what he stresses elsewhere—that the sufferings of the believing community can be faced positively because they are a sharing in the sufferings of Christ (2 Cor 4:7–11; Gal 6:17; Phil 3:10).

[19] Achtemeier, *Romans*, 97.

[20] Martinus de Boer also calls attention to the cosmological characterization of sin, death, grace, and righteousness in Rom 5:12–21 and traces the points of contact with one strand of Jewish apocalyptic eschatology (*The Defeat of Death: Apocalyptic Eschatology in 1 Corinthians 15 and Romans 5* [JSNTSup 22; Sheffield: JSOT Press, 1988] 141–80).

all and that faith is necessary to turn the potentiality into reality. (Certainly death is not pictured as a potential destiny.) There are no restrictions.[21] Paul will get to the moral obligations of his Christian readers in chap. 6. Here, as Käsemann notes, "since death is a force which shapes the cosmos, freedom from it, like the justification which underlies this freedom, has to have universal validity if it is to be seriously maintained."[22]

(3) The statement of the triumph of grace and life over sin and death that concludes Romans 5 becomes the occasion to face the issue of antinomian libertinism. "Should we continue in sin in order that grace may abound?" (6:1). It is the same issue that apparently others raised with Paul (so 3:8), which in terms of this letter has remained unanswered. The response begins with the invitation to readers to recall their baptism and in particular to remember that baptism has to do with a realistic association with the last Adam, whose obedience has made the many righteous.

On the one hand, Christ is described in the passage as one who died, was buried, and was raised from the dead. His resurrection was clearly something different from a resuscitation since "we know that Christ being raised from the dead, will never die again; death no longer has dominion over him" (6:9). He leaves in his wake the broken power of death, the ultimate enemy whose defeat signals the final triumph of God (1 Cor 15:24–28). The death, burial, and resurrection of Christ constitute the decisive apocalyptic event.

On the other hand, the way Paul expounds the association of believers with Christ in baptism means that there remains an incompleteness for the readers.[23] Believers are united with Christ in his death and burial in the sacrament, but they await their resurrection with him (6:5, 8).[24] For the present, the newness of life to which they are called is a cruciform life. In Christ the new age has come, but "this age" has not yet gone, with the result that the age of sin

---

[21] A case has sometimes been made for interpreting the phrase of 5:17 "those who receive the abundance of grace and the free gift of righteousness" to mean that faith is the condition for receiving life. See Rudolf Bultmann, *Theology of the New Testament* (London: SCM, 1952) 1. 302–3. But this seems highly unlikely. See the convincing treatment of 5:12–21 by Arland J. Hultgren, *Paul's Gospel and Mission: The Outlook from His Letter to the Romans* (Philadelphia: Fortress, 1985) 86–93.

[22] Käsemann, *Romans*, 141.

[23] David E. Aune comments, "Paul exhibits a tendency to conceptualize human nature and existence as a microcosmic version of a Christianized form of apocalyptic eschatology. In other words, the apocalyptic structure of history was considered paradigmatic for understanding human nature" ("Apocalypticism," in *Dictionary of Paul and His Letters* [ed. G. F. Hawthorne and R. P. Martin; Downers Grove, IL: InterVarsity, 1993] 31).

[24] Käsemann speaks of "a remarkable caveat in the shape of an eschatological reservation" (*New Testament Questions of Today* [Philadelphia: Fortress, 1969] 132).

and death continues to exist alongside the age of righteousness and life. While the ultimacy of sin's threat is removed, the struggle precipitated by the co-existence of the two ages remains.

Thus, the readers are challenged to live out of the new age and not out of the old, to present themselves to God as instruments of righteousness and not let sin exercise dominion over their mortal bodies (6:12–13). The remainder of the chapter reiterates this call using the categories of slavery and freedom. Indicative-mood verbs declaring liberation from sin's clutches (6:17–18) are set alongside imperative-mood verbs demanding allegiance to righteousness (6:19). Those having received the gift of life and freedom are held account-able to the God of life and freedom.

Between chaps. 5 and 6, of course, two significant changes have taken place. First, whereas in 5:6–8 the death of Christ is depicted an unconditional, non-contingent gift of grace to the ungodly, in 6:1–23 those acknowledging the gift must recognize its demand of a transformed life. Second, whereas the con-trast between Adam and Christ in 5:12–21 is depicted in universal categories that encompass all humanity, union with Christ in baptism in 6:1–11 of course limits the matter to the Christian community. The essential paradoxes of predestination and free will, of universalism and particularism remain, as they do elsewhere in the letters, in remarkable tension. The abandoning of either pole leads to the truncation of Paul's gospel.

(4) In a sense, the illustration from marriage law and its explanation (7:1–6) provide yet another answer to the question of libertinism. The death of the husband creates a new situation that means the widow's release from the bind-ing marital code. She is free to marry another husband. Likewise, the death of Christ brings freedom from the law and union with another—in this case, the risen Christ. The result (in line with the logic of chap. 6) is the fruitful service of God.

While the marital illustration itself may not suggest an eschatological mode of thinking, the concluding contrast between "the old written code" and "the new life of the Spirit" (7:6) indicates that such a mode underlies what is said. Here the coexistence of the two ages, which provides the structure for the moral injunctions in chap. 6, reappears, and readers are reminded that they live out of the one and not the other.

(5) The marital illustration and the contrast between "the old written code" and "the new life of the Spirit" force the question of the law's status, whether or not its association with the old age implies an identification with sin. Rom 7:7–25 engages the issue by detailing how sin works in relation to the law. While the law ends up a vulnerable partner serving the aims and schemes of sin, it is sin and not the law that ultimately brings deception and death. In

good apocalyptic fashion, "sin" takes on demonic proportions, a power to which humans become enslaved and which dominates their lives (7:23). The law in turn is vindicated and characterized as holy, just, and good (7:12).

While we cannot linger over the complex exegetical matters in this passage,[25] the final verse of the chapter warrants special attention. Having affirmed deliverance from the wretched situation of "this body of death," Paul concludes, "So then, with my mind I am a slave to the law of God, but with my flesh I am a slave to the law of sin" (7:25b). How is it possible to make such a statement after the victorious cry of 7:25a? Dunn's explanation is helpful. The coexistence of the two ages lies behind the tension between the two types of service depicted. On the one hand, the new age has broken in, the mind is renewed (12:2), and service is rendered the law of God. On the other hand, the old age has not yet passed, the flesh is vulnerable, and service is also given the law of sin. The cry of freedom in 7:25a ("Thanks be to God through our Lord Jesus Christ!") is not the expression of a salvation finished or yet to begin, but of a salvation "under way and still to be completed."[26]

(6) The connection between chaps. 7 and 8 is obvious in that the law remains a matter of concern, but now the emphasis falls on the difference made by the inbreaking of the new age—the sending of the Son and the presence of the Spirit. Readers are reminded that they belong to the new age ("You are in the Spirit, since the Spirit of God dwells in you," 8:9) and are to let their lives be determined by the Spirit of the new age (8:12–13). This means membership by adoption in the family of God (8:14–17).

Perhaps nowhere in these chapters is the apocalyptic structure of the text so evident as in Rom 8:18–39, where many of the urgent themes of 5:1–11 are readdressed. Like an expectant mother, creation groans intensely as it awaits the eschatological dénouement—"the glory about to be revealed" (8:18), "the revealing of the children of God" (8:19), "the freedom of the glory of the children of God" (8:21). The Spirit makes believers participants in the eschatological anguish as creation and community together experience the birth pangs of the new order.

The word of assurance offered the elect community is set over against not only historical threats (like hardship, famine, nakedness, and sword) but also cosmic enemies that can imperil the soul as well as the body (death, rulers,

---

[25] For a recent treatment, see Paul W. Meyer, "The Worm at the Core of the Apple: Exegetical Reflections on Romans 7," in *The Conversation Continues: Studies in Paul and John in Honor of J. Louis Martyn* (ed. Robert T. Fortna and Beverly R. Gaventa (Nashville: Abingdon, 1990) 62–84.

[26] Dunn, *Romans 1–8*, 396–99, 410–12 (quotation from 399).

things present, things to come, powers, height, and depth). The apocalyptic character of this section is prominent.[27]

III. ROMANS 5–8 AND "APOCALYPTIC"

I am quite aware of the difficulties of using the term "apocalyptic" to describe Paul's theology either in general or in Romans 5–8. Despite numerous attempts, "apocalyptic" continues to be a slippery word to define (or to agree about). There are no apocalyptic scenarios in these chapters (as in 1 Thess 4:13–18 and 1 Cor 15:51–57), though the Greek verb "reveal" (ἀπο-καλύπτω) and the noun "revelation" (ἀποκάλυψις) occur in 8:18–19 to depict what creation is eagerly awaiting. Furthermore, Paul borrows from other fields of thought in addition to apocalyptic, and when he employs apocalyptic categories he often substantially modifies them.[28]

What does seem obvious in Romans 5–8, however, is the extensive use of the rhetoric and perspective of apocalyptic eschatology, characteristics that are essential to identify if one is to understand the logic of Paul's argument. Repeatedly, constructs drawn from apocalyptic traditions shape the presentation of the gospel. Furthermore, these apocalyptic notes produce a strong sound of discontinuity between the time before the advent of Christ and the present and declare the present as a tension-filled era, awaiting final fulfillment. We shall need to consider how these notes are to be heard in a composition that also contains notes of continuity.

Before moving to the continuity–discontinuity issue, two summarizing observations about Romans 5–8 are necessary. First, though the word "age" (αἰών) does not appear in these chapters, our reading has suggested that the temporal dualism of apocalyptic eschatology is nevertheless evident in every chapter. The scheme is employed with a great deal of flexibility, sometimes highlighting the significance of the Christ-event as the alternative to what is wrong in the world, at other times showing the present time as tension-filled.

One could argue that the whole line of thought through this section is determined by a number of antinomies[29] that reflect the two-age pattern:

Adam versus Christ (5:12–21)
judgment versus free gift (5:16)
condemnation versus justification (5:16)

---

[27] See the helpful treatment of Rom 8:18–39 in J. C. Beker, *Paul the Apostle: The Triumph of God in Life and Thought* (Philadelphia: Fortress, 1980) 363–67.

[28] See Leander E. Keck, "Paul and Apocalyptic Theology," *Int* 38 (1984) 229–41.

[29] See J. Louis Martyn, "Apocalyptic Antinomies in Paul's Letter to the Galatians," *NTS* 31 (1985) 410–24.

    death versus life (6:23, passim)
    sin versus grace (5:21)
    sin versus righteousness (6:16, passim)
    old versus new (7:6)
    flesh versus Spirit (8:4–13)

The pairs are set in radical opposition to each other, and there is no continuity between the opposites. While some may have parallels in the Old Testament, what makes these sworn enemies distinct is that they are viewed in light of the decisive act of God in Christ. In terms of a biblical story, the dualistic language creates a serious disruption, more "over-against-ness" than succession.

Second, throughout Romans 5–8 there surges a strong element of "not-yet-ness," rooted in the apocalyptic rhetoric of the section. Already in the initial paragraph, attention is called to the future salvation (5:2, 9–11), a future that is kept before the readers by the promise of "eternal life" (5:21; 6:22, 23), by the "eschatological reservation" of baptism evident in the future tense verbs of 6:5, 8, and by a creation that awaits its deliverance (8:19, 21). The believing community is saved "in hope" and waits with expectancy and with patience (8:24–26).

All this "not-yet-ness" raises questions about the definition of fulfillment. If there is a story to be ferreted out of these chapters it is an unfinished one. The unprecedented event of Christ has changed the course of human history (not only Jewish history, but creation's history), but it has not brought history to an end. The people of God are very much in pilgrimage, not yet having arrived at the destination. The salvation of both "the full number of the Gentiles" and "all Israel" still lies ahead. Without an appreciation of the apocalyptic rhetoric of Romans 5–8 it is possible to embrace a thoroughly realized eschatology and miss the force of Paul's realistic analysis of the present.[30]

IV. CONCLUSION

The emphasis on continuity between Paul's letters and the Old Testament has been a characteristic of a number of recent studies of Paul.[31] No doubt it has emerged in reaction to the so-called Lutheran reading of Paul (Luther,

---

[30] In response to a criticism made by Beker, Richard Hays acknowledges this to be a weakness of his study of Paul's use of the Old Testament. See Richard B. Hays, "On the Rebound: A Response to Critiques of *Echoes of Scripture in the Letters of Paul,*" in *Paul and the Scriptures of Israel* (ed. C. A. Evans and J. A. Sanders; Sheffield: JSOT Press, 1993) 94–95. It is also a feature of Thielman's paper.

[31] For example, Richard B. Hays, *Echoes of Scripture in the Letters of Paul* (New Haven: Yale University Press, 1989); and N. T. Wright, *The Climax of the Covenant: Christ and the Law in Pauline Theology* (Minneapolis: Fortress, 1991).

Bultmann, Käsemann), which has seriously underplayed the positive connections between Paul and Judaism (including the Old Testament).[32] To cite one example, Richard Hays, in response to a criticism of his book *Echoes of Scripture in the Letters of Paul*, writes:

> I will acknowledge that my work might occasionally overstate the case for continuity. If so, I have done so in the effort to redress what I perceive to be a drastic imbalance in the literature of the discipline. The task for all of us who seek to interpret Paul is to do justice to both aspects of his thought: he insists on the one hand that the gospel of Jesus Christ is a decisive and radically new manifestation of God's saving power and, at the same time, that this manifestation is fully consistent with—and adumbrated by—God's past gracious dealing with his people Israel.[33]

The issue, however, is complex. It is not a matter of simply getting the right balance—40 percent of discontinuity and 60 percent of continuity—but of discerning the role of each in relation to the other. Martyn's metaphor of marriage is helpful. When partners unite and share their lives together, both will likely change but the two will not be dissolved into one. Each has his or her own particular role to play and only by doing so can the marriage be a mutually enriching union.

The argument of Romans in many places stresses the notion of continuity in God's relationship to Israel, to the church, and to the world. In 3:1–8 the issue of the faithfulness, justice, and truthfulness of God is raised by the faithlessness of the Jews, by human injustice, and by the slanderous charges brought against Paul's gospel. The vindication comes in 3:21–26 in the rectifying action of God in the death of Christ. God is declared to be both just and the justifier of those who share the faith of Jesus. The divine righteousness revealed in Christ is attested by the law and the prophets.[34] The continuity is sketched not in terms of Israel's story but in terms of the story of God and God's dealings with Israel and the church.[35]

Another occasion of clear continuity emerges in Romans 9–11, where in

---

[32] No doubt the recent reevaluation of first–century Judaism has also helped to set the climate for stressing the element of continuity; see, e.g., E. P. Sanders, *Paul and Palestinian Judaism: A Comparison of Patterns of Religion* (Philadelphia: Fortress, 1977).

[33] Hays, "On the Rebound," 93.

[34] See Charles B. Cousar, *A Theology of the Cross: The Death of Jesus in the Pauline Letters* (OBT; Minneapolis: Fortress, 1990) 36–43.

[35] I feel very hesitant about using the term "story" since it is so widely and loosely employed these days that it tends to lose any distinctive meaning. See Ben Witherington III, *Paul's Narrative Thought World: The Tapestry of Tragedy and Triumph* (Louisville: Westminster/John Knox, 1994). Witherington finds four interrelated stories that serve to comprise the one foundational story out of which Paul's discourse emerges.

the image of the olive tree Paul traces the story of God's mercy in grafting in unnatural branches and in promising to regraft the natural branches that have been broken off (11:17–24). In addition to speaking of God's story, in these chapters one could also speak of the story of Israel—its election, its persistent disobedience, its punishment, and its ultimate salvation. The way in which Old Testament texts are cited and reinterpreted underscores a continuity in the people of God.[36]

How then is Romans 5–8 with its emphasis on discontinuity to be understood in light of these (and other) passages that highlight continuity? Is this another one of Paul's notorious contradictions? I want to suggest that in addition to the logical argument that Romans 5–8 carries on, clarifying earlier issues and paving the way for subsequent ones, its contribution of discontinuity serves a critical hermeneutical function. The apocalyptic presentation of Christ provides the essential lens through which God, Israel, and the church are viewed.

It is not as if one could read the story of Israel and logically deduce that someone like Christ should be its conclusion and fulfillment. Instead, Christ comes as God's invasion into human history, unexpected and unparalleled in the way he comes and how he acts, and in turn provides the key for reinterpreting Israel's history.[37]

In both the occasions of continuity mentioned above, the clue to history is the apocalyptically framed disclosure of Christ and his death. In 3:21–26 the basis for trusting the character of God is the revelation of the divine righteousness in Christ's death. In chaps. 9–11 Israel's story has a salvific ending because the last Adam has more than righted the wrongs of the first Adam. "By the one man's obedience the many [including 'the full number of Gentiles' and 'all Israel'] will be made righteous" (5:19). One could not arrive at the positive conclusion about Israel that Paul does in 11:26, apart from the realization of the universal scope of Christ's obedience in 5:15–21.

Paul provides a radical rereading of Israel's history and scriptures in terms of the revealed gospel. It is the latter that defines and determines the former, and not *vice versa*. Chapters 5–8 help to make that point clear in Romans.

---

[36] See Hays, *Echoes of Scripture*, 63–83.

[37] Martyn comments, "When one needs to do so . . . one *can* find in Scripture a voice that testifies to the gospel; but one finds this testifying voice—the voice of God in Scripture—only because one already hears God's voice in the gospel, that is to say in the story of the cross, the story that brings its own criteria of perception, the story, therefore, that brings its own criteria of exegesis" ("Listening to Paul and John on the Subject of Gospel and Scripture," *WW* 12 [1992] 77).

10 ROMANS 9-11

The Faithfulness and Impartiality of God

E. Elizabeth Johnson
New Brunswick Theological Seminary

I

ONE NEED NOT resort to the hyperbole of bankruptcy to lament the widespread disconnection of critical New Testament study from questions of theological and ecclesiastical import. The defensive and even hostile postures of church and academy have only deepened "the strange silence of the Bible"[1] into what Wayne Meeks describes as "the fateful rupture between religious and academic readings [of scripture] that is now so thoroughly institutionalized."[2] A marked exception to this tendency for scholars and church people to speak past one another is discussion of Romans 9–11, which since World War II has been prompted largely by reflection on the very real human concerns raised by the Holocaust. Fifteen years ago, Werner Kümmel called Romans 9–11 a *crux interpretum* in Pauline studies,[3] and exegesis of the passage continues to be at the center of spirited conversation about the *Israelfrage*[4] as

---

[1] James D. Smart, *The Strange Silence of the Bible in the Church: A Study in Hermeneutics* (Philadelphia: Westminster, 1970).

[2] Wayne A. Meeks, "On Trusting an Unpredictable God: A Hermeneutical Reflection on Romans 9–11," in *Faith and History: Essays in Honor of Paul W. Meyer* (ed. Charles H. Cosgrove, John T. Carroll, and E. Elizabeth Johnson; Atlanta: Scholars Press, 1990) 119.

[3] W. G. Kümmel, "Die Probleme von Römer 9–11 in der gegenwärtigen Forschungslage," in *Die Israelfrage nach Römer 9–11* (ed. L. de Lorenzi; Rome: Abtei von St. Paul vor den Mauern, 1977) 13.

[4] Studies of the passage itself, as well as problems it poses about Paul and Judaism, are too numerous to list. Heikki Räisänen's essay "Römer 9–11: Analyse eines geistigen Ringens," *ANRW* II.25.4 (1987) 2891–2939 concludes with a selected bibliography that contains over sixty titles appearing in the decade since Kümmel's 1977 *Forschungsbericht*. Earlier significant surveys of research appear in Peter Stuhlmacher, "Interpretation von Römer 11.25–32," in *Probleme biblischer Theologie: Festschrift für Gerhard von Rad zum 70. Geburtstag* (ed. H. W. Wolff;

well as about broader concerns. The nature of religious pluralism in a post-modern age raises serious questions about the so-called uniqueness of Christianity or the absoluteness of Christian claims. Paul's use of scripture here confronts his readers more pointedly than does any other exegetical discussion in his letters with the difficulties inherent in the claim to possess a sacred book.[5] And the relation between voluntarism and determinism, between human and divine initiative, is at the heart of modern people's struggle to appropriate ancient religious convictions.

The most recurrent critical questions about the passage, though, continue to revolve around Paul's attitude toward Jews and Judaism, with the implicit—and sometimes explicit—assumption that descriptive studies should yield normative results: if Paul can be shown to be tolerant of or sympathetic to or even "positive" about non-Christian Judaism,[6] then late-twentieth-century Christians can with biblical support repent of their complicity in violent anti-Semitism, affirm the legitimacy of Judaism as a religion parallel to Christianity, and advance the goals of interreligious dialogue and cooperation.[7] As valuable as these goals are,[8] there remains behind their pursuit by some New Testament exegetes an unexamined theological assumption that the imperative for contemporary Christians to repent of statements and actions hostile to Jews requires the same of New Testament writers. Typical is Lloyd Gaston's posing of the problem:

> A Christian Church with an anti-Semitic New Testament is abominable, but a Christian church without a New Testament is inconceivable. . . . Whatever the general effect of the gospels, it is Paul who has provided the theoretical structure for Christian anti-Judaism.[9]

Munich: Kaiser, 1971) 555–70; and Dieter Zeller, *Juden und Heiden in der Mission des Paulus: Studien zur Römerbrief* (2d ed; Stuttgart: Katholisches Bibelwerk, 1976) 108ff.

[5] See particularly Meeks, "On Trusting an Unpredictable God"; and Richard B. Hays, *Echoes of Scripture in the Letters of Paul* (New Haven/London: Yale University Press, 1989) 63–83.

[6] Which generally means that Paul thinks non-Christian Judaism as a religion retains abiding salvific validity.

[7] Hans Küng's claim about Christian–Muslim relations is typical of Jewish–Christian conversations as well: "My thesis, therefore, is: no world peace without peace among religions, no peace among religions without dialogue between the religions, and no dialogue between the religions without accurate knowledge of one another" ("Christianity and World Religions: Dialogue with Islam," in *Toward a Universal Theology of Religion* [ed. Leonard Swidler; New York: Orbis, 1987] 194).

[8] And as much as I myself participate in the conversation—see my "Jews and Christians in the New Testament: John, Matthew, and Paul," *Reformed Review* 42 (1988–89) 113–28.

[9] Lloyd Gaston, "Paul and the Torah," in *Anti-Semitism and the Foundations of Christianity* (ed. A. T. Davies; New York: Paulist, 1979) 54. Gaston, of course, echoes the charge of Rosemary Ruether, *Faith and Fratricide: The Theological Roots of Anti-Semitism* (New York: Seabury, 1974).

While Western Christianity has found theologically legitimate ways to change its mind and behavior in regard to other important human matters (the social and religious roles of women, for example, or the institution of human slavery) without claiming that the Bible was written by people who operated from similar perspectives,[10] the debate about Romans 9–11 has often reflected Gaston's anxiety that post-Holocaust Christian responses to Jews require the New Testament (or at least parts of it) to share modern convictions about multiculturalism and tolerance, so the conversation has focused on Paul's guilt or innocence in this regard.

A change is now evident in the works of those who prescind from a rescue of the apostle and claim that he is well-meaning but confused, that in Romans 9–11 Paul argues himself into a theological corner by holding irreconcilable religious convictions and becoming a necessary (albeit unwitting) accomplice to Christian anti-Semitism.[11]

It may well be that drawing the parameters of the exegetical conversation so narrowly in terms of the question of Israel has unnecessarily limited interpreters' readings of Romans 9–11. If the crucial issue concerns only whether or not Paul believes that non-Christian Jews retain a saving relationship with God, then one is left with an alternative: either one must read the entire passage as unambiguously "positive" about Israel[12] or one must acknowledge that

---

He has been followed by John G. Gager, *The Origins of Anti-Semitism: Attitudes Toward Judaism in Pagan and Christian Antiquity* (New York: Oxford University Press, 1983), who describes Gaston's exegetical and historical "reinvention of Paul" as nothing short of a "paradigm shift" in Pauline studies (p. 198).

[10] See, e.g., the collection of essays in *The Women's Bible Commentary* (ed. Carol Newsom, Sharon Ringe, and Cynthia Thompson; Louisville: Westminster/John Knox, 1992).

[11] E. P. Sanders, *Paul, the Law, and the Jewish People* (Philadelphia: Fortress, 1983) 192–99; Heikki Räisänen, "Paul, God, and Israel: Romans 9–11 in Recent Research," in *The Social World of Formative Christianity and Judaism: Essays in Tribute to Howard Clark Kee* (ed. Jacob Neusner et al.; Philadelphia: Fortress, 1988) 178–206; idem, "Römer 9–11," 2930–36.

[12] This generally results in some form of a "two-covenant" line of thought—that is, that Paul argues Gentiles are saved by faith in Christ, Jews by traditional covenant faithfulness. The theological case for "two religions, two chosen people" was offered nearly thirty-five years ago by J. Parkes, *The Foundations of Judaism and Christianity* (Chicago: Quadrangle, 1960) and endorsed by the exegesis of (among many) Peter Richardson, *Israel in the Apostolic Church* (Cambridge: Cambridge University Press, 1969); Krister Stendahl, *Paul Among Jews and Gentiles and Other Essays* (Philadelphia: Fortress, 1976); Franz Mussner, "'Christus (ist) des Gesetzes Ende zur Gerechtigkeit für jeden, der glaubt' (Röm. 10,4)," in *Paulus: Apostat oder Apostel? Jüdische und Christliche Antworten* (ed. Marcus Barth et al.; Regensburg: Pustet, 1977) 31–44; Lloyd Gaston, "Abraham and the Righteousness of God," *HBT* 2 (1980) 39–68; idem, "Angels and Gentiles in Early Judaism and in Paul," *SR* 11 (1982) 65–75; idem, "Paul and the Torah"; idem, "Works of Law as Subjective Genitive," *SR* 13 (1984) 39–46; and Gager, *Origins of Anti-Semitism*. I argue at length in *The Function of Apocalyptic and Wisdom Traditions in Romans 9–11* (SBLDS 109; Atlanta: Schol-

the passage is logically incoherent since Paul's "positive" and "negative" attitudes seem to negate each other.[13] Since we have allowed Paul to be inconsistent from one letter to the next, we now seem to take greater freedom to label an individual argument inconsistent.[14] I am not sure this is altogether helpful. While it is indeed the case that Paul's logic falters at various points in his letters, it is also the case that the history of exegesis is littered with claims of faulty logic in passages that subsequent interpreters have made comprehensible. We do well, then, to be chary of labeling a text nonsense when it may be that we have not yet made sense of it. One suspects in the case of Romans 9–11 that allegations of Paul's inconsistency may also stem from interpreters' fundamental disagreement with the apostle's premises. Paul is more confident about his grasp of things eternal than most moderns are of their handle on things temporal. His certainty about God's way with the world strikes us as a violation of tolerance, a value we share more with his Greco-Roman contemporaries (outside the synagogue) than with the apostle himself.

Heikki Räisänen, who has done as much as anyone of late to stir up the debate, concedes with the great majority of interpreters that the "real concern [in Romans 9–11] is the question of the *trustworthiness of God* as regards his promises to Israel,"[15] but he then proceeds to address a series of questions that concern God only derivatively, beginning with "What do the chapters tell of *Paul's attitude toward Israel?*"[16] As historically and religiously significant as those questions are, it may just be the asking of them in this way that unnecessarily distorts interpretation of the passage. A Christian "attitude toward Israel" stands at the heart of our modern religious problem, because the failure to convert Jews to Christianity has not merely disappointed Christian expectations and called into question Christian claims but has drawn Christians into

---

ars Press, 1989) 176–205 that, for all its attractiveness in the context of interreligious dialogue, the claim that Paul holds such a "two-covenant" position is historically and exegetically indefensible. Räisänen's rebuttal of the argument in "Paul, God, and Israel" is decisive, although it will doubtless nevertheless continue to be attractive, particularly in popular circles.

[13] Sanders, *Paul, the Law, and the Jewish People*; Räisänen, "Paul, God, and Israel"; W. D. Davies, "Paul and the People of Israel, *NTS* 24 (1977–78) 4–39. The description of the three chapters as logically inconsistent comes most recently from Terence L. Donaldson, "'Riches for the Gentiles' (Rom 11:12): Israel's Rejection and Paul's Gentile Mission," *JBL* 112 (1993) 81–98: "There is nothing unclear about the goal of the argument in chaps. 9–11. . . . But the route [Paul] traces out to reach it is virtually unnavigable" (p. 89).

[14] Jouette M. Bassler, "Preface" to *Pauline Theology Volume I: Thessalonians, Philippians, Galatians, Philemon* (ed. Jouette M. Bassler; Minneapolis: Fortress, 1991) ix–x.

[15] Räisänen, "Paul, God, and Israel," 178 (emphasis original); see also idem, "Römer 9–11," 2930–36.

[16] Räisänen, "Paul, God, and Israel," 179 (emphasis added).

unspeakable violation of our own values.[17] Our inclination is thus to assume that the failure of the Jewish mission is what prompts Paul's reflection because it is what provokes our own.

The apparent failure of the Jewish mission is undeniably one of the factors that prompt Romans 9–11, as the immediate literary context attests. Paul claims that the church's election (8:28–30) undergirds the reliability of its hope (οὖν, "therefore," 8:31), and any uncertainty about Israel's election would vitiate the trustworthiness of God's promise to the church.[18] But Israel's fate is only part of the problem Paul addresses in Romans 9–11. The question that prompts the passage concerns not only the belief or unbelief of Israel but also the character and actions of God in relation to the whole world. Clearly, Christian discussion of and relation to Judaism cannot and should not be divorced from language about God (any more than Paul's is), but the choice of a starting point inevitably shapes the direction of an exegetical argument. The point Wayne Meeks makes at the beginning of his discussion of the passage is germane: "for anyone who still hopes to find some guidance from the Bible in trying to form a Christian life today, there is a more urgent question: not whether Paul is consistent but whether God is."[19]

The two questions are not unrelated, since to take the latter as Paul's starting point is one way to address the former. If Romans 9–11 indeed represents two or three distinct and mutually exclusive attempts to resolve Paul's personal dilemma about the eternal destiny of his non-Christian kinfolk, if the passage is therefore innocent of logical coherence or internal consistency, then there is properly no theology to be discerned in this section of the letter and what we have are instead only Paul's competing religious convictions, whose individual historical antecedents and social or ecclesiological functions we can

---

[17] Richard L. Rubenstein and John K. Roth observe that throughout history, "Jews and Christians could not help but disconfirm each other's religious traditions" (*Approaches to Auschwitz: The Holocaust and its Legacy* [Atlanta: John Knox, 1987] 9), and they quote Raoul Hilberg who describes the intimate and necessary relationship among "three fundamental anti-Jewish policies: conversion, expulsion, and annihilation. The second appeared as an alternative to the first, and the third emerged as an alternative to the second. . . . The missionaries of Christianity had said in effect: You have no right to live among us as Jews. The secular rulers who followed had proclaimed: You have no right to live among us. The German Nazis at last decreed: You have no right to live" (*The Destruction of the European Jews* [New York: Holmes & Meier, 1985] 1. 8–9; cited in *Approaches to Auschwitz*, 9).

[18] "If God has abandoned that 'chosen people' and taken another—as later Christian interpreters, beginning with Matthew, would claim, then how can we really be sure that God will not eventually do the same with this 'new Israel'—as later interpreters, but never Paul, would call the church?" (Meeks, "On Trusting an Unpredictable God," 109).

[19] Ibid., 105.

discuss.[20] If, on the other hand, a defensible case can be made that a single meaningful argument concerning the character of God unites the three chapters, then it may be appropriate to speak of Paul's coherent theological reflection in this part of Romans, regardless of whether or not it coheres with reflection in other letters on the same subject. For the sake of conversation at the most disputed points of the passage, then, and admittedly swimming against a rising tide,[21] this essay argues two points: that a single argument holds Romans 9–11 together and that its internal coherence is both consistent with the letter as a whole and susceptible of theological (rather than only sociological) discussion.

II

The literary unity of the passage—as distinct from any putative logical consistency—is marked first by the opening oath (9:1–6) and closing hymn (11:33–36) which begin and end the passage with the praise of God who is ἐπὶ πάντων ("above all," 9:5) and from whom, through whom, and to whom are τὰ πάντα ("all things," 11:36). A second literary clue to the unity of the passage is its apparently being structured by a series of three rhetorical questions, each of which is followed by further questions which develop the theme or meet potential objections:[22]

(1) 9:6   God's word has not failed [has it?]
      9:14   There is no injustice with God, is there?
      9:19   Why then does God still find fault?
(2) 9:30–32 Why did the Gentiles who did not pursue righteous-

---

[20] This is precisely what H. Räisänen claims is the necessary and proper response. See his *Beyond New Testament Theology: A Story and a Programme* (Philadelphia: Trinity Press International, 1990). Such revival of Wrede's program for so-called New Testament theology ("The Task and Methods of 'New Testament Theology'" [1897], reprinted in *The Nature of New Testament Theology* [ed. Robert Morgan; SBT 2/25; London: SCM, 1973] 68–116) only exacerbates the distance between church and academy.

[21] What follows here is very much the case I make in *Romans 9–11*, 110–75. The temptation to consider an argument more persuasive simply because it is reiterated is, I trust, balanced by genuine desire for engagement and response. The very helpful reviews of and responses to my dissertation have generally attended to aspects of it other than the claim that Romans 9–11 can make sense as a single coherent argument.

[22] Johnson, *Romans 9–11*, 144. Although 9:6 is not put in the grammatical form of a question, οὐχ οἷον δὲ ὅτι ("it is not as though") is surely a denial of one possible answer to a question much like that posed in 3:3, which makes τὴν πίστιν τοῦ θεοῦ καταργηθῆναι ("to nullify God's faithfulness") functionally equivalent τὸν λόγον τοῦ θεοῦ ἐκπεπτωκέναι ("God's word to fail"). See also the structural argument made by James W. Aageson, "Scripture and Structure in the Development of the Argument in Romans 9–11," *CBQ* 48 (1986) 265–89.

ness receive it while Jews who pursued the law did not
attain it?

	10:14–15	How are they to call upon one whom they have not believed? (believe . . . heard? hear . . . preaching? preach . . . sent?)
	10:18	They have heard, have they not?
	10:19	Israel has understood, has it not?
(3)	11:1	God has not rejected his people, has he?
	11:11	Israel has not stumbled so as to fall, has it?

There is widespread assumption among interpreters that the three primary
questions asked in 9:6; 9:30; and 11:1 are synonymous, that each is a different
way of asking why the Jewish majority is not Christian. The problem
addressed in 9:6–29 is then seen to be whether or not God's word of election
to Israel has been abrogated; in 9:30–10:21, the question concerns why Israel's
election has in fact been rescinded; and in 11:1–27, Paul considers whether or
not God might have rejected Israel permanently. So long as all three questions
are understood to address the same phenomenon—Jewish unbelief—then the
chapters take on the incoherent character of three unrelated and mutually
exclusive answers to the same question: part of ethnic Israel's exclusion from
the elect is a function of God's sovereign freedom to redefine community
boundaries (9:6–29); Israel is nevertheless responsible for its own fate because
it refuses to convert to Christianity (9:30–10:21); but despite God's elective
freedom and Israel's culpability, God will nevertheless save all Israel
(11:1–32).[23] Paul's two incompatible convictions—that God saves all through
faith in Christ alone and that God will save Israel—thus drive him to the "desperate expedient"[24] of trying on theological hats until he finds one that fits
him, unfortunately neglecting to discard the unsuitable ones once he finds it
and leaving the reader to surmise that the last of the three is the hat that
"really" fits.[25] Even J. Christiaan Beker, who otherwise defends the coherence

[23] Räisänen's summary of the chapters is nearly a caricature: "[Paul] . . . contradicts himself
when discussing the . . . problem of Israel's reluctance to accept the gospel. In Rom 9 he resorts
to the extreme explanation of divine hardening which takes place regardless of any of man's
doings (9.6–23), whereas he in the very next chapter puts all emphasis on Israel's own notorious disobedience. In chapter 11, at last, Paul definitely discards his predestinarian construction
and replaces it with the statement that Israel's obduracy is of a temporary nature" (*Paul and the
Law* [Philadelphia: Fortress, 1986] 264).

[24] Sanders, *Paul, the Law, and the Jewish People*, 198.

[25] "It would not surprise me a great deal to discover—although such a discovery will always
lie beyond the powers of exegesis—that the quotation in Rom. 11:26b–27 represents Paul's
'real' view" (Sanders, *Paul, the Law, and the Jewish People*, 195–96).

of Paul's fundamental convictions more staunchly than anyone else, laments: "Romans 9–11 is simply inconsistent in its argumentation. It is the only place in the Pauline letters where Paul is engaged in an on-going experiment of thought rather than in the expression of a finalized thought."[26]

There is some good reason to suppose that the single problem of Jewish unbelief prompts Romans 9–11, although in the final analysis it is insufficient. The questions raised in Rom 3:1–8 and left unfinished there are indeed picked up in 9:1. The question of the περισσόν ("advantage") of the Jew raised by 2:17–29 is answered only partially by the claim in 3:2 that circumcision identifies Jews as recipients of divine oracles. There exists also the very real danger, given Paul's claim that circumcision has no necessary relationship to legal obedience, that God will be attacked with the same slanderous charge (that good ends might be pursued by evil means) that is leveled at Paul himself (3:8). God's covenant faithfulness to Israel is relinquished if Israel has no faithful relationship with God (ἀπιστία αὐτῶν, "their faithlessness," 11:20, 23). This perspective on Romans 9–11—that it is simply the delayed conclusion to 3:1–8—then gives the passage the character of theodicy, an attempt to rescue God's covenant integrity from accusations of caprice or malice. The problem with this view of the chapters as no more than the delayed conclusion to 3:1–8 is that it ignores everything else that is accomplished between 3:9 and 8:39, a point to which we shall return.

The assumption that all three major sections of Romans 9–11 address the same reality of Jewish unbelief relies, second, on a backward reading of the passage itself, taking the pruning of branches because of ἀπιστία in 11:20 to be the single source of Paul's anxiety that his non-Christian kinfolk will be ἀνάθεμα ("cursed," 9:3). When he responds to such a possibility with the claim that God's word has in fact not collapsed because not all from Israel are Israel (9:6),[27] the assumption is then that the whole of 9:6–29 constitutes a tortured redefinition of "Israel" in nonethnic (that is, Christian) terms. This is then seen as the first of three mutually exclusive answers to the problem of Israel's unbelief. If, on the other hand, one refrains from knowing ahead of time that Paul will divide Israel into the "elect" and the "rest" in 11:7, then 9:6–29 does not necessarily redefine Israel at all. It describes instead the consistency of redemptive election as divinely rather than humanly initiated.

---

[26] J. Christiaan Beker, "Romans 9–11 in the Context of the Early Church," *Princeton Seminary Bulletin*, Sup 1 (1990) 45.

[27] Mary Ann Getty rightly points out that the perception that Romans 9 contradicts Romans 11 rests on the assumption that Paul's thesis is stated not in 9:6a, "God's word has not collapsed," but in 9:6b, "not all Israel is Israel" ("Paul and the Salvation of Israel: A Perspective on Romans 9–11," *CBQ* 50 [1988] 465).

Although the pathos of 9:1–5 alerts the reader to the potential for Israel's separation from God, Paul does not explicitly raise that possibility until 9:31 and 11:1, and the argumentative function of 9:6–29 (as well as of 9:30–10:21, it might be added) is therefore much more penultimate than is often claimed.

Third, the assumption that all three questions (in 9:6, 9:30–31, and 11:1) are synonymous ignores the fact that the question asked in 9:30–31 explicitly names *two* phenomena as problematic: the arrival of Gentiles at δικαιοσύνη ("righteousness") and the failure of Israel to arrive at νόμον δικαιοσύνης ("the law of righteousness"). Not only do most Jews not embrace Paul's gospel, and thus apparently put themselves "for the moment outside the sphere of salvation,"[28] but Gentiles who never sought salvation have unexpectedly stumbled onto it. Both realities—Jewish unbelief and Gentile belief—are under consideration in Romans 10, which calls into question the claim that God's covenant faithfulness to Israel is alone at stake in the whole argument of chaps. 9–11.

Finally, the first eight chapters, which bring Paul to Rom 9:1, raise more problems than the incomplete discussion in 3:1–8 of Jewish advantage. From the statement of his theme in 1:16–17, Paul has repeatedly made two parallel claims: that God is utterly impartial, dealing with Jew and Gentile on precisely the same terms, and that God is also abidingly faithful to Israel. Salvation is παντὶ τῷ πιστεύοντι ("to everyone who believes"), without regard to ethnic identity or religious behavior, and it is also Ἰουδαίῳ . . . πρῶτον ("to the Jew first," 1:16). Paul explicitly asserts God's impartiality five times in the letter (1:16; 2:11; 3:9, 22; 10:12), and Jew and Gentile are named side by side no fewer than nine times (1:16; 2:9–10; 3:9, 29; 9:24, 30–21; 10:12; 11:25; 15:10). Throughout the first four chapters, God judges Jews and Gentiles alike to be under the power of sin and similarly justified by faith. Specifically at 3:29–30, he asks, "Or is God the God of the Jews alone? Is he not the God of the Gentiles also? Yes, of Gentiles also, since God is one."[29]

God's impartiality can never be construed as reneging on God's promises to Israel, however, which is why Paul avers in 11:29 that God's gifts and election are irrevocable, and this too has marked the argument of the letter from the start. The other half of the affirmation he makes in 1:16 about God's impar-

---

[28] Räisänen, "Paul, God, and Israel," 180.

[29] Jouette M. Bassler makes a compelling case for understanding God's impartiality as the theological conviction which undergirds and structures the opening argument of Romans and plays a role in chaps. 9–11 as well (*Divine Impartiality: Paul and a Theological Axiom* [SBLDS 59; Chico, CA: Scholars Press, 1982] 121–70). Although she shows that Jewish affirmations of God's impartiality are never absolute but are qualified to one extent or another by convictions about God's particular relationship with Israel, she labels the tension between divine impartiality and faithfulness in Romans 9–11 a "logical problem" (p. 187).

tial treatment of Jew and Gentile highlights God's enduring covenant faith-fulness: "to the Jew first and also to the Greek." Five times he reiterates Jew-ish priority and advantage (1:16; 2:9–10; 3:1–2; 9:1–5; and 11:13–16). Although he constantly puts Jew and Gentile on the same footing before God, he also continues to maintain the distinctive identities of the two groups. Even as he mentions Jew and Gentile together nine times, he mentions Jews alone four times (2:17, 28–29; 3:1, 29) and Gentiles alone thirteen times (1:5, 13; 2:14, 24; 4:17; 11:11, 13; 15:9–12, 16, 18, 27; 16:4, [26]). Jews are justified ἐκ πίστεως ("from faith") and Gentiles, διὰ πίστεως ("through faith," 3:30); Abraham is the ancestor of all who follow in his faithful footsteps, both cir-cumcised and uncircumcised believers (4:11–12); matters of food and drink or calendrical observance remain properly within ethnic boundaries, and although those boundaries are not allowed to divide the church in any final sense, neither are they obliterated (14:1–15:13).[30] Christ demonstrates God's truthfulness "in order to confirm the promises given to [Israel], and in order that the Gentiles might glorify God" (15:8–9). Paul preserves the relative uniqueness of both Israel and the Gentiles as well as God's historic promises to Israel, even as he disallows all claims to preferred status before God.

This balanced tension between God's faithfulness and impartiality is what brings Paul to the dilemma he faces head on in Romans 9–11: If God deals with all impartially yet remains faithful to Israel, why is the church full of Gen-tiles and why are Jews staying away in droves? The danger is twofold: either (1) God has ceased to keep promises to Israel and thus cannot be trusted to keep promises to the church, or (2) God has become partial to Gentiles, since it is they who believe Paul's gospel, in which case God is neither impartial nor faithful. To say that Paul believes that God is both impartial and faithful is but another way to name E. P. Sanders's distinction between Paul's convictions about christological exclusivism and covenantal nomism,[31] but it deliberately frames the distinction in terms of God rather than in terms of human com-munities or entrance requirements.

---

[30] See James C. Walters, *Ethnic Issues in Paul's Letter to the Romans: Changing Self-Definition in Earliest Roman Christianity* (Valley Forge, PA: Trinity Press International, 1994) for an adroit discussion of the debate surrounding the ethnic identities of the "weak" and "strong" in Romans 14–15. The objections raised to the labeling of the "weak" as Jews are removed when it becomes clear that Paul's argumentative strategy deliberately avoids specificity so as to avoid exacerbating existing ethnic tensions. *Pace* Wayne A. Meeks, "Judgment and the Brother: Romans 14:1–15:13," in *Tradition and Interpretation in the New Testament: Essays in Honor of E. Earle Ellis* (ed. Gerald F. Hawthorne and Otto Betz; Grand Rapids: Eerdmans, 1987) 292–93.

[31] Sanders, *Paul, the Law, and the Jewish People,* 198; similarly Räisänen, "Paul, God, and Israel," 196.

To speak as Paul does of two natures or impulses or even characters of God is remarkably common, although his precise formulation of the relationship between impartiality and faithfulness in Romans is distinctly his own. The Bible itself refuses to allow God's universal sovereignty to compromise God's particular relationship to Israel or to permit God's חֶסֶד ("covenant faithfulness") to be restricted by nationalism. Isaiah's vision of Egypt and Assyria's joining Israel in the worship of God preserves the centrality of Israel (Isa 19:19–25; cf. 45:20–25),[32] and the classic statement of divine impartiality in Deut 10:17 is prefaced by an equally strong reminder of divine faithfulness:[33]

> Although heaven and the heaven of heavens belong to the Lord your God, the earth with all that is in it, yet the Lord set his heart on your ancestors alone and chose you . . . the great God, mighty and awesome, who is not partial and takes no bribe, . . . and who loves the strangers. (Deut 10:14–18)

In a similar vein, other Jews of Paul's time frequently speak of God's wrath and mercy as together constitutive of God's character. The clearest examples are in Sirach: "both mercy and wrath are with [God]" (5:5); "mercy and wrath are with the Lord; he is mighty to forgive—but he also pours out wrath. Great as his mercy, so also is his chastisement" (16:11–12). Philo, too, speaks of the two "powers" of God, and the rabbis describe God's two "measures" as ways of describing God's nature.[34] What is most characteristic of the rabbis, though, as E. P. Sanders points out, is that for them God's merciful nature always outweighs divine wrath:

> If one asks how the idea that God is just and pays to each his due is to be reconciled into a doctrinal unity with the statement that God's mercy predominates over his justice, the answer is, as before, that this is not a doctrinal system in which every statement has a logical place. One thing or the other would be said depending on the particular needs of the instance. But there should be no doubt that the latter type of statement—that mercy outweighs justice—reflects the Rabbinic attitude towards God at its most basic level.[35]

---

[32] Dale Patrick, "Election, Old Testament," in *ABD,* 2. 434–41.

[33] Bassler, *Divine Impartiality,* 9–13.

[34] Cf. also "Look at all the works of the Most High; they come in pairs, one the opposite of the other" (Sir 33:15); "All things come in pairs, one opposite the other, and he has made nothing incomplete. Each supplements the virtues of the other. Who could ever tire of seeing [God's] glory?" (42:24–25). Further, see Nils A. Dahl, "Contradictions in Scripture," in *Studies in Paul: Theology for the Early Christian Mission* (Minneapolis: Augsburg, 1977) 159–77; G. Stählin, "ὀργή, κτλ," in *TDNT* 5. 419–47; E. P. Sanders, *Paul and Palestinian Judaism: A Comparison of Patterns of Religion* (Philadelphia: Fortress, 1977) 117–47.

[35] Sanders, *Paul and Palestinian Judaism,* 124.

In Romans, on the other hand, Paul maintains the tension between divine impartiality and faithfulness to Israel without allowing one to overcome than the other. Just as χρηστότης, ἀνοχή, and μακροθυμία ("goodness," "forbearance," and "long-suffering") serve the purposes of God's ὀργή ("wrath") in 2:4–5, so ἀγαπάω ("love") parallels μισέω ("hate") in 9:13, and ἐλεέω ("have mercy") stands beside σκληρύνω ("harden") in 9:18, ὀργή ("wrath") beside δόξα ("glory") in 9:23, and χρηστότης ("goodness") beside ἀποτομία ("severity") in 11:22. The gospel is God's power, the revelation of God's righteousness, precisely because it is both "to everyone" and "to the Jew first" (1:16).

It is this balanced tension which drives not only chaps. 9–11 but the entire argument of Romans, and which contributes to the notorious difficulty of its interpretation. Most clearly in the conclusion to chaps. 1–11 does Paul reiterate the dynamic equilibrium between God's impartiality and faithfulness with which he began in 1:16–17:

A[1]   On the one hand, as regards the gospel,
          they are enemies for your sake,
B[1]   but on the other hand, as regards election, they are beloved
          for the sake of the ancestors,
C[1]   because the gifts and election of God are irrevocable.
A[2]   Just as you were once disobedient to God,
          but now you have received mercy because of their disobedience,
B[2]   so they are now disobedient because of your having received
          mercy,
          in order that they also might receive mercy,
C[2]   because God has shut up all to disobedience
          in order to have mercy on all (11:28–32).

The two C lines, which interpret the A and B lines, set God's faithfulness to Israel and God's impartial treatment of all side by side without resolving the tension. This means that God's impartiality cannot nullify God's covenant promises to Israel, but neither can God's faithfulness be construed as loyalty that can somehow be manipulated by human behavior or identity. God's mercy is just and God's justice is merciful. The argument is advanced in three related stages.

Romans 9:1–29

The supreme confidence in the trustworthiness of God's love which Paul expresses in 8:31–39 is followed by a remarkable shift in tone in 9:1 that has tended to suggest more of a break than is there. Nothing can separate us from God's love, not even Paul's λύπη . . . μεγάλη καὶ ἀδιάλειπτος ὀδύνη ("great sorrow and unceasing anguish," 9:3) for his kinfolk, precisely because (as he will argue for three chapters) God's word has not collapsed (9:6). The same word that assures the apostle that believers can reliably hope in God also assures that "all Israel will be saved" (11:26).

Three sets of parallel assertions structure the first step in the argument:[36]

(1) Ancestry is determined by God's promise rather than by human descent (vv. 6–9).
Election is based on God's call rather than on human works (vv. 10–13).

(2) God's call is not arbitrary, but serves the purposes of divine wrath and mercy—e.g., Pharaoh (vv. 14–18).
God's call is not arbitrary, but serves the purposes of divine wrath and mercy—e.g., a potter's vessels (vv. 19–23).

(3) Both Jews and Gentiles have been called in the same way (v. 24):
God mercifully calls Gentiles (vv. 25–26); and
God mercifully calls Israel (vv. 27–29).

The first two assertions outline aspects of common Jewish election theology: God's election is independent of human identity or behavior. Ishmael's genetic relationship to Abraham and Esau's moral superiority to Jacob are irrelevant to their ultimate roles in the people of God: Ishmael was Abraham's firstborn, but Isaac was his heir; God determined to love Jacob before either he or Esau had done anything at all—and it is Jacob who is the scoundrel.[37] "What Paul is arguing is that 'ethnic Israel,' the Israel of every contemporary Jew's self-understanding, is already, on Judaism's own terms, not coterminous with the physical descendants of Abraham, for it does not include the descendants of Ishmael and Esau."[38] Even Pharaoh, whom everyone knows to have been the very embodiment of malice toward Israel, is finally a useful tool in God's hands, a means of proclaiming God's power and name, just as clay pots perform their intended functions in the hands of their creator. All four illustrations—Isaac, Jacob, Pharaoh, and the clay pots—are designed to make the

---

[36] Johnson, *Romans 9–11*, 147–48.

[37] Lloyd Gaston's collection of the evidence to show that Ishmael's and Esau's children are commonly viewed as outside Israel is the most helpful contribution of his reading of Romans 9 ("Israel's Enemies in Pauline Theology," *NTS* 28 [1982] 405–6).

[38] Paul Meyer, "A Response" to Heikki Räisänen's address, "Romans 9–11 and the History of Early Christian Religion," Society of Biblical Literature annual meeting, 1992. I am grateful to Professor Meyer for sharing with me a typescript of his response.

same point: that God elects on the basis of and for the sake of God's own mercy, power, and glory, rather than because of human identity or behavior.

The repeated claims by commentators that Pharaoh "stands for" non-Christian Jews or that Christians are represented by the vessels of mercy over against the nonbelieving vessels of wrath miss the point of Paul's developing thought by focusing—as Paul does not—on the human characters rather than on God. C. E. B. Cranfield notes Paul's marked preference for Ἰσραήλ ("Israel") over Ἰουδαῖοι ("Jews") in Romans 9–11 and opines that it is "no doubt because in them he is particularly concerned with the Jewish people as the object of God's election."[39] But the choice of language signals rather the opposite, that individual human beings are not in view so much as is the one God of Israel. It is not the individual Ἰουδαῖος who is in focus but rather the whole of Ἰσραήλ whom God has elected. The subject of election is "not the one who wills nor the one who runs but the God who has mercy" (9:16). Paul Meyer rightly observes that "Paul is rejecting at every point that rigid determinism of conventional religion that divides humanity into the saved and the damned."[40] No one—neither Paul nor his non-Christian Jewish contemporaries—ever considers Ishmael, Esau, or Pharaoh to have a legitimate claim to identity as Israelites, so it is difficult to see why modern readers of Romans persist in their lament that Paul excludes them from Israel.

Räisänen speaks as though the notion of "double predestination"[41] in Romans 9 were somehow a Pauline innovation, but the quotation of Exod 9:16 in Rom 9:17 and the allusion to Wis 12:12–13 in Rom 9:20–23[42] demonstrate the rather traditional nature of the claim that God elects some and not others.[43] What is distinctive in Paul's discussion is his application of the notion to the whole world on precisely the same terms of divine mercy. God's call has always been independent of human deserving, he says, and that is as true of the Gentiles as of Israel.

Although the passage addresses only the consistently merciful nature of

---

[39] C. E. B. Cranfield, *A Critical and Exegetical Commentary on The Epistle to the Romans* (2 vols.; ICC; Edinburgh: T. & T. Clark, 1979) 2. 538.

[40] Paul W. Meyer, "Romans," *HBC*, 1159.

[41] Räisänen, "Paul, God, and Israel," 183–84.

[42] Although the opening clause of the pot's question in 9:20 comes from Isa 29:16, the rest of it does not. The function of the image of the potter in Romans 9 is quite different from the prophetic usage. Isaiah and Jeremiah (18:1–11) both speak of God as a potter and Israel as a pot in order to describe God's sovereignty in judgment. In Wisdom 12, however, there are two sorts of vessels, just as in Romans 9, created for "clean" and "contrary" purposes (see also Sir 33:13, "blessed . . . cursed"). See Johnson, *Romans 9–11*, 132–33.

[43] See Patrick, "Election," 439–40.

divine election, it is understandable that commentators assume Romans 9 deals with the exclusion of non-Christian Jews from Israel: Paul uses the biblical language of σκληρύνειν ("harden") to describe Pharaoh's role in God's salvation of Israel (9:18) and then later uses similar vocabulary (πωροῦν, "harden") at 11:7, 25 to speak of Israel's hardening. Without the idea that part of Israel has been hardened to the gospel, however, which will not be mentioned until chap. 11, Pharaoh's being hardened in chap. 9 means no more and no less than Exod 9:16 says it does—that no human action lies outside God's sovereign mercy. To say that "empirical Israel—the unbelieving majority—should be identified with Ishmael and Esau" and that Pharaoh "here stands for the [non-Christian] Jews of Paul's time"[44] requires one to have read chap. 11 before chap. 9, and to consider the question of 11:1 identical to that of 9:6. Paul indeed speaks of a distinction within Israel between Christian and non-Christian Jews, but not until 11:7, 25.

The question in chap. 9, then, concerns not who is in the family and who is out but who is in charge and to what purposes. The issue is the consistency and reliability of God's election: καταρτίζειν and προετοιμάζειν ("adjust" and "prepare") in 9:22–23 mean just what προγινώσκειν and προορίζειν ("foreknow" and "predestine") mean in 8:29–30: God calls in order to give descendants (9:6–13), to make known divine power (9:14–18), and to demonstrate divine glory (9:19–24). Prior to 9:24, there is nothing particularly "Christian" in Paul's reasoning. His employment of Isaac, Jacob, Pharaoh, and the clay pots as parallel images uses biblical language and thought to say what Jews often say: that God alone initiates a saving relationship with the world. With the claim that God calls "not only from among Jews but also from among Gentiles" in v. 24, however, Paul does add a new aspect to the otherwise traditional picture he has painted and proceeds to redefine God's people (but *not* Israel) by including believing Gentiles rather than excluding unbelieving Jews.[45] There is no question that 11:17–24 raises the potential for such exclusion, but it is important to say that this is not in view in chap. 9.

The string of biblical proofs Paul offers in vv. 25–29 supports his claim that God's self-revelation is to be found most compellingly not in the fact of an elect people but in its being elected solely by God's mercy, apart from human claims or actions. Hosea's description of God who loves the unloved and creates a people out of no people (9:25–26) recalls the earlier descriptions of the God who justifies, raises the dead, and creates *ex nihilo* (4:5, 17). And although

---

[44] Räisänen, "Paul, God, and Israel," 182–83.
[45] Johnson, *Romans 9-11,* 148-49.

the emphatic ὑπὲρ τοῦ Ἰσραήλ ("concerning Israel") that introduces Isa 10:22 suggests that Hos 2:25 and 2:1 are to be applied to God's call of Gentiles, in a very real sense the words from Hosea are equivalent to Isaiah's description of Israel as rescued solely by divine mercy. Both passages highlight God's creative and redemptive action in contrast to human worth. Those who are by nature unloved un-people become God's beloved people against all odds; those who grow as numerous "as the sand of the sea" are nevertheless rescued by God's swift and sure salvation of the remnant rather than by their numbers or strength. Both these realities are encompassed by Isaiah's prophecy that, apart from God's merciful sparing of σπέρμα (which recalls Abraham's σπέρμα, "seed," in 9:7) no one would survive. Although he reads vv. 6–24 as excluding Jews, Richard Hays's sense of the function of vv. 27–29 is on target: "Indeed, if we remember that Paul is adducing prooftexts in support of his claim that God has called vessels of mercy from among Jews and Gentiles alike (Rom. 9:24), it makes much better sense to read the Isaiah prophecy as a positive word of hope rather than as a word of condemnation."[46]

The presence of ὑπόλειμμα ("remnant") in the citation from Isaiah 10 in v. 27 inevitably calls Rom 11:5 (λεῖμμα κατ᾽ ἐκλογὴν χάριτος, "a remnant according to the election of grace") to the minds of interpreters and wrenches attention away from God's mercy to the individual identities and confessional stances of human beings, but here again a backward reading tends to cloud interpretation of Romans 9. The movement of the argument since 9:24 has been to enlarge rather than reduce the people of God who are created by unmerited and unmanipulated mercy, so there is no reason to suppose that the direction of Paul's thought reverses itself here. The gratuitous "only" inexplicably retained by the NRSV in v. 27 to qualify "a remnant" is indicative of the widespread assumption that 9:6–29 answers the question of 11:1 rather than the question of 9:6.[47] Isa 10:22 and 1:9 function for Paul to compare Israel favorably with the rest of the world by pointing to God's continual rescue of the people. Without God's preemptive mercy, Israel's peculiar relationship to the Lord of Hosts would indeed have been lost many times over and Israel would have fared no better than Sodom and Gomorrah. This means that in chap. 9 Paul is looking at God's *past* faithfulness to Israel rather than predicting the future. That will remain for chap. 11, where the image of the remnant will no longer suffice for the whole, and instead all Israel will be saved.[48]

---

[46] Hays, *Echoes of Scripture*, 68.

[47] The choice by the NRSV of "execute his sentence" to render λόγον . . . ποιήσει similarly reflects an interpretive history that hears judgment rather than mercy in Paul's quotation from Isaiah.

[48] By pointing to the historical identity of the remnant as Paul refers to it here I do not mean

Paul's provisional conclusion, then, is that God's redemptive word of election (cf. λόγος, "word," 9:6, 28) has not collapsed with the inclusion of Gentiles because that inclusion has been accomplished on precisely the same terms as God's call of Israel. That call comes only at God's initiative, independent of human right or worth. God's impartial treatment of Jews and Gentiles is therefore a demonstration of God's faithfulness to Israel rather than an abrogation of it.

Romans 9:30–10:21

Such an affirmation raises yet another question, however, in view of the contemporary ethnic imbalance in the church. "Now for the first time Paul's readers get a clear glimpse of the reason for his pain in 9:2," says Meyer.[49] If God consistently calls impartially and also keeps faith with Israel, then why have Gentiles reached the finish line and left Israel in the dust? The answer is that God has rigged the racecourse. Just as 9:16 explicitly precludes running as a means to attain God's mercy, so in 9:30 the image of a footrace functions to underscore divine sovereignty. Astonishingly, it is those who do not run who are the winners in this race. Paul's combination of Isa 28:16 and 8:14 identifies the very foundation stone of God's righteousness as the cause of offense. Meyer notes that "v. 33 must count as the most remarkable of Paul's OT quotations because of what it attributes to God: placing in the midst of his people a base of security that is at the same time an obstacle over which they will stumble."[50]

The zeal of the runners (10:2) is ironically the source of their undoing. They stumble, Paul says, because they run, because they pursue the goal ὡς ἐξ ἔργων ("as if from works") rather than ἐκ πίστεως ("from faith," 9:32), which means that they seek to establish their own righteousness rather than submitting to God's righteousness (10:3). James Dunn has demonstrated that the language of zeal in Jewish contexts consistently refers to "a dedicated defence of Israel's distinctiveness."[51] To establish one's own righteousness is

---

to affirm the proposed chronological structure of Romans 9–11 that sees chap. 9 to describe the past, chap. 10 to describe the present, and chap. 11 to describe the future. See Ulrich Luz, *Das Geschichtsverständnis des Paulus* (BEvT 49; Munich: Kaiser, 1968); Mary Ann Getty, "An Apocalyptic Perspective on Rom. 10:4," *HBT* 4–5 (1982–83) 79–131. The problem with such a neat division of the argument into discrete historical moments is that it ignores the present reality of Gentile inclusion at 9:24 and the accomplished spread of the gospel in 10:18.

[49] Meyer, "Romans," 1156; see also idem, "Romans 10:4 and the 'End' of the Law," in *The Divine Helmsman* (ed. James L. Crenshaw and Samuel Sandmel; New York: Ktav, 1980) 59–78.

[50] Meyer, "Romans," 1157.

[51] James D. G. Dunn, *The Partings of the Ways Between Christianity and Judaism and their Significance for the Character of Christianity* (London: SCM, 1991) 121.

not simply to grasp after God's righteousness by individual legal perfection, which is neither what Jews do nor what Paul accuses them of doing. To establish one's own righteousness is rather to misunderstand the nature of righteousness, to consider it a human possession rather than divine, to be ignorant (10:3) of its impartiality as well as its faithfulness, to construe God's faithfulness *as* partiality.

The shift from the relatively passive image of stumbling over an obstacle to the more active image of refusing to submit to God's righteousness introduces an element of human responsibility into what has heretofore been an argument solely about God's power. Even Israel's failure to submit to God's righteousness and seeking to establish its own, however, is within God's design as Paul attributes its cause to the gospel proclamation. God's tripping of Israel is designed not to shame (9:33) but to save (10:1), because the very stone that causes stumbling is the rock that saves, "the word of faith which we preach" (10:8). The string of γάρ ("for") clauses in vv. 2, 3, 4, and 5 explains Israel's unenlightened zeal as ignorance of God's righteousness, which righteousness is in turn identified as τέλος νόμου Χριστός ("Christ [is] the end of the law"), and is interpreted by the exegesis of Deut 30:12–14 in Rom 10:6–8. The elaborate explanatory *pesher* on Deuteronomy 30 is deeply indebted to Baruch's exegesis of the passage (Bar 3:29) and thus predicates of the gospel what Baruch says of God's wisdom: that it is near to all without distinction (10:12). That Paul's exegesis explains what he means by saying τέλος νόμου Χριστὸς εἰς δικαιοσύνην παντὶ τῷ πιστεύοντι ("Christ [is] the end of the law for righteousness to everyone who believes") in 10:4 can be seen in the fact that each element of that claim is addressed and expanded in 10:5–13:[52]

end of the law	for Moses writes of the righteousness from the law, Lev 18:5 (Rom 10:5)
Christ	but the righteousness from faith, Deut 30:12–14 (Rom 10:6–8) if you confess . . . and believe (10:9)
for righteousness	for righteousness . . . for salvation (10:10)
to everyone who believes	it is believed (10:10); everyone who believes (10:11); everyone who calls on the name (10:12–13)[53]

---

[52] Johnson, *Romans 9–11*, 156.

[53] τέλος νόμου　　Μωϋσῆς γὰρ γράφει τὴν δικαιοσύνην τὴν ἐκ νόμου, Lev 18:5 (Rom 10:5)
　　Χριστός　　ἡ δὲ ἐκ πίστεως δικαιοσύνη, Deut 30:12–14 (Rom 10:6–8) ὁμο-
　　　　　　　　λογήσῃς . . . καὶ πιστεύσῃς (10:9)
εἰς δικαιοσύνην　εἰς δικαιοσύνην . . . δὲ . . . εἰς σωτηρίαν (10:10)

The law itself, Paul says, guards against a misconstrual of God's righteousness as Israel's possession alone. In the first place, Deut 9:4 ("do not say in your heart") warns against the human attempt to do what God has already done by bringing Christ down from heaven and raising him from the dead. In the second place, by identifying the apostolic proclamation ("the word of faith which we preach") with the wisdom of God, as Baruch does with Torah in Bar 3:29–30, Paul claims that the gospel is the goal of God's law, near to all and alone able to make righteous.

Hays finds Robert Badenas's argument that "the end of the law" in 10:4 is its "destination"[54] so compelling that he says, "The burden of proof [now] lies strongly on any interpreter who reads τέλος ["end"] as 'termination.'"[55] Although I concur with his judgment, it is clear that the case is not yet universally persuasive.[56] Even if the long-standing division between Lutheran and Calvinist readings of τέλος were to be resolved in Calvin's favor, however, the traditional identification of the "stone of stumbling" in 9:33 with "Christ" in 10:4 would largely prevail. In a 1980 essay, Meyer showed that the so-called stone passages in Rom 9:33 fail to carry the christological freight later Christian interpreters like Mark, Matthew, and 1 Peter place on them, and argued that Paul intends the rock in Israel's path to refer to the law itself.[57] More recently, Meyer has amended his position to say the rock is instead God, since Paul's restatement of Isa 28:16 in Rom 10:11 following 10:5–10 makes it unlikely that the law is intended. "As in many of Paul's quotations from the OT, 'Lord' stands for the name of God himself in 10:12 and does not refer separately to Christ."[58] Meyer's careful attention to the literary context of v. 4 exposes the dogmatic blinders common among interpreters, whether of Calvinist or Lutheran persuasion, who assume that what trips up Israel is the person of Jesus, not only because the "stone" vocabulary is so frequently christological in early Christianity but also because the dividing line between Christians and Jews is so often solely christological. Yet another factor that

---

παντὶ τῷ πιστεύοντι   πιστεύεται (10:10); πᾶς ὁ πιστεύων (10:11); πᾶς ὁ ἐπι-
                        καλουμένος (10:12–13)

[54] Robert Badenas, *Christ the End of the Law: Romans 10:4 in Pauline Perspective* (JSOTSup 10; Sheffield: JSOT Press, 1985).

[55] Hays, *Echoes of Scripture,* 208 n. 83.

[56] E.g., John Paul Heil, *Romans: Paul's Letter of Hope* (AnBib 112; Rome: Biblical Institute, 1987) 71. Heil's review of my dissertation, for example, addresses only my own case for "end" as "goal," and alleges that "the majority position" is that τέλος means "termination" (*CBQ* 53 [1991] 138–41).

[57] Meyer, "Romans 10:4"; cf. J. E. Toews, "The Law in Paul's Letter to the Romans: A Study of Rom. 9.30–10.13" (Ph.D. diss., Northwestern University, 1978).

[58] Meyer, "Romans," 1157.

contributes to the highly controverted interpretation of 10:4 is the widespread tendency to treat it in isolation from its context.[59]

To remove the christological baggage artificially added to Paul's invocations of Isa 28:16 in 9:33 and 10:12, however, while claiming that the rock is to be identified with God, similarly isolates 10:4 from its context, apparently shifting the force of the argument from God's trustworthiness to the person of Christ and back to God again. Meyer brings the two foci together by saying, "the real goal of the law *as reached in Christ* is to lead to righteousness for everyone who trusts in God,"[60] but Paul's further explanation makes clear that it is not the person of Christ but what God has accomplished which brings the law to its intended purpose of making righteous. Χριστός ("Christ," 10:4), ῥῆμα τῆς πίστεως ("word of faith," 10:8), and ῥῆμα Χριστοῦ ("word of Christ," 10:17) are parallel ways of referring to the gospel,[61] the proclamation of God's righteousness which includes but is not limited to the person of Christ. The stone of stumbling, which ultimately saves all who trust in it, is the proclamation of God's righteousness in Christian preaching. This theocentric definition of the gospel, which resists a reduction of it to christology, is in keeping with the rest of Romans in general and chaps. 9–11 in particular, where numerous interpreters have noted the remarkable paucity of language about Jesus.[62]

Because the gospel is near to all without distinction, it bears witness to God's impartiality, but the fact that Israel has stumbled over it suggests that the gospel does not bear witness to God's faithfulness. The second half of chap. 10, therefore, addresses this potential weakness in Paul's argument by asking the rhetorical questions of 10:14–15, which set up a causal chain of calling upon God's name, believing, hearing, preaching, and being sent. The world-

---

[59] Rudolf Bultmann's essay on the verse, for example, deals nowhere with any other part of Romans 9–11 ("Christ the End of the Law," in *Essays Philosophical and Theological* [London: SCM, 1955] 36–66).

[60] Meyer, "Romans," 1157 (emphasis added).

[61] Similar shorthand reference to the gospel is expressed by ὁ λόγος τοῦ σταυροῦ ("the word of the cross") in 1 Cor 1:18; ὁ λόγος μου ("my word"), which is parallel to τὸ κήρυγμα μου ("my proclamation") in 1 Cor 2:4 (cf. ὁ λόγος ἡμῶν, "our word," 2 Cor 1:18; ὁ λόγος τοῦ θεοῦ ("the word of God," 1 Cor 14:36; 2 Cor 2:17; 4:2); ὁ λόγος τῆς καταλλαγῆς ("the word of reconciliation," 2 Cor 5:19); ὁ λόγος ζωῆς ("the word of life," Phil 2:16); and simply ὁ λόγος ("the word," Phil 1:14). Repeatedly, the emphasis is on the word of what God has accomplished in Christ rather than on any particular word(s) spoken (Johnson, *Romans 9–11*, 158 n. 141). See Robert G. Hamerton-Kelly's discussion of Paul's use of Χριστός ("Christ") as a synecdoche for the gospel in 1 Corinthians 1–2 in *Pre-Existence, Wisdom, and the Son of Man: A Study in the Idea of Pre-Existence in the New Testament* (Cambridge: Cambridge University Press, 1973) 115.

[62] Stendahl makes a particular point of this in *Paul Among Jews and Gentiles*, 3–7.

wide proclamation of the gospel (v. 18) has resulted not in faith but in jealousy and anger. Paul's interpretation of Deut 32:21 by means of Isa 65:2 ("I will make you jealous of a non-nation, I will make you angry at a foolish nation. . . . I was found among those who do not seek me, I became visible to those who do not ask for me") reiterates the point of 9:30–33 by pointing to God's use of Gentiles to provoke Israel to jealousy. Although they have heard (10:18) and understood the gospel (10:19), they have not believed, and this too is by God's design.

It is fair to ask in what sense the combined citation of Deut 32:21 and Isa 65:1–2 is an answer to the question about Israel's understanding. The Bible verses do not describe human resistance to God or human response to God's words but speak instead of God's action: the psalmist's depiction of the creation in praise of God (Ps 18:5 LXX) again gives Paul the language to describe Christian proclamation, in the language of divine wisdom,[63] as universally accessible. Then in Deut 32:21 Moses predicts what in fact has taken place in Israel's encounter with the gospel. The worldwide proclamation has resulted in the unexpected finding of God by Gentiles. But far from sealing Israel's guilt, as is so often claimed, the universal preaching of the gospel serves to confirm God's faithfulness to Israel. It is not to Gentiles only that the word has been sent but to Israel as well, which scripture confirms. Paul rearranges the words of Isa 65:2, shifting "all day long" to the beginning, to highlight God's *continual* reaching out to Israel.[64]

Romans 11:1–36

The third stage of the argument arises from the claim that God's abiding mercy to Israel is in no way compromised by God's self-revelation to Gentiles. The question "God has not rejected his people, has he?" is answered with Paul's second use of "remnant" language (the first in 9:27 is borrowed from Isaiah). Although the apostle himself is an illustration of the contemporary "remnant according to the election of grace" (11:5), he emphasizes the rescue of that remnant for God's own sake by adding ἐμαυτῷ ("for myself") to the citation from 1 Kgs 19:18. Believers like Paul are the current evidence (ἐν

---

[63] It is not coincidental that Paul chooses a wisdom psalm (James L. Crenshaw, *Old Testament Wisdom: An Introduction* [Atlanta: John Knox, 1981] 184; Gerhard von Rad, *Wisdom in Israel* [Nashville: Abingdon, 1972] 225) to bear witness to the universality of Christian preaching. In view of what 10:4–13 has said about the gospel as God's wisdom, it makes great sense to invoke the psalmist, who predicates of both creation and Torah the praise of God's glory. Hays notes, "Paul transmutes the psalmist's graceful depiction of the heavens' glory into a description of the universal scope of Christian preaching" (*Echoes of Scripture*, 175).

[64] Johnson, *Romans 9–11*, 159.

τῷ νῦν καιρῷ, "at the present time") that God has not transferred loyalty from Israel to the Gentiles. But unlike the traditional uses of the theme by the prophets, Paul's usage does not allow the remnant to suffice for the whole, as will become clear in 11:11–27. Although he appears to hold unbelieving Israel accountable for its disobedience and contrary behavior toward the gospel in 10:21, he refuses to take credit for his own status before God in 11:6. Paul has "heard" and "known" the same gospel he says Israel has "heard" and "known" in 10:18–21. The difference is that God has called Paul but not all Israel—at least not yet. Paul will not allow human willing or running—or even believing—to manipulate God's favor. Paul's being part of the remnant is by grace alone (11:6). The division of the runners into winners (ἐκλογή, "elect") and losers (λοίποι, "rest") in 11:7 reprises the metaphor of 9:16, 30–32 within Israel. But this time, God hardens rather than trips some of the contestants by blinding, deafening, and bowing them down.

The result of such hardening, of course, is that the runners hardened by God do after all stumble, as in 9:32, but in 11:11–12 Paul addresses the temporary nature of the stumbling and its evangelical function. He reiterates what Deut 32:21 and Isa 65:1 predicted for him earlier in 10:19–21, that the purpose for Israel's stumbling/hardening is to allow for the Gentile mission. Just as the supposedly stronger runners in 9:30–33 are tripped up and the nonparticipants have become the surprise winners, so Israel's misstep means salvation and wealth for the Gentiles in 11:11–12, and Paul glorifies his Gentile mission in 11:13–16 because it in turn serves Israel's salvation. Sanders asks incredulously, "Does [Paul] really think that jealousy will succeed where Peter failed?"[65] The answer is yes; he apparently does, although the sharp distinction between the two may force an alternative Paul would not recognize. He speaks as though Israel's salvation is God's doing rather than his or Peter's, and the worldwide proclamation of the gospel in 10:18–21 presumably encompasses the missions to both circumcised and uncircumcised.

Paul shares with several of his Jewish and Christian contemporaries a conviction that Israel's repentance and faithfulness to God will inaugurate the eschaton.[66] From that vantage point, Israel's immediate positive response to the gospel would have initiated the judgment and left the Gentile world under a death sentence. Only by God's gracious restraint of Israel are the Gentiles successfully evangelized, and that without compromising the πρῶτον ("first")

---

[65] Sanders, *Paul, the Law, and the Jewish People*, 198.

[66] E.g., 4 Ezra 4:35-37; *2 Bar.* 23:4-5; *T. Dan.* 6:4; Acts 3:19–20; and 2 Pet 3:11-12. Dale C. Allison also examines several later rabbinic texts that give voice to the same conviction ("The Background of Romans 11:11–15 in Apocalyptic and Rabbinic Literature," *Studia Biblica et Theologica* 10 [1980] 229–234).

of the Jewish mission. The "rest" or "part" of Israel who wait for the πλήρ-ωμα ("fullness") of the Gentiles to enter God's salvation are, like Pharaoh in 9:17 (Exod 9:16), the means of demonstrating God's power and name. Terence L. Donaldson draws a helpful distinction between "delay" and "displacement" in describing Paul's understanding of Israel's redemption.[67] Rather than replacing Israel as God's elect, Gentile Christians step in line ahead of part of Israel. The metaphor of the olive tree in vv. 17–24 envisions branches broken off and regrafted after the inclusion of wild shoots, provided they do not persist in unbelief.

To raise the possibility that some might culpably persist in unbelief (11:17–24) after the assurance that God is in essence responsible for that unbelief (11:7–16) sharpens the tension between divine and human initiative which has been building from the start of this argument. On the one hand, God has held back part of Israel from responding to the gospel to make room for the Gentiles; on the other hand, branches have been broken off because of faithlessness and can be regrafted only if they do not persist in faithlessness. Put in these dichotomous terms, this is the "Catch-22" that Sanders and Räisänen claim dooms Paul's argument to inconsistency, his simultaneous, irreconcilable convictions that God saves those who believe in Jesus only and that God saves all Israel with or without faith in Jesus. To pose the problem this absolutely, however, is finally anachronistic, "a construction of Paul's situation that goes beyond recognizing natural human inconsistencies and imposes on Paul polarities that have no real resonance in his theological reflection."[68]

> This false dilemma pits "faith in Jesus" against the faith of Abraham who trusted in the God who gives life to the dead, where Paul aligns the two. It pits the "Father of Jesus Christ" against the God of Abraham, where Paul aligns the two. It pits Christianity against Judaism in Paul's own breast, his Christian identity against his Jewish, where Paul aligns the two. It pits individual salvation against corporate, human freedom in believing against divine determinism, where Paul at least intertwines the two.[69]

The mystery revealed in 11:25–26 discloses God's wise plan to save the whole world, restoring the ethnic balance in the church and maintaining both God's impartiality and God's faithfulness to Israel. Rather than a sudden insight reached in the midst of anguished wrestling,[70] the interdependence

---

[67] Donaldson, "'Riches for the Gentiles,'" 92–98.

[68] Meyer, "A Response," 7.

[69] Ibid., 7–8.

[70] Bent Noack is so hard-pressed to fit the three chapters into a single argument that he says,

between Israel and the Gentiles has been hinted at already in 9:30–31 and
10:18–21 and described rather explicitly in 11:11–24. Even the picture in
chap. 9 of God who uses unexpected means and inappropriate people to
accomplish the goals of elective mercy prefigures this description of the way
"God's word has not collapsed" (9:6).

Chapters 9–11 in Relation to Chapters 12–15

This reading of Romans 9–11 both depends on and contributes to an
understanding of the entire letter as Paul's self-introduction to a congregation
from which he seeks support. His own expressed purposes for writing in
1:8–15; 15:14–32 deal not with Roman congregational matters but with
apostolic ones, and attempts to reconstruct specific conflicts between Christians in Rome invariably rest on a good bit of speculation. To suggest that the
letter has a fundamentally pastoral intention, which is the implication of interpretations that see anxiety about Israel's eternal destiny as Paul's primary motivation in chaps. 9–11, makes rather cynical the principle of nonintervention
he articulates at 15:20. Even the direct address of 11:13–27, with its blatantly
parenetic aims, rests on the premise of and seeks to defend the authenticity of
Paul's apostleship. Potential Gentile boasting jeopardizes Paul's apostleship
because it misconstrues Paul's gospel by making people's response to it their
own doing rather than God's. Having maintained consistently for eight chapters that God's radically new deed in Christ is utterly consistent with God's
prior self-revelation, in chaps. 9–11 Paul must interpret the largely Gentile
composition of the church or risk that his readers will draw Marcion's conclusion about God. One can scarcely hope in God's future, as he exhorts the
Romans to do at the conclusion of the body of his letter (15:14), if God's past
and present have been and can be manipulated by human beings.[71]

Meeks correctly identifies the relationship between the parenesis in chaps.
12–15 (particularly 14:1–15:13) and the argument of chaps. 9–11 when he
describes the function of 15:8–9:

> Christ accepted the *Gentile* Christians by being a διάκονος ["servant"]
> of the *Jews*, in order to fulfill promises made in the Jewish scriptures to

---

"The solution is granted Paul . . . at the very moment of his dictating the second part of ch. xi,
vv. 13-36" ("Current and Backwater in the Epistle to the Romans," *ST* 19 [1965] 165).

[71] See J. Christiaan Beker, "Conversations With a Friend about Romans," in *Faith and History: Essays in Honor of Paul W. Meyer* (ed. Charles H. Cosgrove, John T. Carroll, E. Elizabeth
Johnson; Atlanta: Scholars Press, 1990) 90–98; he calls the doxology of 15:13 "the climax to
the letter as a whole" and claims that "the trajectory of hope is crucial to Paul's theological
intent in Romans" (p. 97).

Jewish patriarchs about Gentiles. This extraordinarily compact statement constitutes a reprise of the themes Paul has developed in chaps 9–11 and, more than that, in the whole letter, leading up to Paul's restatement of the goal of his own mission, which follows in the remainder of this chapter (n.b. 15:16, 18, 27). . . . Paul takes up the topic [of ethnic differences] out of his experience, not theirs [i.e., the Romans'], because it is well suited to show in behavioral terms the outworking of the main themes of the letter.[72]

The trustworthiness of God's impartial mercy means that believers of all ethnic identities can "welcome one another, therefore, just as Christ has welcomed you" (15:7), knowing that God deals with all on the same righteous terms and will never renege on covenant promises.

III

Paul's argument in Romans 9–11, then, proceeds in three intimately related stages. The three chapters are neither separate nor separable stabs at making sense of Israel's destiny but represent instead a single sustained case for God's integrity. In 9:6–29, Paul argues that God's call of Gentiles does not jeopardize God's faithfulness to Israel (and therefore God's faithfulness to the church) because God has called Gentiles on precisely the same terms as God has previously called Israel. This claim demands defense, though, because the overwhelming Gentile response and puny Jewish response to the gospel suggest rather the opposite—that God has transferred loyalty from Israel to the Gentiles. Thus, 9:30–10:21 explains that the divergent responses to the gospel are themselves encompassed by God's wise design. God's righteousness has always been intended to be universal in its scope and power (10:4; note the reaffirmation of impartiality in 10:12); the gospel itself reveals the universality of God's righteousness even as it deliberately scandalizes Israel. The end of chap. 10 then prepares for chap. 11 by explicitly introducing God's purpose for tripping up Israel—that is, to provide for Gentile salvation, and the assurance that the engrafting of Gentiles in no way compromises Israel's eventual salvation but rather serves it. The mechanics of God's evenhandedness with Israel and the Gentiles are detailed finally in 11:11–27, first as Israel's hardening allows for the Gentiles to be welcomed, and then as Gentile redemption paves the way for the restoration of Israel. At each moment of God's back-and-forth attention to Israel and the Gentiles, the historic relationship between the people of God and outsiders is surprisingly reversed, but at no point is God's promise to Israel broken.

---

[72] Meeks, "Judgment and the Brother," 292.

The tension Paul maintains so persistently between God's impartiality and faithfulness results in a refinement of each as traditionally understood. Because he allows neither to overwhelm the other, divine faithfulness never becomes blind loyalty nor does divine impartiality obliterate God's eternal promises. This is admittedly an argument that only a Christian understands; there is nothing particularly compelling about it to a non-Christian Jew. That does not mean it is incoherent or even logically inconsistent. In Romans 9–11 Paul refashions the priority of Israel, which he has asserted repeatedly since 1:16, into an interdependent relationship with the Gentiles that moves far beyond what any of his contemporaries affirm. Israel's privileges are real and irrevocable, but some of them (adoption, glory, worship, and promises) are granted also to Gentiles. Israel's redemptive relationship with God is both first and last chronologically, before and after the Gentiles' inclusion. Paul's substitution of ἐκ for ἕνεκεν ("from" for "on behalf of") when he quotes Isa 59:20 (Rom 11:26) is crucial here. The redeemer comes from Zion to establish God's covenant with the whole world, including but not limited to Jacob. God himself will banish the impiety and forgive the sin of Israel, even as he has that of the Gentiles. The universal mercy of God as Paul describes it necessarily modifies the traditional self-understanding of Israel as having favored standing with God and the traditional function of the law as protection from sin, but both those points are argued in Romans well before chaps. 9–11.

This mutual modification by divine faithfulness and impartiality of each other results in a much more subtle balance in Paul's argument between God's sovereignty and human accountability than is sometimes acknowledged. Stephen Westerholm says, "while we do not expect of Paul a systematic treatment of the relation between God's foreknowledge and plan on the one side and human responsibility on the other, we do him an injustice if we fail to see that he deliberately and persistently affirms both principles,"[73] but in Romans 9–11 there is more than a mere affirmation of two distinct claims. As substantially as God's power figures in this argument—and thus seems to lessen the weight of human responsibility—Romans 9–11 has a hortatory purpose: to forbid Gentile boasting over Israel's apparent rejection and to urge the church to remain faithful. The warning in 11:21–22 cuts both ways: God's kindness and severity are for Israel and the Gentiles alike.

The extent to which unbelieving Israel remains in unbelief and Christian Gentiles remain in God's kindness is a matter of human response that is itself empowered by God's grace, much as the Roman Christians have become

---

[73] Stephen Westerholm, *Israel's Law and the Church's Faith: Paul and His Recent Interpreters* (Grand Rapids: Eerdmans, 1988) 175.

"obedient from the heart" to the saving gospel to which God has handed them over (6:17).[74]

> What we have, in other words, in this matter of determinism and freedom is not a simple inconsistency, certainly not simple determinism pitted against a simple human choice, but a complex psychological, social, and *theo*logical insight in which Paul displays some significant consistency, at least throughout this letter.[75]

This tension between determinism and voluntarism, between divine initiative and human response, is finally truer to religious experience than is either one alone. A contemporary confession of faith puts it this way: "In all these things [repentance and faith] we are responsible for our decisions. But after we have trusted and repented we recognize that the Spirit enabled us to hear and act."[76] To locate one's experience in this theological context accomplishes more than to explain one's inclusion in the elect and to justify the exclusion of others. It is also to make a particular claim about God. To affirm human responsibility this way, without in any sense limiting divine sovereignty, is to say that God's engagement with the world is intimate, complex, and subtle, neither overpowering the creation with holiness nor relinquishing holiness to accommodate human frailty.

The subtlety and complexity of this situation—that God alone hardens and has mercy and that human beings also participate in the maintenance of their own citizenship among God's people—are difficult to overestimate. Paul's failure to share the later church's expectation of a mass Jewish conversion at the parousia is a function of his unshakable confidence in God's power to save the world rather than any neatly worked-out logical or chronological scheme for holding his competing convictions together. Paul believes that nothing— neither Jewish unbelief nor Gentile presumption—will be able to thwart God's redemptive purpose, but his apostolic commission also underscores the urgent necessity of preaching and hearing the gospel. This does not mean he is incoherent in Romans 9–11 or that he stubbornly refuses to give up Jewish faith for Christian, but somehow holds them both. In Paul's mind, the two are the same because his faith is first and finally in God.

In Paul we are dealing with a man who simply has not yet learned enough church history to understand the differences between Christianity and Judaism, much less to recognize the distinction between two religious com-

---

[74] Meyer says of the stone of stumbling in 9:33 that it "combines the same fatefulness and freedom that have appeared in Paul's earlier analyses (Rom. 1:21–23; 5:12; 6:17; 8:12–14)" ("Romans," 1157), but the same can be said of the entire argument of Romans 9–11.

[75] Meyer, "A Response," 3 (emphasis original).

[76] *A Declaration of Faith* (Presbyterian Church in the United States, 1977) V.3.36–38.

munities. Paul's place at the center of the canon inevitably tempts us to read his letters through the lenses of the evangelists, his own theological descendants, and the apologists, and to forget that he stands historically prior to them all. By the end of the first century, Christians are nearly unanimous in their desire to shake the dust of the Jewish mission from their feet, but Paul does not yet share their frustration, if indeed he would ever have shared it. The person of Jesus is consistently the focus of debate between those other early Christians and their Jewish neighbors, and they draw emphatically christological lines in the sand. Paul does not. Yes, the Christ is from Israel and the redeemer comes from Zion (Rom 9:5; 11:26); Israel's salvation is without question achieved by means of Christ's death and resurrection, as is the redemption of the whole world. But for Paul those affirmations are of a piece with his claim that Abraham trusted the God who justifies the ungodly, raises the dead, and creates out of nothing, and is thus the rightful ancestor of all who believe (4:5, 17, 24).

It is not only Paul's chronological primacy that determines his distinctive perspective. Paul is a qualitatively different sort of Christian from Matthew or John or the writer of Hebrews or Justin Martyr, whose attitudes toward non-Christian Israel are finally far more influential in church history. Paul's experience of Christ crucified and raised never replaces the one God of Israel as the source and object of his faith, but is rather incorporated into it in ways that most of his successors are unable to manage. Nowhere is this so prominently manifested as in Romans, and nowhere in Romans so much as in chaps. 9–11.

Paul says the righteousness of God is God's power to save precisely because it both judges and redeems the world's unrighteousness. This can be true only if God remains utterly impartial and also keeps promises. The God whose righteousness Paul preaches continues to shape and reshape the creation with wisdom that is as unsearchable as it is trustworthy. The hymn he quotes in Rom 11:33–36 in praise of God's wisdom is borrowed from the very synagogue which has shaped his knowledge and experience of God, to affirm the continuity of God's saving mercy.[77] The God whose wisdom is both universally accessible and humanly inscrutable is always trustworthy but never predictable. Meeks asks:

> Is it possible for us, as it evidently was for Paul, to hold fast to Christ as
> the image of God, the πνεῦμα ["spirit"] that takes away the veil from

---

[77] The abundance of traditional material, most of it drawn from Hellenistic Judaism, the presence of unusual vocabulary and vocabulary used in uncharacteristic ways, and the intricacy of the hymn's structure combine to fuel the suspicion that the piece has independent origins (Johnson, *Romans 9–11*, 164–74).

the heart and from the reading of scripture, the goal of the Torah, the embodiment of the wisdom and the righteousness of God—and still affirm with equanimity that not Christ but God is ultimate? In the necessary and desirable pluralism of the world we have now irreversibly entered, this is a question of fundamental significance. The alternative to pluralist relativism need not be fanaticism, although evidence for that kind of religious and cultural polarization is all around us. A faithful hermeneutic of the Pauline kind, however, requires confidence in the God who, determined to have mercy on all and to bring into being the things that are not, will astonish those who are loyal to the story of God's past actions, but will not abandon them.[78]

The radical newness of the gospel[79] poses for Paul a challenge not only to his kinfolk's eternal destiny but, more importantly, to God's trustworthiness and the reliability of Paul's gospel. In the transforming present of the Christ-event as Paul preaches it, there lurks the danger that God's past was fruitless and the consequent risk that God's future will similarly disappoint. The apostle responds in Romans 9–11 not by denying the severity of the challenge or stubbornly maintaining contradictory convictions but by calling the Bible as a witness to God's consistently innovative actions throughout history. Paul reframes the threat to God's integrity and thus disarms it without relaxing the necessary balance between the constitutive qualities of God's righteousness: impartiality and faithfulness.

---

[78] Meeks, "On Trusting an Unpredictable God," 124.

[79] Romans is punctuated throughout with νῦν, νυνί ("now"), more than twice as often as any other letter.

11 THE THEOLOGY OF ROMANS 9-11

A Response to E. Elizabeth Johnson

Douglas Moo
Trinity Evangelical Divinity School

ELIZABETH JOHNSON correctly identifies the key issue in current study of the theology of Romans 9–11: Does the apostle's argument, as a whole, make sense? The number and influence of scholars claiming that Paul's argument in this section of Romans is incoherent are increasing rapidly. Indeed, many scholars working on these chapters assume that the incoherence of Paul's argument has been demonstrated, and they therefore spend their time assessing the implications of that assumption or the factors that produced it. I think Johnson's assessment of the implications of this trend in current scholarship is on target. If Paul asserts contradictory viewpoints about the implications of the gospel for Israel in Romans 9–11, then his right to inform our own views of this matter is jeopardized. Why should I take seriously the opinions of someone who is himself so confused that he contradicts himself in the space of fifteen hundred words—and contradicts himself not on some incidental point to which he was not giving his full attention but on a matter central to these chapters and critical to the argument of the letter as a whole? There is another implication that we must face. Those who argue that Paul is inconsistent in these chapters usually claim that Paul's "positive" attitude toward Israel in chap. 11 stands out as an anomaly in Paul's letters and in the entire New Testament. If this is so, it is difficult to see how we can ascribe much theological value to that viewpoint or to claim it as a genuinely Christian perspective. Paul's positive evaluation of Israel in Romans 11 becomes a New Testament aberration arising from an emotional attachment to his own people (e.g., C. H. Dodd) or from the need to handle a particular pastoral or sociological problem (e.g., F. Watson). To claim New Testament or early Christian warrant for so marginal a perspective seems dubious. It is difficult on these grounds to see how Romans 11 can justifiably be used as a *Christian* foundation for dialogue with Jews.

But with Johnson, I am not persuaded that we are forced to this conclusion, and I agree with her two basic points: "that a single argument holds Romans 9–11 together and that its internal coherence is both consistent with the letter as a whole and susceptible of theological (rather than only sociological) discussion" (p. 216). This being the case, I am probably not the best choice of respondent. Nevertheless, while endorsing her general conclusions, I do not endorse all the steps that she takes in order to justify those conclusions. In what follows, I will raise some questions about Johnson's identification of the purpose, structure, and issue of Romans 9–11. I will then build on this discussion in tackling the areas of theological tension in Romans 9–11.

I. THE STRUCTURE, OCCASION, AND PURPOSE OF ROMANS

Johnson claims that we must play down the role of Jewish unbelief in Romans 9–11 if we are to find coherence in these chapters and to make sense of their place within the argument of Romans. Her depreciation of the place of Jewish unbelief is reflected in her discussion of the occasion, purpose, and structure of these chapters.

Most scholars emphasize Jewish rejection of the gospel as the *occasion* for Paul's teaching in Romans 9–11. Johnson acknowledges that Jewish unbelief was an important factor, but she argues that acceptance of the gospel among great numbers of Gentiles was equally significant. This great influx of Gentiles into the community of the saved vindicates God's impartiality, demonstrating him to be the God who is "rich in mercy to *all* who call on him" (10:12). But the twin phenomena of Jewish exclusion and Gentile inclusion raise also the problem of God's faithfulness to Israel. Paul's *purpose*, therefore, is to reconcile God's impartiality and his faithfulness—not, as a too-myopic focus on Jewish exclusion would suggest, to explain Israel's role in salvation history or to reconcile God's word of promise to Israel with Jewish unbelief.

In Johnson's explanation of the *structure* of Romans 9–11, she shows how Paul goes about reconciling God's impartiality and his faithfulness. She divides the body of these chapters into the traditional three sections—9:6–29; 9:30–10:21; 11:1–32—but she criticizes the tendency to find in each section a response to the problem of Israel's unbelief, claiming that the result is incoherence. Instead, she argues, each section provides a different justification for the compatibility of God's impartiality and faithfulness. (1) God's inclusion of Gentiles, which demonstrates his impartiality, has not compromised his faithfulness, for he has called Gentiles on the same basis as he called Israel (9:6–29). (2) The "ethnic imbalance" of the church in Paul's day vindicates God's impartiality while not violating God's faithfulness, since Israel has wrongly misunderstood God's faithfulness to Israel as partiality toward Israel (9:30–10:21). (3) God remains faithful to his people Israel even as he expresses his impartiality in including Gentiles; indeed, the inclusion of the Gentiles is a means to express his faithfulness to his people (11:1–32). Recognizing the focus on the relationship between God's faithfulness and his impartiality enables us to view Romans 9–11 as a natural and integral part of Romans, for these themes have dominated the letter since the beginning.

Anyone who has struggled to make sense of the argument of Romans 9–11 must admire Johnson's lucid and comprehensive summary. She has admirably integrated the various strands of these chapters and located them securely within the argument of the letter as a whole. And she is certainly right to insist that we not neglect the part that Gentile acceptance of the gospel plays in Paul's discussion. Nevertheless, I think she has overemphasized this point, as I will argue by examining her arguments about the occasion, purpose, and structure of the section.

Structure

Johnson uses Paul's rhetorical questions to divide the body of Romans 9–11 into three major sections. I have two problems with this procedure. First, 9:6–29 is introduced not with a rhetorical question but with an assertion: "It is not as though the word of God had failed." Johnson argues that this assertion implies a question (n. 22); and probably it does. But Paul's failure to record that question must suggest caution in using it as a clue to his intended structure. Second, while no one would want to give all the rhetorical questions in Romans 9–11 equal structural value, I think that the question in 11:11 might have more importance than Johnson gives it. It is identical in form to the question in 11:1: λέγω οὖν ("I say, therefore"), μή ("not") + question; and both are rejected with μὴ γένοιτο ("May it never be!"). The parallelism suggests that 11:1–10 and 11:11–32 should be identified as two discrete stages in Paul's argument. Confirmation of this proposal comes from the catena of Old Testament quotations in 11:8–10, matching similar catenas or mixed quotations in the conclusions of the other major parts of Romans 9–11: cf. 9:25–29; 10:18–21; and 11:26b–27.

Johnson is right to question the neat division of Romans 9–11 into three parallel defenses of the proposition that "the word of God has not failed" (9:6a). Paul argues in a more "linear" fashion, with each new section building on, or responding to, points in the previous section (or sections):

(1) 9:9–29 is a defense of the proposition in v. 6a—"the word of God has not failed." Paul argues that God's word never promised salvation to all the

biological descendants of Abraham (9:6b–13). Salvation is never a birthright, even for Jews, but always a gift of God's electing love (vv. 14–23), a gift he is free to bestow on Gentiles as well as Jews (vv. 24–29).

(2) 9:30–10:21 is connected to 9:6b–29 (and especially vv. 25–29) with the rhetorical question "What then shall we say?" Paul uses his understanding of the gospel to explain the surprising turn in salvation history, as Jews are cast aside while Gentiles stream into the kingdom.

(3) 11:1–10 is connected to 9:30–10:21 (especially vv. 20–21) and indirectly to 9:6b–29 with the rhetorical question, "I ask, then . . . ." Paul summarizes the situation of Israel he has outlined in the previous two sections and prepares for the next section by affirming the continuation of Israel's election.

(4) 11:11–32 is connected to 11:1–10 (especially v. 7a) with the rhetorical question, "I ask then . . . ." Paul argues that Israel's current hardened state is neither an end in itself nor permanent. God is using Israel's casting aside in a salvific process that reaches out to Gentiles and will include Israel once again.[1]

This pattern of initial positive exposition followed by clarifications and expansions introduced with rhetorical questions matches what Paul has done earlier in the letter: compare 2:1–29 with 3:1–8; 3:21–26 with 3:27–31, 4:1–25; 5:1–21 with 6:1–14, 15–23; 7:1–6 with 7:7–12, 13–25. To be sure, we must not minimize the importance of these clarifications and expansions, which are often lengthy and substantive. But the way in which chaps. 9–11 appear to reflect this pattern should warn us against emphasizing chap. 11 at the expense of the argument in 9:6–13. If this outline of the structure is right, then 9:6–29 (esp. 6–13 and 24–29[2]) has a more central place in these chaps. than Johnson acknowledges; and 9:6a, the "starting point" of the entire discussion, may well represent Paul's chief concern in these chapters.

---

[1] For a similar suggestion about the structure of these chapters, see S. Hafemann, "The Salvation of Israel in Romans 11:25–32: A Response to Krister Stendahl," *Ex Auditu* 4 (1988) 45–46.

[2] Paul's argument and vocabulary choices suggest that 9:14–23 is something of an excursus within the section. God's "calling" of a "people" is the topic of the passage, and Paul characteristically points us to that topic by both beginning (v. 7) and ending (v. 29) the section on that note. Two of the key words of the paragraph occur in the Old Testament quotations in these verses (Gen 21:12 and Isa 1:9): καλέω ("call") (cf. also vv. 12, 24, 25, 26 and ἐκλογή ["election"] in v. 11) and σπέρμα ("seed") (cf. also v. 8 and the related terms υἱός ("son") (vv. 9, 26, 27) and τέκνον ("child") (vv. 7 and 8). The two quotations thus form an *inclusio* (see, e.g., Richard B. Hays, *Echoes of Scripture in the Letters of Paul* [New Haven: Yale University Press, 1989] 65; P. E. Dinter, "The Remnant of Israel and the Stone of Stumbling in Zion according to Paul [Romans 9–11]" [Ph.D. dissertation, Union Theological Seminary, 1980] 10–22; J. D. G. Dunn, *Romans 9–16* [WBC 38b; Waco: Word, 1988] 537; J.-N. Aletti, "L'argumentation paulinienne en Rm 9," *Bib* 68 [1987] 42–43).

Occasion

Johnson is justified in singling out the inclusion of Gentiles as an important factor generating Paul's discussion in Romans 9–11, but I think she gives too much weight to this factor and too little to the problem of the apparent exclusion of the majority of Jews from God's salvation in Christ.[3] Certainly Paul applies his vision of God's sovereignty in election to the calling of both Jews *and* Gentiles in 9:6–29; cf. v. 24. But the apostle's focus is not on Gentile inclusion but on the limitation of the recipients of God's word of promise *within* Israel. This is the essence of Paul's argument in vv. 6–13, which is reiterated in vv. 27–29. The enlargement of God's people beyond the bounds of Israel is one implication of God's freedom in election; but the restriction of those people ("seed of Abraham," vv. 7–8; cf. v. 29; "vessels of honor/mercy," vv. 21, 23) within Israel is the focal point. Nor are we thereby guilty, as Johnson argues, of reading later parts of Paul's argument (e.g., 11:21–24) into this section. Paul's expression of anguish for his fellow Jews and his offer to take their place under the curse at the very beginning of the whole argument (9:1–3) make clear that he is going to be addressing the failure of so many Jews to enter into the messianic salvation.

The rhetorical question in 9:30—τί οὖν ἐροῦμεν ("What then shall we say?")—introduces a new stage in Paul's discussion. Johnson is right to think that 9:30–10:21 is not simply a second (after 9:6–29) answer to the question, Why aren't more Jews Christians? As our structural analysis suggested, its place in Paul's argument is more subordinate than this. Specifically, Paul is showing how the surprising turn in salvation history that he has sketched in 9:24–29 can be understood in terms of the gospel, and especially its central component, "the righteousness of faith."[4] Explanation of Gentile inclusion is certainly a significant part of Paul's discussion (9:30; 10:19–20; cf. 10:10–13). But the weight of emphasis falls on Israel's failure to attain the righteousness

---

[3] Although Johnson never directly addresses the matter, she implicitly rejects the idea that the only problem Paul had with the Jews was their failure to agree to his vision of the inclusion of Gentiles. This view was popularized by L. Gaston (see the collection of essays in *Paul and the Torah* [Vancouver: University of British Columbia, 1987]) and J. Gager (e.g., *The Origins of Anti-Semitism: Attitudes toward Judaism in Pagan and Christian Antiquity* [New York: Oxford University Press, 1985] 197–264 [esp. 223–25 on Romans 9–11]); and see recently S. G. Hall III, *Christian Anti-Semitism and Paul's Theology* (Minneapolis: Fortress, 1993) 113–27.

[4] One of the most striking features about 9:30–10:21 is the way it reverts to the key theological language about the gospel that Paul has used earlier. Every component of Paul's "definition" of the gospel in the theme of the letter (1:16–17) is taken up in 9:30–10:21: "gospel" (see 10:15, 16); "salvation"/"save" (see 10:1, 9, 10, 13); "all" (10:4, 11, 12, 13); "Jew and Greek" (10:12); "faith" (passim); and "the righteousness of God" (10:3). But language of righteousness provides the basic structural foundation for the section.

of God in Christ. Johnson argues that Paul's real concern in this section is not Israel's failure but the sovereign role of God in determining the inclusion of Gentiles. Noting that Paul uses racecourse imagery in presenting the success of the Gentiles and the failure of the Jews in 9:30–32a, she claims that the Gentiles have finished ahead of the Jews because God "has rigged the race-course" (p. 227). Paul probably does imply that the Gentiles' surprising "attaining" of "the righteousness of faith" is the result of God's election (compare 9:30 with 9:16), but I think Johnson has seized on what is implicit at the expense of what is explicit. What Paul emphasizes here is the fact that the Gentiles attained righteousness because of *faith* (v. 30), while Israel missed "the torah in its promise of righteousness" because they *lacked faith* (v. 32a). In 9:32b–10:13 Paul unpacks this basic point, but again with particular reference to the Jews (as is revealed by his use of scripture and critique of the law). Rom 10:14–21 continues this focus: Gentile inclusion is mentioned only briefly (vv. 19–20), while Israel's failure to believe is again explicitly condemned (see vv. 16–17; cf. v. 21).[5]

Both Rom 11:1–10 and 11–32 confirm this focus on the Jews. Johnson claims that the argument of chap. 11 "arises from the claim that God's abiding mercy to Israel is in no way compromised by God's self-revelation to Gentiles" (p. 231). Yet the assertion that leads to the question, "God has not rejected his people, has he?" in 11:1 is not about God's self-revelation to the Gentiles but about Israel's disobedience and obstinance (10:21). As 11:11–24 and 11:32 reveal, Paul again assumes as basic to his discussion the failure of Israel: they have "stumbled," "been cut off," been "disobedient." And it is this failure of the Jews, not the inclusion of Gentiles, that drives the argument. This is made clear in the fact that Paul sees the salvation of the Gentiles is a means[6] to reach the Jews. Paul is arguing *from* the fact of Gentile inclusion and the Gentile mission *to* God's faithfulness to Israel. The direction of his argument suggests again that it is Israel's plight that gives rise to his discussion.

Purpose

By minimizing the role of Israel's plight in Romans 9–11, Johnson shifts the focus from the tension between God's word of promise and Israel's exclusion

---

[5] I think it likely that the third person plural verbs in vv. 14–15 refer to the Jews, resuming the implicit subject from v. 3 (see, e.g., C. E. B. Cranfield, *A Critical and Exegetical Commentary on the Epistle to the Romans* [2 vols.; ICC; Edinburgh: T. & T. Clark, 1975, 1979] 2. 533; H. Schlier, *Der Römerbrief* [HTKNT; Freiburg/Basel/Vienna: Herder, 1979] 316), but this point is not essential to my argument.

[6] Although, as Johnson rightly stresses (p. 232), this should be seen as only one means among others.

from the messianic salvation (as in most approaches to the chapters) to the tension between God's faithfulness to Israel and his impartiality toward all. As I have argued in the last section, I think that the problem of Israel's failure to respond to the gospel is, on the contrary, basic to these chapters. This historical fact is what sets up the basic tension in Romans 9–11: the apparent contrast between God's word expressed in the scriptures and God's word in the gospel. The former makes repeated and significant promises to Israel as a people; the latter appears to disenfranchise Israel and to fly in the face of those promises. It is this contrast that Paul implicitly raises in the opening verses of the section: Israel, despite the promises and privileges granted to it in scripture (vv. 4–5) is, in light of the gospel, in need of salvation (vv. 1–3). In contrast to Johnson's interpretation, I find this same tension repeated in 11:28: "from the standpoint of the gospel [the Jews] are enemies for your sakes; but from the standpoint of election [e.g., the word of promise to Israel in scripture] they are beloved because of the fathers."[7] Paul's assertion here of Israel's dual status succinctly summarizes the dilemma that drives the whole argument of these chapters: the Israel now at enmity with God because of the gospel is nevertheless the Israel to whom God has made irrevocable promises of blessing. In broad terms, as 9:30–10:21 elaborates the former, negative side of this dilemma, so 9:6b–29 and 11:1–27 explain the second, positive side.[8] These texts frame Paul's discussion, setting forth the essential tension that Paul seeks to resolve.

If 9:6–13 is as basic to Paul's argument as my understanding of the structure suggests, then the widespread assumption that 9:6a states the basic theme of Romans 9–11 receives confirmation: "the word of God has not failed." As Johnson recognizes, this assertion implies a question; and in light of 9:1–5, that question must be: Does not the apparent exclusion of Israel from the people of God through the preaching of the gospel render null and void God's earlier promises to Israel? It is for this reason that Paul quotes the scriptures so often in Romans 9–11 (almost a third of all Paul's quotations are found in these chapters): he is seeking to demonstrate "the congruity between God's

---

[7] Johnson's description of the structure of vv. 28–32 is accurate, but I question whether vv. 29 and 32 (the "C" lines in her diagram) "interpret," respectively, v. 28 and vv. 30–31. Rather, I think that vv. 29 and 32 ground (γάρ, "for") the assertions in v. 28 and vv. 30–31. And these assertions focus on the salvation of Jews, with Gentile inclusion introduced only as it relates to the Jews. Speaking broadly, one may say that v. 32 asserts God's impartiality. But it is not set in tension with God's faithfulness (v. 28); the two are parallel bases for God's mercy to Israel.

[8] See R. Schmitt, *Gottesgerechtigkeit—Heilsgeschichte—Israel in der Theologie des Paulus* (Europäische Hochschulschriften 23/240; Frankfurt: Peter Lang, 1984) 111. Note the verbal parallels with earlier sections: ἐκλογή ("election," v. 28; cf. 9:11; 11:5, 7); πατέρας ("fathers," v. 28; cf. 9:5); κλῆσις ("calling," v. 29; cf. καλέω, "call," in 9:7, 12, 24, 25, 26); ἀπειθέω ("disobey," vv. 30–31; cf. 10:21); ἐλεέω ("have mercy on," vv. 30–32; cf. 9:15, 18).

word in Scripture and God's word in Paul's gospel."[9] Johnson is right, therefore, to locate the essence of Romans 9–11 in a question about God. We disagree, however, on what that exact question is: she stresses the tension between two revealed characteristics of God; I stress the historical tension between God's word to Israel and his word of good news in Jesus Christ.

Any satisfactory interpretation of Romans 9–11 must be able to integrate these chapters with the argument of the letter as a whole, and here is one of the strengths of Johnson's position. She argues that the topic of Romans 9–11, the tension between God's faithfulness to Israel and his impartiality to all, is precisely what "drives" the entire argument of Romans (p. 222). However, while these themes are important in Romans, I am not convinced that they are as central as Johnson makes them. Paul certainly stresses the universal significance of the gospel (e.g., 1:16; 3:9, 19, 22–23, 29–30; 4:12, 16–17; 5:12–19; 9:24; 10:10–13, 19–20; 11:32; 15:7–12), and the extension of God's grace to Gentiles as well as Jews may perhaps be interpreted as a reflection of his impartiality. But the language of "impartiality" occurs only once in Romans—and then with respect not to the gospel but to the assessment of human beings at the judgment (2:11).[10] Moreover, as Johnson notes (n. 29), Jewish writers did not see any conflict between God's impartiality and his favor to Israel. It seems difficult to think, then, that the doctrine of God's impartiality would have created a tension with God's faithfulness strong enough to drive the argument of Romans 9–11. Neither is God's faithfulness (to Israel? to the world?) as dominant a theme as Johnson suggests.[11]

Current scholarly preoccupation with the "for all who believe, but to the Jew first" element of Rom 1:16–17 in explanations of the letter as a whole may be an overreaction to a former preoccupation with "the one who is righteous by faith will live." Both these themes, however, are subordinate to the concept that leads off Paul's statement of the theme of the letter in 1:16–17: the gospel. As I understand the letter, Paul is presenting and defending the gospel against a backdrop of controversy over the relationship between Judaism and the church. Paul, the "apostle to the Gentiles," found himself at

---

[9] Hays, *Echoes of Scripture*, 64; cf. F. Watson, *Paul, Judaism and the Gentiles: A Sociological Approach* (SNTSMS 56; Cambridge: Cambridge University Press, 1986) 160–62.

[10] J. Bassler nevertheless argues that God's impartiality is the central theme in 1:16–2:29, and perhaps in 1:16–3:20 as a whole (*Divine Impartiality: Paul and a Theological Axiom* [SBLDS 59; Chico, CA: Scholars Press, 1982] 122–37, 154–65). But it seems to me that Bassler has placed more emphasis on this theme than the structure of the passage and its key summary assertions (1:18–19; 3:9, 19–20) would justify.

[11] Even if δικαιοσύνη θεοῦ ("the righteousness of God") is interpreted in these terms (which I question), significant sections of Romans (e.g., chaps. 5–8) cannot be subsumed under the theme of God's faithfulness.

the vortex of this debate. A decade of struggle to preserve the integrity and freedom of the gospel from a fatal mixture with the Jewish torah lies behind him; a critical encounter with Jews and Jewish Christians suspicious of him because of his outspoken stance in this very struggle lies immediately ahead (cf. Rom 15:30–33). And reinforcing Paul's own reasons for being preoccupied with the relation of Jew and Gentile is the situation in the Roman church. Rom 14:1–15:13 reveals a split along largely Jewish–Gentile lines; and although this problem is not the main motivation for the letter, it is (contra Johnson) surely one reason for Paul's focus in Romans on the theological and historical continuity between the Old Testament and the New Testament, "law" and "gospel."[12]

Romans 9–11 has an integral role in this explanation and defense of the gospel. It is no excursus or afterthought; neither is it, however, the center or climax of the letter.[13] Paul demonstrates in these chapters the compatibility between the gospel and scripture in order to vindicate a crucial claim he makes for that gospel: that it is "the gospel of God" (1:1). Paul's argument earlier in the letter might have seemed to jeopardize that claim. He has denied that Jews

---

[12] For substantiation of these points, see my *Romans 1–8* (Chicago: Moody, 1991) 16–28.

[13] F. C. Baur paved the way for this view of the centrality of Romans 9–11. He contested the "dogmatic" interpretation of Romans, with its focus on justification by faith in chaps. 1–8, and argued for a historical interpretation of the letter, focused on the debates between Jews and Christians and with chaps. 9–11 the "germ and centre" of the letter (*Paul the Apostle of Jesus Christ: His Life and Work, His Epistles and His Doctrine* [2 vols.; 2d ed.; London: Williams & Norgate, 1876] 315–41, esp. 315). For recent defenses of the centrality of Romans 9–11, see K. Stendahl, *Paul Among Jews and Gentiles and Other Essays* (Philadelphia: Fortress, 1976) 4; J. C. Beker, *Paul the Apostle: The Triumph of God in Life and Thought* (Philadelphia: Fortress, 1980) 87.

Romans 9–11 reveals many specific textual and thematic contacts with chaps. 1–8. Many scholars see a close relationship with 3:1–8 (e.g., E. Brandenburger, "Paulinische Schriftauslegung in der Kontroverse um das Verheissungswort Gottes (Röm 9)," *ZTK* 82 [1985] 3–5; Schlier, *Römerbrief*, 283) and chap. 8 (e.g., B. Byrne, *'Sons of God'—'Seed of Abraham': A Study of the Idea of Sonship of God of all Christians in Paul against the Jewish Background* [AnBib 83; Rome: Biblical Institute, 1979] 127–29; N. Elliot, *The Rhetoric of Romans: Argumentative Constraint and Strategy and Paul's "Dialogue with Judaism"* [JSNTSup 45; Sheffield: JSOT Press, 1990] 261–63). For a complete list and full discussion of these contacts, see H.-M. Lübking, *Paulus und Israel im Römerbrief: Eine Untersuchung zu Römer 9–11* (Europäische Hochschulschriften 23/260; Frankfurt: Peter Lang, 1986) 21–51. But the very number of these contacts suggests that chaps. 9–11 form a discrete argument, relating generally to the argument of chaps. 1–8 without being tied to any one text or theme. See W. G. Kümmel, "Die Probleme von Römer 9–11 in der gegenwärtigen Forschungslage," in *Die Israelfrage nach Röm 9–11* (ed. L. de Lorenzi; Monographische Reihe von 'Benedictina' 3; Rome: St. Paul's Abbey, 1977) 15; D. E. Aune, "Romans as a *Logos Protreptikos*," in *The Romans Debate* (ed. K. P. Donfried; rev. ed.; Peabody, MA: Hendrickson, 1991) 294–95; H. Räisänen, "Paul, God, and Israel: Romans 9–11 in Recent Research," in *The Social World of Formative Christianity and Judaism: Essays in Tribute to Howard Clark Kee* (ed. J. Neusner et al.; Philadelphia, Fortress, 1988) 179–80.

are guaranteed salvation through the Mosaic covenant (chap. 2, especially). What, then, becomes of their scripturally based status as "God's chosen people"? Magnifying the problem is Paul's repeated insistence that what once apparently belonged to, or was promised to, Israel now belongs to believers in Jesus Christ, whether Jew or Gentile. Christians are Abraham's heirs (chap. 4), God's adopted children (8:14–17), possessors of the Spirit (chap. 8), and heirs of God's own glory (5:2; 8:18–30). Therefore, although I think that Johnson overemphasizes it, she is certainly justified in bringing out the significance of Gentile inclusion for the situation addressed in Romans 9–11. I think that it is Jewish rejection of the gospel that creates the problem Paul grapples with in Romans 9–11; but Gentile acceptance of that same gospel exacerbates it. Paul could have cut the Gordian knot by claiming that the church had taken over Israel's position and leaving it at that. This Paul refuses to do; in his view, to jettison God's promises to Israel is to jettison the gospel.

II. THEOLOGICAL TENSIONS IN ROMANS 9–11

The issues we have examined in section I are important in their own right. But, in the context of present academic discussion of Romans 9–11, they are also preliminary to the more critical question of the theological integrity of Paul's argument. Johnson sets her own analysis of the argument of Romans 9–11 in the context of this debate. As I made clear at the outset of my response, I am entirely supportive of Johnson's effort to find theological coherence in these chapters. But my differences with her over the general shape of Romans 9–11 will mean that I also disagree with some elements of her solution to this problem. In this section, I want to air those disagreements at the same time as I tentatively suggest some alternate approaches to these issues.

Divine Sovereignty and Human Responsibility

As Johnson notes, those scholars who find in 9:6–29 and 9:30–10:21 parallel responses to the question Why hasn't Israel responded to the gospel? are faced with an apparent contradiction. In 9:6–29 Paul answers this question with reference to the sovereign decision of God: he has chosen some to participate and has rejected others. But in 9:30–10:21 Paul argues that the Jews' failure to believe is why they have been excluded from salvation. In the first section the Jews are not included because *God* chose that they would not be; in the second that are not included because *they* chose not to be.

Johnson takes some of the force from this apparent contradiction by arguing that Paul's election teaching in 9:6–29 is directed to the inclusion of Gentiles rather than to the exclusion of Jews. While I cannot follow her interpretation at this point, I do think she is right to argue that 9:6–29 and 9:30–10:21 are not two answers to the same question. The relationship between these two units is more subtle. Nevertheless, as Johnson also realizes, these considerations do not remove the problem. Some scholars seek to "explain" the tension by making human response (9:30–10:21; 11:17–24) the basis for God's election (9:6–29; 11:5–7)[14] or by making human response the outcome of God's election.[15] While Johnson appears to lean toward the latter solution (see p. 233), she ultimately affirms the integrity of both God's sovereignty and human responsibility. I entirely agree. God's control of all things and the full seriousness and integrity of human decision making are found together throughout the scriptures and in many Jewish writings.[16] Their interplay is woven into the warp and woof of biblical religion, and while their relationship may finally defy logical resolution, we are not thereby left only with an *il*logical contradiction, but with a paradox or antinomy that is perhaps the inevitable product of a powerful and holy God's intervention in human affairs (as Johnson notes).

The Election of Israel

For various reasons, current study of Romans 9–11 is preoccupied with the teaching of these chapters about the role of Israel in God's purposes. Johnson suggests that this might not be the best starting point and that those who begin here might end up with a distorted picture of the chapters. Her warning is well taken. For all our (appropriate) concern with the implications of Paul's teaching for the issues we face in our day, we will fail to understand his teaching if we impose on the apostle our own issues and agendas. What results from such a procedure might be interesting and applicable, but its claim to be *Paul's* teaching may be questionable. Nevertheless, as my comments in section I above indicate, I am not sure that Johnson's warnings in this case are on target. I think that the large-scale Jewish rejection of the gospel, with the implication that these Jews are thereby excluded from God's salvation in Christ, *is* the driving force behind Romans 9–11. The questions that this circumstance

---

[14] E.g., Melanchthon: "Here he [Paul] expressly sets down the cause of reprobation, namely, because they are not willing to believe the Gospel" (*Commentary on Romans* [ed. and trans. F. Kramer; St. Louis: Concordia, 1992] 193).

[15] E.g., G. Maier, *Mensch und freier Wille nach den jüdischen Religionsparteien zwischen Ben Sira und Paulus* (WUNT 12; Tübingen: Mohr [Siebeck], 1971) 385.

[16] See, e.g., D. A. Carson, *Divine Sovereignty and Human Responsibility: Biblical Themes in Tension* (Atlanta: John Knox, 1981).

raises for the integrity of God's word, filled as it is with strong and sweeping promises to those same apparently rejected Jews, force Paul to put the place of Israel in God's purposes at the forefront of this discussion.

It is just because the issue of Israel is so central to Romans 9–11 that Paul's alleged contradictions in his teaching about Israel are so serious. Isolated voices in the past have identified contradictions in Paul's discussion of Israel in these chapters. But recent years have seen those voices swell into a chorus. Several points of contradiction are often noted, but they boil down to the question of election. Has God elected only some—and apparently, indeed, a small minority—of Jews to be saved, or has he elected the entirety of Israel? Rom 9:6–29 seems to affirm the former; as Paul summarizes in v. 27, "the *remnant* will be saved." Yet 9:4–5; 11:1–2; and 11:11–24 hint at a different answer, spelled out in 11:25–32 and stated in v. 26a: "*all Israel* will be saved."

Johnson rejects two methods of resolving this conflict, one explicitly and the other implicitly. In n. 12 she cites and criticizes the "two-covenant" theory. While its advocates do not usually advance this theory as a means of solving the apparent contradiction in Romans 9–11 about Israel's election, it has the potential for doing so. The salvation of the remnant could be based on God's election of the church through Jesus Christ, while the salvation of "all Israel" could be based on God's election of Israel through the "torah covenant." I agree with Johnson's decision to reject this alternative and cite her own fine and detailed critique of the proposal for substantiation.[17]

Another way to resolve the tension in Paul's treatment of Israel's election and salvation is to deny, in effect, that 11:25–32 is speaking about Israel's election. That is, we may understand the "all Israel" of 11:26a to refer not to the nation of Israel but to the people of God generally, composed of both Jews and Gentiles. This interpretation, which has a long pedigree, has been advanced recently by N. T. Wright as a way of resolving the apparent contradiction about Israel's election in Romans 9–11.[18] I am not clear about Johnson's view of this interpretation.[19] In any case, I think that 11:25–26 refers to or at least presup-

---

[17] E. E. Johnson, *The Function of Apocalyptic and Wisdom Traditions in Romans 9–11* (SBLDS 109; Atlanta: Scholars Press, 1989) 176–205. Another fine rebuttal of this view is R. Hvalvik, "A 'Sonderweg' for Israel: A Critical Examination of a Current Interpretation of Romans 11.25–27," *JSNT* 38 (1990) 87–107.

[18] N. T. Wright, *The Climax of the Covenant: Christ and the Law in Pauline Theology* (Minneapolis: Fortress, 1992) 236–46.

[19] In her rejoinder to my response at the conference, Johnson claims that Paul failed to share my "expectation of a mass Jewish conversion" (p. 237). But, according to her paper, she also finds in 11:11–27 a "back-and-forth" movement from Israel's hardening to Gentile inclusion to "the restoration of Israel."

poses large-scale conversion of Jews[20] at the time of the return of Christ.[21] As attractive at it might be in some ways, then, I cannot adopt Wright's solution to the tension about Israel in Romans 9–11.

If N. T. Wright and others resolve the apparent conflict between 9:6–29 and 11:25–26 by removing 11:25–26 from consideration, Johnson suggests that she would resolve it by removing, or at least playing down, 9:6–29. I say "suggests," because Johnson never spells out her resolution. But I think that this is the tendency of her exposition. As we noted above, she argues that 9:6–29 "concerns not who is in the family and who is out but who is in charge and to what purposes" (p. 225); exclusion of unbelieving Jews from the people of God, she argues, is "not in view in chap. 9" (p. 225). I indicated above my unease with this approach to 9:6–29; I will now give some further reasons for it.

Johnson argues that 9:6–23 is a general argument about God's way of "initiating a saving relationship with the world," while 9:24–29, which focuses explicitly on the implications of this teaching for Christian experience, has the purpose not of reducing the people of God (by excluding Jews) but of enlarging that people (by including Gentiles) (p. 225). But there are difficulties with both these conclusions.

While 9:6–23 is an important statement about God's sovereignty in election to salvation,[22] these verses have a specific purpose within their context: to justify Paul's assertion in v. 6b that "not all who are of Israel are Israel."[23] This assertion grounds (γάρ, "for") Paul's denial that the word of God has failed (v. 6a); and this denial, in turn, comes in response to the apparent conflict between by Israel's plight (vv. 1–3) and its scriptural privileges (vv. 4–5). Exclusion of some Israelites is the issue that Paul claims to be addressing at this

---

[20] πᾶς Ἰσραήλ ("all Israel") occurs 143 times in the LXX, where it usually denotes not every single Israelite but a representative number of Israelites—Israel as a corporate entity (see, e.g., Josh 7:25; 1 Sam 14:22; Ezra 2:70; Neh 7:73; Jdt 15:14).

[21] The temporal delimitation of Israel's salvation is based not on οὕτως ("in this way"), which probably has no temporal nuance, but on the emphasis on temporal sequence in vv. 11–24 (οὕτως refers, then, to this sequence as the manner of Israel's salvation) and on the probable identification of the coming of the deliverer (v. 26b) with the parousia.

[22] Despite the weight of current scholarship, I am convinced that these verses are speaking about God's election of individuals to salvation. See esp. J. Piper, *The Justification of God: An Exegetical and Theological Study of Romans 9:1–23* (2d ed.; Grand Rapids: Baker, 1993); T. R. Schreiner, "Does Romans 9 Teach Individual Election unto Salvation? Some Exegetical and Theological Reflections," *JETS* 36 (1993) 25–40.

[23] While I think that Paul does use Ἰσραήλ ("Israel") to denote the elect from among both Jews and Gentiles in the much-debated Gal 6:16 (so, recently R. N. Longenecker, *Galatians* [WBC; Waco: Word, 1990] 297–99), the context here shows that he intends the second occurrence of Ἰσραήλ in 9:6b to denote the "remnant" of the elect within national Israel (see vv. 7–13, 27).

point; 9:6–23 must have application to it. This being the case, I am inclined to think, despite Johnson's denial (p. 224), that Paul intends his readers to see behind the figures of Esau (vv. 10–13), Pharaoh (vv. 17–18), and "the vessels of dishonor/wrath" (vv. 21–22) unbelieving Jews of his own day.[24]

Similarly, to claim that the function of vv. 24–29 is to "enlarge" and not "reduce" the people of God is reductionistic. Paul is doing both in these verses. He uses scripture to validate God's freedom to call Gentiles as well as Jews (vv. 25–26) *and* to call only *some* Jews (vv. 27–29; cf. v. 24: ἐκάλεσεν ἡμᾶς . . . ἐξ Ἰουδαίων, "He called us . . . from among Jews"). By stressing that God's calling of Jews and Gentiles takes place in parallel fashion (a selection of some from among each ethnic group), Paul implies a radically new understanding of the election of Israel. And the fact that v. 24 so clearly speaks of God's calling of Christians requires that vv. 27–29 refer not just to Israel's past (as Johnson argues) but to Israel's present. That Paul uses scripture to affirm God's continuing faithfulness to Israel is clear from the quotation of Isa 1:9 in v. 29: God is still preserving a "seed." But the note of discrimination within Israel is heard here again also: not all of Israel is Israel (v. 6b). While Johnson is right to note that there is no explicit warrant in the Greek of v. 27b for the "only" of the NRSV (and the NIV, TEV, REB, and JB), the logical relationship between the first part of the verse—"even if the number of the children of Israel is as the sand of the sea"—justifies its inclusion as an interpretive paraphrase. The continuation of the quotation from Isa 10:22–23 in v. 28 probably reinforces the note of judgment.[25] But if Paul is true to the scriptures in finding in the doctrine of the remnant a word of judgment—"it is *only* a remnant that will be saved"—he also follows scripture and Jewish tradition in finding in the doctrine a word of hope—"a remnant *will be* saved."[26] This, at least, seems to be an implications of his use of the concept of the remnant in 11:1–10, when we consider its relationship to 11:11–32.

But it is just in this conviction—that the present remnant within Israel will one day expand to include "all Israel"—that Paul is said to contradict his teaching in 9:6–29 and 11:5–10. I have already rejected two methods of rec-

---

[24] Cranfield, *Romans,* 2. 488; Byrne, *Sons of God and Seed of Abraham,* 135; Räisänen, "Paul, God, and Israel," 182–83.

[25] Paul follows the LXX at this point, which radically revises the Hebrew. The meaning of the LXX rendering (and of Paul's application of its rendering) is debated, but there is good reason to think that it carries over the note of judgment plainly present in the Hebrew. See, e.g., U. Wilckens, *Der Brief an die Römer* (3 vols.; EKK; Neukirchen-Vluyn: Neukirchener Verlag, 1978–1981) 2. 207.

[26] On the Old Testament remnant concept, see particularly G. F. Hasel, *The Remnant: The History and Theology of the Remnant Idea from Genesis to Isaiah* (Andrews University Monographs 5; Berrien Springs, MI: Andrews University Press, 1972).

onciling this tension, and I have raised doubts about Johnson's own approach. Of course, it is easy to criticize: difficult (and perilous!) to come up with viable alternatives. Nevertheless, I want to offer some tentative suggestions about resolving the apparent contradiction on this matter. It is, of course, all too easy to impose a unity on Paul by means of arbitrary exegesis and "harmonizing expedients." But we must beware the other extreme also: failing to give due attention to larger theological presuppositions and frameworks of reference that may enable us to solve apparent contradictions at the conceptual level.[27]

In Romans 9–11, a critical frame of reference in Paul's treatment of Israel's salvation is a distinction between corporate and individual election. Some traditional explanations of Romans 9–11 have overemphasized the individual perspective, viewing the chapters as an exposition on predestination. But some contemporary approaches err in the opposite direction. The situation Paul confronted required him to integrate the two perspectives or, better, to interpret one in the light of the other. Paul inherited from the scriptures and his Jewish heritage the teaching of a corporate election of all Israel. But his experience of and understanding of the gospel required a serious revision of this perspective. That not all Jews were responding to the gospel did not itself overturn the traditional understanding of Israel's election; for that tradition never insisted that Israel's election required the salvation of every single Israelite. On the other hand, the relatively small number of Jews responding to the gospel required a serious recasting of that tradition. But it was the great influx of Gentiles—as individuals, not as a "people"—that broke those boundaries altogether. Paul thus did what some Jewish "sectarian" groups before him had done: he "individualized" election by insisting that membership in the true people of God was reserved for certain people rather than for a nation.[28] Paul's doctrine, of course, was far more radical, for he not only restricted election within Israel but expanded it to include Gentiles.

Once we recognize that Paul must deal with both individual and corporate election in Romans 9–11, it is no "harmonizing expedient" to ask which perspective Paul might have in mind in a given text. Paul has framed his discussion in Romans 9–11 with reassertions of the continuing validity of Israel's "corporate" election (9:4–5; 11:28b–29; cf. also 11:1–2).[29] But Paul's key task

---

[27] See, e.g., Wright, *Climax of the Covenant*, 4–13.

[28] Thus, e.g., covenantal membership was reserved at Qumran for the "sons of light" and in *Psalms of Solomon* for the "pious." See esp. M. Seifrid, *Justification by Faith: The Origin and Development of a Central Pauline Theme* (NovTSup 68: Leiden: Brill, 1992) 81–133.

[29] The present tense verb (εἰσιν, "are") in 9:4 and the relationship between 9:4–5 and 11:28–29 show that the privileges Paul lists in 9:4–5 are fraught with continuing significance for Israel as a people. In each of these texts, the reference is to the corporate entity of Israel (see F. Dreyfuss, "Le passé et le présent d'Israel [Rom 9:1–5, 11:1–24]," in *Die Israelfrage*, 143–44).

is to explain how individual election qualifies the nature and significance of this corporate election.[30] This he does in 9:6–29. This text does not revoke Israel's election,[31] but shows that it does not require the salvation of every Israelite at every point in history. To be sure, virtually all Jews could agree with Paul at this point. But Paul's view is different from standard Jewish views of election in two related ways. First, he reduces the number of Jews who belong to the people of God in a given generation much further than most Jews were willing to do. Second, he bases election on God's free and sovereign calling of an individual in a way distinct from the syncretism of most Jewish views of salvation. What sets Paul's teaching in Rom 9:6b–29 apart from Jewish perspectives is the starting point. While "mainstream" Jewish theology held that Jews were within the covenant unless and until they apostatized, Paul presumes that Jews, like Gentiles, can "get in" only through a positive and specific decision of God on that person's behalf. Thus, within and outside the corporate election of Israel, there is operating, Paul shows, an election of individuals. And Paul's exclusivist soteriology requires that the corporate election of Israel be a nonsalvific election: an election to privilege and blessing for a nation in contrast to the election of individuals to salvation.

With this perspective in place, we may turn to the texts in which the tension between two conceptions of election is greatest: 9:6–29, which affirms that "(only) a remnant (of Israel) will be saved" (v. 27c) because God has chosen only some Jews (v. 24); and 11:26–28, which affirms that "all Israel will be saved" (v. 26a) because Jews, generally, are "according to election beloved because of the fathers" (v. 28b). Three considerations ease the tension between these texts.

First, Paul is pursuing contrasting rhetorical purposes in the two texts. In the former, Paul is denying that the exclusion of many Jews from the messianic people of God means that "the word of God had failed" (9:6a). He is countering the Jewish assumption that God's word of promise required that Jews would always make up the great bulk of the people of God. Against this assumption Paul emphasizes God's freedom to choose whomever he wants, Jew or Gentile. But in 11:11–32, Paul counters the arrogance of Gentile Christians who are convinced that God has put the Jews into a permanent minority position within the people of God. To them, Paul reveals God's

---

[30] Cf. O. Hofius: "Paul fully acknowledges that God's election and rejection within Israel is *set in the broader framework* of God's election of *all* Israel . . ." ("'All Israel will be Saved': Divine Salvation and Israel's Deliverance in Romans 9–11," *Princeton Seminary Bulletin* Sup 1 [1990] 32); cf. also P. von der Osten-Sacken, *Christian–Jewish Dialogue: Theological Foundations* (Philadelphia: Fortress, 1986) 70–72 (although he comes to conclusions quite different from mine).

[31] *Contra*, e.g., Watson, *Paul, Judaism and the Gentiles*, 164, 228 n. 10.

abiding commitment to his covenant with the people of Israel and claims that this commitment will be manifested in a great influx of Jews into the kingdom before the end. Recognizing these different purposes does not, in itself, remove possible contradictions between the passages, but it does warn us about an "overinterpretation" in which statements from one text or the other are cut loose from their own contexts and given an absolute status that Paul never intended.

Second, we must understand correctly the biblical concept of "remnant." The scriptural/Jewish concept of "remnant" is not a quantitative one; the remnant can include a very small percentage of Israel (as in Elijah's day; cf. 11:3–4) or a very large percentage of Israel. "(Only) a remnant will be saved" (9:27) need not mean that the number of Jews to be saved will always be a very small one.[32] When, therefore, Paul predicts in 11:26a that a large number of Jews in the last days will be saved, he is doing no more than claiming that the remnant will experience a great numerical expansion.[33] No contrast between 9:27 and 11:26 need be seen.

Third, applying the two conceptions of election that we have seen in Romans 9–11 removes the apparent contradiction in the bases for salvation in the two passages. In 9:6–29, the basis for the salvation of both Jews and Gentiles is God's free and sovereign choice of each person, individually. By relating the salvation of "all Israel" to God's election of the Jewish people generally (11:26 and 28–29), Paul is not introducing a different basis for God's saving of individuals. He is simply pointing out that God's free and sovereign election to salvation of so many Jews in the last days is a corollary of his corporate election of the Jewish people to privilege and blessing. Paul is following a widespread scriptural eschatological pattern: God manifests his faithfulness by preserving a remnant of believers throughout the vicissitudes of her sin and struggle, but he will one day regather lost and scattered Jews and definitively make them "his people."[34]

---

[32] B. W. Longenecker correctly emphasizes the importance of temporality in Paul's teaching about the place of Israel and the Gentiles in salvation history ("Different Answers to Different Issues: Israel, the Gentiles and Salvation History in Romans 9–11," *JSNT* 36 [1989] 95–123). (Although I am not sure that we can apply it to the issue of ethnicity and election in the way that he does.)

[33] Nor need there be any contradiction between such an expansion and Paul's teaching that God has "hardened" Jews (implied in 9:17–18, 22, and stated in 11:7–10). Paul's references to the removal of Israel's hardening in 11:11ff. and 11:25a may suggest that God's hardening of the Jews is a temporary blinding rather than a permanent act of reprobation. Or we may apply the distinction between individual and corporate perspectives here also, with 9:17–23 treating the hardening of the individual (as a permanent state) and 11:11–26 treating it as corporate (God's limitation of his salvific grace to Israel as a whole).

[34] This expectation is, of course, a staple of the prophetic preaching and of the peoples' hope.

To be sure, Paul implies a relationship between God's corporate election of Israel and his election of individual Jews to salvation: God's saving of "all Israel" in the end (v. 26a) is a manifestation of his irrevocable covenant love for the Jewish people (vv. 28b–29). All Jews are "beloved of God"; but, as Paul has made clear, this status will eventuate in salvation only for those whom God individually chooses for salvation in this age (the remnant) and in the last days (the expanded remnant, "all Israel"). But this connection between God's election of Israel and the salvation of "all Israel" in the end times does not threaten the sovereignty of God in the process. For God's sovereignty does not mean, as, for instance, H. Räisänen claims, that "God's action is incalculable."[35] It means, rather, that God's actions are not based on anything outside his own will. And God's salvation of many Jews at the time of Christ's return will be based not on "human will or exertion" (9:16) but entirely on God's own merciful call. Salvation, then, as always, will be a gift of God's grace. But could not Jews in that day rightly claim that God was constrained to save them? No, and for two reasons. First, as we have seen, "all Israel" does not mean "every Israelite"; even at that time, a choice among Jews to be saved will be made, a choice based on God's decision and not human merit. Second, we must remember that even God's original choosing of Israel to a position of special blessing was a product of sheer grace.[36] God's salvation of many Jews in the last day originates from nothing outside his own will.

N. T. Wright has recently suggested that Paul was influenced by one specific form of this tradition: that Jews in the Second Temple period viewed themselves as still in "exile" (*The New Testament and the People of God* [Minneapolis: Fortress, 1992] 268–72; see also J. M. Scott, "'For as Many as are of the Works of the Law are under a Curse' [Galatians 3.10]," in *Paul and the Scriptures of Israel* [ed. C. A. Evans and J. A. Sanders; JSNTSup 83; Sheffield: Sheffield Academic Press, 1993] 197–213; both refer especially to M. A. Knibb, "The Exile in the Literature of the Intertestamental Period," *HeyJ* 17 [1976] 253–72, which I have not had time to check). Some texts that support this contention are Neh 9:30–37; Zech 8:1–23; 10:8–12; Sir 36:1–22. However widespread this tradition may have been (and there is evidence of many other competing "patterns"), it is doubtful whether Paul takes it over. There is no evidence that the pre-Christian Paul thought of Israel as a whole as being still in "exile"; rather, it was the coming of Christ that revealed to him the seriousness of Israel's plight (see M. Seifrid, "Blind Alleys in the Controversy over the Paul of History," *TynBul* 45 [1994] 86–92).

[35] Räisänen, "Paul, God, and Israel," 193. Although Johnson does not mention this particular point, it certainly is one of those instances in which she is quite justified in accusing Räisänen of caricaturing Paul's arguments in a way that creates unnecessary tensions in the apostle's thinking (see n. 23).

[36] "Because of the fathers" in 11:28b does not mean that God entered into covenant with Israel because of the "merits of the fathers"; as he makes clear in, e.g., Galatians 3 and Romans 9, the patriarchs are significant as bearers of God's merciful promise. See, for a slightly different approach to the relationship between God's covenant with Israel and the salvation of "all

Nor does Paul reintroduce here in Romans 11 an ethnic element in election that he has removed in Romans 9. For Paul does not remove all ethnic element from God's election in Romans 9. God is free, Paul argues, to save anyone he wants. This means that no individual Jew can claim salvation as a birthright; and that God can reach out and save Gentiles just as he does Jews. But Paul is not saying that God's own free decision to choose certain individuals to be saved cannot take into account ethnic origin. God is, indeed, free to save anyone he wants. In his own time, Paul says, God is saving many Gentiles, while many Jews are hardened. In the last days, however, he will manifest his love for Israel as a people by saving many Jews. Neither the Gentile in this age nor the Jew in the last days will be able to claim that his or her election was a result of anything he or she had done. It is, in each case, a matter of "the God who calls."[37]

The reconciliation of Romans 9 and 11 that I have suggested does not follow exactly the same lines as Johnson lays down, but I do not think that the differences between our views are all that great. Both of us, I think, want to maintain a balance in Paul's teaching on Israel that avoids the extremes of a traditional "displacement" model on the one hand and of a modern "bi-covenantal" model on the other.[38] And we both insist on the importance of finding coherence in Paul's argument if his theology is ultimately to inform our own perspectives and behavior.

Israel," D. A. Hagner, who calls the large-scale conversion of Israel "part of the extravagance of God" ("Paul's Quarrel with Judaism," in *Anti-Semitism and Early Christianity: Issues of Polemic and Faith* [ed. C. A. Evans and D. A. Hagner; Minneapolis: Fortress, 1993] 146).

[37] Paul's teaching about a final gathering of Jewish people has no parallel elsewhere in his writings. But this may be because it was only in Romans that Paul faced a situation in which he needed to remind Christians of the continuing significance of Israel's election of the Jewish people. Ultimately, of course, one would want to seek to integrate Paul's perspective in Rom 11:25–32 with his teaching elsewhere. This is no easy task (and 1 Thess 2:13–16 is particularly difficult—for which see the recent discussion in Hagner, "Paul's Quarrel," 130–36). But a recognition of the contingency of those writings goes far to mitigate the differences.

[38] We can apply the concept of displacement to Paul's teaching in the sense that he allows for salvation only through Christ (cf. J. C. Beker, "Romans 9–11 in the Context of the Early Church," *Princeton Seminary Bulletin* Sup 1 [1990] 51–52). Faith in Christ thus "displaces" the Jewish covenant and Torah observance as the basis for membership in the people of God—forever and for everyone. But Paul does not allow that these had ever been the basis for salvation (e.g., Romans 4). Nor does Paul teach that the church displaces Israel in any final or total sense. As his "olive tree" image suggests (11:17–24), Paul insists that Christians, both Jews and Gentiles, find their relationship to God in a community that is the continuation and fulfillment of the Israel of the scriptures (see, e.g., B. Witherington III, *Jesus, Paul and the End of the World: A Comparative Study in New Testament Eschatology* [Downers Grove, IL: InterVarsity, 1992] 117–28).

12 THE RULE OF FAITH IN ROMANS 12:1-15:13

The Obligation of Humble Obedience to Christ as the Only Adequate Response to the Mercies of God

William S. Campbell
Westhill College, University of Birmingham

I. INTRODUCTION: INTERPRETIVE TENDENCIES IN THE UNDERSTANDING OF THE LETTER

CHAPTERS 12–15 of Romans have been allowed in some instances to be determinative of the interpretation of the entire letter.[1] However, this approach has not met with wide acclaim, and any interpretation of these chapters must take into account the wider issues that affect the understanding of the letter as a whole.[2]

There has been in recent years a growing tendency to note the verbal and argumentative connections between chaps. 1–11 and chaps. 12–15/16.[3] Earlier emphasis on how little Paul could be expected to know about the Roman Christians' situation had tended in the opposite direction, but the increasing awareness of the contingency of many of Paul's statements in his letters was bound eventually to force commentators to pay strict attention to the relation between argument and the context addressed. This was complicated by another factor—namely, the dialogical style in which major sections of the letter were formulated. Earlier discussions about whether or not such a genre as the diatribe actually existed in ancient times have given way to a full-blown discussion of Paul's rhetoric generally and that of Romans in particular.[4]

---

[1] See Paul S. Minear, *The Obedience of Faith: The Purpose of Paul in the Epistle to the Romans* (London: SCM, 1971).

[2] See C. E. B. Cranfield, *A Critical and Exegetical Commentary on the Epistle to the Romans* (2 vols.; ICC; Edinburgh: T. & T. Clark, 1775, 1979) 2. 820–22.

[3] See James D. G. Dunn, *Romans 1–8, Romans 9–16* (WBC 38a, b; Dallas: Word, 1988).

[4] See S. Stowers, *The Diatribe and Paul's Letter to the Romans* (SBLDS 57; Chico, CA: Scholars Press, 1981); and N. Elliott, *The Rhetoric of Romans: Argumentative Constraint and Strategy and Paul's Dialogue with Judaism* (JSNTSup 45; Sheffield: Sheffield Academic Press 1990).

But the crucial issue still requiring to be addressed is this: Having clarified, to some extent at least, the role played by certain elements in the rhetorical argumentation in Romans, how can we determine their relation to actual positions held by Christians in Rome? It is precisely at this point that interpretative presuppositions and tendencies come into play. Because of the stylistically necessary dissociation between the argumentative strategy and that to which it is addressed, scholarly subjectivity and selectivity once again have space in which to maneuver.

The dominant tendency of exegesis of Romans in this century has been the tendency to interpret its contents as Paul's critique of Judaism in contrast to his own law-free gospel. Since the Reformation, scholars have implicitly or explicitly interpreted Paul's arguments in the context of a debate with Judaism. However unsure a scholar may have been about Paul's knowledge of the Romans' context, one thing remained unquestioned: that Paul in Romans confronts Judaism polemically as the apostle to the Gentiles.[5] Even in contemporary scholarship, wherever there is interpretative uncertainty this assumption tends to creep in.[6] In my own research, I found it most obviously emerging in scholars' interpretations of Paul's citation of biblical texts in chaps. 9–11. Even the RSV in 9:27 adds a gratuitous *"only"* before the reference to a remnant being saved. Again in similar vein in 11:17 according to the RSV the wild olives are not grafted in among the remaining branches on the olive tree, but are situated *"in their place."* The NRSV remains unchanged at this point!

What is the significance of this for interpreting Romans 12–15? It is that since the approach to these chapters not only depends on but also reinforces one's view of the preceding chapters, then what one *brings to* the understanding of the section is vitally important because it is bound up with one's approach to the entire letter.[7] My own conclusion on Paul's attitude to Judaism in Romans, particularly in chaps. 9–11, I will state clearly rather than attempt to argue in detail. Paul, because of nascent anti-Judaism among the Roman Gentile Christians, finds himself cast in the role of defender of Israel against Gentiles, probably for the first time in his apostolic career.[8] If it is true

---

[5] The antithesis with Judaism is not integral to justification by faith (which can also serve an apologetic purpose); *contra* Ernst Käsemann, *Commentary on Romans* (London: SCM, 1980) 85. On Paul's critique of Judaism and of legalism in general, see E. P. Sanders, *Paul, the Law, and the Jewish People* (Philadelphia: Fortress, 1983) 154–60.

[6] On this, see my *Paul's Gospel in an Intercultural Context: Jew and Gentile in the Letter to the Romans* (Frankfurt/New York: Peter Lang, 1992) esp. 136–40.

[7] Francis Watson holds that Romans 1–11 is "the theoretical legitimation for the social reorientation called for in Rom. 14:1–15:13" (*Paul, Judaism and the Gentiles: A Sociological Approach* [SNTSMS 56; Cambridge: Cambridge University Press, 1986] 107).

[8] See Campbell, *Paul's Gospel*, 201.

that Paul is here actually forced to defend Israel against Gentile prejudice, then any residue of anti-Jewish interpretation is bound to distort the understanding of this letter more than any other.

The real issue at stake is to try to determine how Paul meant his arguments to be understood.[9] Is the apostle always equally fair and balanced to both Jew and Gentile at *each* point in the letter? This may not be his strategy. For instance James Dunn's generally well balanced approach to Romans concludes the exposition of chap. 11 by stressing Paul's use of Job to maintain that God "owes no one anything." Dunn then goes on to state:

> The thought is particularly appropriate in the epilogue to an argument intended to confront and refute the assumption of most of Paul's Jewish contemporaries that God's mercy was their national prerogative, for such an *assumption* too easily becomes the *presumption* that God's mercy is Israel's right, something God owes to them, as some later rabbinic statements show."[10]

This particular statement seems to imply that it is mainly the Jews who need such a corrective. Whether or not Dunn is right to see this as directed mainly toward Jewish assumptions and presumptions, the Gentile Christians recently addressed in 11:13 also needed to hear that God owes them nothing. This understanding would concur better with Paul's universal emphasis in Romans and the entire letter can be regarded not just as a warning against *Jewish* presumption but against *all human* presumption, which I understand the doctrine of justification essentially to preclude.[11]

Where we are not sure whether Paul addresses Jews or Gentiles, it is only appropriate to apply the argument universally rather than selectively to Jews. Otherwise we risk dealing in generalizations or stereotypes rather than actualities.[12]

Thus, the crucial question in relation to the example cited above is whether Rom 11:33–36 is the conclusion to the immediately preceding section, which opposes Gentile arrogance and presumption (which 12:2–3 would

---

[9] See J. L. Martyn, "Listening to John and Paul on the Subject of Gospel and Scripture," *WW* 12 (1992) 61–81, esp. 69–70.

[10] Dunn, *Romans 9–16*, 703.

[11] Which Dunn likewise stresses: "a consistent concern throughout the letter is to puncture presumption, wherever he finds it" ("The Formal and Theological Coherence of Romans," in *The Romans Debate* [ed. K. P. Donfried; rev. ed.; Peabody, MA: Hendrickson, 1991] 245–50, esp. 150).

[12] On this, see Sanders, *Paul, the Law*, 154–60. M. Barth criticized Käsemann for the assertion that "the apostle's essential enemy is the pious Jew" (Barth, "St. Paul—a good Jew," *HBT* 1 [1979] 7–8).

seem to imply), or whether, on the other hand, it is designed to serve as a conclusion for all of chaps. 1–11, in which case it *is* legitimate to speak at this point of Jewish presumption as well as Gentile, but certainly not the one *without* the other.

If Romans could simply be regarded as Paul's theology per se and not the contingent set of specifically targeted words that most scholars now recognize it to be, then we would not need to question Paul's stance or strategy in the epistle. But since this is not the case, how can we be sure about Paul's stance toward Judaism? Is Paul's dialogue with the Jew in 2:17–29 to be regarded as a polemical attack on contemporary Judaism, and is his "pro-Jewish" conclusion in 11:25–32 to be viewed as somehow at odds with it?[13] Paul does appear to oscillate somewhat: sometimes he seems critically anti-Jewish, but at other points so pro-Jewish that C. H. Dodd considered that here his Christian apostleship had been subsumed under a residual Jewish patriotism![14]

Only by finding some congruence between Paul's purpose in writing the letter, the argumentative style and strategy he employs in the text, and the theological arguments undergirding the whole, can we hope to reach any measure of agreement on the relative significance of the diverse statements Paul somehow fuses together in this document. One of the most complicating factors in all this is the question of the diatribe style, and it is to this that we must now turn.

II. THE DIATRIBE STYLE AS INDIRECT WITNESS TO WHAT PAUL IS NOT SAYING: HE INTENDS TO PRECLUDE AN ANTI-JEWISH INTERPRETATION OF HIS GOSPEL

Amid all the intricacies of interpretation of the significance of the diatribe style, what may be missed is the obvious point, the fact that by mentioning a particular interpretation at all (even to refute or disown it), Paul indicates his awareness of theological stances and conclusions which he chooses not to follow or which he even explicitly disowns. The actual outcome of the uncertainty about how to interpret the diatribe style is a weakening of confidence

---

[13] On the possibility of contradictions in Paul's thought, see Watson, *Paul, Judaism and the Gentiles,* 170–73; and H. Räisänen, *Paul and the Law* (WUNT 29; Tübingen: Mohr, 1983). See also Sanders, *Paul, the Law,* 144–54; and J. A. Fitzmyer, *Romans: A New Translation with Introduction and Commentary* (AB 33; New York: Doubleday, 1993) 131–32.

[14] On this, see L. Gaston, *Paul and the Torah* (Vancouver: University of British Columbia Press, 1987) 92 and 217 n. 60; cf. W. Marxsen, *Introduction to the New Testament* (Oxford: Blackwell, 1968) 103.

about what Paul did intend to say or even to refute. It is in order to counter-act this debilitating malaise that I wish to point to another aspect of dialogical style as such.

If one deals with issues directly or in a straightforward manner, it will be evident what one supports or promotes but not perhaps so clear *what one rejects*. The advantage of Paul's dialogical approach in Romans is that along-side the letter he actually wrote, we can to some extent at least, envisage the letter *he chose not to write*.

In my own work on Romans, I have tried to demonstrate that when one puts together Paul's ten rejected theses, one gets a sort of summary outline of the issues the apostle faced in writing the letter.[15] Paul's strategy appears to be to highlight his own stance by a categorical rejection of extreme positions adopted by, or available to, at least some of the Roman Christians. A crucial indicator of the interpreter's stance is usually presented in the approach to 2:1–29. Neither grammar nor rhetoric constrains us to presume that the Jew explicitly addressed in 2:17 is already presupposed in 2:1; yet this interpreta-tion still dominates in the literature. S. Stowers's careful rhetorical analysis demonstrates that the admonitory apostrophe beginning in 2:1 clearly addresses the Greek. Only at 2:17 does Paul turn to an imaginary Jew, a pre-tentious teacher of the law. The fictitious persona and life situation depicted here—a well-known character type that appears as a Gentile in 2:1–5 and as a Jew in 2:17–29—are used by Paul as an argument against pretension and boasting. By applying the type to both Greek and Jew, he reinforces the theme of equity. Despite its precise targeting of the pretentious Jewish teacher (who thinks he holds the cure to the moral and religious malaise of Gentiles), even 2:17–29 criticizes "not Jews or Judaism as such but teachers who in Paul's view stand in antithesis to his own gospel concerning justification of the Gen-tile peoples."[16] We are forced to the conclusion here that while "an anti-Jewish interpretation of Romans has been a frequent phenomenon, it was certainly not the original historical meaning of Romans as a public text."[17]

---

[15] See Campbell, *Paul's Gospel*, 178–84. See also Robert Jewett, "Following the Argument of Romans," in *The Romans Debate*, ed. Donfried, 265–77.

[16] S. Stowers, *A Rereading of Romans: Justice, Jews and Gentiles* (New Haven: Yale University Press, 1994) 153.

[17] *Contra* C. H. Cosgrove, "The Justification of the Other: An Interpretation of Romans 1:18–4:25," in *Society of Biblical Literature 1992 Seminar Papers* (Atlanta: Scholars Press, 1992) 613–34, esp. 631. Cosgrove thinks that Paul leaned in the direction of the privileged Gentile majority. See also Paul Meyer, "The Justification of God" (a paper read at the SBL Pauline The-ology Group meeting in 1992 in response to Cosgrove's paper).

III. THE SITUATION PAUL ADDRESSES
IN ROMANS 12–15

Recent research would appear to indicate that several factors were influential in producing the situation that Paul addressed in Romans.

Political Factors

A unique factor of the "Roman context" was that the emperor Claudius, during the period 41–49 CE, was forced to intervene at least once in disputes among the Jews in Rome.[18] As a result, it seems that there may have been a prohibition of synagogal meetings, and there is evidence that a number of Jews were expelled from the city in 49 CE. It would appear that at least the leaders of the Jewish Christians were temporarily absent from Rome. Some Gentiles in close adherence to the synagogue may also have been expelled, since to the Romans they would appear to be living as Jews. Whether or not the expulsion led to a complete severance between house groups and synagogues, it probably did contribute to a splintering into the diverse groups that were typical of Roman Christianity several decades later. In any case, what is fundamental to the Roman situation is that political factors may have been instrumental in encouraging a rupture in relations between the Gentile churches and the synagogues.

Peter Lampe maintains that by the time Romans was written the Christians were certainly separated from the synagogue. Recent proselytes and God-worshipers would also have been forced to reconsider their adherence to the Jewish community.[19] Some doubtless would conclude that it was politic to sever these links. The ejection of Jews from Rome may have encouraged feelings that God's purpose had now moved on from the Jews, bringing a status reversal which some welcomed (Jews were now the adherents and fringe members).[20]

We would not wish to claim a complete break between house groups and synagogues *prior* to Paul's writing to the Romans. It is true that Paul seems to

---

[18] See E. M. Smallwood, *The Jews under Roman Rule* (Leiden: Brill, 1981) 251. See also G. Lüdemann, *Paul, Apostle to the Gentiles: Studies in Chronology* (Philadelphia: Fortress, 1982) 164–65; and R. Brändle and E. W. Stegemann, "The Emergence of the First Christian Community in Rome in the Context of the Jewish Communities" (a paper read at the 1993 SNTS meeting in Chicago).

[19] Peter Lampe considers that the Gentiles in Rome were predominantly "God-fearers," both because this was normal in many early Christian communities and also because of the "Jewish" context of Romans (*Die stadtrömischen Christen in den ersten beiden Jahrhunderten: Untersuchungen zur Sozialgeschichte* [2d ed.; WUNT 2/18; Tübingen: Mohr (Siebeck), 1989] 56–58).

[20] See Dunn, *Romans 9–16*, 662.

openly acknowledge little positive response to the gospel from Jews (see Rom 9:30). It is also clear that those Gentiles who boasted over the branches broken off (11:19) are unlikely to be part of a synagogue community. But, despite this, there is evidence throughout Romans, and especially in chaps. 14–15, of a form of Christianity that is still attached to the synagogue. Romans, in our view, represents not the final divorce in the "marriage" between house groups and synagogues but only the beginnings of that separation—the marriage is in trouble but it's not yet clear that it is irreparably damaged.[21]

As it is unlikely that up to fifty thousand Jews were expelled from Rome, some form of Jewish community activities would probably continue. But the point we wish to stress here is that the political factors we have noted may have caused, or at least encouraged, a period of relative separation of Gentile Christians from the synagogue.

Theological Factors

This period came to an end when expelled Christians such as Aquila and Priscilla returned to Rome after Nero came to power. Those Christians who previously had had close links with the synagogue may have found they were no longer welcome there lest future disturbances ensue. They may not have been able to return to the same area of the city, so that it may have been difficult to find ceremonially pure food, and a type of vegetarianism may have been temporarily practiced.[22] Neither were they necessarily welcomed by all the Gentile Christians at Rome. Most Pauline Christians would doubtless have welcomed such people. But there seems to be some diversity in theology among the Roman Christians. Despite the clear evidence for Gentile Christianity evinced by Paul's letter to Rome, there is good reason to believe that the earlier forms of Christianity that existed there, both Jewish and Gentile, were strongly influenced by Jewish teaching and practice. There is a growing scholarly consensus that the earliest Christianity in Rome was an intra-Jewish phenomenon.[23] Alongside this there are signs of a radical Hellenist Christianity, also of early origin.[24] There is evidence of frequent jour-

---

[21] See Campbell, *Paul's Gospel*, 150–53.

[22] See Watson, *Paul, Judaism and the Gentiles,* 95.

[23] See Lampe, *Stadtrömischen Christen*, 10–35; and James C. Walters, *Ethnic Issues in Paul's Letter to the Romans: Changing Self-Definitions in Earliest Roman Christianity* (Valley Forge, PA: Trinity Press International, 1993) esp. chapter 2, which deals with Jewish socialization in ancient Rome (pp. 19–58).

[24] See R. E. Brown, "Not Jewish Christianity and Gentile Christianity but Types of Jewish/Gentile Christianity," *CBQ* 45 (1983) 74–79. This essay is similar to Brown's introduction (with John P. Meier) *Antioch and Rome: New Testament Cradles of Catholic Christianity* (New York: Paulist, 1983).

neys by Jews between Rome and Jerusalem, and it is quite likely that Hellenists like Pauline converts would migrate to the imperial city.[25]

The disturbances in 49 CE may not have been caused by the advent of Christianity in Rome, which probably should be dated some years earlier. The riots possibly resulted from radical Hellenists preaching a law-free gospel to Gentiles and God-worshipers associated with the synagogue. With the expulsion of Jewish Christian leaders, it may be that more radical forms of Gentile Christianity developed in the house-churches in the period prior to the succession of Nero.[26] An alternative scenario is that the radicals were internal to the Roman congregations and that the anti-Jewish bias developed out of disputes about the relevance of Torah to Christians (see 16:17).

Beyond the fact that we know for certain that Claudius moved against the Jews in Rome at least once, we have no real evidence concerning the precise significance of this political factor for understanding Romans. All we can claim with any degree of certainty is that the daily life and worship of both Roman Jews and Christians were *in all probability* strongly influenced in certain factors.

A heightened consciousness of ethnic differences in relation to Roman legal status would necessarily emerge, since the Jews were those officially targeted, despite a historic regard for their special status. Jews in Rome as a close-knit immigrant ethnic community would already have a very strong sense of identity, but the edict may well have accentuated this and also encouraged a comparable Gentile response. Anti-Jewish sentiments common among the Romans may have become intensified. The outcome of all this would necessarily lead to divergent self-definitions by the different strands of Roman Christianity. James C. Walters has given a good rationale for the view that the intervention of Claudius led to *changing* self-definitions among the Roman groups.

> The turmoil that Jewish Christians and God–fearing Gentiles experienced was compounded in the aftermath of the edict; not only were they separated from their "ethnos," but they had at the same time to deal with the heightened dissonance caused by changes in the Roman communities. . . . The pressure that law–abiding Christians felt under these circumstances must have been enormous.[27]

---

[25] See Brown and Meier, *Antioch and Rome,* 110; also E. A. Judge and G. S. R. Thomas, "The Origin of the Church at Rome: A New Solution," *Reformed Theological Review* 25 (1966) 81–93. Lampe estimates that two thirds of the names of the Christians mentioned in Romans 16 indicate Greek background, and hence immigrant status (*Stadtrömischen Christen,* 153).

[26] See Robert Jewett, "Tenement Churches and Communal Meals in the Early Church: The Implications of a Form-Critical Analysis of 2 Thessalonians 3:10," *BR* 38 (1993) 23–43. Jewett argues against the traditional dominance of the house-church model (pp. 29–30).

[27] See Walters, *Ethnic Issues,* 64.

We can reasonably assume, therefore, that the Edict of Claudius had a lasting divisive influence on the situation of the Roman Christians. As already noted, the growing consensus is that almost all of the Roman Christians had had contact with Judaism at some point in their lives.[28] So we can posit that when Paul wrote his letter there were probably some Christians of Jewish background or at least proselytes and former God-worshipers who by conviction still sought to follow the law and who, given the opportunity, would have preferred to keep their connection with synagogue worship.[29]

But there were probably other Christians who had never had this close contact with the synagogue. Among these we would expect to find converts from Paul's mission in the east. Others also may have found in Christianity freedom from the constraints of their previous adherence to Judaism. Yet others, caught up in the problems resulting from the expulsion, may have been rejected by Jews who blamed the advent of the Christian message for their punishment.[30]

Major studies such as those of James D. G. Dunn and Robert Jewett, among others, see the theme of the relation of Jew and Gentile as a constituent element in the discussion in chaps. 14–15.[31] With H. W. Bartsch one can affirm the connection of 11:25 via 12:3 to chaps. 14–15.[32] But from F. C. Baur to G. Bornkamm, Robert Karris, and others, the precise identification of specific groups has been deeply disputed.[33] If the thesis that the Roman Christians are essentially Gentile (at least by birth) could be sustained—and it *does* have some substance—then where can we locate the (Jewish) Christians frequently identified as "the weak"? What is required to make sense of the content of Romans is not Jewish *Christians* as such but a context in which *Judaism* plays a role, even if that role is simply to provide a foil for Gentile Christian arrogance. It would make better sense, however, if there were lively social links between Gentile Christian assemblies and local synagogues.

---

[28] In addition to the views noted above in n. 23, see A. J. M. Wedderburn, *The Reasons for Romans* (Studies in the New Testament and Its World; Edinburgh: T. & T. Clark, 1988) 50–54; Fitzmyer, *Romans,* 33–34; and Brändle and Stegemann, "Emergence."

[29] Watson suggests that Jewish success in attracting proselytes led to the expulsion of Jews in 19 CE (*Paul, Judaism and the Gentiles,* 93).

[30] Ibid., 95.

[31] See Jewett, "Following the Argument"; idem, *Christian Tolerance: God's Message to a Modern Church* (Philadelphia: Westminster, 1982) esp. 43–67.

[32] H. W. Bartsch, "Die antisemitischen Gegner des Paulus in Römerbrief," in *Antijudaismus in Neuen Testament?* (ed. W. Eckert et al.; Munich: Kaiser, 1969) 27–43.

[33] G. Bornkamm's essay "The Letter to the Romans as Paul's Last Will and Testament" and R. J. Karris's essay "The Occasion of Romans: A Response to Professor Donfried" are both included in *The Romans Debate* (rev. ed.), 16–28 and 65–84, respectively. Recent research has demonstrated the specificity in the application of Paul's parenesis within each letter, even though not all of the content may be unique to a particular letter.

But even if the great majority of the Roman Christians *were* Gentile (with only a few Jewish leaders such as Aquila and Priscilla), we are not obligated to accept the hypothesis that the weak were all Jewish by birth (and the resultant correlation of Jewishness with weakness). It is feasible that many of them were Gentiles influenced in different degrees by Jewish practices. Thus, the debates may be mainly between Gentile Christians about the degree of Jewishness (if any) obligatory on such Christians. The issue at stake must then be the legitimacy of the residual Judaism still prevailing in the life-style of certain Gentile Christians and, issuing from that, the fundamental question of the relationship of the Pauline movement to Judaism and its ultimate identity.

Social Factors: The Weak and the Strong in First-Century Roman Society

Some recent studies suggest that the alienation between weak and strong in Rome may have been due to social factors as much as to political or theological ones. Mark Reasoner has recently drawn attention to the social connotations of the words for strong and weak which Paul uses in Rom 15:1: δυνατός ("strong") and ἀδύνατος ("weak") are nearly exact Greek counterparts of the Latin *potens, firmus,* and *vis,* on one hand, and *inferior, tenuus,* and *invalidus* on the other.[34] Roman society at this period had a very fixed social order; however, within the given social divisions there also operated a *potentior/inferior* distinction. Social strength consisted of some kind of prestige "from physical strength to financial wealth to *auctoritas.*"[35]

Reasoner finds it instructive to consider the ideology of weakness in Roman society: "The *inferiores* appear in the literature of the late Republic and early Empire to be those who were vulnerable to exercises of social power from those above them on the social ladder."[36] In such a society, where people measured their worth by the people over whom they could exercise social power, it is significant that Paul uniquely in Romans uses the terms δυνατός and ἀδύνατος and does not mention categories otherwise used to describe Roman society, as, for example, the imperial distinction in orders, categories related to status such as patron/client or citizen/peregrinus, or categories related to class such as rich/poor or free/servile.

---

[34] See Mark Reasoner, "Potentes and Inferiores in Roman Society and the Roman Church" (a paper read at the 1992 SBL meeting in San Francisco). See also his "The 'Strong' and 'Weak' in Rome and in Paul's Theology" (Ph.D. dissertation, University of Chicago, 1990).

[35] Reasoner, "Potentes," 12 . I am indebted also to Carolyn Osiek's paper read at the 1993 SNTS meeting in Chicago, "The Oral World of the First Christians at Rome."

[36] See Reasoner, "Potentes," 12.

If we were to attempt to determine which group in Rome was the more likely to be considered "weak" in social terms, it is quite likely that a Jewish Christian group would be a better candidate than a Gentile one; however, Reasoner holds that the household of Aristobulus (if, as is likely, he belonged to the Herodian family and was a friend of Claudius) would count among the *potentes* of the Roman church.[37] The "strong" in terms of social significance would most naturally refer to Roman citizens or foreign-born who display a proclivity toward things Roman. Such persons would exercise their *auctoritas* over those whom Roman society placed below them in status. Freedmen who had risen in status, social influence, and property holdings above the freeborn within the lower population might form a significant proportion of the group.

Carolyn Osiek thinks that "if the language of weak and strong had such inescapably social connotations, then its use in Romans 14–15 must have referred not primarily to legal or moral differences, but to differences in social status."[38] She goes on to note that "a possible qualification for being assigned to the category of the weak is having foreign lower class connections, in this case the foreign religion of Judaism." Other factors such as the degree of romanization in language, customs, and so on, and the degree of literacy and Roman citizenship may also have been factors. Osiek holds that κρίνειν ("to judge") and ἐξουθενεῖν ("to despise") in Romans 14 denote the language of power and that "the entire persuasive strategy of Paul's rhetoric is to convince the powerful that they are not to oppress the weak by exerting social pressure on them in the matter of diet."[39]

Paul ranks himself with the δυνατοί ("strong") on the basis of the criterion of conscience in regard to diet (14:14). But do his Roman citizenship and literacy also contribute to this social strength? It is exceedingly difficult to distinguish the relative significance of the social and theological factors. Perhaps it is the combination of them that is so powerful. Paul uses every theological weapon at his disposal to convince his fellow δυνατοί not only not to exploit the "weak" believers, nor simply to *tolerate* them, but rather positively *to bear with*, to *support*, the powerless after the example of Christ.[40]

What emerges from this discussion is that it is unlikely that we can say with any confidence that either group, Jewish Christians or Gentile Christians, as such was clearly identifiable as being socially weak or strong, though Jewish Christians for cultural and other reasons might be less likely to have been regarded as the strong.[41] The exhortation not to be high-minded but to asso-

---

[37] Ibid. Lampe has identified Marsfield and Aventine as districts where Christians of higher social status lived (*Stadtrömischen Christen*, 46–52). See also Jewett, "Tenement Churches," 6–7.

[38] Osiek, "Oral World," 9.

[39] Ibid., 11.

[40] βαστάζειν (15:1) means "to protect and support" (cf. 11:18); see Osiek, "Oral World," 11.

[41] See Reasoner, "Potentes," 11.

ciate with the lowly (12:16) would have much greater weight if "the weak" are identified as those of low social status.

Stanley Stowers also acknowledges that "the weak" and "weakness" were well-established concepts in Greco-Roman society. Stowers holds that Paul employed categories such as mature or immature, weak (or sick) and strong in his communities. These are not fixed roles but relative categories. Nor are they groups, parties, or theological positions; they are dispositions of character. Stowers reads Romans very much in the light of the current first-century interest in an ethic of self-mastery (though this is not its most important theme).[42] "Until recently scholars have not noted that the concept of weakness so prominent in Paul's letters had its cultural home at the very heart of Greco-Roman discourse about the passions and self-mastery." Romans 14–15 can be "read as a hortatory distillation of Paul's advice to gentile converts who sought to learn mastery of their passions and desires through psychagogic practices within the community of Christ." This influence derived "either from popular moral philosophy or from the kind of Judaism we meet in Philo." Despite the fact that "the weak hold to false beliefs about things like food and special days"—which causes them to reject the strong—the latter are not to approach the weak like philosophers who subjected the foolish to "therapy of the passions with reason." "Paul did not consider the church a school for self-mastery." As God and Christ have accepted the weak and strong alike, so too the weak and the strong must adapt themselves to one another in the same way. The paradigm of the Pauline ethic is ultimately not the "mastery of emotion and desire" but "adaptability to the needs of others."[43]

IV. THE IDENTITY OF THE WEAK AND THE STRONG IN ROMANS 14–15

In a recent article on the weak and the strong, Paul Sampley notes that the direct data about these "groups" is extremely slight.[44] There are only three explicit references to the weak: τὸν ἀσθενοῦντα (14:1), ὁ ἀσθενῶν (14:2), and τῶν ἀδυνάτων (15:1); the use of different terms suggests no formal identification of a group. The "profile of the weak" indicates only that he is "weak in faith or with respect to faith" (14:1) and a vegetarian (14:2). Paul then opposes

---

[42] Stowers, *A Rereading*, 66.

[43] Ibid., 45, 322, 323, 258.

[44] Sampley's paper was read at the 1993 SNTS meeting in Chicago. It has been printed as "The Weak and the Strong: Paul's Careful and Crafty Rhetorical Strategy in Romans 14:1–15:13," in *The Social World of the First Christians: Studies in Honor of Wayne A Meeks* (ed. L. Michael White and O. Larry Yarbrough; Minneapolis: Fortress, 1994) 40–52.

anyone interfering "in the relationship of a house servant (οἰκέτης) with his master (κύριος)" and insists "that preferences regarding meat and vegetables are extraneous to one's relationship to one's Lord." A possible third clue in the profile of the weak is that "one prefers one day over another; another regards all days alike" (14:5). Scholars have tended to identify weak and strong respectively here, but Paul does not. So Sampley claims that "even if a modern interpreter insisted on carrying Paul's mention of weak and strong in 14:1–2" into the subsequent verses, "it is not a priori clear who might be better identified as the weak person." Sampley concludes that this minimal information concerning the weak and the strong surely gives us "scant basis to profile them onto either extreme of what was in reality more likely a continuum among the house churches of Rome."[45]

In contrast to the attempts to give precise specific identification concerning the profile of the weak and the strong, Sampley holds that 14:1–15:13 is "laced with exhortations and definitional declarations that are designed to *be equally applicable to all the Roman believers*" (emphasis mine). "These claims rehearse the common ground and calling that all believers share and give a powerful context in which to consider anew individual differences with regard to practice." While we may speculate that "one point of contention among Roman believers was in fact the sabbath," Paul does not actually say this was so. Gentiles also honored special days—so Paul deftly moves the sabbath issue "onto neutral ground." Thus "Paul's rhetorical strategy" involves an "oblique approach" that puts no Roman group in the spotlight." Paul had done the same earlier in this chapter on the issue of keeping *kashrut* by moving the discussion over into the "neutral and mutually accessible grounds of vegetarianism" so that when he "finally brings to the surface . . . what indeed must have been a contentious issue, viz. what is κοινός ("common, impure, unclean," 14:14), he has assiduously prepared a context within which it can be considered afresh and on different grounds by all the parties among the Roman believers."[46]

While supporting the scholarly consensus that stresses the connection of 12:1–2 with all that follows, Sampley insists that 14:1–15:13 cannot be adequately grasped apart from its links to 12:3. Two elements prepare for what succeeds 12:3: (1) the significant "individuated 'measure of faith'" that "provides the conceptual framework within which one could recognize stronger and weaker faith" and (2) the "caution against *over*-evaluation"—Paul does not warn against under-evaluation of oneself, so unwarranted "high self-evaluation" must be the problem of all in Rome. Thus, Sampley claims that

---

[45] Ibid., 41–42.
[46] Ibid., 42–43.

when "Paul broaches the Roman divisiveness with his figured speech in 14:1–15:13, he urges the strong to welcome the one who is weak in faith—and in so doing assumes that all parties may well identify themselves as strong in faith" ("presuming *all* will identify themselves as strong in faith"). He also urges them to realize that "each believer has the obligation to welcome and nurture others, just as 'Christ did not please himself' (15:1–3)."[47] We find ourselves in broad agreement with Sampley's approach.

However, we can only accept with reservation the thesis that "the rhetorical notations of "weak" and "strong" have no objective referents in the Roman congregations." We can accept the more dynamic notion of a continuum of various "types" of Christians,[48] but this does not necessarily entirely remove the need to posit the existence of certain groups across whose divisiveness Paul proposes to build rhetorical bridges.[49]

It will greatly assist our understanding here if we can be clear about Paul's intention. Is Paul seeking to remove diversity in order to produce a more monochrome Christianity in the Pauline mold? This is certainly not the case. Paul's intention is to promote harmony *within* diversity rather than to remove the diversity—otherwise what could be the significance of saying, "Let everyone be fully convinced in his own mind" or "whatever is not of faith is sin"?

I have previously argued that ethnic distinctions are far from being unimportant for Paul.[50] Although for the apostle, Jew and Gentile are one in Christ according to Gal 3:28, this statement is too often generalized by correlating it with the twice-repeated thesis in Romans—"there is no distinction"—as if Paul had written the two phrases side by side in the same letter. The Galatian text signifies the equality of access to salvation rather that the removal of distinctions between Jew and Gentile (or male and female). I have maintained that it was in fact Paul's own theology that legitimated the right of Jews to live *as Jews* in Christ.[51] The alternative to this is the traditional understanding of Paul's gospel which inevitably turns out to be a pro-Gentile or an anti-Jewish message. Because Paul fought for the right of Gentiles to be accepted in faith as Gentiles, scholars have failed to recognize that Jews have not in fact been allowed a similar privilege—that is, to be accepted in faith *as*

---

[47] Ibid., 47–48.

[48] We need to distinguish "groups" of Christians from "types" of Christians. R. E. Brown refers to "types" in his article "Not Jewish Christianity," but in *Antioch and Rome* he speaks of "groups," reflecting a certain ambiguity.

[49] Sampley, "The Weak and the Strong," 48.

[50] Paul denies ultimate significance to ethnic distinctions rather than their continuing existence. See Campbell, *Paul's Gospel*, 98–131.

[51] Ibid., 99–100.

Jews. They are expected to become like Gentiles and to conform to a Gentile Christian life-style upon coming to faith in Christ.

Such a gospel is essentially biased and therefore flawed, because it destroys the very equality and correlation it is designed to promote: God becomes the God of Gentiles rather than the one God of Israel and the nations. But an even greater consequence of this theology is that theologically Judaism, as such, and Jewishness—even in its manifestation as an element within Christianity—has no longer any actual right to exist.

Paul does identify himself as strong, but he is realistic enough to acknowledge continuing diversity within the house-churches, as Jewett has clearly recognized: "Faith for Paul is not a single dogmatic standard . . . faith in Jesus Christ has pluralistic possibilities."[52]

But the question that now requires answer is: What kind of pluralism? "Let each be fully convinced in his own mind" too readily suggests to modern interpreters the contemporary Western individualistic view of society as comprised solely of separate individuals who freely choose their own particular life-styles without reference to cultural groupings or corporate loyalties, shared traditions, and so on. It is our contention, however, that Paul is dealing here with conflicting *groups* rather than with differing types of individual Christians. This perspective will become clearer if we consider the alternative scenario. If Paul is dealing only with a variety of individuals who are situated at various points on a continuum that stretches from "conservative," law-abiding Jewish Christians to radical (possibly Hellenist) Christians, then why should individual believers be vulnerable or threatened? With such diversity of opinion and such freedom for individual conviction, this inherent pluralism of belief should in fact prove to be a source of security for the diverse individuals that produced it. "Weak" and "strong" would be almost completely relativized. If there were no groupings or if the groups were so numerous and diverse that everyone could be easily accommodated, then there would be no vulnerable "weak" torn with divided loyalties or troubled conscience.

We need to distinguish here between a continuum of ideas and a continuum of organizations. Doubtless, every shade of Christian opinion was represented among the Christians in Rome. But this does not mean that there was freedom and opportunity in every instance for believers to follow their own individual convictions. The diversity in belief was probably not exactly matched by diversity of organization, and individuals would have to conform to the mores of the group to which they wished to be attached.

The fact that Romans 14 indicates that there are weak Christians who are

---

[52] See Jewett, *Christian Tolerance*, 62.

extremely vulnerable (see vv. 13, 15, 16, 20, 21) may be taken as an indication that there were individuals who were torn between adherence to conviction and adherence to a group. If groups were in contention and in competition with each other, individuals would feel under pressure to conform to the dominant behavior patterns of such groups, especially if they were well-defined groups.[53]

Paul's clear advice and stance are that the strong ought in some way to support and accommodate the weak (15:1). If his advice had been that the weak should yield to the strong, then the problem would be solved. The Christians with synagogue connections and a Jewish life-style would simply relinquish both of these and form one mixed Pauline community. But what then would be the relevance of the measure of faith meted out to each if this inherent charismatic diversity is simply obliterated? The provision for ongoing diversity which seems to be such a fundamental premise in the discussion means that yet another possible solution is thereby excluded. If Paul's advice were that the strong should simply accommodate the weak by giving up their own life-style and conforming completely to that of the weak, this would mean that the life-style of the latter would become the norm for both the house-churches and (Christian) synagogues in Rome, a position that begins to appear very different from the contemporary understanding of Paul.

A radical review of Paul's attitude to Judaism and to the weak has recently been proposed by Mark D. Nanos, who, claims that "the weak in faith" was Paul's phrase to describe the faith of those he still considered part of the people of God but who had not yet recognized that Jesus was the Christ of Israel: non-Christian Jews. Nanos links the stumbling of the weak in chaps.14–15 to 9:30–33, where the stone over which Jews stumble is the refusal to accept the equal co-participation of Gentiles in God's grace because of an ethnocentric definition of entrance requirements.[54] The church in Rome was not yet separate from the synagogue, but this mainly Gentile community was becoming arrogant, boasting in freedom from the law as the new people of God in a way that would cause Jewish people "to blaspheme" the grace of God supposedly enjoyed by such Gentiles. Paul writes to exhort the strong Christians to help support the weak Jewish brother to prevent him stumbling and thus to

---

[53] See *Differentiation between Groups: Studies in the Social Psychology of Intergroup Relations* (ed. H. Tajfel; London: Academic Press, 1979).

[54] Mark D. Nanos, *The Mystery of Romans: The Jewish Context of Paul's Letter* (Minneapolis: Fortress, forthcoming); see esp. chapter 3, "Who were the 'weak' and 'strong' in Rome?" Although Nanos's work was unknown to me when I read the initial version of this paper at the 1993 SBL meeting in Washington, I am delighted that the author has kindly shared his forthcoming work with me.

encourage him toward faith in Christ. The strong must in fact behave like righteous Gentiles for the sake of the weak.

Nanos's arguments are compelling and make excellent sense of many verses and sections of Romans. Reluctantly, I find myself not fully convinced by some aspects of his comprehensive reworking of the letter. I am still inclined to the view that the weak are Christians—the measure of faith of 12:2 in my view implies a christological foundation (rather that just a theological one). Further, Paul argues for the continuance and maintenance of the diversity that springs from the differing measures of faith gifted to believers. This could not be the case if the Jewish believers were not yet committed to faith in Christ.

It seems best therefore to envisage a scenario something like this. Paul is essentially dealing with differing groups of Christians in the context of on-going links with synagogues. Whether we should envisage the Christians who feel obligated to a Jewish life-style as being a *part* of a synagogue or, alternatively, as comprising a separate assembly of Jews who had faith in Jesus, it is impossible to determine. What we can be reasonably sure about is that there were groups of Christians in Rome who by conviction followed the broad lines of a Jewish life-style in relation to purity laws, festivals, and so on. Alongside these there were other groups of Christians, probably in the majority, who were mainly of Gentile origin, although some at least of these would previously have had contact with the synagogues in some form or another. These despised the scruples of their "Jewish" brethren and were arrogant in their self-confidence as the new people of God. They now worshiped only in their house groups and saw little reason why they should maintain any social contacts with Jews as such.[55]

Thus, we have a context in which groups of Christians were divided over their attitude toward (and therefore their connections with) the law and the synagogue. The organizational issue that we posited above as a necessary constituent of the situation in Rome could then take the form of the question whether or not Gentile Christians and former God-fearers should sever their links with the synagogue. This hypothesis would make even better sense if in fact the troublemakers of 16:17 were suggesting precisely this—that is, advocating a separatist "Gentile" Christianity. The assumption implicit in this interpretation is that most of the Christian groups in Rome had hitherto been subgroups of the synagogues, even though there is no indication of any pressure to judaize.

---

[55] See Jewett, "Tenement Churches." If the majority of Roman Jews were poor—as seems likely from Philo's comment that the Jewish population of Rome was concentrated in the Transtibernine region—then most of them would have lived in mass housing (*insulae*) rather than in their own *domus* (see Walters, *Ethnic Issues*, 31–32).

We ought also to consider here the role of leaders, especially in relation to synagogue groups. Paul himself was not disinterested in promoting order and discipline in his communities. He urged the Corinthians to submit to such men as Stephanus and to every fellow worker and laborer (1 Cor 16:15–16). Contrary to earlier interpretations of Paul's charismatic theology, the apostle himself saw no inherent contradiction between charisma, structure, and order (to a limited extent at least) within his communities.[56]

Synagogues in Rome were organized independently rather than under a central *ethnarch* or γερουσία (council) as was the case in Alexandria. Each synagogue group may have had its own γερουσία, though there may have been a designated leader (ἄρχων) (cf. Rom 13:3) from within the γερουσία. The house-churches would also have their leaders. If "those who create doubts and cause stumblings (σκάνδαλα) in opposition to the teachings you have been taught" are themselves ("Gentile") leaders *within* the house groups in Rome (rather than [judaizing] interlopers from outside), then their self-serving associated with the creation of dissensions and the causing of stumbling may consist in their putting severe pressure on weaker individuals to conform to their (new) perceptions of what faith means.[57]

Thus, the role of leaders is a further element in the organizational or supraindividual features of the Roman context that must necessarily be considered alongside any understanding of the continuum of ideas. The attitudes and activities of the leaders may well have accentuated differences between groups and led to the persecution and stumbling of individuals (cf. 12:14; 14:21). If Nanos's view is correct, then the Roman Christians were to be subordinate to the synagogue leaders, to obey the apostolic decree in keeping the Noachic commandments and to pay the temple tax.[58] Christians subject to the discipline of the synagogue could have suffered prescribed beatings for association with Gentiles (2 Cor 11:24). Some of them could have been excluded if others refused to eat or worship with them.

---

[56] Cf. B. Holmberg, *Paul and Power: The Structure of Authority in the Primitive Church as Reflected in the Pauline Epistles* (Philadelphia: Fortress, 1980).

[57] The tendency to see all Paul's opponents as judaizers has not assisted a clear understanding of 16:17, *contra* M. Kettunen, *Der Abfassungszweck des Römerbriefes* (Annales Academiae Scientiarum Fennicae, Hum.-litt. 18; Helsinki: Suomalainen Tiedeakatemia, 1979) 192–96. See Campbell, *Paul's Gospel*, 165–70; see also Fitzmyer, *Romans*, 34. Wedderburn admits that evidence for the nature of Christian traditions in Rome remains scanty, "that they were originally of a Judaizing character must remain a hypothesis, nothing more" (*Reasons*, 54).

[58] Chapter 6 of Nanos's study, entitled "Romans 13:1–7: Christian Obedience to Synagogue Authority," integrates Rom 13:1–7 into the theme of the letter. For evidence of Gentiles with formal links with a Jewish community, see M. Goodman, "Who was a Jew" (The Yarnton Trust Lecture, The Oxford Centre for Postgraduate Hebrew Studies, Oxford 1994) 1–20.

A vital concern for a new religious movement engaged in the process of self-definition is a fresh understanding of its past. This pre-history must be reviewed and reinterpreted in order to affirm the newly acquired identity of the movement. For Christians with a previous association with the synagogue, Judaism itself, its failings and its virtues, must be called in question. The tendency to define oneself over against those Jews still rejecting the gospel would be hard to resist—"branches were broken off so that I might be grafted in" (11:19).

Thus we can envisage a situation in which the significance of the Jewish roots of their faith was being debated by the emergent Christians. Accordingly, the appropriate life-style for the members of the new communities would also become a bone of contention. We have envisaged competing communities and leaders along a continuum that stretched from "synagogue" Christians to "Gentile" house-churches with an aversion to Judaism and the law.

Our discussion of the identity of "the weak" has revealed a wide diversity of opinion. It is no longer feasible simply to designate them as Jewish Christians. The reference to what is κοινός ("unclean") and to σκάνδαλα ("stumbling[s]") denotes that Jewish purity laws constituted one element in the debate. There is evidence of judging one another's life-style and of adherence to practices that may be mainly or partly attributable to Judaism or earlier Jewish socialization of Gentiles. But we find no evidence of judaizing. The opponents in 16:17 may as readily be designated "gentilizers" as judaizers, since their identity derives from one's perspective on chaps. 1–15.

That Paul sent Romans to "all God's beloved in Rome," but primarily addressed Gentiles, must indicate a community(s) of Gentile believers living in a context involving some relationship with Judaism. A pronounced Gentile ethnic self-consciousness is also evident in 11:17–24. Boasting with an element of ethnic superiority appears both in the latter passage and also in the apostrophe to the Jew in 2:17–29. Our knowledge of the Roman context indicates that there were probably also social dimensions to the disunity among "God's beloved" in Rome. Differences in social status (see 12:16) and differences in knowledge related to this may have combined with the unrest resulting from the disturbances under Claudius to create insecurity for a significant proportion of believers. We conclude therefore that the division between "the weak" and "the strong" "did not correspond to the division between Jewish and Gentile Christians, but cut across it."[59]

---

[59] See John Ziesler, *Paul's Letter to the Romans* (London: SCM, 1989) 325. The approach of the Pauline Theology Group has been to study each letter of Paul separately; on the weak in 1 Corinthians, see G. Theissen, *The Social Setting of Pauline Christianity: Essays on Corinth* (Philadelphia: Fortress, 1982) 137–40.

It is not in fact the differences in life-style that concern Paul—the kingdom of God is not meat and drink (14:17). Righteousness and the unity of the church are his concern. Since he clearly states that his policy is "not to build on another man's foundation" (15:20), it must certainly follow from this that he also would have made it his policy not to destroy another man's foundation (even if Rome was somewhat of an anomaly in this respect). Since Paul himself had not founded the churches in Rome, he is faced with diversity as a given factor in the situation, and one he must acknowledge rather than seek to demolish.[60] The fact that Paul's own theological thinking is contextually related and influenced means that the apostle must take into account the Roman context as part of the reality within which he is called to operate.[61] The church for Paul is truly a church of Jews and Gentiles, not a third entity that is neither of these. Viewed from this perspective, Romans 12–15 may be adequately described as Paul's argument for the legitimation and maintenance of diversity among the Christians in Rome. We must now consider the theological rationale on which Paul bases his argument for this.

V. THE RULE OF FAITH: NORMS FOR THE BELIEVING COMMUNITY

Paul provides both a positive and a negative application of faith to everyday issues of conduct. In Romans, faith is not only individuated, as 12:3 asserts; faith is also demonstrated in one's choice of life-style and in one's attitude toward the differing life-styles of other Christians. Both righteousness and faith were practical issues for the Romans. Orthopraxy rather than orthodoxy was a central concern; however, it is not choice but *conviction* that determines how one lives the life in Christ, and one does not lightly change one's convictions.[62] Here Paul is a true charismatic. The Holy Spirit gives gifts to all and

---

[60] Paul envisages a permanent pluralism in Rome; see Jewett, *Christian Tolerance*, 134.

[61] See my essay "The Contribution of Traditions to Paul's Theology," in *Pauline Theology II*, 234–54. Wayne Meeks argues that since Paul's normal practice was to establish house-churches that were, from their origin, fundamentally independent of Jewish communities, then the Roman Christian community would differ radically from the norm in that, unlike the others, this community was shaped by having its origin within a Jewish context ("Breaking Away: Three New Testament Pictures of Christianity's Separation from the Jewish Communities," in *To See Ourselves as Others See Us: Christians, Jews and 'Others' in Late Antiquity* [ed. J. Neusner and E. S. Frerichs; Chico, CA: Scholars Press, 1985] 93–115, esp. 108).

[62] Fitzmyer, NRSV, and RNEB translate πίστις as "conviction" in 14:22. The RNEB and Fitzmyer are consistent, repeating this translation in 14:23 and Fitzmyer translates πίστις in 14:1 also as "conviction." For a good discussion of the issues here, see Fitzmyer, *Romans*, 698–700; and Cranfield, *Romans*, 2. 698–701.

through the Christian community will guide each one (whether as individual or group) to live in obedience to Christ.[63]

Thus, to take one's own "measuring rod" of faith—that is, the norm that each person is provided in the appropriation of the grace of God—and to seek to impose it as a norm upon others is to usurp the function of the Spirit and contradict the meaning of "faith in Christ."[64] The nature and origin of one's own charisma should prevent anyone from attempting to force a brother or sister to adopt his or her particular life-style. This is Paul's positive rationale, but he reinforces it by a negative argument as well. If people are forced to live other than as they are called, they are being forced to sin, for "whatever is not of faith is sin" (14:23). Paul uses here a particular phrase, ἐκ πίστεως ("from faith"), that he has already employed a number of times in earlier chapters (1:17 [twice]; 3:26, 30; 4:16 [twice]; 5:1; 9:30, 32; and 10:6). This recurring theme is obviously of some significance in the letter.[65]

We first meet ἐκ πίστεως in Paul's citation of Hab 2:4 in Rom 1:17; here the phrase occurs in conjunction with εἰς πίστιν ("into faith") and with the phrase "to the Jew first and also to the Greek." In this citation ἐκ πίστεως embraces both God's faithfulness and the human response in faith. Paul cites this text because he wishes to stress both the source of righteousness and its practice in daily life: note ζήσεται ("shall live," 1:17; cf. also 6:11; 8:13; and 10:5).[66] We find ἐκ πίστεως again in Rom 3:26 and 3:30. The Christ-event is intended to demonstrate that God himself is righteous and that he justifies the one who has faith in Jesus (τὸν ἐκ πίστεως Ἰησοῦ). Paul interprets this to maintain that all boasting is excluded on the principle or rule of faith (note the similarity with 14:23).[67] The alternative to this is to make God "the God of Jews only" (3:29). But "God is one"; "he will justify the circumcised on the ground of faith (ἐκ πίστεως) and the uncircumcised through faith (διὰ τῆς πίστεως, 3:30).

If Paul's main purpose in this passage is to argue for the equality of Jew and Gentile in salvation, it seems strangely unwarranted for him to use differing prepositions in respect to the two peoples whose distinctiveness he apparently wishes to eliminate. The equality of Jew and Gentile in faith must therefore constitute only *one* aspect of Paul's argument; the other is that even as he

---

[63] On this, see Käsemann, *Romans*, 334–35.

[64] See ibid., 379; Jewett, *Christian Tolerance*, 59–67.

[65] See Dunn, *Romans 9–16*, 828–29.

[66] We use the terms "Jewish" and "Gentile" Christianity to indicate life-style rather than ethnic origin; cf. Gal 2:14.

[67] On whether νόμος should be taken figuratively here, see Fitzmyer, *Romans*, 363; but cf. Cranfield, *Romans*, 1. 220.

argues for equality he acknowledges their continuing distinctiveness within the divine purpose.[68]

Paul next uses ἐκ πίστεως in 4:16, where he summarizes a major section of his argument by a cryptic phrase διὰ τοῦτο ἐκ πίστεως ἵνα κατὰ χάριν, "that is why it depends on faith in order that the promise may rest on grace." Only as it is dependent on grace can the promise be guaranteed to all Abraham's seed. "The seed" (σπέρμα) here is not Christ, as in Gal 3:16, but refers to two distinct groups—τῷ ἐκ τοῦ νόμου and τῷ ἐκ πίστεως 'Αβραάμ—those who adhere to the law and those who share the faith of Abraham. Rom 4:16 is essentially inclusive (not only but also), and since it maintains the necessity of faith, the two groups listed here must signify the Jewish Christian and Gentile Christian "branches" on "the tree of Abraham." Only thus in Paul's view can God's promise to make Abraham "the father of many nations," the father of us all (4:16–17), be realized.

Paul's emphasis on Abraham as an inclusive figure for all peoples of faith would appear to indicate that the Roman Christians were disputing what walking in the faith and footsteps of Abraham should mean for the pattern of daily life—in particular, how they should relate to the law. What is to be noted here is that though Paul argues for a common paternity for all believers in Abraham, he again acknowledges the difference between Jew and Gentile. The implication of this may turn out to be that two differing life-styles are permissible within the family of Abraham's children. Significantly, Paul in 4:16 uses the phrase τῷ ἐκ τοῦ νόμου ("the adherent of the law") in a neutral rather than a pejorative sense. This description of Jewish Christians demonstrates that in Paul's theology there was no absolute opposition between Christ and the law.

Paul begins a new section of the letter in 5:1, which continues the inclusive emphasis of 4:16. He uses ἐκ πίστεως here in an opening summary in which all believers are included as those who have been justified and who (therefore) should enjoy peace. Their boasting is not of ethnic distinctions but of hope, of afflictions, or of God (5:2, 3, 11).

We find ἐκ πίστεως again in 9:30 and 10:6. Israel's failure in its race toward righteousness is explained as a result of its not being "from faith." In 10:6 this mistaken faith is contrasted with the true righteousness (ἐκ πίστεως). The difference noted here is not that between those who had the law and those who had not, but that between those who *acted* from faith and those who did not.

---

[68] See S. Stowers, "Ἐκ πίστεως and διὰ τῆς πίστεως in Rom 3:30," *JBL* 108 (1989) 665–74. Following Origen and Theodore of Mopsuestia, Stowers holds that Paul's use of different prepositions is significant, concluding that διά appears when the Gentiles are in view, and ἐκ when either or both Jews and Gentiles are under discussion.

Significant discussions of faith (and unbelief) occur in 11:13–24 (cf. 11:20) and in 12:3, although the precise phrase ἐκ πίστεως does not recur there. In 14:23 Paul gives a crucial role to faith (ἐκ πίστεως) as the principle or rule by which the life-style that is in accordance with the will of God is discerned. If we consider the various occurrences of ἐκ πίστεως noted above, alongside the frequent use of the verb πιστεύειν ("to have faith"), it is apparent that this word group is of central significance in Romans.[69] It is no surprise therefore that Paul's doxological conclusion in 15:13 reads "May the God of hope fill you with all joy and peace ἐν τῷ πιστεύειν ("in believing").

From this cursory survey it would appear that Paul wishes to demonstrate to the Roman Christians that the life of faith is a life of commitment rather than of vacuous freedom, of obligation to Christ and to other humans. Yet the *obedience that faith produces*, though in continuity with Israel's faith, is not the same as obedience to the law.[70] Moreover, although all true faith has one divine source, it may be differentiated in practice in the differing life-styles of Jewish Christians and Gentile Christians.

Paul warns against pressuring people to conform to other people's life-styles in contradiction to their own faith conviction. Such conformity to the world Paul repudiates in his important introductory exhortations in 12:1–2. The significance that Paul gives to mutual recognition and admonition between Christians with differing life-styles should not be underestimated. The Christian faith was still very young; the church in Rome was lacking in any unified understanding of what should be normative, and the whole movement would be at risk if it came to the attention of the authorities.

Bearing in mind also the previous disturbances in Rome and the resultant expulsion of the Jews, Paul's call for subjection to the governing authorities in 13:1–7 makes good sense.[71] The Romans are advised to be submissive and

---

[69] As H. W. Bartsch has emphasized ("The Concept of Faith in Paul's Letter to the Romans," *BR* 13 [1968] 41–53). Bartsch notes that the word faith occurs forty times, more often than in any other biblical book and that the concept appears twice in the beginning of the letter in unique usages (1:5 and 1:17) which Paul obviously assumed his readers would understand (p. 45). See also D. R. Lindsay, *Josephus and Faith: Πίστις and Πιστεύειν as Faith Terminology in the Writings of Flavius Josephus and the New Testament* (Leiden: Brill, 1993).

[70] We take ὑπακοὴ πίστεως as a genitive of source; see D. B. Garlington, *"The Obedience of Faith": A Pauline Phrase in Historical Context* (WUNT 38; Tübingen: Mohr [Siebeck], 1990) esp. 205–6. See also Fitzmyer, *Romans*, 449. "Obedience of faith" signifies not a polemical thrust against the law but continuity with the faith of Israel; see Nanos, *Mystery of Romans*, chapter 4, *contra* Garlington, *Obedience*, 247–59.

[71] Paul must have been aware of the reaction of people in the empire to the conduct of the *publicani* and the tax situation under Nero. Christian reactions to the cult of the emperor may also be in view here; see J. Friedrich, W. Pöhlmann, and P. Stuhlmacher, "Zur historischen Sit-

obedient citizens meeting all their debts—above all the debt to love one another (13:8). The commandments are summed up in "the Golden Rule" and "love does no wrong to a neighbor—therefore love is the fulfilling of the law" (13:9–10).

In stressing the demands inherent in his gospel, Paul is seeking an "obedience of faith" that seems to bring together somewhat disparate elements. A congruence hinted at earlier in 3:27 and in 8:1–4 (cf. also 10:4) now becomes explicit, and a positive relation between the commandments and Christian love is established. The δικαίωμα of the law is love.[72] This leads us to believe that, in showing the congruence, Paul is seeking to minimize the force of the conflicts about the law and its relevance for the daily life of the Christian community.

Paul has prepared for this emphasis in chaps. 5–6 in a major contrast between obedience (Christ) and its effects and disobedience (Adam) and its effects. Righteousness is also linked with obedience and slavery to Christ, while sin and death are linked with disobedience and slavery to sin's rule. Paul's own mission is to win *obedience* from the Gentiles (15:18).

This emphasis on the obedience of faith is further strengthened when we note the strong correspondence in vocabulary between chaps. 6–8 and 12:1–21, as Victor Furnish and J. D. G. Dunn have emphasized.[73] The imagery of slavery to Christ significantly reappears in 14:18. According to 6:17 the Romans had previously received catechetical instruction. As former slaves who transferred to a new master, they "became obedient to the standard of teaching or *rule of faith* (Moffatt) to which they had been entrusted."[74] Paul writes to bring to their remembrance aspects of this they may have forgotten or neglected (15:15).

VI. THE FAILURE OF THE ROMANS TO ACCEPT ONE ANOTHER: BOASTING IN DISTINCTIONS AND IGNORING COMMON ALLEGIANCE TO CHRIST

Our study to this point leads us to the conclusion that diversity in life-style was not the most serious problem; it was rather the attitude of Christians to

---

uation und Intention von Röm 13, 1–7," *ZTK* 73 (1976) 131–66; also E. Bammel, "Romans 13," in *Jesus and the Politics of His Day* (ed. E. Bammel and C. F. D. Moule; Cambridge: Cambridge University Press, 1984) 365–83.

[72] See L. E. Keck, "What makes Romans Tick" (pp. 3–29 in this volume); see also Glenn N. Davies, *Faith and Obedience in Romans: A Study in Romans 1–4* (JSNTSup 39; Sheffield: JSOT Press, 1990) 173–75.

[73] Victor Paul Furnish, *Theology and Ethics in Paul* (Nashville: Abingdon, 1968) 103–4; Dunn, *Romans 9–16*, 708–9.

[74] See Fitzmyer, *Romans*, 449–50.

this diversity. Provided their own calling or faith conviction calls them to this life-style, Paul has no quarrel with those who continue to observe the law so long as they do not seek to compel others to live like them! *Gentiles must not regard observance of the Jewish law as incompatible with Christian faith, and Jews must not regard it as essential to Christian faith.*[75] Justification by faith demands freedom of life-style *in faith*.

But there were some in Rome—evidenced in 11:13–24 as well as in chaps.14–15—who felt that freedom in Christ in no wise obligated them to the Jewish law. This attitude combined with other factors already noted to make the Gentile Christians feel that they were superior to non-Christian Jews, and probably also to those Christians still committed to a Jewish life-style. Paul does not wish to encourage such attitudes. He opposed all boasting in human achievement such as the idealized self-image of the Jew in 2:17–24, but an inflated self-image was not the exclusive prerogative of the Jews in Rome.[76] It is instructive in this regard to consider Paul's use of the verb φρονεῖν and related terms in Romans.[77] The neutral use, meaning "to think, form or hold an opinion, have an understanding" is found in Paul as in 12:3, but the term can be given a more particular and often negative force by its context; in the New Testament this usage is almost wholly Pauline as in 11:20 and 12:16.[78]

This accusation of "high-mindedness" follows on from 11:13–24, where it is specifically Gentiles whom Paul targets. In contrast to ὑπερφρονεῖν ("arrogant thinking"), Paul places σωφρονεῖν ("think wisely"); the latter featured widely in popular Hellenistic philosophy, denoting modesty or restraint and would have been familiar to Paul's readers. Paul's wordplay shows he also is aware of this.[79]

Thus, a characteristic of some of the Roman Christians was that they held an inflated self-estimate, and this may have included elements of religious, ethnic, and cultural superiority. They tended to boast in their *distinctions* rather than in their *common faith*. It was arrogant attitudes that were the root of the problem. This arrogance destroyed community harmony and was characterized by a presumptuous pride. Pride and boasting contradict faith, transform-

---

[75] See Watson, *Paul, Judaism and the Gentiles*, 96.

[76] See Wedderburn, *Reasons*, 126.

[77] Φρονεῖν occurs in 8:15; 11:20; 12:3, 16 (twice); 14:6 (twice); 15:5; φρόνιμος in 11:25; 12:16; and φρόνημα in 8:6 (twice); 8:7; and 8:27. See Wedderburn, *Reasons*, 76–77. Paul tells his readers "not to be super-minded above what one ought to be minded, but (to) set your mind on being sober-minded" (Jewett, *Christian Tolerance*, 66).

[78] See Dunn, *Romans 9–16*, 721.

[79] Ibid., 721–22.

ing πίστις ("faith") into ἀπιστία ("unfaith"), and Paul in Romans opposes Gentile as well as Jewish misconceptions of faith.

Bornkamm noted this drawing of distinctions behind Paul's statements in 1:18–2:29. Paul's strategy was to free the natural understanding of God and the world from its Greek presuppositions through specific Jewish terms and thoughts, and again in the second part of his argument to burst the boundaries of the Jewish understanding of law and judgment through the reference to the law that Gentiles know. By dealing separately and in rather stereotyped ways with the traditions and practice of the different groups, whether Jewish or Gentile, and by stressing God's judgment upon all, Paul showed that none may boast because the gospel relativizes their exaggerated distinctions.[80]

Judging and despising one another are also for Paul in direct contradiction to the acceptance that the gospel demands (see chap. 2; 14:1; 15:7 [11:15]).[81] The gospel requires of both Jew and Gentile that they reevaluate all their past, including their cultural presuppositions; such "judging" will prevent inflated self-images and self-understanding, and promote a better appreciation of their common humanity as God's creation.[82]

In the face of assumed cultural and ethnic superiority, in opposition to boastful, imperialist faith, Paul uses his weapon of a justifying faith centered on the cross, before which no human may boast of any achievements or attributes. The earliest form of this justification by faith argument *may* have been formulated in reaction to Judaism or judaizers, but its presentation in Romans has a more universal focus; the target is not just Judaism or judaizers but *all* Christians. So Paul addresses the Gentile Christians and reminds them that they do not bear the branches but they themselves are borne on the root of Abraham; they are wild and unproductive olives cultivated by divine grace.[83] And to Israel he says that were it not for divine mercy that chose not always the firstborn or the mighty, but the weak and younger, then not even a remnant would have been saved.[84]

Before God Jews cannot boast of their Jewishness and Gentiles dare not presume. *The life-style to which their faith commits them is not something about which*

---

[80] G. Bornkamm, "The Revelation of God's Wrath: Romans i–iii," in his *Early Christian Experience* (London: SCM, 1969) 46–70, esp. 61.

[81] The root κριν becomes a leitmotif in Romans and thereby connects the judging in chap. 2 with that of chaps. 14–15; see W. Meeks, "Judgment and the Brother: Romans 14:1–15:13," in *Tradition and Interpretation in the New Testament: Essays in Honor of E. Earle Ellis* (ed. G. F. Hawthorne with Otto Betz; Grand Rapids: Eerdmans, 1987) 290–300, esp. 296.

[82] As Marxsen correctly perceived (*Introduction*, 92–109).

[83] See W. D. Davies, "A Suggestion concerning Romans 11:13–24," in *Jewish and Pauline Studies* (Philadelphia: Fortress, 1985) 153–63.

[84] See F. Thielman, "Unexpected Mercy: Echoes of a Biblical Motif in Romans 9–11," *SJT*

to boast above other believers. Nor is it legitimate to condemn or despise the believer whose convictions bind him or her to a different pattern of life. The harmonious solution to the disputes among the Roman Christians demands a recognition that faith must determine what is the right life-style for everyone. Love, rather than domination, will liberate and take care of the weak; diversity is to be acknowledged and allowed to continue.[85] Ultimately it is not birth or public pressure, or even Torah, but only *faith* that should be determinative of life-style.[86]

VII. CONCLUSION: PAUL'S THEOLOGY OF FAITH IN ROMANS

Because of the Romans' misconceptions about the meaning of faith, Paul's major concern in writing to them is with the nature of obedient faith. The translation of a Semitic faith into Hellenistic culture may have allowed the Romans to miss some of the content πίστις normally carried for those of Jewish background, familiar with the Septuagint.[87] Paul reinterprets the meaning of faith in such a way as to stress positive continuity with the faith of Abraham and equality for Jew and Gentile within this faith.

Instead of positing that Paul opposes judaizing tendencies or "works of law" in Romans, it makes better sense to view the discussion of faith and merit as related to the human problems of boasting and judging, whether by Jew or Gentile. A true understanding of faith counteracts arrogance over against one's neighbor and confirms the right of persons to live by their own "rule of faith." To counteract misconceptions of faith, Paul uses both Abraham and Christ as originators and exemplars of faith. Abraham found grace, unmerited favor, but even he had nothing to boast about. He became "strong in faith" because his faith was not determined by earthly realities such as his old age. Thus the present reality of lack of faith in Christ among the Jews must not lead the Roman Christians into boasting.

To further counteract a presumptuous type of faith, the provisional aspect

---

47 (1994) 169–81, esp. 178–79. Thielman notes that God often communicates his blessing through the very candidate whom cultural norms would exclude.

[85] "Paul does not assimilate Jew and Gentile into a generic Christianity" (Stowers, "Εκ πίστεως," 674; see also J. C. Beker, "The Faithfulness of God and the Priority of Israel in Paul's Letter to the Romans," in *Christians among Jews and Greeks: Festschrift for Krister Stendahl* [ed. G. W. E. Nickelsburg and G. W. MacRae; Philadelphia: Fortress, 1986] 16).

[86] On the uniqueness of the "μέτρον πίστεως" for each believer, see Käsemann, *Romans*, 334–35; and Dunn, *Romans 9–16*, 721–22.

[87] See D. R. Lindsay "The Roots and Development of the 'pist' Word Group as Faith Terminology," *JSNT* 49 (1993) 103–18.

of salvation is stressed in Rom 8:14–39. Those with faith already enjoy the firstfruits of the Spirit (8:23), but they *await* adoption as sons. They dare not boast over those Jews who reject the Gospel, for until God's purpose for Jew and Gentile comes to fruition there is no salvation for either. Paul claims that Christ came to *confirm* the promises, but he avoids the language of fulfillment that might encourage presumption. Paul is certain that God's consistency and integrity (ἀλήθεια) are greater than human faithlessness. God's faithfulness is demonstrated in Christ's becoming and continuing to be "servant to the circumcised" (15:8).[88]

Remarkably, Paul does not use the term Israel but prefers circumcision despite all its ethnic connotations.[89] This surely points to the fact that *ethnicity and cultural divisions were crucial factors in the Roman situation.* Christian leaders in Rome should not selfishly seek their own factional interests thereby causing the weak to stumble but, out of concern for the weak, should follow the example of Christ, the servant of Israel.

Paul's collection for and his relationship to Jerusalem would suffer if anti-Judaism were to develop among the Gentile Christians in Rome.[90] Paul seeks to deny legitimacy to a Christianity that defines itself over against Judaism. He secures the new movement to its historical roots in Judaism and that not only at the new point of departure in the revelation of Christ. He binds it to Israel's origins with Abraham and to Israel's ultimate salvation (see 11:25).

---

[88] See Stowers, "Εκ πίστεως," 673; and Bartsch, "Concept of Faith," 48–49.

[89] See J. Marcus, "The Circumcision and the Uncircumcision in Rome," *NTS* 35 (1989) 67–81.

[90] The importance of the collection within the context of Romans is often overlooked. "It gave concrete expression to Jewish and Gentile Christians' common sharing in the spiritual heritage of Israel" (Wedderburn, *Reasons*, 40).

13 THE THEOLOGY OF ROMANS 12:1-15:13

Mark Reasoner
Bethel College

MY GOAL IN THIS RESPONSE is twofold: (1) to highlight and respond to aspects of William Campbell's essay that are noteworthy or problematic and (2) to offer a unified statement of the theology of Rom 12:1–15:13 that shows how the parts fit together.

I. RESPONSE TO WILLIAM CAMPBELL

Paul's Attitude to Judaism in Romans

Campbell helpfully draws our attention to past biases against Judaism in the interpretation of Paul's letter to the Romans. He is right in asserting that this letter is directed against all human presumption, both from within Judaism and from the Gentile world. But because Paul's gospel in Romans is directed against all human presumption, it is simplistic to state that "Paul . . . finds himself cast in the role of defender of Israel against Gentiles."[1] It is true that Paul catalogs the rich heritage of Judaism in 3:1–2 and 9:4–5, and he warns against Gentile boasting in 11:13–24. But he also attacks Judaism at two of its most celebrated points—possession of the Mosaic Law and circumcision (2:17–29)—after attacking Gentile religiosity in the preceding context (1:18–32). And though affirming the election of the Jews (9:4–5), he states that they have not arrived at righteousness and have stumbled (9:31–10:4). At the close of the letter Paul requests prayer for deliverance "from the disobedient in Judea"

---

[1] William S. Campbell, *Paul's Gospel in an Intercultural Context: Jew and Gentile in the Letter to the Romans* (Studies in the Intercultural History of Christianity 69; Frankfurt: Peter Lang, 1991) 201. Campbell affirms this in the first section of his essay in this volume.

(15:31). He cannot be considered a defender of a religion whose strongest adherents he feared. A more nuanced statement about Paul's relation to Judaism is necessary, a statement that can account both for Paul's positive and negative statements toward Judaism in Romans.[2]

In Romans, Paul's first goal is not to defend Israel but to defend his own gospel. In so doing he finds a place for both Jew and Gentile within the plan of God. Paul is more affirming of Gentiles than some in his audience expected. For example, in 13:1–7, he defends the practice of paying taxes to Caesar. This certainly offended some of his Jewish readers.[3] At the same time, Paul is more affirming of Judaism and its adherents than others in his audience expected. Paul's remarks in 3:1–2 and 9:4–5 show that he has a high view of Judaism and its heritage.

Rom 15:7–9, coming as it does at the conclusion of our section in Romans, shows how this synthesis works in Paul's mind. God will be faithful to his promises to the Jews (11:26). At the same time, there is now a new people of God, composed of both Jews and Gentiles who attach themselves to the Messiah.

Identification of the "Weak" and "Strong"

I agree with Campbell that the "weak" and the "strong" refer to real groups in the Roman churches to which Paul is writing. Together we agree against J. Paul Sampley and Robert Karris on this point.[4] I think that the differences between 1 Corinthians 8–10 and Rom 14:1–15:13 are significant enough to take the latter passage as directed to a real situation in Rome that was distinct from that in Corinth.[5] Those who take Rom 14:1–15:13 to refer only to an

---

[2] In the introductory section of his essay, Campbell states that Paul seems to oscillate in his presentation of Judaism, though the footnote that follows, with its quotation from W. Marxsen, seems more balanced in its assessment of Paul's posture toward Judaism in Romans.

[3] See Josephus, *Ant.* 18.23, on the Fourth Philosophy.

[4] J. Paul Sampley, "The Weak and the Strong: Paul's Careful and Crafty Rhetorical Strategy in Romans 14:1–15:13," in *The Social World of the First Christians: Studies in Honor of Wayne A. Meeks* (ed. L. Michael White and O. Larry Yarbrough; Minneapolis: Fortress, 1994) 40–52. Sampley's statement that these terms have "no objective referents in the Roman congregations" follows Robert J. Karris's classic statement of this position in "Romans 14:1–15:13 and the Occasion of Romans," in *The Romans Debate* (ed. K. P. Donfried; rev. ed.; Peabody, MA: Hendrickson, 1991) 65–84. For a similar position, see also William Sanday and A. C. Headlam, *A Critical and Exegetical Commentary on the Epistle to the Romans* (13th ed.; ICC 32; New York: Charles Scribner's Sons, 1911) 401–2.

[5] "Food offered to idols" is mentioned in 1 Cor 8:1, 4, 7, 10; 10:19, but is missing in Romans. "Knowledge" is a key concept in 1 Cor 8:1, 7, 10, 11; it is not emphasized as a difference in Romans. "Conscience" is found in 1 Cor 8:7, 10, 12; 10:25, 27–29, but is missing

imagined or potential difference in Rome cannot explain why Paul, well informed about the Roman churches as he was (Rom 1:8; 16:1–22[6]), would risk misunderstanding by writing to the Romans churches, whom he wanted to win to his side (1:11–12, 15; 15:22–32), as if they had a problem that they did not actually have. It is also worth noting J. C. Brunt's point that there is clearly a controversy, or dispute, in Rome, while such a division of church groups is not evident in 1 Corinthians 8–10.[7]

I also agree with Campbell that the "weak" are Christians. Besides the "christological foundation" he sees at 12:3 for this whole section of Romans, I note also that 14:4–6, 9; 15:5 also locate the difference as occurring between parties that identify with Jesus as Lord.

But it is difficult to understand exactly what Campbell sees behind the terms "strong" and "weak," and certainly the opaque character of Rom 14:1–15:13 on this point is partially responsible for this ambiguity. Campbell hesitates to equate the "weak" with Jews, partly because this "contains an implicit denigration of Judaism." This is methodologically suspect, since our goal in interpreting this section of the letter is to determine what sort of social division Paul is describing within the Roman churches, regardless of how biased or prejudiced its basis might seem to us. All of us want to avoid anti-Semitism, but many people in first-century Rome had no such concern.[8]

---

in Rom 14:1–15:13. These differences have been noted by J. D. G. Dunn (Romans 9–16 [WBC 38b; Dallas: Word, 1988] 795) and others. The key imperative of Rom 14:1–15:13— "accept" (Rom 14:1, 3; 15:7 [twice])—is missing from 1 Corinthians. The stated difference in Romans seems to be centered around faith (14:1, 22, 23 [twice]). This word is not found in 1 Corinthians 8–10. It appears that the Roman "weak" considered meat to be "common" (κοινός, 14:14 [three times]), and this word is not found in 1 Corinthians.

[6] Based on arguments in Kurt Aland, "Der Schluss und die ursprüngliche Gestalt des Römerbriefes," in Neutestamentliche Entwürfe (Munich: Kaiser, 1979) 284–301; J. A. Fitzmyer, Romans: A New Translation with Introduction and Commentary (AB 33; Garden City, NY: Doubleday, 1993) 55–65; Peter Lampe, Die stadtrömischen Christen in den ersten beiden Jahrhunderten (2d ed.; WUNT 2/18; Tübingen: Mohr [Siebeck], 1989) 124–35; Wolf-Henning Ollrog, "Die Abfassungsverhältnisse von Röm 16," in Kirche: Festschrift für Günther Bornkamm zum 75. Geburtstag (ed. D. Lührmann and G. Strecker; Tübingen: Mohr [Siebeck], 1980) 221–44, I take Romans 16 to be part of the letter.

[7] J. C. Brunt, "Paul's Attitude toward and Treatment of Problems Involving Dietary Practice: A Case Study in Pauline Ethics" (Ph.D. dissertation, Emory University, 1978) 124–25.

[8] Besides the following quotation from Horace, see Cicero, Pro Flacco 66–69. Secondary sources include J. G. Gager, The Origins of Anti-Semitism: Attitude Toward Judaism in Pagan and Christian Antiquity (Oxford: Oxford University Press, 1983) 39–88 (both positive and negative portraits of Jews in Roman sources); A. Momigliano, Alien Wisdom: The Limits of Hellenization (Cambridge: Cambridge University Press, 1975) 121–22 (on Apollonius Molon); and A. N. Sherwin-White, Racial Prejudice in Imperial Rome (1966 J. H. Gray Lectures; Cambridge: Cambridge University Press, 1967) 97–100.

We do have clear evidence that Jews could be considered "weak" in Rome, as the following quotation illustrates. Horace describes a conversation in Rome in which one person has reminded another that the latter had wanted to tell him something in private:

> "I mind it well, but I'll tell you at a better time. Today is the thirtieth Sabbath. Would you affront the circumcised Jews?"
> "I have no scruples," say I.
> "But I have. I'm a somewhat weaker brother, one of the many. You will pardon me; I'll talk another day."[9]

Besides this parallel, which links the concept of weakness with Judaism in the Roman context, we have philological evidence from the word "common" in 14:14. This word is used to describe food as unclean only in contexts related to Jewish dietary laws; it is therefore good evidence that the differences over diet in the Roman churches were due to concerns related to the *kashrut* laws.[10]

I am therefore more ready to link the "weak" party with Jewish Christians in Rome than Campbell is. Of course, we cannot say that only people with a Jewish heritage were on the "weak" side of the continuum. Vegetarianism was a perfectly legitimate choice for good Romans, and so there may have been some on the "weak" side who were vegetarian for typically Greco-Roman reasons.[11]

Faith

I can agree with the two principles that Campbell presents in his section, "The Rule of Faith": (1) that Paul sees the source of the Romans' faith in the faithfulness of God; and (2) that Paul allows that the Romans' faith may show

---

[9] "Memini bene, sed meliore tempore dicam; hodie tricesima sabbata: vin tu curtis Iudaeis oppedere?"

"Nulla mihi," inquam, "religio est."

"At mi; sum paulo infirmior, unus multorum. ignosces; alias loquar."

Horace, *Sat.* 1.9.68–72 (trans. H. R. Fairclough; rev. ed.; LCL; London: William Heinemann, 1929).

[10] Nélio Schneider, "Die 'Schwachen' in der christlichen Gemeinde Roms" (D.Th. dissertation, University of Wuppertal, 1989) 91–92, 108–115.

[11] These reasons for vegetarianism include the Romans' positive appraisal of vegetarianism in popular culture (Horace, *Sat.* 2.1.73–74; Pliny, *Hist. nat.* 18.33; Quintus Metellus, *Strateg.* 2); Roman sumptuary laws, which limited meat consumption (Aulus Gellius, *Noc. Att.* 2.24.1; laws are listed in J. Haussleiter, *Der Vegetarismus in der Antike* [Religionsgeschichtliche Versuche und Vorarbeiten 24; Berlin: Töpelmann, 1935] 389); Stoic arguments for vegetarianism in Rome (Musonius Rufus 18A; Seneca, *Ep.* 108.16–22); and Pythagorean teachings in favor of vegetarianism in first-century Rome (Quintus Sextius, s.v. "Sextius [2], Quintus, *OCD*, 2d ed.).

itself in different ways. The latter is a point of significant agreement. Both Campbell and I understand Rom 14:1–15:13 as allowing for ongoing difference in the Roman churches. There is no indication from Paul that he is trying to move the "weak" from their position of abstinence and day observance. Nor is there any indication that Paul wants the "strong" to view meat as contaminating in itself.

I agree with Campbell that the "obedience of faith" (1:5) is a determining factor in our understanding of how faith functions in Rom 12:1–15:13. In Rom 1:5 this phrase, with "faith" functioning as a genitive of source, refers to the obedience that arises out of faith. As obedience and faith are inseparable in this letter,[12] so in 12:1–15:13 Paul is out to specify what living in faith will mean for the covenant community.

I differ with Campbell on the relationship of the "measure of faith" that Paul mentions in Rom 12:3 to the "faith" mentioned in 14:1, 22, 23. Certainly Campbell's general formulation for "measure of faith" ("the norm that each person is provided in the appropriation of the grace of God") fits with both contexts, but this formulation may be too general to be of help in either passage. It is true that in both places the faith distinguishes members of the community from one another. Yet "the measure of faith" in 12:3 is with reference to the spiritual gifts that arise out of one's faith, as 12:4–8 makes clear.

"Faith" in Romans 14 is more than the "conviction" that Campbell suggests. Note how cognitive this faith is in 14:1–15:13. To judge and to observe days (14:5–6) implies a conscious thought process of evaluation, and not simple conviction. Similarly, in 14:14, Paul states that to the one who *thinks* some food to be unclean, it is unclean. The faith of the "weak" is "an insufficiently enlightened faith"; that is, there are cognitive differences between their faith and that of Paul or of the "strong" in Rome.[13] So I want to nuance Campbell's discussion on "the rule of faith" to say that this phrase in Rom 12:3–8 refers to spiritual gifts, and one's self-evaluation in relation to them, but the "faith" in Rom 14 refers both to the content of the Roman believers' faith *(fides quae creditur)* and the response of conviction toward God *(fides qua creditur)*. The Romans' idea of *fides* was broad, and since they would not expect Paul to use the term in the same way throughout a letter of this length, neither should we.

---

[12] C. E. B. Cranfield pairs Rom 1:8 with 16:19; 10:16a with 10:16b; 11:23 with 11:30–31; and 15:18 with 1:5 to show how inseparable faith and obedience are in this letter *(A Critical and Exegetical Commentary on the Epistle to the Romans* [2 vols.; ICC; Edinburgh: T. & T. Clark, 1975] 66 n. 3).

[13] The quoted phrase comes from Fitzmyer, *Romans,* 688. Paul's words in the beginning of Rom 14:14 also show that there is a difference in cognition: "I know and am convinced in the Lord Jesus. . . ."

II. THE THEOLOGY OF ROMANS 12:1–15:13

The theology of Rom 12:1–15:13 is a theology of obligation within the new covenant community.[14] This theology of obligation is clearly worked out in a covenantal framework. The new covenant community is to be led by the Spirit in its exercise of gifts and in its unifying, upbuilding attitude. Paul wants to reaffirm that love, the central element of the Mosaic covenant, is still upheld in the new covenant community, while at the same time he contends that some features of the Mosaic covenant are no more (14:14). Paul argues that faith that grasps the benefits of Christ works itself out in obligation to God, church members, government, one's neighbors in society, and even feuding church parties. Before I show how the parts of Rom 12:1–15:13 give rise to this theology of obligation, several big issues that affect our understanding of this section deserve comment.

The Significance of 12:1–15:13 within Romans

In this volume on Pauline theology it needs to be made clear that after centuries of neglect, Rom 12:1–15:13 is now recognized as crucial to our understanding of the letter. In particular, one's reading of Rom 14:1–15:13 certainly affects how one construes Paul's theology in the rest of the letter. If we accept Romans 14–15 as directed to a real situation in Rome, that means we will read the rest of the letter as an occasional letter addressed to a church about which Paul was informed, and not as a *compendium doctrinae Christianae* (summation of Christian doctrine).[15] If we understand the "strong" and "weak" division in these chapters to reflect mainly a Gentile *versus* Jew difference, we will be more likely to rate the ethnic question as important throughout the letter, listening for Gentile or Jewish voices in the interlocuter's questions.

Rom 12:1–15:13 therefore cannot be ignored when one begins to study Romans. It is just as important as the preceding eleven chapters and cannot be relegated to second place.[16]

---

[14] I am indebted to my teacher, H. D. Betz, for first showing me the role that obligation plays in Rom 12:1–15:13.

[15] The phrase is Melanchthon's and represents the perspective on Romans that Paul is writing a general letter that he intended to be equally applicable to all churches, as though it were a theology textbook and not a letter focused on the concerns of the Roman churches.

[16] For an argument that Rom 12:1–15:13 is *more* important than the preceding part of the letter, see Paul Minear, *The Obedience of Faith: The Purpose of Paul in the Epistle to the Romans* (SBT 2/19; Naperville, IL: Allenson, 1971). Jürgen Becker illustrates the past tendency to ignore this part of the letter: "Romans 1–8 does present the last unfolding of the Pauline gospel" (*Paul: Apostle to the Gentiles* [Louisville: Westminster/John Knox, 1993] 351). But in his section on Romans 1–8, he appeals several times to texts from Rom 12:1–15:13!

Jesus Traditions in Romans 12:1–15:13

This section of Romans contains more allusions to teachings of Jesus attested in the Gospels than we find anywhere else in the Pauline corpus. Its theology is therefore marked by Jesus traditions to an extent not found elsewhere in Paul. Thus, his directions to the Roman churches to pay their taxes may arise from his knowledge of Jesus' saying on paying taxes to Caesar.[17] Love is seen to be the fulfillment of the law as Jesus taught.[18] Similarly, Paul states that he knows "in the Lord Jesus" that no food is unclean in itself (14:14), a truth that he perhaps knew from traditions preserved for us in Mark 7:14–19. The best recent statement of these Jesus traditions in this section of Romans is Thompson's *Clothed with Christ.*[19]

Romans 12:1–15:13 and the Apocalyptic Paul

Campbell helpfully emphasizes salvation as a future hope in Romans. Although he does not use "the apocalyptic Paul" as a term in his chapter, as I have in the above heading, I think he would agree that Paul does hold an apocalyptic hope. By this I mean the common hope in some Jewish literature of the Hellenistic era that at the end of history a large number of Gentiles will join Israel in following God.[20] Paul of course is not just concerned with the ingathering of the Gentiles. He has already made clear that in his understanding, "all Israel will be saved" after the Gentiles turn to God (11:26).[21] In this section of Romans, Paul looks ahead to a time when God will intervene in history and vindicate his covenant community of Jew and Gentile. Rom

---

[17] Rom 13:6–7; cf. Matt 22:21; Mark 12:17; Luke 20:25.

[18] Rom 13:8–10; cf. Matt 5:43; 19:19; 22:39; Mark 12:31; Luke 10:27.

[19] Michael Thompson, *Clothed with Christ: The Example and Teaching of Jesus in Romans 12.1–15.13* (JSNTSup 59; Sheffield: Sheffield Academic Press, 1991).

[20] Scot McKnight discusses this as a theme in Jewish literature of the Second Temple period (*A Light among the Gentiles: Jewish Missionary Activity in the Second Temple Period* [Minneapolis: Fortress, 1991] 47–48). Though not all the texts he cites are commonly considered apocalyptic literature, this hope surely is, since it involves divine intervention along with the vindication of Israel. McKnight cites Tob 13:11; Sir 36:11–17; *1 Enoch* 48:4; *T. Sim.* 7:2; *T. Levi* 18:2–9; *T. Jud.* 24:6; 25:5; *T. Zeb.* 9:8; *T. Benj.* 10:5–10; *Sib. Or.* 5:493–500; 4 Ezra 6:26; *2 Bar.* 68:5; *b. Ber.* 57b. McKnight also mentions J. Jeremias, *Jesus' Promise to the Nations* (1953 Franz Delitzsch Lectures; SBT 24; London: SCM, 1958) 56–73, for a description of the ingathering of the Gentiles as a theme in Jewish literature.

[21] While I agree with N. T. Wright (*The Climax of the Covenant: Christ and the Law in Pauline Theology* [Minneapolis: Fortress, 1991] 248) that Paul envisions Jews coming to faith in Jesus; I disagree that the "all Israel" of 11:26 refers to a redefined Israel of Jewish and Gentile believers (p. 250). Wright has not explained how 11:11–12, 15, 23–24, which seem to anticipate the fullness of ethnic Israel, fit with his idea that 11:26 describes how a redefined Israel is saved.

13:12a employs a metaphor to suggest the end of history. The judgment scene in 14:11–12 also fits into this apocalyptic mindset. The conclusion of the section (15:7–13), with its scripture quotations from Law, Prophets, and Writings, is used to give the reader a sense that God will accomplish his promises (v. 8), so that Gentiles and Jews will praise God together (v. 10) and all will hope in the Davidic king, the "root of Jesse" (v. 12).

Not only is our acknowledgment of this hope in Paul helpful for our sense of Paul's self–understanding; it also helps us see how Rom 12:1–15:13 relates to chaps. 9–11. Romans 9–11 ends with Paul's vision of God bringing the elect, both Jews and Gentiles, to salvation (11:25–36). Similarly, Rom 12:1–15:13 ends with a picture of Jews and Gentiles praising God as delivered people (15:8–12). This leads to the conclusion that Rom 12:1–15:13 gives a picture of how the new covenant community of both Jew and Gentile is to live now (12:1–15:6) in light of their spectacular destiny (15:8–12).[22]

12:1–2

These two verses anchor what is to follow to the preceding chapters and provide a programmatic statement for 12:1–15:13. The "mercies of God" include the benefits of Christ—freedom from death (chap. 5), freedom from sin (chap. 6), freedom from the law (chap. 7), life with God through the Spirit (chap. 8)—as well as God's covenant faithfulness that is examined and re-affirmed in Romans 9–11.

"Reasonable worship" is certainly the best reading of λογικὴ λατρεία. It comes here as the fulcrum for a letter body that begins (1:20–21, 25b) and ends with worship (15:9–13). "Reasonable worship" means in this context the worship that is expected, given all that belongs to those who are in Christ. Worship is the first obligation of the believer and therefore comes first in this section that spells out the obligations of the new covenant community.

"Reasonable worship" according to Paul also signifies worship that is performed with a knowledge of God's plan for the world. The worship (λατρεία) had belonged to ethnic Jews, those physically descended from Abraham (9:4). But though zealous, they did not pursue God in a reasonable way (10:2–3). Having redefined Israel in 9:6–8, Paul has to redefine what belongs to the new Israel. Rom 12:1–15:13 is thus the new covenant counterpart to 9:4–5. In those two verses Paul gave a shorthand description of what belongs to ethnic Jews. Now after sounding an echo of the new covenant (Jer 31:33–34 in Rom 11:27a), Paul seeks to spell out in detail the marks of the new covenant community in 12:1–15:13.

---

[22] See also J. C. Beker, *Paul's Apocalyptic Gospel: The Coming Triumph of God* (Philadelphia: Fortress, 1982) 29–77; idem, *The Triumph of God* (Minneapolis: Fortress, 1990) 61–103.

This community is to be separate from the world in its mindset, dedicated to God (12:2).[23] Yet Paul will continue to spell out their obligations for life in the community of faith and in secular society.

12:3–8

After the principle of obligation is described in 12:1–2, Paul begins to discuss the obligation of living in the church. We know that it is an issue of obligation, for Paul writes that one should not think more highly than one *ought* to think in 12:3. An underlying obligation is at work in 12:6, where we read that the gifts are given according to the grace given to us. As in 12:1–2, obligation results from the grace that is bestowed by God.

The "measure of faith" (12:3) is surely a guiding principle for 12:1–15:13, though "faith" is used in a slightly different connotation in 14:1, 22, 23. Here it is one's unique "measure" with regard to the gifts that arise out of faith.[24] But in 14:1, 22–23 it is one's own knowledge and conviction of how one approaches God through Christ.

Rom 12:3–8 is also programmatic for this section of Romans because of its mention of the χαρίσματα ("gifts") in 12:6. Though I do not link these "gifts" here with the "strong" and "weak" difference as Campbell does, I do agree that the Holy Spirit is definitely in Paul's mind throughout chaps. 12–15. Though explicit reference to the Spirit is infrequent (14:17; 15:13), the Spirit's work is assumed in ways that show how vital Paul considers the Spirit's role in the church to be (12:1–2, 6–8; 13:12–14; 15:5–6). Paul's references to the Spirit in this section seem analogous to how an orchestra's musical director might use both explicit and implicit references to the conductor when discussing the orchestra's performance.[25]

12:9–21

These verses comprise a ring composition of maxims, based on the theme of love. Their Hellenistic Jewish character[26] makes them especially appropri-

---

[23] The echoes of Exod 19:5–6 reverberate here.

[24] Dunn, *Romans 9–16*, 721–22.

[25] For further insight on the place of the Spirit in Romans, see Gordon Fee, *God's Empowering Presence: The Spirit in the Letters of Paul* (Peabody, MA: Hendrickson, 1994) 594–624; Fitzmyer, *Romans*, 124: "In Romans, when Paul speaks of the Spirit, he does not understand *pneuma* as in the Hellenistic world of his time, as the power of thaumaturgy and ecstasy, but rather as an apocalyptic manifestation of the endtime, as in the OT."

[26] Walter T. Wilson, *Love without Pretense: Romans 12:9–21 and Hellenistic-Jewish Wisdom Literature* (WUNT 2/46; Tübingen: Mohr [Siebeck], 1991).

ate to an audience of churches in Rome that certainly included believers from a Jewish background. The force of the verses certainly rides on an underlying obligation that one ought to live in a certain way with one's fellow church members.

These verses contain another clue of a distinctive characteristic of Romans 12–15, an allusion to a Jesus-saying. Though Rom 12:14 could simply have arisen out of a Jewish matrix, in light of the attention Paul gives to Jesus' teachings in this letter, it is best to see in this verse an allusion to traditions preserved in Luke 6:28a.[27] The use of Jesus as an example continues on through 15:13.

The significance of this section of Romans 12–15 for the theology of these chapters as a whole is that it sets up the moral obligation upon believers in light of the love command. Paul gives basic guidelines, centered on the love command, for living in the new covenant community. The measure of faith that believers share places them under a common obligation to love one another.

13:1–7

The measure of faith that believers share places them all under a second common obligation—to obey the government. Paul is no doubt aware of the severe discontent over taxes at this time, and writes to make sure that the Roman believers bring no reproach by neglecting to pay.[28] While this and the preceding commands for obedience are certainly based on Paul's understanding of the believers' common obligation, he is also concerned lest any disobedience bring against the Roman churches the charge of *superstitio*, and so lead to persecution or expulsion.[29]

13:8–14

Here at the center of this section of Romans, Paul most explicitly expresses the main obligation that is at work from Rom 12:1–15:13, the obligation to love one's neighbor. It is supported from the moral teaching of the Mosaic Law. The faith that appropriates the benefits of one who has become the goal of the law (10:4) still lives itself out in love. Paul has already defended himself against the charge of antinomianism in 3:31 and 6:1–2; now he shows how the new covenant community can use the law. As he wrote to judaizers in Gal

---

[27] Against Wilson (*Love without Pretense*, 169–71), here I follow Thompson, *Clothed with Christ*, 96–105.

[28] Tacitus, *Ann.* 13.50–51. See also J. Friedrich, W. Pöhlmann, and P. Stuhlmacher, "Zur historischen Situation und Intention von Röm 13,1–7," *ZTK* 73 (1976) 131–66; and J. D. G. Dunn, "Romans 13:1–7—A Charter for Political Quietism?" *Ex Auditu* 2 (1986) 55–68.

[29] Robert Hodgson, "Superstition," in *ABD*, vol. 6.

5:13–16, so here in Rom 13:8–10 Paul places the love command in a prominent position. I have already noted above how Paul's use of the love command reminds us of Jesus. In 13:14 Paul presents Jesus as the example of how faith gives rise to a holy love.

The commands against partying and carousing (13:13) may be focused on the Roman situation. This picture fits with the "strong" who eat everything (14:2), as well as Juvenal's description of first-century gluttonous Romans, bedridden with undigested food in their stomachs (*Sat.* 3.234).

14:1–15:6

In this section we have Paul's description of how divided church groups are obligated to live in relation to each other. The "weak in faith" are probably Jewish Christians and their sympathizers who have some qualms about eating meat and drinking wine in Rome (14:1–2, 14, 21) and appear scrupulous in their observance of the sabbath (14:5–6). Because of God's ability to uphold the believer and each believer's appointment at the divine court for judgment, these "weak" are obligated not to judge the "strong," those who do not share their qualms or scruples (14:3–4, 10–12). Because of God's ability to uphold the believer, the reality of a scruple or reservation in the mind of the "weak," and the example of Christ, the "strong" are obligated not to despise or offend the "weak" but to respect their scruples, to see to it that the "weak" are not grieved, and to support them (14:3–4, 14–15, 21; 15:1–3). The burden of obligation in this section surely falls on the "strong." There is no sense in which Paul is trying to move the "weak" out of their scrupulous positions. He rather respects their scruples and asks the "strong" to do so as well.

When we read this section in light of Rom 15:7–12, Paul's underlying theology seems to be that Christ's death allows the promises to Abraham to be opened up to the Gentiles. Since he died under the curse of the Mosaic Law, its provisions are now changed (14:14), so that no food is unclean. But still the law's underlying message of love is to be viewed as the obligation on all who identify with Jesus (14:15; 15:3–4).

Verse 23b is further evidence that Paul is crafting this section to fit his audience. "Whatever is not of faith is sin" is very close to a Roman maxim:

> It is, therefore, an excellent rule that they give who bid us not to do a thing, when there is a doubt whether it be right or wrong; for righteousness shines with a brilliance of its own, but doubt is a sign that we are thinking of a possible wrong. (Cicero, *Off.* 1.30)[30]

---

[30] Quocirca bene praecipiunt, qui vetant quicquam agere, quod dubites aequum sit an iniquum. Aequitas enim lucet ipsa per se, dubitatio cogitationem significat iniuriae (trans. by

Paul therefore uses a Roman saying (14:23b) and an Old Testament quotation (15:3) to show the Romans that they must respect the doubts some have about food in order to live in love with others in the new covenant community.

The christological reading of Ps 68:10 LXX that Paul uses in 15:3 is probably pre-Pauline. Davidic psalms were read in the light of the Messiah, who was to represent the people of the covenant.[31] Paul considers it fitting to use this text, therefore, since he is outlining the obligations for people in the new covenant community.

The mention of hope in 15:4 signals to us the eschatological horizon Paul has in mind for this community. The perfect will of God (12:2) finally comes to fruition in the *eschaton*, in light of which we are now called to live.

The benediction in 15:5–6 assumes the Spirit's help in moving the divided community back to its first obligation, proper worship of God. The believers were divided because they did different things with their mouths, both at the table and in conversation (14:1–3). Paul therefore prays that they might use one mouth to glorify God.

15:7–13

Here we have Paul's fitting conclusion to the section on "strong" and "weak" and the body of the letter. The description of Christ as "minister of the circumcision" emphasizes his role as the representative of Israel. The global result of his death and resurrection is that the curse of the law, which kept the Abrahamic promises for the world from being fulfilled, can now be overcome so that the promises can be actualized. The significance of the Deuteronomy quotation in 15:10 cannot be overestimated. Here Paul goes to the Mosaic law, at times a source of pride and Jewish distinctiveness, and finds in it a clear signal of God's purpose for choosing Israel, praise to God by the nations and the Jews. It illustrates precisely his point in the preceding two verses. The promises God gave to the Jews had the world in view.

The string of scripture proofs are meant to support Paul's contention that God's purpose in election all along was to bless the world.[32] A realization of this must inevitably involve acceptance and fellowship of ethnically different groups in the Roman churches. The hope of the nations in the Messiah (Isa

---

Walter Miller; LCL; London: William Heinemann, 1913). J. J. Wettstein has noted Pliny's version of the maxim (*Ep.* 1.18.5) in *Novum Testamentum*, 2. 91. Cf. also *1 Clem.* 23.2.

[31] Here I follow Richard B. Hays, "Christ Prays the Psalms: Paul's Use of an Early Christian Exegetical Convention," in *The Future of Christology: Essays in Honor of Leander E. Keck* (ed. A. J. Malherbe and W. A. Meeks; Minneapolis: Fortress, 1993) 130–32.

[32] Wright, *Climax of the Covenant*, 248, 262–63; Hays, "Christ Prays the Psalms," 136.

11:10 LXX quoted in 15:12) again shows us that Paul's eyes are on the escha-tological horizon as a guide for life in the new covenant community. Hope is reaffirmed in 15:13, Paul's concluding benediction. Here he is explicit in his reference to the Spirit; it is by the Spirit's power that such unity-bringing hope will come to the Roman churches.

III. CONCLUSION

Rom 12:1–15:13 works out how the Roman believers, as members of the new covenant community, are to live in the world. Their obligations to wor-ship God and love others are based on God's covenant faithfulness, made avail-able to them in Christ. God's power that leads to salvation (1:16–17) is brought into the new covenant community through the Spirit's transforming and hope-instilling activity (12:1–2; 15:13). Their life in the church and the world is to be lived in consciousness of the glorious finale to which they are destined, the praise of God and his Messiah by the Gentiles and the Jews.

BIBLIOGRAPHY

Compiled by
Robert Jewett

Aageson, James W. "Scripture and Structure in the Development of the Argument in Romans 9– 11." *CBQ* 48 (1986) 265–89.
———. *Written Also for Our Sake: Paul and the Art of Biblical Interpretation.* Louisville: Westminster/John Knox, 1993.
Achtemeier, Paul J. *Romans.* Interpretation: A Bible Commentary for Teaching and Preaching. Atlanta: John Knox, 1985.
Aland, Kurt. "Der Schluss und die ursprüngliche Gestalt des Römerbriefes." In *Neutestamentliche Entwürfe*, 284–301. TBü NT 63. Munich: Kaiser, 1979.
Aletti, Jean-Noël. "L'Argumentation paulinienne en Rm 9." *Bib* 68 (1987) 41– 56.
———. *Comment Dieu est-il juste? Clefs pour interpréter l'épître aux Romains.* Parole de Dieu. Paris: Seuil, 1991.
Allison, Dale C., Jr. "The Background of Romans 11:11–15 in Apocalyptic and Rabbinic Literature." *Studia Biblica et Theologica* 10 (1980) 229–34.
———. "Romans 11:11–15: A Suggestion." *Perspectives in Religious Studies* 12 (1985) 23–30.
Althaus, Paul. *Der Brief an die Römer.* NTD 6. 1932. Göttingen: Vandenhoeck & Ruprecht, 1966.
Amiot, François. *The Key Concepts of St. Paul.* Translated by J. Dingle. Edinburgh/London: Nelson, 1962.
Aune, David E. *The New Testament in Its Literary Environment.* Philadelphia: Westminster, 1987.
———. "Romans as a *Logos Protreptikos.*" In *The Romans Debate,* edited by K. P. Donfried, 278–96. Revised and expanded edition. Peabody, MA: Hendrickson, 1991.
Aus, Roger D. "Paul's Travel Plans to Spain and the 'Full Number of the Gentiles' of Rom 11:25." *NovT* 21 (1979) 232–62.

Badenas, Robert. *Christ the End of the Law: Romans 10:4 in Pauline Perspective.* JSNTSup 10. Sheffield: JSOT Press, 1985.

Baeck, Leo. "The Faith of Paul." In *Judaism and Christianity*, 139–68. Translated by W. Kaufmann. New York: Atheneum, 1958.

Balz, Horst Robert. *Heilsvertrauen und Welterfahrung: Strukturen der paulinischen Eschatologie nach Römer 8, 18–39.* BEvT 59. Munich: Kaiser, 1971.

Bammel, Ernst. "Romans 13." In *Jesus and the Politics of His Day*, edited by E. Bammel and C. F. D. Moule, 365–83. Cambridge: Cambridge University Press, 1984.

Barrett, C. K. *A Commentary on the Epistle to the Romans.* 2d ed. London: Black, 1991.

———. "I am Not Ashamed of the Gospel." In *Foi et salut selon S. Paul*, edited by M. Barth et al., 19–41. AnBib 42. Rome: Biblical Institute Press, 1970. Reprinted in *New Testament Essays*, 116–43. London: SPCK, 1972.

———. *Paul: An Introduction to His Thought.* Louisville: Westminster/John Knox; London: Chapman, 1994.

Barth, Markus. *Justification: Pauline Texts Interpreted in the Light of the Old and New Testaments.* Grand Rapids: Eerdmans, 1971.

———. *The People of God.* JSNTSup 5. Sheffield: JSOT Press, 1983.

———. "St. Paul—A Good Jew." *HBT* 1 (1979) 7–45.

Bartsch, Hans-Werner. "Die antisemitischen Gegner des Paulus im Römerbrief." In *Antijudaismus im Neuen Testament*, edited by W. Eckert et al., 27–43. Munich: Kaiser, 1967.

———. "The Concept of Faith in Paul's Letter to the Romans." *BR* 13 (1968) 41–53.

———. "Zur vorpaulinischen Bekenntnisformel im Eingang des Römerbriefes." *TZ* 23 (1967) 329–39.

Bassler, Jouette M. *Divine Impartiality: Paul and a Theological Axiom.* SBLDS 59. Chico, CA: Scholars, 1982.

———. "Paul's Theology: Whence and Whither?" In *Pauline Theology, Volume II: 1 & 2 Corinthians*, edited by D. M. Hay, 3–17. Minneapolis: Fortress, 1993.

———. "Preface." In *Pauline Theology, Volume I: Thessalonians, Philippians, Galatians, Philemon*, edited by J. M. Bassler, ix–xi. Minneapolis: Fortress, 1991.

Baumgarten, Jörg. *Paulus und die Apokalyptik.* WMANT 44. Neukirchen-Vluyn: Neukirchener Verlag, 1975.

Baur, Ferdinand Christian. *Paul the Apostle of Jesus Christ: His Life and Work, His Epistles and His Doctrine.* Translated by A. Menzies. 2 vols. London: Williams & Norgate, 1875.

Beck, Norman A. *Mature Christianity in the 21st Century: The Recognition and Repudiation of the Anti-Jewish Polemic in the New Testament.* Expanded and revised edition. Prologue and Introduction by C. M. Leighton. New York: Crossroad, 1994.

Becker, Jürgen. *Auferstehung der Toten im Urchristentum.* Stuttgart: Katholisches Bibelwerk, 1976.

———. *Paul: Apostle to the Gentiles.* Translated by O. C. Dean, Jr. Louisville: Westminster/Knox, 1993.

Beker, J. Christiaan. "The Challenge of Paul's Apocalyptic Gospel for the Church Today." *JRT* 40 (1983) 9–15.

———. "The Faithfulness of God and the Priority of Israel in Paul's Letter to the Romans." *HTR* 79 (1986) 10–16. Reprinted in *Christians Among Jews and Gentiles: Essays in Honor of Krister Stendahl on his Sixty-fifth Birthday,* edited by G. W. E. Nickelsburg and G. W. MacRae, 10–16. Philadelphia: Fortress, 1986.

———. *Paul the Apostle: The Triumph of God in Life and Thought.* Philadelphia: Fortress, 1980.

———. *Paul's Apocalyptic Gospel: The Coming Triumph of God.* Philadelphia: Fortress, 1982.

———. "Paul's Theology: Consistent or Inconsistent?" *NTS* 34 (1988) 364–77.

———. "Romans 9–11 in the Context of the Early Church." *Princeton Seminary Bulletin* Sup 1 (1990) 40–55.

———. "Suffering and Triumph in Paul's Letter to the Romans." *HBT* 7 (1985) 105–19.

Bell, Richard H. *Provoked to Jealousy: The Origin and Purpose of the Jealousy Motif in Romans 9–11.* WUNT 63. Tübingen: Mohr (Siebeck), 1994.

Ben-Chorin, Shalom. *Paulus: Der Völkerapostel in jüdischer Sicht.* Munich: List, 1970.

Benoit, Pierre. "Genèse et évolution de la pensée paulinienne." In *Paul de Tarse, Apôtre de notre temps,* edited by P. Benoit, 75–100. Série monographique de "Benedictina" Section Paulinienne 1. Rome: Abbaye de S. Paul, 1979.

Berger, Klaus. *Gottes einzinger Ölbaum: Betrachtungen zum Römerbrief.* Stuttgart: Quell, 1990.

Betz, Hans Dieter. "Christianity as Religion: Paul's Attempt at Definition in Romans." *JR* 71 (1991) 315–44. Reprinted in *Paulinische Studien,* 206–39.

———. *Paulinische Studien: Gesammelte Aufsätze III.* Tübingen: Mohr (Siebeck), 1994.

Bindemann, Walther. *Die Hoffnung der Schöpfung: Römer 8:18–27 und die Frage einer Theologie der Befreiung von Mensch und Natur.* Neukirchener Studienbücher 14. Neukirchen-Vluyn: Neukirchener Verlag, 1983.

Binder, Hermann. *Der Glaube bei Paulus*. Berlin: Evangelische Verlag, 1968.

Bockmuehl, Markus N. A. *Revelation and Mystery in Ancient Judaism and Pauline Christianity*. WUNT 36. Tübingen: Mohr (Siebeck), 1990.

Boers, Hendrikus. "The Foundations of Paul's Thought: A Methodological Investigation—The Problem of the Coherent Center of Paul's Thought." *ST* 42 (1988) 55–68.

———. *The Justification of the Gentiles: Paul's Letters to the Galatians and Romans*. Peabody, MA: Hendrickson, 1994.

———. "The Meaning of Christ in Paul's Writings: A Structuralist Semiotic Study." *BTB* 14 (1984) 131–44.

———. "The Problem of Jews and Gentiles in the Macro-Structure of Romans." *SEÅ* 47 (1982) 184–96.

Borg, Marcus. "A New Context for Romans XIII." *NTS* 19 (1972–73) 205–18.

Bornkamm, Günther. "The Letter to the Romans as Paul's Last Will and Testament." In *The Romans Debate*, edited by K. P. Donfried, 16–28. Revised and expanded edition. Peabody, MA: Hendrickson, 1991.

———. "The Revelation of God's Wrath: Romans i–iii." In *Early Christian Experience*, translated by P. L. Hammer, 46–70. London: SCM, 1969.

Bouwman, Gijs. *Paulus aan de romeinen: Een retorische analyse van Rom 1–8*. Abjij Averbode: Werkgroep voor levensverdieping, 1980.

Bovon, François. "Paul aux côtes d'Israël et des nations (Rm 9–11)." *Bulletin du Centre Protestant d'Etudes et de Documentation* 44 (1992) 6–15.

Brandenburger, Egon. *Adam und Christus: Exegetisch-religionsgeschichtliche Untersuchungen zu Röm 5:12–21 (1 Kor 15)*. WMANT 7. Neukirchen-Vluyn: Neukirchener Verlag, 1962.

———. "Alter und neuer Mensch, erster und letzter Adam-Anthropos." In *Vom alten zum neuen Adam: Urzeitmythos und Heilsgeschichte*, edited by W. Strolz, 182–223. Freiburg: Herder, 1986.

———. "Paulinische Schriftauslegung in der Kontroverse um das Verheissungswort Gottes (Röm 9)." *ZTK* 82 (1985) 1–47.

Breytenbach, Cilliers. *Versöhnung: Eine Studie zur paulinischen Soteriologie*. WMANT 60. Neukirchen-Vluyn: Neukirchener Verlag, 1989.

Brown, Raymond E., and John P. Meier. *Antioch and Rome: New Testament Cradles of Catholic Christianity*. New York: Paulist, 1983.

———. "Further Reflections on the Origins of the Church of Rome." In *The Conversation Continues: Studies in Paul and John in Honor of J. Louis Martyn*, edited by R. T. Fortna and B. R. Gaventa, 98–115. Nashville: Abingdon, 1990.

———. "Not Jewish Christianity and Gentile Christianity but Types of Jewish/Gentile Christianity." *CBQ* 45 (1983) 74–79.

Bruce, Frederick F. *Paul: Apostle of the Free Spirit.* Exeter: Paternoster, 1977. American title: *Paul: Apostle of the Heart Set Free.* Grand Rapids: Eerdmans, 1977.

Bultmann, Rudolf. "Christ the End of the Law." In *Essays Philosophical and Theological,* translated by J. D. G. Grieg, 36–66. London: SCM; New York: Macmillan, 1955.

———. *The Old and New Man in the Letters of Paul.* Translated by K. R. Crim. Richmond: John Knox, 1967.

___. *Theology of the New Testament.* Translated by K. Grobel. 2 vols. London: SCM; New York: Scribner, 1965.

Burger, Christoph. *Jesus als Davidssohn: Eine traditionsgeschichtliche Untersuchung.* FRLANT 98. Göttingen: Vandenhoeck & Ruprecht, 1970.

Bussmann, Claus. *Themen der paulinischen Missionspredigt auf dem Hintergrund der spätjüdisch-hellenistischen Missionsliteratur.* Europäische Hochschulschriften 23.3. Bern/Frankfurt: Lang, 1975.

Byrne, Brendan. *"Sons of God"–"Seed of Abraham": A Study of the Idea of the Sonship of God of All Christians in Paul Against the Jewish Background.* AnBib 83. Rome: Biblical Institute Press, 1979.

Caird, G. B. *New Testament Theology.* Completed and edited by L. D. Hurst. Oxford: Clarendon; New York: Oxford, 1994.

Calvin, John. "The Theme of the Epistle of Paul to the Romans." Translated by R. Mackenzie. In *The Epistles of Paul to the Romans and to the Thessalonians.* Grand Rapids: Eerdmans, 1960.

Campbell, Douglas A. *The Rhetoric of Righteousness in Romans 3.21–26.* JSNTSup 65. Sheffield: JSOT Press, 1992.

Campbell, William S. "The Contribution of Traditions to Paul's Theology." In *Pauline Theology II,* edited by D. M. Hay, 234–54. Minneapolis: Fortress, 1993.

———. *Paul's Gospel in an Intercultural Context: Jew and Gentile in the Letter to the Romans.* Studies in the Intercultural History of Christianity 69. Frankfurt: Lang, 1992.

Capes, Donald B. *Old Testament Yahweh Texts in Paul's Christology.* WUNT 2/47. Tübingen: Mohr (Siebeck), 1992.

Carrez, Maurice. *De la souffrance à la glorire: De la doxa dans la pensée paulinienne.* Bibliothèque théologique. Neuchâtel/Paris: Delachaux et Niestlé, 1976.

Carson, Donald A. *Divine Sovereignty and Human Responsibility: Biblical Themes in Tension.* Atlanta: John Knox, 1981.

Cerfaux, Lucien. *Christ in the Theology of St. Paul.* Translated by G. Webb and A. Walker. New York: Herder & Herder, 1959.

Collins, John N. *Diakonia: Re-interpreting the Ancient Sources*. New York/Oxford: University Press, 1990.

Conzelmann, Hans. *An Outline of the Theology of the New Testament*. Translated by J. Bowden. New York: Harper & Row, 1969.

Cosgrove, Charles H. "Justification in Paul: A Linguistic and Theological Reflection." *JBL* 106 (1987) 653–70.

————. "The Justification of the Other: An Interpretation of Rom. 1:18–4:25." In *Society of Biblical Literature 1992 Seminar Papers*, edited by E. H. Lovering, Jr., 613–34. Atlanta: Scholars Press, 1992.

Court, John M. "Paul and the Apocalyptic Pattern." In *Paul and Paulinism: Essays in Honour of C. K. Barrett*, edited by M. D. Hooker and S. G. Wilson, 56–66. London: SPCK, 1982.

Cousar, Charles B. *A Theology of the Cross: The Death of Jesus in the Pauline Letters*. Minneapolis: Fortress, 1990.

Crafton, Jeffrey A. "Paul's Rhetorical Vision and the Purpose of Romans: Toward a New Understanding." *NovT* 32 (1990) 317–39.

Cranfield, C. E. B. *A Critical and Exegetical Commentary on the Epistle to the Romans*. 2 vols. ICC. Edinburgh: T. & T. Clark, 1975, 1979.

Cullmann, Oscar. *The Christology of the New Testament*. Translated by S. C. Guthrie and C. A. M. Hall. Philadelphia: Westminster, 1959.

Dabelstein, Rolf. *Die Beurteilung der "Heiden" bei Paulus*. BEvT 14. Bern/Frankfurt: Lang, 1981.

Dahl, Nils Alstrup. "The Messiahship of Jesus in Paul." In *The Crucified Messiah and Other Essays*, 37–47. Minneapolis: Augsburg, 1974.

————. *Studies in Paul: Theology for the Early Christian Mission*. Minneapolis: Augsburg, 1977.

Davies, Glenn N. *Faith and Obedience in Romans: A Study in Romans 1–4*. JSNTSup 39. Sheffield: JSOT Press, 1990.

Davies, W. D. *Jewish and Pauline Studies*. Philadelphia: Fortress, 1985.

————. *Paul and Rabbinic Judaism: Some Elements in Pauline Theology*. London: SPCK, 1958.

————. "Paul and the Gentiles: A Suggestion concerning Romans 11:13–24." In *Jewish and Pauline Studies*, 153–63, 356–60. Philadelphia: Fortress, 1985.

————. "Paul and the Law: Reflections on Pitfalls in Interpretation." *The Hastings Law Journal* 29 (1978) 1459–1504. Abbreviated in *Paul and Paulinism: Essays in Honour of C. K. Barrett*, edited by M. D. Hooker and S. G. Wilson, 4–16. London: SPCK, 1982.

————. "Paul and the People of Israel." *NTS* 24 (1977–78) 4–39. Reprinted in *Jewish and Pauline Studies*, 123–52. Philadelphia: Fortress, 1985.

de Boer, Martinus C. *The Defeat of Death: Apocalyptic Eschatology in 1 Corinthians 15 and Romans 5*. JSNTSup 22. Sheffield: JSOT Press, 1988.

Deidun, T. J. *New Covenant Morality in Paul.* AnBib 89. Rome: Biblical Institute Press, 1981.

Dietzfelbinger, Christian. *Die Berufung des Paulus als Ursprung seiner Theologie.* WMANT 58. Neukirchen-Vluyn: Neukirchener Verlag, 1985.

———. *Heilsgeschichte bei Paulus? Eine exegetische Studie zum paulinischen Geschichtsdenken.* Theologische Existenz heute 126. Munich: Kaiser, 1965.

———. *Paulus und das Alte Testament: Die Hermeneutik des Paulus, untersucht an seiner Deutung der Gestalt Abrahams.* Theologische Existenz heute 95. Munich: Kaiser, 1961.

———. "Sohn und Gesetz: Überlegungen zur paulinischen Christologie." In *Anfänge der Christologie: Festschrift für Ferdinand Hahn zum 65 Geburtstag,* edited by C. Breytenbach and H. Paulsen, 111–19. Göttingen: Vandenhoeck & Ruprecht, 1991.

Dodd, C. H. *The Epistle of Paul to the Romans.* MNTC. London: Hodder & Stoughton, 1932. Rev. ed. London: Collins, 1959.

Donaldson, Terence L. "'Riches for the Gentiles' (Rom 11:12): Israel's Rejection and Paul's Gentile Mission." *JBL* 112 (1993) 81–98.

Donfried, Karl P. "Justification and Last Judgement in Paul." *ZNW* 67 (1976) 90–110.

———, ed. *The Romans Debate.* Minneapolis: Augsburg, 1977. Revised and Expanded Edition. Peabody, MA: Hendrickson, 1991.

Drane, John W. *Paul: Libertine or Legalist? A Study in the Theology of the Major Pauline Epistles.* London: SPCK, 1975.

Dreyfus, François. "Le Passé et le présent d'Israël (Rom 9,1–5; 11,1–24)." In *Die Israelfrage nach Römer 9–11,* edited by L. de Lorenzi, 131–92. Rome: Abtei von St. Paul, 1977.

Dugandzic, Ivan. *Das "Ja" Gottes in Christus: Eine Studie zur Bedeutung des Alten Testaments für das Christusverständnis des Paulus.* Würzburg: Echter, 1977.

Dunn, James D. G. *Christology in the Making.* London: SCM, 1980.

———. "The Formal and Theological Coherence of Romans." In *The Romans Debate,* edited by K. P. Donfried, 245–50. Revised and expanded edition. Peabody, MA: Hendrickson, 1991.

———. *Jesus and the Spirit.* London: SCM, 1975.

———. "Jesus—Flesh and Spirit: An Exposition of Rom 1.3–4." *JTS* 24 (1973) 40–68.

———. "The Justice of God: A Renewed Perspective on Justification by Faith." *JTS* 43 (1992) 1–22.

———. "The New Perspective on Paul." *BJRL* 65 (1983) 95–122.

———. *The Partings of the Ways between Christianity and Judaism and their Sig-*

nificance for the Character of Christianity. London: SCM; Philadelphia: Trinity Press International, 1991.

———. "Paul's Epistle to the Romans: An Analysis of Structure and Argument." *ANRW* 2.25.4 (1987) 2842–90.

———. "Paul's Understanding of the Death of Jesus." In *Reconciliation and Hope: New Testament Essays on Atonement and Eschatology presented to L. L. Morris on his 60th Birthday,* edited by R. J. Banks, 125–41. Exeter: Paternoster, 1974. Revised as "Paul's Understanding of the Death of Jesus as Sacrifice," in *Sacrifice and Redemption: Durham Essays in Theology,* edited by S. W. Sykes. Cambridge: Cambridge University Press, 1989.

———. *Romans 1–8; Romans 9–16.* 2 vols. Word Biblical Commentary 38a, 38b. Dallas: Word, 1988.

———. "Romans 13:1–7—A Charter for Political Quietism?" *Ex Auditu* 2 (1986) 55–68.

———, and James P. Mackey. *New Testament Theology in Dialogue.* London: SPCK, 1987.

du Toit, A. B. "Faith and Obedience in Paul." *Neot* 25 (1991) 65–74.

———. "Die Kirche als doxologische Gemeinschaft im Römerbrief." *Neot* 27 (1993) 69–77.

———. "Persuasion in Romans 1:1–17." *BZ* 33 (1989) 192–209.

———. "Romans 1,3–4 and the Gospel Tradition: A Reassessment of the Phrase κατὰ πνεῦμα ἁγιωσύνης." In *The Four Gospels 1992: Festschrift Frans Neirynck,* edited by F. van Segbroeck et al., 1. 249–56. BETL 100. Louvain: Leuven University and Peeters, 1992.

Eichholz, Georg. *Die Theologie des Paulus im Umriß.* 4th ed. Neukirchen-Vluyn: Neukirchener Verlag, 1983.

Elliott, R. Neil. *The Rhetoric of Romans: Argumentative Constraint and Strategy and Paul's Dialogue with Judaism.* JSNTSup 45. Sheffield: JSOT Press, 1990.

Epp, Eldon J. "Jewish-Gentile Continuity in Paul: Torah and/or Faith? (Romans 9:1–5)." *HTR* 79 (1986) 80–90. Reprinted in *Christians among Jews and Gentiles: Essays in Honor of Krister Stendahl on his Sixty-fifth Birthday,* edited by G. W. E. Nickelsburg and G. W. MacRae. Philadelphia: Fortress, 1986.

Fee, Gordon D. *God's Empowering Presence: The Holy Spirit in the Letters of Paul.* Peabody, MA: Hendrickson, 1994.

Feuillet, André. "Loi de Dieu, loi du Christ et loi de l'Esprit d'après les Epîtres pauliniennes: Les rapports de ces trois lois avec la Loi Mosaïque." *NovT* 22 (1980) 29–65.

Fitzmyer, Joseph A. *According to Paul: Studies in the Theology of the Apostle.* New York/Mahwah: Paulist, 1993.

————. "The Gospel of the Theology of Paul." *Int* 33 (1979) 339–50.

————. *Paul and His Theology: A Brief Sketch.* 2d ed. Englewood Cliffs, NJ: Prentice-Hall, 1989.

————. "Paul and the Law." In *To Advance the Gospel*, 186–201. New York: Crossroad, 1981.

————. "Reconciliation in Pauline Theology." In *No Famine in the Land: Studies in Honor of John L. McKenzie*, edited by J. W. Flanagan and A. W. Robinson, 155–77. Claremont: Scholars Press for the Institute of Antiquity and Christianity, 1975.

————. *Romans: A New Translation with Introduction and Commentary.* AB 33. New York: Doubleday, 1993.

Friedrich, J., W. Pöhlmann, and Peter Stuhlmacher. "Zur historischen Situation und Intention von Röm 13:1–7." *ZTK* 73 (1976) 131–66.

Froitzheim, Franzjosef. *Christologie und Eschatologie bei Paulus.* FB 35. Würzburg: Echter, 1979.

Fuller, Reginald H. *The Foundations of New Testament Christology.* New York: Scribner, 1965.

Furnish, Victor P. *Theology and Ethics in Paul.* Nashville: Abingdon, 1968.

————. *The Love Command in the New Testament.* Nashville: Abingdon; London: SCM, 1973.

————. *The Moral Teaching of Paul.* Nashville: Abingdon, 1979.

Gager, John G. *The Origins of Anti-Semitism: Attitudes Toward Judaism in Pagan and Christian Antiquity.* Oxford: Oxford University Press, 1983.

Gamble, Harry, Jr. *The Textual History of the Letter to the Romans: A Study in Textual and Literary Criticism.* Studies and Documents 42. Grand Rapids: Eerdmans, 1977.

Garlington, Don B. '*The Obedience of Faith': A Pauline Phrase in Historical Context.* WUNT 38. Tübingen: Mohr (Siebeck), 1990.

Gaston, Lloyd. "Abraham and the Righteousness of God." *HBT* 2 (1980) 39–68. Reprinted in *Paul and the Torah*, 45–63. Vancouver: University of British Columbia Press, 1987.

————. "Angels and Gentiles in Early Judaism and in Paul." *SR* 11 (1982) 65–75. Reprinted in *Paul and the Torah*, 35–44. Vancouver: University of British Columbia Press, 1987.

————. "Israel's Enemies in Pauline Theology." *NTS* 28 (1982) 400–423. Reprinted in *Paul and the Torah*, 80–99. Vancouver: University of British Columbia Press, 1987.

————. *Paul and the Torah.* Vancouver: University of British Columbia Press, 1987.

————. "Paul and the Torah." In *Antisemitism and the Foundations of Christianity*, edited by A. T. Davies, 48–71. New York: Paulist, 1979.

Reprinted in *Paul and the Torah*, 15–34. Vancouver: University of British Columbia Press, 1987.

———. "Works of Law as a Subjective Genitive." *SR* 13 (1984) 39–46. Reprinted in *Paul and the Torah*, 100–106. Vancouver: University of British Columbia Press, 1987.

Gebauer, Roland. *Das Gebet bei Paulus: Forschungsgeschichtliche und exegetische Studien*. Theologische Verlagsgemeinschaft Monographien und Studienbücher 349. Giessen: Brunnen, 1989.

Georgi, Dieter. *Theocracy in Paul's Praxis and Theology*. Translated by D. E. Green. Minneapolis: Fortress, 1991.

Getty, Mary Ann. "An Apocalyptic Perspective on Rom. 10:4." *HBT* 4–5 (1982–83) 79–131.

———. "Paul and the Salvation of Israel: A Perspective on Romans 9–11." *CBQ* 50 (1988) 456–69.

Gibbs, John G. *Creation and Redemption: A Study in Pauline Theology*. NovTSup 26. Leiden: Brill, 1971.

Giblin, Charles Homer. *In Hope of God's Glory: Pauline Theological Perspectives*. New York: Herder & Herder, 1970.

Gnilka, Joachim. *Theologie des Neuen Testaments*. Freiburg/Basel: Herder, 1994.

Gooch, Paul W. *Partial Knowledge: Philosophical Studies in Paul*. Notre Dame: University of Notre Dame Press, 1987.

———. "St. Paul on the Strong and the Weak: A Study in the Resolution of Conflict." *Crux* 13 (1975–76) 10–20.

Goppelt, Leonhard. *Theology of the New Testament: Vol. 2, The Variety and Unity of the Apostolic Witness to Christ*. Translated by J. E. Alsup. Edited by J. Roloff. Grand Rapids: Eerdmans, 1982.

Grässer, Erich. *Der Alte Bund im Neuen: Exegetische Studien zur Israelfrage im Neuen Testament*. WUNT 35. Tübingen: Mohr (Siebeck), 1985.

———. "'Ein einziger ist Gott' (Röm 3,30): Zum christologischen Gottesverständnis bei Paulus." In *"Ich will euer Gott werden": Beispiele biblischen Redens von Gott*, edited by N. Lohfink, 177–205. SBS 100. Stuttgart: Katholisches Bibelwerk, 1981. Reprinted in *Der Alte Bund im Neuen: Exegetische Studien zur Israelfrage im Neuen Testament*, 231–58. WUNT 35. Tübingen: Mohr (Siebeck), 1985.

Grenholm, Cristina. *Romans Interpreted: A Comparative Analysis of the Commentaries of Barth, Nygren, Cranfield and Wilckens on Paul's Epistle to the Romans*. Acta Universitatis Upsaliensis 30. Stockholm: Almqvist & Wiksell, 1991.

Güttgemanns, Erhardt. *Der leidende Apostel und sein Herr: Studien zur paulinische Christologie*. FRLANT 90. Göttingen: Vandenhoeck & Ruprecht, 1966.

Gyllenberg, Rafael. *Rechtfertigung und Altes Testament bei Paulus*. Stuttgart: Kohlhammer, 1973.

Haacker, Klaus. "Der Römerbrief als Friedensmemorandum." *NTS* 36 (1990) 25–41.

Hafemann, Scott. "The Salvation of Israel in Romans 11:25–32: A Response to Krister Stendahl." *Ex Auditu* 4 (1988) 38–58.

Hagner, Donald A. "Paul's Quarrel with Judaism." In *Anti-Semitism and Early Christianity: Issues of Polemic and Faith*, edited by C. A. Evans and D. A. Hagner, 128–50. Minneapolis: Fortress, 1993.

Hahn, Ferdinand. *The Titles of Jesus in Christology: Their History in Early Christianity*. Translated by H. Knight and G. Ogg. New York: World, 1969.

———. "Gibt es eine Entwicklung in den Aussagen über die Rechtfertigung bei Paulus?" *EvT* 53 (1993) 342–66.

———. "Taufe und Rechtfertigung: Ein Beitrag zur paulinischen Theologie in ihrer Vor- und Nachgeschichte." In *Rechtfertigung: Festschrift für Ernst Käsemann zum 70. Geburtstag*, edited by J. Friedrich et al., 95–124. Tübingen: Mohr (Siebeck), 1976.

Hainz, Josef. *Koinonia: "Kirche" als Gemeinschaft bei Paulus*. Biblische Untersuchungen 16. Regensburg: Pustet, 1982.

Hall, Sidney G., III. *Christian Anti-Semitism and Paul's Theology*. Minneapolis: Fortress, 1993.

Hamerton-Kelly, Robert G. *Sacred Violence: Paul's Hermeneutic of the Cross*. Minneapolis: Fortress, 1992.

———. "Sacred Violence and Sinful Desire: Paul's Interpretation of Adam's Sin in the Letter to the Romans." In *The Conversation Continues: Studies in Paul and John. In Honor of J. Louis Martyn*, edited by R. T. Fortna and B. R. Gaventa, 35–54. Nashville: Abingdon, 1990.

Hanson, Anthony T. *Studies in Paul's Technique and Theology*. London: SPCK, 1974.

Harrisville, Roy A. *Romans*. Augsburg Commentary on the New Testament. Minneapolis: Augsburg, 1980.

Hartman, Lars. *"Auf den Namen des Herrn Jesus": Die Taufe in den neutestamentlichen Schriften*. SBS 148. Stuttgart: Katholisches Bibelwerk, 1992.

Hasel, Gerhard F. *New Testament Theology: Basic Issues to the Current Debate*. Grand Rapids: Eerdmans, 1978.

———. *The Remnant: The History and Theology of the Remnant Idea from Genesis to Isaiah*. Andrews University Monographs 5. 2d ed. Berrien Springs: Andrews University Press, 1972. 2d ed., 1974.

Hay, David M. "*Pistis* as 'Ground for Faith' in Hellenized Judaism and Paul." *JBL* 108 (1989) 461–76.

Hays, Richard B. "Christ Prays the Psalms: Paul's Use of an Early Christian

Exegetical Convention." In *The Future of Christology: Essays in Honor of Leander E. Keck*, edited by A. J. Malherbe and W. A. Meeks. Minneapolis: Fortress, 1993.

———. *Echoes of Scripture in the Letters of Paul*. New Haven: Yale University Press, 1989.

———. *The Faith of Jesus Christ: The Narrative Substructure of Galatians 3:1–4:11*. SBLDS 56. Chico, CA: Scholars, 1983.

———. "'Have We Found Abraham to Be Our Forefather According to the Flesh?' A Reconsideration of Rom. 4:1." *NovT* 27 (1985) 76–98.

———. "ΠΙΣΤΙΣ and Pauline Christology." In *Society of Biblical Literature 1991 Seminar Papers*, edited by E. H. Lovering, Jr., 714–29. Atlanta: Scholars Press, 1991.

Heil, John Paul. *Paul's Letter to the Romans: A Reader-response Commentary*. New York–Mahwah, NJ: Paulist, 1987.

———. *Romans—Paul's Letter of Hope*. AnBib 112. Rome: Biblical Institute Press, 1987.

Heiligenthal, Roman. "Strategien konformer Ethik im Neuen Testament am Beispiel von Röm 13.1–7." *NTS* 29 (1983) 55–61.

———.*Werke als Zeichen: Untersuchungen zur Bedeutung der menschlichen Taten im Frühjudentum, Neuen Testament und Frühchristentum*. WUNT 2/9. Tübingen: Mohr (Siebeck), 1983.

Heine, Susanne. *Leibhafter Glaube: Ein Beitrag zum Verständnis der theologischen Konzeption des Paulus*. Vienna/Freiburg/Basel: Herder, 1976.

Hermann, Ingo. *Kyrios und Pneuma: Studien zur Christologie der paulinischen Hauptbriefe*. SANT 2. Munich: Kösel, 1961.

Herold, Gerhart. *Zorn und Gerechtigkeit Gottes bei Paulus: Eine Untersuchung zu Röm 1.16–18*. Europäische Hochschulschriften 23/14. Bern/Frankfurt: Lang, 1973.

Hester, James D. *Paul's Concept of Inheritance: A Contribution to the Understanding of Heilsgeschichte*. Scottish Journal of Theology Occasional Papers 14. Edinburgh: Oliver & Boyd, 1968.

Hofius, Otfried. "'All Israel Will be Saved': Divine Salvation and Israel's Deliverance in Romans 9–11." *Princeton Seminary Bulletin* Sup 1 (1990) 19–39.

———. *Paulusstudien*. WUNT 51. Tübingen: Mohr (Siebeck), 1989.

Holmberg, Bengt. *Paul and Power: The Structure of Authority in the Primitive Church as Reflected in the Pauline Epistles*. Philadelphia: Fortress, 1980.

Hooker, Morna D. *From Adam to Christ: Essays on Paul*. Cambridge: Cambridge University Press, 1990.

———. "Paul and Covenantal Nomism." In *Paul and Paulinism: Essays in Honour of C. K. Barrett*, edited by M. D. Hooker and S. G. Wilson, 47–56.

London: SPCK, 1982. Reprinted in *From Adam to Christ: Essays on Paul,* 155–64. Cambridge: Cambridge University Press, 1990.

Horn, Friedrich Wilhelm. *Das Angeld des Geistes: Studien zur paulinischen Pneumatologie.* FRLANT 154. Göttingen: Vandenhoeck & Ruprecht, 1992.

Hübner, Hans. *Biblische Theologie des Neuen Testaments:* Vol. 2, *Die Theologie des Paulus und ihre neutestamentliche Wirkungsgeschichte.* Göttingen: Vandenhoeck & Ruprecht, 1993.

———. *Gottes Ich und Israel: Zum Schriftgebrauch des Paulus in Römer 9–11.* FRLANT 136. Göttingen: Vandenhoeck & Ruprecht, 1984.

———. *Law in Paul's Thought.* Translated by J. C. G. Grieg. Studies in the New Testament and Its World. Edinburgh: T. & T. Clark, 1984.

———. "Pauli Theologiae Proprium." *NTS* 26 (1979–80) 445–73.

Hultgren, Arland J. *Paul's Gospel and Mission: The Outlook from His Letter to the Romans.* Philadelphia: Fortress, 1985.

Hurtado, Larry W. *One God, One Lord: Early Christian Devotion and Ancient Jewish Monotheism.* Philadelphia: Fortress, 1988.

Hvalvik, R. "A 'Sonderweg' for Israel: A Critical Examination of a Current Interpretation of Romans 11.25–27." *JSNT* 38 (1990) 87–107.

Iori, Renata. *La solidarietà nelle prime communità cristiane: La dottrina degli Atti e di san Paolo.* Rome: Città Nuova, 1989.

Jaquette, James L. "Paul, Epictetus, and Others on Indifference to Status." *CBQ* 56 (1994) 68–80.

Jeremias, Joachim. *Jesus' Promise to the Nations.* Translated by S. H. Hooke. SBT 24. London: SCM; Naperville, IL: Allenson, 1958.

Jervell, Jacob. *Imago Dei: Gen 1,26f im Spätjudentum, in der Gnosis und in der paulinischen Briefen.* Göttingen: Vandenhoeck & Ruprecht, 1960.

Jervis, L. Ann. *The Purpose of Romans: A Comparative Letter Structure Investigation.* JSNTSup 55. Sheffield: JSOT Press, 1991.

Jewett, Robert. *Christian Tolerance: Paul's Message to the Modern Church.* Philadelphia: Westminster, 1982.

———. "Following the Argument of Romans." *WW* 6 (1986) 382–89. In *The Romans Debate,* edited by K. P. Donfried, 265–77. Revised and expanded edition. Peabody, MA: Hendrickson, 1991.

———. "Paul, Phoebe, and the Spanish Mission." In *The Social World of Formative Christianity and Judaism: Essays in Tribute to Howard Clark Kee,* edited by P. Borgen et al., 144–64. Philadelphia: Fortress, 1988.

———. *Paul's Anthropological Terms: A Study of Their Use in Conflict Settings.* Leiden: Brill, 1971.

———. *Paul the Apostle to America: Cultural Trends and Pauline Scholarship.* Louisville: Westminster/John Knox, 1994.

———. "The Redaction and Use of an Early Christian Confession in Romans 1:3–4." In *The Living Bible Text: Essays in Honor of Ernest W. Saunders*, edited by D. E. Groh and R. Jewett, 99–122. Lanham, MD: University Press of America, 1985.

———. *Romans*. Basic Bible Commentary 22. Nashville: Abingdon, 1994.

———. "Romans as an Ambassadorial Letter." *Int* 36 (1982) 5–20.

Johnson, E. Elizabeth. *The Function of Apocalyptic and Wisdom Traditions in Romans 9–11*. SBLDS 109. Atlanta: Scholars, 1989.

———. "Jews and Christians in the New Testament: John, Matthew, and Paul." *Reformed Review* 42 (1988–89) 113–28.

Jones, F. Stanley. *"Freiheit" in den Briefen des Apostels Paulus: Eine historische, exegetische und religionsgeschichtliche Studie*. GTA 34. Göttingen: Vandenhoeck & Ruprecht, 1987.

Jüngel, Eberhard, and Dietrich Rössler. *Gefangenes Ich, befreiender Geist: 2 Tübinger Römerbrief–Auslegungen*. Munich: Kaiser, 1976.

Käsemann, Ernst. *Commentary on Romans*. Translated by G. W. Bromiley. London: SCM; Grand Rapids: Eerdmans, 1980.

———. *New Testament Questions of Today*. Translated by W. J. Montague. London: SCM; Philadelphia: Fortress, 1969.

———. *Perspectives on Paul*. Translated by M. Kohl. London: SCM, 1971.

Karris, Robert J. "The Occasion of Romans: A Response to Prof. Donfried." In *The Romans Debate,* edited by K. P. Donfried, 125–27. Revised and expanded edition. Peabody, MA: Hendrickson, 1991.

———. "Romans 14:1–15:13 and the Occasion of Romans." In *The Romans Debate,* edited by K. P. Donfried, 65–84. Revised and expanded edition. Peabody, MA: Hendrickson, 1991.

Kaylor, R. David. *Paul's Covenant Community: Jew and Gentile in Romans*. Atlanta: John Knox, 1988.

Keck, Leander E. "The Function of Rom 3:10–18: Observations and Suggestions." In *God's Christ and His People: Studies in Honour of Nils Alstrup Dahl*, edited by J. Jervell and W. A. Meeks, 141–57. Oslo: Universitetsforlaget, 1977.

———. "Justification of the Ungodly and Ethics." In *Rechtfertigung: Festschrift für Ernst Käsemann zum 70. Geburtstag*, edited by J. Friedrich et al., 179–209. Tübingen: Mohr (Siebeck), 1976.

———. "Paul and Apocalyptic Theology." *Int* 38 (1984) 229–41.

———. *Paul and His Letters*. Philadelphia: Fortress, 1979.

———. "Paul as a Thinker." *Int* 47 (1993) 27–38.

Kertelge, Karl. "Adam und Christus: Die Sünde Adams im Lichte der Erlösungstat Christi nach Röm 5,12–21." In *Anfänge der Christologie:*

Festschrift für Ferdinand Hahn zum 65 Geburtstag, edited by C. Breytenbach and H. Paulsen, 141–53. Göttingen: Vandenhoeck & Ruprecht, 1991.

———. *The Epistle to the Romans*. Translated by F. McDonagh. New Testament for Spiritual Reading 23. New York: Herder & Herder, 1972.

———. *Grundthemen paulinischer Theologie*. Freiburg: Herder, 1991.

———. *"Rechtfertigung" bei Paulus: Studien zur Struktur und zum Bedeutungsgehalt des paulinischen Rechtfertigungs-Begriffs*. Münster: Aschendorff, 1967, 1971.

———. "Das Verständnis des Todes Jesu bei Paulus." In *Der Tod Jesu: Deutungen im Neuen Testament*, edited by J. Beutler et al., 114–36. Freiburg: Herder, 1976.

Kettunen, Markku. *Der Abfassungszweck des Römerbriefes*. Annales Academiae Scientiarum Fennicae. Helsinki: Suomalainen Tiedeakatemia, 1979.

Kim, Seyoon. *The Origin of Paul's Gospel*. WUNT 2/4. Tübingen: Mohr (Siebeck), 1981.

Kitzberger, Ingrid. *Bau der Gemeinde: Das paulinische Wortfeld οἰκοδομή/ (ἐπ)οἰκοδομεῖν*. FB 53. Würzburg: Echter, 1986.

Klaiber, Walter. *Rechtfertigung und Gemeinde: Eine Untersuchung zum paulinische Kirchenverständnis*. FRLANT 127. Göttingen: Vandenhoeck & Ruprecht, 1982.

———, et al. *Rechenschaft über den Glauben. Römerbrief*. Bibelauslegung für die Praxis 21. Stuttgart: Katholisches Bibelwerk, 1989.

Klein, Günter. "Apocalyptische Naherwartung bei Paulus." In *Neues Testament und christliche Existenz: Festschrift für Herbert Braun*, edited by H. D. Betz and L. Schottroff, 241–62. Tübingen: Mohr (Siebeck), 1973.

———. "Präliminarien zum Thema 'Paulus und die Juden.'" In *Rechtfertigung: Festschrift für Ernst Käsemann zum 70. Geburtstag*, edited by J. Friedrich et al., 229–43. Tübingen: Mohr (Siebeck), 1976.

———. "Ein Sturmzentrum der Paulusforschung." *VF* 33 (1988) 40–56.

———. "Sündenverständnis und Theologie crucis bei Paulus." In *Theologie Crucis—Signum Crucis: Festschrift für Erich Dinkler zum 70. Geburtstag*, edited by C. Andresen and G. Klein, 249–82. Tübingen: Mohr (Siebeck), 1979.

Kleinknecht, Karl Theodor. *Der leidende Gerechtfertigte: Die alttestamentlich-jüdische Tradition von 'leidenden Gerechten' und ihre Rezeption bei Paulus*. WUNT 2/13. Tübingen: Mohr (Siebeck), 1984.

Knox, John. "The Epistle to the Romans." In *The Interpreter's Bible*, edited by G. A. Buttrick, 9. 355–668. Nashville: Abingdon, 1954.

———. *Life in Christ Jesus: Reflections on Romans 5–8*. Greenwich: Seabury, 1961.

Koch, Dietrich-Alex. *Die Schrift als Zeuge des Evangeliums: Untersuchungen zur*

Verwendung und zum Verständnis der Schrift bei Paulus. Tübingen: Mohr (Siebeck), 1986.

Koenig, John. *Charismata: God's Gifts for God's People.* Philadelphia: Westminster, 1978.

———. "The Jewishness of the Gospel: Reflections by a Lutheran." *JES* 19 (1982) 57–68.

Koskenniemi, Heikki. *Studien zur Idee und Phraseologie des griechischen Briefes bis 400 n. Chr.* Helsinki: Suomalainen Tiedeakatemia, 1956.

Kraus, Wolfgang. *Der Tod Jesu als Heiligtumsweihe: Eine Untersuchung zum Umfeld der Sühnevorstellung in Römer 3,25–26a.* WMANT 66. Neukirchen-Vluyn: Neukirchener Verlag, 1991.

Kreitzer, L. Joseph. "Christ and the Second Adam in Paul." *Communio viatorum* 32 (1989) 55–101.

———. *Jesus and God in Paul's Eschatology.* JSNTSup 19. Sheffield: JSOT Press, 1987.

Krentz, Edgar. "The Spirit in Pauline and Johannine Theology." In *The Holy Spirit in the Life of the Church: From Biblical Times to the Present*, edited by P. D. Opsahl, 47–65. Minneapolis: Augsburg, 1978.

Kümmel, Werner G. "Die Probleme von Römer 9–11 in der gegenwärtigen Forschungslage." In *Die Israelfrage nach Römer 9–11*, edited by L. de Lorenzi, 13–33. Rome: Abtei van St. Paul vor den Mauern, 1977.

———. *Römer 7 und die Bekehrung des Paulus.* UNT 17. Leipzig: Hinrichs, 1929. Reprinted, Munich: Kaiser, 1974.

———. *The Theology of the New Testament according to Its Major Witnesses Jesus—Paul—John.* Translated by J. S. Steely. Nashville: Abingdon, 1973.

Kuss, Otto. *Paulus: Die Rolle des Apostels in der theologischen Entwicklung der Urkirche.* Auslegung und Verkündigung 3. Regensburg: Pustet, 1971.

———. *Der Römerbrief übersetzt und erklärt.* 3 vols. Regensburg: Pustet, 1957–78.

Ladd, George Eldon. *A Theology of the New Testament.* Revised edition by D. A. Hagner. Grand Rapids: Eerdmans, 1993.

Lambrecht, Jan. *The Wretched "I" and its Liberation: Paul in Romans 7 and 8.* Louvain Theological and Pastoral Monographs 14. Louvain: Peeters; Grand Rapids: Eerdmans, 1992.

Lambrecht, Jan, and Richard W. Thompson. *Justification by Faith: The Implications of Romans 3:27–31.* Zaccheus Studies. Wilmington: Glazier, 1989.

Lampe, Peter. "The Roman Christians of Romans 16." In *The Romans Debate*, edited by K. P. Donfried, 216–30. Revised and expanded edition. Peabody, MA: Hendrickson, 1991.

———. *Die stadtrömischen Christen in den ersten beiden Jahrhunderten.* WUNT 2/18. Tübingen: Mohr (Siebeck), 1987, 1989.

Liebers, Reinhold. *Das Gesetz als Evangelium: Untersuchungen zur Gesetzeskritik des Paulus.* ATANT 75. Zurich: Zwingli, 1989.

Lincoln, Andrew T. "Abraham Goes to Rome: Paul's Treatment of Abraham in Romans 4." In *Worship, Theology and Ministry in the Early Church,* edited by M. J. Wilkens et al., 163–79. JSNTSup 87. Sheffield: JSOT Press, 1992.

Lindsay, Dennis R. *Josephus and Faith: Pistis and Pisteuein as Faith Terminology in the Writings of Flavius Josephus and the New Testament.* Leiden: Brill, 1993.

Ljungman, Henrik. *PISTIS: A Study of its Presuppositions and its Meaning in Pauline Use.* Translated by W. F. Salisbury. Acta reg. societatis humaniorum litterarum Lundensis 64. Lund: Gleerup, 1964.

Lohmeyer, Ernst. *Probleme paulinischer Theologie.* Darmstadt: Wissenschaftliche Buchgemeinschaft, 1954; Stuttgart: Kohlhammer, 1955.

Longenecker, Bruce W. "Different Answers to Different Issues: Israel, the Gentiles and Salvation History in Romans 9–11." *JSNT* 36 (1989) 95–123.

———. *Eschatology and the Covenant: A Comparison of 4 Ezra and Romans 1–11.* JSNTSup 57. Sheffield: JSOT Press, 1991.

Longenecker, Richard N. *Paul: Apostle of Liberty.* New York: Harper & Row, 1964.

Lübking, Hans–Martin. *Paulus und Israel im Römerbrief: Eine Untersuchung zu Römer 9–11.* Europäische Hochschulschriften 23/260. Frankfurt: Lang, 1986.

Lüdemann, Gerd. *Paulus und das Judentum.* Theologische Existenz heute 215. Munich: Kaiser, 1983.

Lührmann, Dieter. "Christologie und Rechtfertigung." In *Rechtfertigung: Festschrift für Ernst Käsemann zum 70. Geburtstag,* edited by J. Friedrich et al., 351–63. Tübingen: Mohr (Siebeck), 1976.

———. *Glaube im frühen Christentum.* Gütersloh: Mohn, 1976.

———. *Das Offenbarungsverständnis bei Paulus und in paulinischen Gemeinden.* WMANT 16. Neukirchen-Vluyn: Neukirchener Verlag, 1965.

Luz, Ulrich. "Zum Aufbau von Röm 1–8." *TZ* 25 (1969) 161–81.

———. *Das Geschichtsverständnis des Paulus.* BEvT 49. Munich: Kaiser, 1968.

Maier, Gerhard. *Mensch und freier Wille: Nach den jüdischen Religionsparteien zwischen Ben Sira und Paulus.* WUNT 12. Tübingen: Mohr (Siebeck), 1971.

Marcus, Joel. "The Circumcision and the Uncircumcision of Rome." *NTS* 35 (1989) 67–81.

————. "'Let God Arise and End the Reign of Sin!' Contribution to the Study of Pauline Parenesis." *Bib* 69 (1988) 386–95.

Martin, Ralph P. *Reconciliation: A Study of Paul's Theology.* Atlanta: John Knox, 1981. Revised Edition, 1989.

Mayer, Bernhard. *Unter Gottes Heilsratschluss: Prädestinationsaussagen bei Paulus.* FB 15. Würzburg: Echter, 1974.

Meeks, Wayne A. "Breaking Away: Three New Testament Pictures of Christianity's Separation from the Jewish Communities." In *To See Ourselves as Others See Us: Christians, Jews and 'Others' in Late Antiquity,* edited by J. Neusner and E. S. Frerichs, 93–115. Atlanta: Scholars Press, 1985.

————. "Judgment and the Brother: Romans 14:1–15:13." In *Tradition and Interpretation in the New Testament: Essays in Honor of E. Earle Ellis,* edited by G. F. Hawthorne and O. Betz, 290–300. Grand Rapids: Eerdmans; Tübingen: Mohr (Siebeck), 1987.

————. *The Moral World of the First Christians.* Library of Early Christianity 6. Philadelphia: Westminster, 1986.

————. "On Trusting an Unpredictable God: A Hermeneutical Reflection on Romans 9–11." In *Faith and History: Essays in Honor of Paul W. Meyer,* edited by J. T. Carroll, C. H. Cosgrove, and E. E. Johnson, 105–24. Atlanta: Scholars Press, 1990.

————. "The Social Context of Pauline Theology." *Int* 36 (1982) 266–77.

Mell, Ulrich. *Neue Schöpfung: Eine traditionsgeschichtliche und exegetische Studie zu einem soteriologischen Grundsatz paulinischer Theologie.* BZNW 56. Berlin: Töpelmann, 1989.

Merk, Otto. *Handeln aus Glauben: Die Motivierungen der paulinischen Ethik.* Marburger theologische Studien 5. Marburg: Elwert, 1968.

Merklein, Helmut. *Studien zu Jesus und Paulus.* WUNT 43. Tübingen: Mohr (Siebeck), 1987.

Meyer, Ben F. "The Pre-Pauline Formula in Rom 3:25–26a." *NTS* 29 (1983) 198–208.

Meyer, Paul W. "The Holy Spirit in the Pauline Letters: A Contextual Exploration." *Int* 33 (1979) 3–18.

————. "A Response." Typescript of a Response to Heikki Räisänen. "Romans 9–11 and the History of Early Christian Religion." Presented at the 1992 SBL Meeting in San Francisco.

————. "Romans." In *Harper's Bible Commentary,* edited by J. L. Mays, 1130–67. San Francisco: Harper & Row, 1988.

————. "Romans 10:4 and the 'End' of the Law." In *The Divine Helmsman: Studies on God's Control of Human Events, Presented to Lou H. Silberman,* edited by J. L. Crenshaw and S. Sandmel, 59–78. New York: Ktav, 1980.

————. "The Worm at the Core of the Apple: Exegetical Reflections on

Romans 7." In *The Conversation Continues: Studies in Paul and John. In Honor of J. Louis Martyn*, edited by R. T. Fortna and B. R. Gaventa, 62–84. Nashville: Abingdon, 1990.

Minear, Paul S. *The Obedience of Faith: The Purpose of Paul in the Epistle to the Romans*. SBT 2/19. London: SCM, 1971.

Moo, Douglas J. *Romans 1–8*. Chicago: Moody, 1991.

Morris, Leon. *New Testament Theology*. Grand Rapids: Academie, 1986.

———. "The Theme of Romans." In *Apostolic History and the Gospel: Biblical and Historical Essays Presented to F. F. Bruce*, edited by W. W. Gasque and R. P. Martin, 9–63. Exeter: Paternoster; Grand Rapids: Eerdmans, 1970.

Moxnes, Halvor. *Theology in Conflict: Studies in Paul's Understanding of God in Romans*. NovTSup 53. Leiden: Brill, 1980.

Müller, Christian. *Gottes Gerechtigkeit und Gottes Volk: Eine Untersuchung zu Römer 9–11*. FRLANT 86. Göttingen: Vandenhoeck & Ruprecht, 1964.

Müller, Peter. "Grundlinien paulinischer Theologie (Röm 15,14–33)." *KD* 35 (1989) 212–35.

Mullins, Michael. *Called to be Saints: Christian living in First-Century Rome*. Dublin: Veritas, 1991.

Munck, Johannes. *Christ and Israel: An Interpretation of Romans 9–11*. Translated by I. Nixon. Foreword by K. Stendahl. Philadelphia: Fortress, 1967.

———. *Paul and the Salvation of Mankind*. Translated by F. Clarke. London: SCM; Richmond: Knox, 1959.

Murray, John. *The Epistle to the Romans: The English Text with Introduction, Exposition, and Notes*. NICNT. 2 vols. London: Marshall, Morgan & Scott; Grand Rapids: Eerdmans, 1959–65. Reprinted in 1 vol., 1975.

Mussner, Franz. "Christus, des Gesetzes Ende zur Gerechtigkeit für jeden der glaubt (Röm 10,4)." In *Paulus-Apostat oder Apostel? Jüdische und christliche Antworten*, edited by M. Barth et al., 31–44. Regensburg: Pustet, 1977.

———. "Heil für Alle: Der Grundgedanke des Römerbriefes." *Kairos* 23 (1981) 207–14.

———. *Die Kraft der Würzel: Judentum–Jesus–Kirche*. Freiburg: Herder, 1987.

Nanos, Mark D. *The Mystery of Romans: The Jewish Context of Paul's Letter*. Minneapolis: Fortress, forthcoming.

Nebe, Gottfried. *"Hoffnung" bei Paulus: Elpis und ihre Synonyme im Zusammenhang der Eschatologie*. SUNT 16. Göttingen: Vandenhoeck & Ruprecht, 1983.

Neugebauer, Fritz. *In Christus/EN XPIΣTΩ: Eine Untersuchung zum paulinischen Glaubensverständnis*. Göttingen: Vandenhoeck & Ruprecht, 1961.

Newton, Michael. *The Concept of Purity at Qumran and in the Letters of Paul*. Cambridge: Cambridge University Press, 1985.

Neyrey, Jerome H. *Paul in Other Words: A Cultural Reading of His Letters.* Louisville: Westminster/John Knox, 1990.

Niebuhr, Karl-Wilhelm. *Heidenapostel aus Israel: Die jüdische Identität des Paulus nach ihrer Darstellung in seinen Briefen.* WUNT 62. Tübingen: Mohr (Siebeck), 1992.

Noack, Bent. "Current and Backwater in the Epistle to the Romans." *ST* 19 (1965) 155–66.

Nygren, Anders. *Commentary on Romans.* Translated by C. C. Rasmussen. Philadelphia: Muhlenberg, 1949; London: SCM, 1952.

O'Grady, J. F. *Pillars of Paul's Gospel: Galatians and Romans.* New York: Paulist, 1992.

O'Neill, John C. *Paul's Letter to the Romans.* Harmondsworth: Penguin, 1975.

Ollrog, Wolf–Hennig. "Die Abfassungsverhältnisse von Röm 16." In *Kirche: Festschrift für Günther Bornkamm zum 75. Geburtstag*, edited by D. Lührmann and G. Strecker, 221–44. Tübingen: Mohr (Siebeck), 1980.

————. *Paulus und seine Mitarbeiter: Untersuchungen zu Theorie und Praxis der paulinischen Mission.* WMANT 58. Neukirchen-Vluyn: Neukirchener Verlag, 1979.

Ortkemper, Franz-Josef. *Leben aus dem Glauben: Christliche Grundhaltungen nach Römer 12–13.* NTAbh 14. Münster: Aschendorff, 1980.

Patte, Daniel. *Paul's Faith and the Power of the Gospel: A Structural Introduction to the Pauline Letters.* Philadelphia: Fortress, 1983.

Perkins, Pheme. *Love Command in the New Testament.* New York: Paulist Press, 1982.

————. "Theological Implications of New Testament Pluralism." *CBQ* 50 (1988) 5–23.

Pickett, Raymond W. "The Death of Christ as Divine Patronage in Romans 5:1–11." In *Society of Biblical Literature 1993 Seminar Papers*, edited by E. H. Lovering, Jr., 726–39. Atlanta: Scholars, 1993.

Piper, John. *The Justification of God: An Exegetical and Theological Study of Romans 9:1–23.* 2d ed. Grand Rapids: Baker, 1983.

Plag, Christoph. *Israel's Wege zum Heil: Eine Untersuchung zu Römer 9 bis 11.* Arbeiten zur Theologie 40. Stuttgart: Calwer, 1969.

Pohle, Lutz. *Die Christen und der Staat nach Röm 13, 1–7 in der neueren deutschsprachigen Schriftauslegung.* Mainz: Grünewald, 1984.

Popkes, Wiard. *Christus Traditus: Eine Untersuchung zum Begriff der Dahingabe im Neuen Testament.* ATANT 49. Zurich: Zwingli, 1967.

Prat, Ferdinand. *The Theology of Saint Paul.* Translated by J. L. Stoddard. 2 vols. London: Burns, Oates & Washburne, 1926–27.

Räisänen, Heikki. *Beyond New Testament Theology: A Story and a Programme.* London: SCM; Philadelphia: Trinity Press International, 1990.

———. "Legalism and Salvation by the Law: Paul's Portrayal of the Jewish Religion as a Historical and Theological Problem." In *Die Paulinische Literatur und Theologie*, edited by S. Pedersen, 63–83. Aarhus: Aros; Göttingen: Vandenhoeck & Ruprecht, 1980. Reprinted in *The Torah and Christ: Essays in German and English on the Problem of the Law in Early Christianity*, 25–54. Publications of the Finnish Exegetical Society 45. Helsinki: Finnish Exegetical Society, 1986.

———. *Paul and the Law.* WUNT 29. Tübingen: Mohr (Siebeck), 1983; Philadelphia: Fortress, 1986.

———. "Paul, God, and Israel: Romans 9–11 in Recent Research." In *The Social World of Formative Christianity and Judaism: Essays in Tribute to Howard Clark Kee*, edited by J. Neusner et al., 178–206. Philadelphia: Fortress, 1988.

———. "Paul's Conversion and the Development of his View of the Law." *NTS* 33 (1987) 404–19.

———. "Paul's Theological Difficulties with the Law." In *Studia Biblica 1978*, edited by E. A. Livingstone, 3. 301–20. JSNTSup 3. Sheffield: JSOT Press, 1980. Reprinted in *The Torah and Christ: Essays in German and English on the Problem of the Law in Early Christianity*, 3–24. Publications of the Finnish Exegetical Society 45. Helsinki: Finnish Exegetical Society, 1986.

———. "Römer 9–11: Analyse eines geistigen Ringens." *ANRW* 2.25.4 (1987) 2891–2939.

———. *The Torah and Christ: Essays in German and English on the Problem of the Law in Early Christianity.* Publications of the Finnish Exegetical Society 45. Helsinki: Finnish Exegetical Society, 1986.

Reasoner, Mark. "*Potentes* and *Inferiores* in Roman Society and the Roman Church." In *Society of Biblical Literature Seminar 1993 Seminar Papers*, edited by E. H. Lovering, Jr., 1–17. Atlanta: Scholars Press, 1993.

———. "The 'Strong' and the 'Weak' in Rome and in Paul's Theology." Dissertation, University of Chicago, 1990.

Refoulé, François. "*. . . Et ainsi tout Israël sera sauvés*": *Romains 11,25–32*. LD 117. Paris: Cerf, 1984.

Reumann, John Henry Paul. *Creation and New Creation: The Past, Present and Future of God's Creative Activity.* Minneapolis: Augsburg, 1973.

———, et al. *Righteousness in the New Testament.* Philadelphia: Fortress; New York: Paulist, 1982.

Richardson, Peter. *Israel in the Apostolic Church.* SNTSMS 10. Cambridge: Cambridge University Press, 1969.

Ridgway, John K. "'By the Mercies of God . . .'—Mercy and Peace in Romans 12." *IBS* 14 (1992) 170–91.

Ridderbos, Herman. *Paul: An Outline of His Theology.* Translated by J. R. DeWitt. Grand Rapids: Eerdmans, 1975.

Riekkinen, Vilho. *Römer 13: Aufzeichnung und Weiterführung der exegetischen Diskussion.* Annales academiae scientiarum fennicae: Dissertationes humanarum litterarum 23. Helsinki: Suomalainen Tiedeakatemia, 1980.

Robinson, Donald. *Faith's Framework: The Structure of New Testament Theology.* Sutherland: Albatross; Exeter: Paternoster, 1985.

Röhser, Günter. *Metaphorik und Personifikation der Sünde: Antike Sündenvorstellungen und paulinische Hamartia.* WUNT 25. Tübingen: Mohr (Siebeck), 1987.

Roetzel, Calvin J. *Judgement in the Community: A Study of the Relationship between Eschatology and Ecclesiology in Paul.* Leiden: Brill, 1972.

———. *The Letters of Paul: Conversations in Context.* 3d ed. Atlanta: John Knox, 1975. Louisville: Westminster/John Knox, 1991.

Roloff, Jürgen. *Apostolat–Verkündigung–Kirche: Ursprung, Inhalt und Funktion des kirchlichen Apostelamtes nach Paulus, Lukas und den Pastoralbriefen.* Gütersloh: Mohn, 1965.

Rubenstein, Richard L. *My Brother Paul.* New York: Harper & Row, 1972.

Sampley, S. Paul. "Romans and Galatians: Comparison and Contrast." In *Understanding the Word: Essays in Honor of Bernhard W. Anderson,* edited by J. T. Butler et al., 315–40. JSOTSup 37. Sheffield: JSOT Press, 1985.

———. *Walking Between the Times: Paul's Moral Reasoning.* Minneapolis: Fortress, 1991.

———. "The Weak and Strong: Paul's Careful and Crafty Rhetorical Strategy in Romans 14:1–15:13." In *The Social World of the First Christians: Studies in Honor of Wayne A. Meeks,* edited by L. M. White and O. L. Yarbrough, 40–52. Minneapolis: Fortress, 1995.

Sanders, E. P. *Paul and Palestinian Judaism: A Comparison of Patterns of Religion.* London: SCM; Philadelphia: Fortress, 1977.

———. *Paul, the Law, and the Jewish People.* Philadelphia: Fortress, 1983.

Sandnes, Karl Olav. *Paul—One of the Prophets? A Contribution to the Apostle's Self-Understandng.* WUNT 2/43. Tübingen: Mohr (Siebeck), 1991.

Sänger, Dieter. *Verkündigung des Gekreuzigte und Israel: Studien zum Verhältnis von Kirche und Israel bei Paulus und im frühen Christentum.* WUNT 75. Tübingen: Mohr (Siebeck), 1994.

Schade, Hans-Heinrich. *Apokalyptische Christologie bei Paulus: Studien zum Zusammenhang von Christologie und Eschatologie in den Paulusbriefen.* GTA 18. Göttingen: Vandenhoeck & Ruprecht, 1981.

Schlier, Heinrich. *Besinnung auf das Neue Testament: Exegetische Aufsätze und Vorträge*, vol. 2. Freiburg: Herder, 1967.

―――. "Eine Christologische Credo-Formel der römischen Gemeinde: Zu Röm 1:3f." In *Neues Testament und Geschichte: Historisches Geschehen und Deutung im Neuen Testament: Oscar Cullmann zum 70. Geburstag*, edited by H. Baltensweiler and B. Reicke, 207–18. Zurich: Theologischer; Tübingen: Mohr (Siebeck), 1972.

―――. *Das Ende der Zeit: Exegetische Aufsätze und Vorträge*. Freiburg: Herder, 1971.

―――. "Εὐαγγέλιον im Romerbrief." In *Wort Gottes in der Zeit: Festschrift Karl Hermann Schelke zum 65. Geburtstag*, edited by H. Feld and J. Nolte, 127–42. Düsseldorf: Patmos, 1973.

―――. *Grundzüge einer paulinischen Theologie*. Freiburg: Herder, 1978. 2d ed., 1979.

―――. *Der Römerbrief*. HTKNT. Freiburg: Herder, 1977.

―――. *Die Zeit der Kirche: Exegetische Aufsätze und Vorträge*. Freiburg: Herder, 1955, 1967, 1972.

Schmeller, Thomas. *Paulus und die "Diatribe": Eine vergleichende Stilinterpretation*. NTAbh 19. Münster: Aschendorff, 1987.

Schmithals, Walter. *Paul and the Gnostics*. Translated by J. E. Steely. Nashville: Abingdon, 1972.

―――. *Der Römerbrief als historisches Problem*. SNT 9. Gütersloh: Mohn, 1975.

―――. *Der Römerbrief: Ein Kommentar*. Gütersloh: Mohn, 1988.

―――. *Die theologische Anthropologie des Paulus: Auslegung von Röm 7.17– 8.39*. Stuttgart: Kohlhammer, 1980.

Schmitt, Rainer. *Gottesgerechtigkeit–Heilsgeschichte–Israël in der Theologie des Paulus*. Europäische Hochschulschriften 23/240. Frankfurt: Lang, 1984.

Schnackenburg, Rudolf. "Christologie des Neuen Testaments." In *Mysterium Salutis: Grundriss heilsgeschichtlicher Dogmatik*, edited by J. Feiner and M. Löhrer, 3.1. 227–388. Einsiedeln: Benziger, 1970.

―――. *Neutestamentliche Theologie: Der Stand der Forschung*. Munich: Kösel, 1963, 1965.

Schnelle, Udo. *Gerechtigkeit und Christusgegenwart: Vorpaulinische und paulinische Tauftheologie*. GTA 24. Göttingen: Vandenhoeck & Ruprecht, 1983.

Schoeps, Hans Joachim. *Paul: The Theology of the Apostle in the Light of Jewish Religious History*. Translated by H. Knight. Philadelphia: Westminster, 1961.

Schottroff, Luise. "Die Schreckensherrschaft der Sünde und die Befreiung durch Christus nach dem Römerbrief des Paulus." *EvT* 39 (1979) 497–510.

Schrage, Wolfgang. *The Ethics of the New Testament.* Translated by D. E. Green. Philadelphia: Fortress, 1988.

Schreiner, T. R. "Does Romans 9 Teach Individual Election unto Salvation? Some Exegetical and Theological Reflections." *JETS* 36 (1993) 25–40.

Schulz, Siegfried. "Der frühe und der späte Paulus: Überlegungen zur Entwicklung seiner Theologie und Ethik." *TZ* 41 (1985) 228–36.

Schunack, Gerd. *Das hermeneutische Problem des Todes: Im Horizont von Römer 5 untersucht.* HUT 7. Tübingen: Mohr (Siebeck), 1967.

Schweitzer, Albert. *The Mysticism of Paul the Apostle.* Translated by W. Montgomery. New York: Holt, 1931; London: Black, 1953. Reprinted with a note by F. C. Burkitt. Northhampton: Dickens, 1967.

Schweizer, Eduard. *Church Order in the New Testament.* Translated by F. Clarke. SBT 32. London: SCM; Naperville, IL: Allenson, 1961.

———. *Neotestamentica: Deutsche und Englische Aufsätze 1951–1963. German and English Essays 1951–1963.* Zurich: Zwingli, 1963.

———. "Römer 1,3f. und der Gegensatz von Fleisch und Geist vor und bei Paulus." *EvT* 15 (1955) 563–71. Reprinted in *Neotestamentica: Deutsche und Englische Aufsätze 1951–1963. German and English Essays 1951–1963,* 180–89. Zurich: Zwingli, 1963.

Scott, James M. *Adoption as Sons of God: An Exegetical Investigation into the Background of ΥΙΟΘΕΣΙΑ in the Pauline Corpus.* WUNT 2/48. Tübingen: Mohr (Siebeck), 1992.

Scroggs, Robin. *Christology in Paul and John: The Reality and Revelation of God.* Proclamation Commentaries. Philadelphia: Fortress, 1988.

———. *The Last Adam: A Study in Pauline Anthropology.* Oxford: Blackwell, 1966.

———. "Paul as Rhetorician: Two Homilies in Romans 1–11." In *Jews, Greeks, and Christians: Religious Cultures in Late Antiquity: Essays in Honor of William David Davies,* edited by R. G. Hamerton-Kelly and R. Scroggs, 271–98. SJLA. Leiden: Brill, 1976.

Segal, Alan F. *Paul the Convert: The Apostolate and Apostasy of Saul the Pharisee.* New Haven: Yale University Press, 1990.

Seifrid, Mark A. "Blind Alleys in the Controversy over the Paul of History." *TynBul* 45 (1994) 86–92.

———. *Justification by Faith: The Origin and Development of a Central Pauline Theme.* NovTSup 68. Leiden: Brill, 1992.

Siker, Jeffrey S. *Disinheriting the Jews: Abraham in Early Christian Controversy.* Louisville: Westminster/John Knox, 1991.

Sloan, Robert B. "Paul and the Law: Why the Law cannot Save." *NovT* 33 (1991) 35–60.

Snodgrass, Klyne R. "Justification by Grace—to the Doers: An Analysis of the Place of Romans 2 in the Theology of Paul." *NTS* 32 (1986) 72–93.

Stalder, Kurt. *Das Werk des Geistes in der Heiligung bei Paulus.* Zurich: EVZ, 1962.

Stendahl, Krister. *Paul Among Jews and Gentiles and Other Essays.* Philadelphia: Fortress, 1976.

Stowers, Stanley K. *The Diatribe and Paul's Letter to the Romans.* SBLDS 57. Chico: Scholars, 1981.

―――. "Ἐκ πίστεως and διὰ τῆς πίστεως in Romans 3:30." *JBL* 108 (1989) 665–74.

―――. "Paul on the Use and Abuse of Reason." In *Greeks, Romans and Christians: Essays in Honor of Abraham J. Malherbe,* edited by D. L. Balch et al., 253–86. Minneapolis: Fortress, 1980.

―――. *A Rereading of Romans: Justice, Jews, and Gentiles.* New Haven: Yale University Press, 1994.

Strecker, Georg. "Befreiung und Rechtfertigung: Zur Stellung der Rechtfertigungslehre in der Theologie des Paulus." In *Eschaton und Historie: Aufsätze,* 229–59. Göttingen: Vandenhoeck & Ruprecht, 1979.

Strobel, Adolf. *Erkenntnis und Bekenntnis der Sünde in neutestamentlicher Zeit.* Stuttgart: Calwer, 1968.

―――. *Untersuchungen zum Eschatologischen Verzögerungs-problem auf Grund der spätjudisch-urchristlichen Geschichte von Habakuk 2,2ff.* NovTSup 2. Leiden: Brill, 1961.

Stuhlmacher, Peter. *Paul's Letter to the Romans.* Translated by S. J. Hafemann. Louisville: Westminster/John Knox, 1994.

―――. *Das Evangelium und die Evangelien.* Tübingen: Mohr (Siebeck), 1983.

―――. *Gerechtigkeit Gottes bei Paulus.* FRLANT 87. Göttingen: Vandenhoeck & Ruprecht, 1966.

―――. *Das paulinische Evangelium.* FRLANT 95. Göttingen: Vandenhoeck & Ruprecht, 1968.

―――. "The Purpose of Romans." In *The Romans Debate,* edited by K. P. Donfried, 231–42. Revised and expanded edition. Peabody, MA: Hendrickson, 1991.

―――. *Reconciliation, Law, and Righteousness: Essays in Biblical Theology.* Translated by E. R. Kalin. Philadelphia: Fortress, 1986.

―――. "The Theme of Romans." *AusBR* 36 (1988) 31–44.

___. "Zur Interpretation von Röm 11,25–32." In *Probleme biblischer Theologie: Festschrift für Gerhard von Rad zum 70. Geburtstag,* edited by H. W. Wolff, 555–70. Munich: Kaiser, 1971.

Suggs, M. Jack. "The Word Is Near You: Rom 10:6–10 Within the Purpose of the Letter." In *Christian History and Interpretation: Studies Presented to John Knox*, edited by W. R. Farmer, C. F. D. Moule, and R. R. Niebuhr, 289–312. Cambridge: Cambridge University Press, 1967.

Synofzik, Ernst. *Die Gerichts- und Vergeltungsaussagen bei Paulus: Eine traditions-geschichtliche Untersuchung*. GTA 8. Göttingen: Vandenhoeck & Ruprecht, 1977.

Tannehill, Robert C. *Dying and Rising with Christ: A Study in Pauline Theology*. BZNW 32. Berlin: Töpelmann, 1967.

Theissen, Gerd. *Psychological Aspects of Pauline Theology*. Translated by J. P. Galvin. Philadelphia: Fortress; Edinburgh: T. & T. Clark, 1987.

Theobald, Michael. "'Dem Juden zuerst und auch dem Heiden': Die paulinische Auslegung der Glaubensformel Röm 1:3f." In *Kontinuität und Einheit: Für Franz Mussner*, edited by P.-G. Müller and W. Stenger, 376–92. Freiburg: Herder, 1981.

———. *Die überströmende Gnade: Studien zu einem paulinischen Motivfeld*. FB 22. Würzburg: Echter, 1982.

Thielman, Frank. *From Plight to Solution: A Jewish Framework to Understanding Paul's View of the Law in Galatians and Romans*. NovTSup 61. Leiden: Brill, 1989.

Thompson, Michael. *Clothed with Christ: The Example and Teaching of Jesus in Romans 12.1–15.13*. JSNTSup 59. Sheffield: JSOT Press, 1991.

Thüsing, Wilhelm. *Gott und Christus in der paulinischen Soteriologie:* Vol. 1, *Per Christum in Deum: Das Verhältnis der Christozentrik zur Theozentrik*. NTAbh 1. Münster: Aschendorff, 1965. 3d ed., 1986.

Tobin, Thomas H. "Controversy and Continuity in Romans 1:18–3:20." *CBQ* 55 (1993) 298–318.

Toews, John E. "The Law in Paul's Letter to the Romans: A Study of Romans 9:30–10:13." Dissertation, Northwestern University, 1977.

Tomson, Peter J. *Paul and the Jewish Law: Halakha in the Letters of the Apostle to the Gentiles*. CRINT 3/1. Assen/Maastricht: Van Gorcum; Minneapolis: Fortress, 1990.

van der Minde, Hans–Jürgen. *Schrift und Tradition bei Paulus: Ihre Bedeutung und Funktion im Römerbrief*. Paderborner theologische Studien 3. Munich/ Vienna: Schöningh, 1976.

Via, Dan O., Jr. *Self-Deception and Wholeness in Paul and Matthew*. Minneapolis: Fortress, 1990.

Vielhauer, Philipp. "Ein Weg zur neutestamentlichen Christologie? Prüfung der Thesen Ferdinand Hahns." In *Aufsätze zum Neuen Testament*, 141–98. Munich: Kaiser, 1965.

Volf, Judith M. Gundry. *Paul and Perseverance: Staying In and Falling Away*. Louisville: Westminster/John Knox; Tübingen: Mohr (Siebeck), 1990.

Vollenweider, Samuel. *Freiheit als neue Schöpfung: Eine Untersuchung zur Eleutheria bei Paulus und in seiner Umwelt.* FRLANT 147. Göttingen: Vandenhoeck & Ruprecht, 1989.

von der Osten-Sacken, Peter. *Christian-Jewish Dialogue: Theological Foundations.* Translated by M. Kohl. Philadelphia: Fortress, 1986.

———. *Evangelium und Tora: Aufsätze zu Paulus.* TBü 77. Munich: Kaiser, 1987.

———. *Römer 8 als Beispiel paulinischer Soteriologie.* FRLANT 112. Göttingen: Vandenhoeck & Ruprecht, 1975.

von Dobbeler, Axel. *Glaube als Teilhabe: Historische und semantische Grundlagen der paulinischen Theologie und Ekklesiologie des Glaubens.* WUNT 22. Tübingen: Mohr (Siebeck), 1987.

von Schlatter, Adolf. *Die Botschaft Paulus: Eine Übersicht über den Römerbrief.* Velbert im Rheinland: Freizeiten, 1928.

———. *Der Glaube im Neuen Testament.* 6th ed. Stuttgart: Calwer; Neukirchen-Vluyn: Neukirchener Verlag, 1982.

———. *Gottes Gerechtigkeit: Ein Kommentar zum Römerbrief.* Stuttgart: Calwer, 1935. 4th ed., 1964. 6th ed., with preface by P. Stuhlmacher, 1991.

Wagner, Günter. *Pauline Baptism and the Pagan Mysteries: The Problem of the Pauline Doctrine of Baptism in Romans VI. 1–11, in the Light of its Religio-Historical "Parallels."* Translated by J. P. Smith. Edinburgh: Oliver & Boyd, 1967.

Walters, James C. *Ethnic Issues in Paul's Letter to the Romans: Changing Self-Definitions in Earliest Roman Christianity.* Valley Forge, PA: Trinity Press International, 1994.

Watson, Francis. *Paul, Judaism and the Gentiles: A Sociological Approach.* SNTSMS 56. Cambridge: Cambridge University Press, 1986.

Wedderburn, A. J. M. "Adam in Paul's Letter to the Romans." In *Studia Biblica 1978*, edited by E. A. Livingstone, 3. 413–30. JSNTSup 3. Sheffield: JSOT Press, 1980.

———. *Baptism and Resurrection: Studies in Pauline Theology against Graeco-Roman Background.* WUNT 44. Tübingen: Mohr (Siebeck), 1987.

———. *The Reasons for Romans.* Studies in the New Testament and Its World. Edinburgh: T. & T. Clark, 1988.

———. "Some Observations on Paul's Use of the Phrases 'In Christ' and 'With Christ.'" *JSNT* 25 (1985) 83–97.

Weder, Hans. *Das Kreuz Jesu bei Paulus: Ein Versuch, über den Geschichtsbezug des christlichen Glaubens nachzudenken.* FRLANT 125. Göttingen: Vandenhoeck & Ruprecht, 1981.

Wengst, Klaus. *Christologische Formeln und Lieder der Urchristentum.* Gütersloh: Mohn, 1972.

Westerholm, Stephen. *Israel's Law and the Church's Faith: Paul and His Recent Interpreters*. Grand Rapids: Eerdmans, 1988.

Whiteley, D. E. H. *The Theology of St Paul*. Oxford: Blackwell, 1964.

Wiederkehr, Dietrich. *Die Theologie der Berufung in den Paulusbriefen*. Studia freiburgensia 36. Fribourg: Universitätsverlag, 1963.

Wiefel, Wolfgang. "The Jewish Community in Ancient Rome and the Origins of Roman Christianity." *Judaica* 26 (1970) 65–88. Reprinted in *The Romans Debate*, edited by K. P. Donfried, 85–101. Revised and expanded edition. Peabody, MA: Hendrickson, 1991.

Wilckens, Ulrich. *Der Brief an die Römer*. EKKNT 6. 3 vols. Zurich: Benziger; Neukirchen-Vluyn: Neukirchener Verlag, 1978–82.

———. "Christologie und Anthropologie im Zusammenhang der paulinischen Rechtfertigungslehre." *ZNW* 67 (1976) 64–82.

———. *Rechtfertigung als Freiheit: Paulusstudien*. Neukirchen-Vluyn: Neukirchener Verlag, 1974.

———. "Statements on the Development of Paul's View of Law." In *Paul and Paulinism: Essays in Honour of C. K. Barrett*, edited by M. D. Hooker and S. G. Wilson, 17–26. London: SPCK, 1982.

Williams, Sam K. *Jesus' Death as Saving Event: The Background and Origin of a Concept*. HDR 2. Missoula, MT: Scholars Press, 1975.

———. "The 'Righteousness of God' in Romans." *JBL* 99 (1980) 241–90.

Wilson, Walter T. *Love without Pretense: Romans 12:9–21 and Hellenistic–Jewish Wisdom Literature*. WUNT 2/46. Tübingen: Mohr (Siebeck), 1991.

Winger, Joseph Michael. *By What Law? The Meaning of Νόμος in the Letters of Paul*. SBLDS 128. Atlanta: Scholars Press, 1992.

Wink, Walter. *The Powers*: Vol. 1, *Naming the Powers: The Language of Power in the New Testament*. Philadelphia: Fortress, 1984.

———. *The Powers*: Vol. 2, *Unmasking the Powers: The Invisible Forces That Determine Human Existence*. Philadelphia: Fortress, 1986.

———. *The Powers*: Vol. 3, *Engaging the Powers: Discernment and Resistance in a World of Domination*. Minneapolis: Fortress, 1992.

Witherington, Ben, III. *Jesus, Paul and the End of the World: A Comparative Study in New Testament Eschatology*. Downers Grove: InterVarsity, 1992.

———. *Paul's Narrative Thought World: The Tapestry of Tragedy and Triumph*. Louisville: Westminster/John Knox, 1994.

Wolter, Michael. "Der Apostel und seine Gemeinden als Teilhaber am Leidensgeschick Jesu Christi: Beobachtungen zur paulinischen Leidenstheologie." *NTS* 36 (1990) 535–57.

———. *Rechtfertigung und zukünftiges Heil: Untersuchungen zu Röm 5:1–11*. BZNW 43. Berlin: de Gruyter, 1978.

Wrede, Wilhelm. "The Task and Methods of New Testament Theology." In

The Nature of New Testament Theology, edited by R. Morgan, 68–116. SBT 2/25. London: SCM, 1973.

Wright, N. Thomas. *The Climax of the Covenant: Christ and the Law in Pauline Theology*. Edinburgh: T. & T. Clark; Minneapolis: Fortress, 1991.

————. *The New Testament and the People of God*. London: SPCK; Minneapolis: Fortress, 1992.

Wuellner, Wilhelm. "Greek Rhetoric and Pauline Argumentation." In *Early Christian Literature and the Classical Intellectual Tradition: In honorem Robert M. Grant*, edited by W. R. Schoedel and R. L. Wilken, 177–88. Theologie historique 54. Paris: Beauchesne, 1979.

————. "Paul's Rhetoric of Argumentation in Romans: An Alternative to the Donfried–Karris Debate Over Romans," *CBQ* 38 (1976) 330–51. Reprinted in *The Romans Debate,* edited by K. P. Donfried, 128–46. Revised and expanded edition. Peabody, MA: Hendrickson, 1991.

Zeller, Dieter. *Der Brief an die Römer übersetzt und erklärt*. Regensburger Neues Testament. Regensburg: Pustet, 1985.

————. *Juden und Heiden in der Mission des Paulus: Studien zum Römerbrief*. FB 8. 2d ed. Stuttgart: Katholisches Bibelwerk, 1976.

Ziesler, John A. *The Meaning of Righteousness in Paul*. SNTSMS 20. Cambridge: Cambridge University Press, 1972.

————. *Paul's Letter to the Romans*. Trinity Press International New Testament Commentary. London: SCM; Philadelphia: Trinity Press International, 1989.

Zmijewski, Josef. *Paulus—Knecht und Apostel Christi: Amt und Amsträger in paulinischer Sicht*. Stuttgart: Katholisches Bibelwerk, 1986.

Index of Ancient Sources

Index of Modern Authors

Printed in the United States
113135LV00003B/68/A

9 781589 830547